D0902028

Studies in New Testament Interpretation

Consultant Editor
Robert Morgan

THE INTERPRETATION OF MARK

Second Edition

Edited by

WILLIAM R. TELFORD

T&T CLARK
EDINBURGH

T&T CLARK LTD
59 GEORGE STREET
EDINBURGH EH2 2LQ
SCOTLAND

Contents

Acknowledgements

Eduard Schweizer "Mark's Theological Achievement" is a translation of "Die theologische Leistung des Markus", first published in *Evangelische Theologie* 24 (1964) 337–55, reprinted with slightly expanded footnotes in the author's *Beiträge zur Theologie des Neuen Testaments* (Zurich 1970) and again in R. Pesch (ed.), *Das Markus-Evangelium* (Darmstadt 1979). This English version appears with the author's permission. © Eduard Schweizer 1964.

Theodore J. Weeden "The Heresy that necessitated Mark's Gospel" is reprinted with the author's permission from *Zeitschrift für die neutestamentliche Wissenschaft* 59 (1968) 145–58.

Karl Kertelge "The Epiphany of Jesus in the Gospel (Mark)", translated with the author's permission, first appeared as "Die Epiphanie Jesu im Evangelium (Markus)" in J. Schreiner (ed.), *Gestalt und Anspruch des Neuen Testaments* (Wurzburg: Echter-Verlag, 1969) 153–72, and was reprinted in R. Pesch (ed.), *Das Markus-Evangelium* (Darmstadt 1979).

Norman Perrin "The Christology of Mark: a Study in Methodology" was first published in *The Journal of Religion* 51 (1971) 173–87 and reprinted with slight alterations in M. Sabbe (ed.), *L'Évangile selon Marc. Tradition et Rédaction* (Leuven: University Press, 1974). © University of Chicago Press.

Joanna Dewey "The Literary Structure of the Controversy Stories in Mark 2:1–3:6" was originally published in the *Journal of Biblical Literature* 92 (1973) 394–401, and is reprinted with permission. © *Journal of Biblical Literature* 1973.

The Interpretation of Mark

The Contributors

WILLIAM TELFORD is Lecturer in Religious Studies (Christian Origins and the New Testament) at the University of Newcastle, England. *The Barren Temple and the Withered Tree*, the first of his studies on Mark, was published in 1980.

EDUARD SCHWEIZER was Professor of New Testament Theology and Exegesis at the University of Zurich from 1949 to 1979. His commentaries on the Synoptic Gospels and on Colossians are widely read in English translation.

THEODORE WEEDEN is Pastor of Asbury First United Methodist Church, Rochester, New York, and the author of *Mark. Traditions in Conflict* (1971).

KARL KERTELGE was Professor of New Testament in the Roman Catholic Faculty of Theology at Münster. His books include *Rechtfertigung bei Paulus* (1967), *Die Wunder Jesu im Markusevangelium* (1970) and a popular commentary on Romans in *The New Testament for Spiritual Reading* (1969).

NORMAN PERRIN (1921–76) was Professor at the University of Chicago and wrote extensively on Mark and the teaching of Jesus, notably the parables.

JOANNA DEWEY of the Episcopal Divinity School, Cambridge, Massachusetts is the author of *Markan Public Debate* (1980) as well as of a number of articles on Mark.

ERNEST BEST was Professor of Divinity and Biblical Criticism in the University of Glasgow from 1974 to 1982. His works on Mark include *The Temptation and the Passion* (1965), *Following Jesus* (1981) and *Mark: The Gospel as Story* (1983).

The Interpretation of Mark

ROBERT TANNEHILL is Professor at the Methodist Theological School in Ohio. He has written *Dying and Rising with Christ* (1967), *The Sword of his Mouth* (1975) and *The Narrative Unity of Luke–Acts* (1986/1990).

SIEGFRIED SCHULZ was Professor of New Testament in Zurich and has written extensively on the Synoptic Gospels, Q, New Testament hermeneutics and ethics.

ROBERT FOWLER is Professor of New Testament at Baldwin-Wallace College in Ohio and the author of *Loaves and Fishes* (1981) and *Let the Reader Understand* (1991).

ANDREW LINCOLN is Senior Lecturer in New Testament at the University of Sheffield. Among his publications are *Paradise Now and Not Yet* (1981), the Word Biblical Commentary on *Ephesians* (1990) and *The Theology of the Late Pauline Letters* (1993).

ELIZABETH MALBON is Professor of New Testament in the Department of Religion at the Virginia Polytechnic Institute and State University. Her *Narrative Space and Mythic Meaning in Mark* was published in 1986.

WILLEM VORSTER of the Institute for Theological Research, The University of South Africa, Pretoria was a distinguished and internationally respected New Testament scholar whose untimely death in 1993 has been deeply felt by all his colleagues. A collection of his major articles, which have focused, among other things, on hermeneutics, literary approaches, the Gospels and Mark, is shortly to be published.

FRANK MATERA is a Professor of New Testament at the Catholic University of America, Washington. Among his publications are *The Kingship of Jesus* (1982), *Passion Narratives and Gospel Theologies* (1986) and *What are They Saying about Mark?* (1987).

Series Foreword

"Studies in New Testament Interpretation" is an off-shoot from an earlier series edited by Douglas Knight and myself. Like that series, its successor aims to collect and reproduce key studies, all previously published, which have contributed significantly to our present understanding. In each case, the volume editor introduces the discussion with an original essay which describes the subject and its treatment in religious and theological studies.

Together the essays are intended to present a balanced overview of the problem and various approaches to it. Each piece is important in the current debate, and any older publication included normally stands as a "classical" or seminal work which is still worth careful study. Readers unfamiliar with the issue should find that these discussions provide a good entrée, while more advanced students will appreciate having studies by some of the best specialists on the subject gathered together in one volume. The editor has, of course, faced certain constraints: analyses too lengthy or too technical could not be included, except perhaps in excerpt form; the bibliography is not exhaustive; and the volumes in this series are being kept to a reasonable length. On the other hand, the editor is able to overcome the real problem of inaccessibility. Much of the best literature on a subject is often not readily available to readers, whether because it was first published in journals or books not widely circulated or because it was originally written in a language not read by all who would benefit from it. By bringing these and other studies together in this series, we hope to contribute to the general understanding of these key topics.

The series editor and the publisher wish to express their gratitude to the authors and their original publishers whose works are reprinted or translated here, sometimes with authors' corrections.

ROBERT MORGAN

Abbreviations

AJT	*American Journal of Theology*
BJRL	*The Bulletin of the John Rylands Library*
BR	*Biblical Research*
BTB	*Biblical Theology Bulletin*
BZ	*Biblische Zeitschrift*
CBQ	*Catholic Biblical Quarterly*
ETL	*Ephemerides theologicae lovanienses*
EvT	*Evangelische Theologie*
ExpTim	*Expository Times*
HeyJ	*Heythrop Journal*
HTR	*Harvard Theological Review*
Int	*Interpretation*
JAAR	*Journal of the American Academy of Religion*
JBL	*Journal of Biblical Literature*
JR	*Journal of Religion*
JSNT	*Journal for the Study of the New Testament*
JTS	*Journal of Theological Studies*
NovT	*Novum Testamentum*
NTS	*New Testament Studies*
RB	*Revue Biblique*
SJT	*Scottish Journal of Theology*
StEv	*Studia Evangelica*
TDNT	*Theological Dictionary of the New Testament*, ed. G. Kittel and G. Friedrich
TRu	*Theologische Rundschau*
TTZ	*Trierer theologische Zeitschrift*
TU	*Texte und Untersuchungen zur Geschichte der altchristlichen Literatur*

TS	*Theological Studies*
TZ	*Theologische Zeitschrift*
USQR	*Union Seminary Quarterly Review*
ZNW	*Zeitschrift für die neutestamentliche Wissenschaft*
ZTK	*Zeitschrift für Theologie und Kirche*

Introduction:
The Interpretation of Mark
A History of Developments
and Issues

W. R. TELFORD

A literary explosion has occurred in the field of Marcan studies within the last thirty years.[1] A reviewer of Marcan research in this period, for example, pointed out that one scholar (J. Lambrecht) working on the parables in Mark had been able to list some forty-four books and articles on Mark chapter 4 alone that had appeared between 1967 and 1974.[2] In evaluating the major contributions to Marcan scholarship in recent years and deciding on the eight articles presented in the first edition of this collection (1985), the present reviewer was faced with the formidable task of assessing over 250 essays, articles and books on the Gospel, 90 per cent of which were written after 1960. After what is almost a further decade of scholarly activity on Mark, a similar task faced him in producing this revised edition and in selecting the five further articles (by R. M. Fowler, A. T. Lincoln, E. S. Malbon, F. J. Matera and W. S. Vorster) included here. How are we to make sense of this current interest in a Gospel formerly viewed in a simplistic and indeed frequently patronizing light?

A traditional view of Mark's Gospel has often presumed the work to be unsophisticated and untheological. Writing in 1922, the British scholar, J. V. Bartlet, claimed that the author of the so-called "Second Gospel" had given us "a simple, objective report of things as they had come to him in the tradition".[3] The Gospel was written in Rome in the sixties after the death of Peter, according to a hitherto common view, and represents a relatively faithful and unadorned transmission of the reminiscences of the apostle by the John Mark of the New Testament.[4] These recorded reminiscences give the reader almost direct access to the Jesus of history. The outline of Jesus' ministry by Mark is assumed to be substantially historical. The Marcan portrait of the secrecy surrounding Jesus' person reflects Jesus' own consciousness of his Messianic mission as that of a suffering "Servant" or "Son of Man" in contrast to more militaristic concepts of Messiahship thought to be current at the time.

This traditional view owes much, on the one hand, to the claim by Papias that Mark was the *hermeneutes* (translator, stenographer, interpreter?) of Peter,[5] and, on the other hand, in this century, to the arguments of such British scholars as B. H. Streeter, J. V. Bartlet, H. E. W. Turner, V. Taylor, C. H. Dodd, W. Manson and T. W. Manson.[6]

More recent Marcan studies, however, have tended to move away from the historical (some would even say "romantic") assumptions on which the traditional view is based. Doubts have been raised against the Papias tradition.[7] For lack of evidence, particularly within the Gospel itself, fewer New Testament scholars nowadays address the question of the author's specific identity.[8] While the traditional view still has its defenders (e.g. M. Hengel, 1985; B. Orchard, 1992) a direct and uniform Petrine connection has not in practice been a basic premise of most of the studies appearing in the 1960s onwards. A "new look" at the Gospel, if we may call it that, has been emerging, one characterized, among other things, by an open mind or even lack of interest in such historical questions.

In common with the other Synoptic Gospels, Mark's Gospel is now widely regarded as the product of a more or less creative editorial process upon diverse and discrete oral (and possibly written) traditions which had circulated for a generation within the primitive Christian communities that transmitted them. The basic aim of Marcan research since the 1960s has been to seek to determine what motives and which factors influenced the author (now unknown to us, but for convenience almost invariably designated as "Mark") to select, arrange and edit this traditional material in the way he (or she?) has to produce what is perhaps the first instance of this kind of literature, a genre subsequently labelled a "gospel".[9] The focus, in other words, has been not on the Jesus of history but on the evangelist himself and his contribution to the tradition about Jesus. In the words of one scholar who has himself contributed to the "new look": "the history of recent research on the Gospel of Mark can be seen as the record of an attempt to discern the aim of the evangelist and so to discover the perspective which gives coherence to all the features of the Second Gospel".[10]

In what follows we shall briefly review, and attempt to explain, how we reached the point where we now are in Marcan studies. Notwithstanding the flood of literature on the subject, we shall seek to assess the present state of Marcan research to which the thirteen articles here presented have contributed. The introduction has been revised and the notes and the bibliography at the end have been extensively updated since the first edition and offer a selection of contributions to the subject which have proved important or are likely to prove useful to the student of "the Second Gospel".

Let us begin by summarizing some major developments in Marcan study from the pre-critical period up until the end of the 1950s.[11] The fact that Mark is still referred to as "the Second Gospel" reflects the early Church's traditional view of the order in which the canonical Gospels were written (Matthew, Mark, Luke, John), despite the fact that scholarship for over one hundred years has in general maintained the priority of Mark. While in theory the early Church gave equal prominence to all four Gospels,[12] in practice Mark was neglected in favour of the others, especially Matthew.[13] Augustine in particular gave impetus to this trend by remarking that "Mark follows him (Matthew) closely and looks as if he were his servant (*pedisequus*) and epitomist (*breviator*)".[14] This view of Matthean priority and Mark's dependence upon Matthew's Gospel as a source he has merely abbreviated, held sway largely until the latter half of the eighteenth century when it came to be increasingly challenged.

One of the great achievements of the nineteenth-century scholarship on gospel literary relationships was to establish (to the satisfaction of the majority of critics) that Mark (or some form of Mark) was the earliest, and was used as a source by both Matthew and Luke. The emergence of this "Marcan hypothesis" is associated principally with the names of K. Lachmann, C. G.

3

Wilke, C. H. Weisse and H. J. Holtzmann. When combined with the suggestion that the further common material shared by both Matthew and Luke, but not by Mark, constituted a second original source (designated by the cipher "Q"), one employed independently by both, the groundwork was laid for the "Two Document" hypothesis of Synoptic relationships. This result still stands, and while it has been shaken by the re-opening of the debate in recent times by protagonists of Matthean priority,[15] it continues to command, with varying degrees of qualification, widespread support.[16]

The establishment of Marcan priority in the nineteenth century gave a new impetus to the study of the Gospel. If this was the earliest, and the most primitive, Gospel (the two were often equated), then might it not give us the most dependable historical account of Jesus' ministry? This assumption was the basis of the "traditional" view of Mark outlined above. Even those who were not swayed by the Papias tradition of the Gospel's direct connection with Peter devoted prodigious efforts to determine and isolate the written sources the author may have used. Numerous highly ingenious source theories were proposed, many directed to the recovery of an even earlier form of the Gospel, an "Ur-Markus" deemed to embody the historical stratum of the Jesus tradition.[17]

The first major assault on the historicizing approach to the Gospel was William Wrede's *Das Messiasgeheimnis in den Evangelien* published in 1901, but despite its considerable influence, translated only in 1971. Wrede challenged the assumption that Mark gives us the historical facts about Jesus in as "straight" a form as we are likely to get them. No less so than the other Gospels, he claimed, "the Gospel of Mark belongs to the history of dogma" (1971: 131). By portraying Jesus in an historically implausible way as the bearer of the concealed dignity of the Messiah or Son of God (the two are used interchangeably), by having him recognized as such for the most part by the supernatural world alone, by having Jesus command his disciples and those described as being healed by him not to spread the word of his real identity; in short, by employing a secrecy motif in this work, the author has imposed upon traditions about Jesus that were for the most part originally non-Messianic in nature the estimate of the significance of Jesus adopted with hindsight by the community to and for which Mark speaks. The Messianic

4

christology to which the Gospel bears witness actually developed after the rise of the belief in his resurrection. While Wrede's theory has not survived in the form in which it was presented, his highlighting of the theological ("dogmatic") motivation at work in the composition of the Marcan Gospel is now almost universally acknowledged.[18]

The next major contribution to Marcan studies (as to gospel research as a whole) was the form-critical work in the inter-war period associated principally with the names of K. L. Schmidt, M. Dibelius and R. Bultmann.[19] By proffering a critical method (though not one that has been immune from criticism itself)[20] whereby scholars might recover and examine the tradition behind the Gospel in its pre-literary or oral phase, form criticism offered a way out of the impasse that had been reached as a result of the failure of scholars to establish and isolate specific written sources behind Mark. Schmidt (1919) drew attention to the "unit-structure" of the Gospel, the "pearls and string" pattern evident in its composition. He demonstrated that the Gospel consisted (with the exception of the longer passion narrative) of a whole series of separate and discrete units (pericopae) linked by a largely artificial and extremely loose overall geographical and chronological framework. This framework was for the most part the evangelist's own creation, as evidenced, among other things, by the freedom exhibited by Matthew and Luke in altering it. Much of the traditional material represented by these pericopae-units exhibited a topical arrangement in the Gospel, but not one conditioned by historical actuality.[21] This result, though subsequently qualified, has not been successfully overturned.[22]

Dibelius[23] and Bultmann[24] devoted themselves to the work of isolating and classifying the various forms (e.g. apophthegms, gnomic or wisdom sayings, prophetic or apocalyptic sayings, legal sayings, community rules, christological sayings, parables, miracle stories, historical stories and legends, a passion narrative),[25] establishing the "creative milieu" or function (*Sitz im Leben*) of the piece of tradition in the community (whether in preaching, worship, parenesis, catechesis, apologetic, polemic, etc.) and reconstructing as far as was possible the tradition history of the pericope. Subsequent form-critical investigations have not only continued this work on individual pericopae[26] but have also sought to establish the existence of possible pre-

Marcan collections of pericopae, and their *Sitz im Leben* or function in the Marcan community.[27]

A major result of the form-critical approach was to demonstrate that Mark's Gospel was the product of "community tradition" and not direct eye-witness testimony. This conclusion was to shake further any confidence in the immediate historical value of the Gospel. Building on Bultmann's exposure of the mythological world-view (*Weltanschauung*) which informs the New Testament writers, J. M. Robinson (1957) tackled the problem of history in Mark.[28] Robinson examined the Marcan understanding of history and highlighted the mythological dimension underlying the historical drama he believed the author had created out of his tradition. Mark viewed the history of Jesus in mythic terms as a cosmic struggle between God (or the Spirit) and Satan. The eschatological appearance of Jesus heralded the overthrow of Satan and the supernatural forces of evil. Mark describes in similar terms, and with echoes of "cosmic language", the reaction of Jesus to the Satanic bondage of the demon-possessed and to the supernatural blindness of both his opponents and his disciples. "In the resurrection the force of evil is conclusively broken and the power of God's reign is established in history" (53). For Mark, the experience of his own community is "a continuation within the Church of the same kind of history as characterized Jesus' history, i.e. a struggle between Spirit and Satan, until the final outcome of that struggle is reached and the goal of history attained" (59).

In attempting to uncover a distinctively Marcan understanding of history, Robinson, for all the methodological weaknesses attributed to him,[29] was anticipating subsequent redaction-critical aims and developments. In seeking to discover a unified Marcan theology in this text, he was, to an extent, going against the grain of contemporary form criticism with its emphasis on the fragmentation of the tradition, the compositeness of the Gospel, the diversity of the various materials incorporated in it. Form criticism has in general downplayed the theological contribution of the evangelists themselves in favour of the more important role of the (anonymous) community in shaping the Jesus tradition. A major premise of earlier form-critical studies (prominent in Dibelius, though less so in Bultmann)[30] concerned the nature of the evangelists and their work. "The literary understanding of the Synoptics begins with the recognition that they are collections of material. The composers are only to the smallest extent authors. They are principally collectors, vehicles of tradition, editors" (M. Dibelius, 1934: 3). In other words, to use the much repeated analogy of the scrapbook, Mark was a "scissors-and-paste" man! This preoccupation of form criticism with the individual pre-Gospel units has tended to blind it to what the editorial framework and activity manifest in the text itself might tell us about the Gospel's overall purpose and theological motivation.

This balance was corrected, however, after the Second World War with the advent of redaction criticism (*Redaktionsgeschichte*), a critical method pioneered by the German scholars W. Marxsen (on Mark),[31] G. Bornkamm (on Matthew) and H. Conzelmann (on Luke) and advanced in the English-speaking world by scholars such as N. Perrin whose application of the method in relation to Marcan christology is illustrated in the essay reprinted here. It was Marxsen who made the case for the unique and distinctive contribution of the evangelist to the developing tradition about Jesus. In first committing the diverse and fragmented oral tradition to writing, the author of Mark was engaged in a synthetic and constructive literary exercise of great individual significance for the future of the Christian faith.[32] In the process of selecting, arranging, modifying, altering and even creating the material found in the Gospel, he has been influenced to a greater or lesser extent by his own theological conceptions and tradition. Mark was not merely a "scissors-and-paste" compiler. "On the contrary, the scissors were manipulated by a theological hand, and the paste was impregnated with a particular theology" (R. H. Stein).[33]

Employed in conjunction with its "sister" disciplines, form and tradition criticism, redaction criticism has given a dynamic impetus to gospel research. All three approaches taken together have proved fruitful in uncovering the complex levels in the Gospel tradition as it has come down to us. In its application of a critical method designed to separate redaction from tradition within a particular text, redaction criticism has done much to spotlight the creative role of the evangelist. The popularity of this method has been largely responsible for the flood of literature already referred to which has appeared on the Gospel since the 1960s.

A number of full-length form-, tradition- and redaction-critical investigations have been conducted upon single pericopae (e.g.

the discovery of the empty tomb [Schenke, 1969] or the triumphal entry [März, 1980]) or on groups of pericopae either in proximity with one another or of similar type or content (e.g. the controversy pericopae [Thissen, 1976; Hultgren, 1979; Dewey, 1980; Mudiso Mbâ Mundla, 1984; Kiilunen, 1985; Weiss, 1989], the feeding miracles [Fowler, 1981; Schenke, 1983], the Caesarea Philippi pericope and the transfiguration [Horstmann, 1969], the disciple passages [Reploh, 1969; Stock, 1975], the community rules or *Regelkompendium* of chapter 10 [Busemann, 1983] or the cursing of the fig-tree story and the cleansing of the temple [Telford, 1980]), or on apparently discrete sections of the Gospel (e.g. "the little apocalypse" of Mark 13 [Hartman, 1966; Lambrecht, 1967; Pesch, 1968; Brandenburger, 1984] or the passion narrative as a whole or parts thereof [Schenke, 1971 – on 14:1–42; Donahue, 1973 and Juel, 1977 – on the trial narrative; Dormeyer, 1974, 1979; Kelber, 1976; Matera, 1982 – on chapter 15; Mohr, 1982; Trocmé, 1983; Schreiber, 1986 – on the crucifixion; Feldmeier, 1987 – on the Gethsemane narrative; Ruhland, 1987; Green, 1988]) all with a view to establishing their form, tradition or redaction history.

Other studies have been directed to those parts or aspects of the Gospel in which the evangelist's redactional activity is deemed to be most evident. These have included the "summary passages" (*Sammelberichte*) to which K. L. Schmidt first drew attention,[34] the so-called Marcan "seams", where the redactor has joined together previously separate units of tradition, or the *hermeneiai*, his editorial asides, parentheses or explanatory comments.[35] Building on contributions made by E. von Dobschutz,[36] C. H. Turner (1923–8),[37] R. Bultmann (1968), and M. Zerwick,[38] among others, detailed analyses have been made of the author's language,[39] style[40] and compositional techniques.[41] Key words in Marcan redactional passages (indicative of the evangelist's own special vocabulary) have been examined, important contributions in this regard being those of E. Schweizer, a translation of whose 1964 article, "Die theologische Leistung des Markus", is included in this volume, and F. Neirynck, who has synthesized the progress made (1981, 1987). An emergent result of such investigation has been the gradual recognition of the apparent homogeneity of the evangelist's style and of the concomitant difficulty of establishing the redactional text of the Gospel.

As well as pursuing redaction-critical studies at pericope-level, Marcan scholars have attempted to identify the basic structure of the Gospel and to ask what the overall arrangement of the material may tell us about the evangelist's literary and theological intent. A number of interesting composition theories have been suggested, including the influential structural analysis of E. Schweizer just mentioned.[42] Content, summary and transitional passages, topographical and geographical indices and various patterns or cycles of recurrent or related material have all been invoked as clues to the literary and theological structure of the Gospel. An increasing number of scholars are now proposing chiasmus, or concentric arrangement, as the key, a pervasive rhetorical device in antiquity, used and appreciated both in oral teaching and in written discourse as a structural device (see e.g. B. Standaert, 1978; B. Van Iersel, 1983; A. Stock, 1984, 1989). A concentric or sandwich pattern has been detected not only in individual sections of the narrative (cf. J. Dewey, 1980 – on 2:1–3:6; N. R. Petersen, 1980 – on 4:1–8:26) but also in the Gospel as a whole, though as yet without unanimity (cf. e.g. M. P. Scott, 1985, with W. Stenger, 1988). The general thrust of all these studies has been to further demonstrate that theological rather than historical motives led Mark to arrange the Gospel as he did.

In the continuing search for the evangelist's leading ideas a number of thematic studies have also emerged, some dealing with Mark's redaction of the parables (Boucher, 1977; Marcus, 1986),[43] his understanding of the Kingdom of God (Ambrozic, 1972; Kelber, 1974), his attitude to the law (Sariola, 1990), his use of the miracle traditions (Kertelge, 1970; Koch, 1975), his treatment of the disciples (Schmahl, 1974; Donahue, 1983), his concept of discipleship (Best, 1981), his eschatology and its relation to discipleship (Breytenbach, 1984; Geddert, 1989), his soteriology (Best, 1965) and so on.

While the traditio-historical method continues to be fruitfully employed on Mark by European scholars in search of the pre-Marcan tradition (see review article, Telford, 1992), the pursuit of the organizing principle or principles behind the literary composition of the Gospel has given rise, in the last twenty years, and especially in America, to further and significant methodological developments. In line with a growing consciousness of, and respect for, the literary achievement of the evangelist has come a call for the Gospel to be studied by holistic methods familiar to the secular literary critic (the analysis of narrative, the investigation of plot, characterization, connecting motifs, etc.).[44] A key figure in this regard was the late N. Perrin, whose appeal for investigations along these lines is expressed in the article included here,[45] and whose challenge has been taken up by several of his students (cf. e.g. Kelber, 1979a). Alongside source, form, tradition and redaction criticism, newer disciplines have been emerging in the biblical field (composition criticism, narrative criticism, reader-response criticism, structuralism, (socio-) rhetorical criticism, media criticism, etc.), methods which, though in some cases allied to redaction criticism, are distinguishable from it. These newer methods have promised or threatened (depending on one's viewpoint) to subsume or submerge "traditional" redaction criticism with its historical as well as literary orientation, within the wider field of a literary criticism schooled to detect literary technique but in some cases (e.g. structuralism) deliberately indifferent to historical questions.

One feature of Marcan studies in the late 1970s and 1980s has been a growing consensus that summary passages, seams, insertions or modifications of pericopae are an inadequate base for developing a full picture of Mark's style and theology. Redaction criticism has been giving way, therefore, to a broader composition criticism (cf. S. E. Dowd, 1988) or narrative criticism (cf. e.g. C. D. Marshall, 1989) in its search for the Marcan fingerprints. Applying literary theory to the text, and insisting on the autonomy of the narrative world created by Mark, narrative criticism in particular has generated some fruitful insights and an increasing number of productive studies. All have laid stress on the unity of the narrative Mark created and the importance of reading it as a narrative whole.[46] The Gospel, it has been increasingly said, should be read as a "story" (e.g. W. H. Kelber, 1979a; D. Rhoads and D. Michie, 1982; J. D. Kingsbury, 1989), written with a consistent "point of view" (N. R. Petersen, 1978b). Narrative critics have analysed it, therefore, in terms of its rhetoric, structure, story-line, settings and characters. Some have examined a number of the evangelist's literary devices (cf. J. Sergeant, 1988), for example, his use of irony (J. Camery-Hoggatt, 1992), or explored single motifs like the "garment" references (cf. R. A. Culpepper, 1982, and 2:21; 5:27–30; 6:56; 9:3; 10:50; 11:7–8; 13:16; 15:20, 24) or major themes like faith

(C. D. Marshall, 1989) or disbelief (M. R. Thompson, 1989). Others have approached particular sections of the narrative from a literary point of view – the prologue, little apocalypse or Marcan ending, as in the articles by F. J. Matera (1988), W. S. Vorster (1987) and A. T. Lincoln (1989) included here, the passion narrative (cf. F. J. Matera, 1986) or even the *hermeneiai* or parenthetical comments (C. W. Hedrick, 1987). Narrative structure has been seen as a clue to the Gospel itself by B. Van Iersel (1988; cf. Stock, 1985a, 1985b).

This latter principle has been developed to an even greater extent by the linguistic discipline of structuralism for which it is a fundamental tenet. With its complex analysis of the "deep structures" underlying a text, structuralism explores the way meaning is achieved within that text without reference to its antecedents or pre-history.[47] Significant in this respect for Mark have been the series of Lévi-Straussian studies by E. S. Malbon (1979, 1982, 1984, 1986a), one of which is included here. These reveal Mark not only as a historical narrative but as a religious text with mythic structure and meaning.

Meaning, however, is not only encoded in a text or created by its author, but is also constructed by the reader who receives it. Reception theory, or reader-response criticism, has also therefore played an important role in recent studies (cf. R. M. Fowler, 1983, 1989 – included here, 1991), as has (socio-)rhetorical criticism (cf. J. Dewey, 1980; V. K. Robbins, 1982, 1984; B. L. Mack and V. K. Robbins, 1989), which examines the literary strategies employed by the author to guide, persuade or manipulate the reader engaged in the construction of meaning. While some forms of reader-response criticism are interested only in the "implied" or "ideal" reader or the reader "in" the text (cf. E. V. McKnight, 1989, and the series of essays therein by B. C. Lategan, B. Van Iersel, R. M. Fowler and T. F. Berg), other approaches emphasize the reception of the Marcan text by its ancient readership and hence retain an historical interest (see T. J. Weeden, 1971; N. R. Petersen, 1984; G. Zuntz in H. Cancik (1984); M. A. Beavis, 1987, 1989; W. R. Telford, 1991; cf. also E. Best, 1992).

While approaching the Gospel as fiction and as a self-consciously crafted narrative, recent scholarly concern to establish the literary environment in which it was created (especially its relation to the Graeco-Roman world and its literature) and the social context in which it was read has led to a number of interesting literary-historical readings (cf. e.g. M. A. Tolbert, 1989). Employing a reader-response criticism with its foundations in formalism and the New Criticism, Tolbert's holistic study locates the Gospel within the literary-historical ethos of its own day and highlights the interpretative conventions which governed the way it was read. Concern, too, to establish the original medium in which it was received (an aim of media criticism) – for example, as an oral narrative composed for and experienced in public reading (T. E. Boomershine, 1987; J. Dewey, 1989) – has also contributed some new insights on the Gospel.

Concern, furthermore, to expose the ideology of the evangelist, his sources, his community or even indeed of his modern interpreters (see M. A. Corner and C. R. Rowland, 1990) has resulted in some socio-historical (cf. B. L. Mack, 1988), socio-literary (cf. C. Myers, 1988), socio-political (cf. H. Waetjen, 1989) or even materialist or Marxist (cf. F. Belo, 1981) readings of Mark. The purpose of Mack's controversial book, *A Myth of Innocence* (1988), which one reviewer has described as "the most creatively synthetic work on the gospel of Mark we have received from an author during the latter half of the twentieth century" (Robbins, 1991, p. 20; see n. 1), is to situate the Gospel within the socio-historical currents of the time. Employing sources whose ideologies reflect the plurality of Jesus movements, the evangelist has fashioned, in Mack's view, a myth of origin for social formations in search of a charter. Combining a literary-critical and socio-logical approach, as a number of these studies have done, Myers, too, sees the Gospel as a weapon in a war of myths. With a socio-political stance that may be described as "non-aligned radicalism" or "revolutionary non-violence", the evangelist's aim is to subvert, on behalf of the common people, the dominant ideology of his culture (and ours). The periphery, Mark's story tells us, and not the centre, is where God is at work, the cross representing the beginning of the new world order. Feminist perspectives have also come into play, particularly in the 1980s with the publication of a series of articles examining the image, status and role of women in the Marcan narrative (cf. e.g. M. J. Schierling, 1980; J. J. Schmitt, 1981; W. Munro, 1982; A. B. Lane, 1983; E. S. Malbon, 1983; J. Kopas, 1985; M. A. Beavis, 1988; J. A. Grassi, 1988).

The variety of hermeneutical approaches which have now emerged and their interrelationship to one another has not only generated confusion, but has also sparked off a considerable methodological debate. The advocacy of a "multi-tool" approach has produced a methodological pluralism full of promise but with its own attendant problems. There has been a move towards a sharper definition of the redaction-critical method and its criteria, especially with regard to Mark whose sources, unlike those of Matthew and Luke, cannot be determined with any degree of certainty.[48] In the case of Mark, the selection and arrangement of material and overall composition may provide a better clue to the evangelist's intention than the alterations he is deemed to have made in his source material. Attention has been drawn to the limitations of a purely (German) tradition-redaction approach, with its meticulous division of the text into verses and fractions of verses allocated either to the evangelist or his sources.[49] Some have even announced the demise of redaction criticism (C. C. Black, 1988, 1989), castigating it for the lack of consensus in its results, its "methodological imperialism" and its misplacement of the author (and not the text) at the centre of textual interpretation. Given the often atomistic nature of a strict form- and redaction-critical procedure, and given the complexity revealed by its results in a text once considered simple, it is not surprising that there has been a call for a more holistic approach to the Gospel.[50]

The hermeneutical task should begin with a literary analysis unencumbered with historical suppositions, its proponents claim, and this is surely correct. In its apparent "flight from history", however, in its treatment of the Gospel by the same methods used to analyse fiction, in its overestimation of Mark's literary achievement, in its disregard of the evidence for textual compositeness (discrepancies, contradictions, etc.) and in its disparagement, in some cases, of the admittedly complex and difficult historical task faced by the exegete,[51] it may, say its critics, be doing us a disservice. This would be an extreme judgement. The newer literary criticism, of which the articles by J. Dewey, R. M. Fowler, A. T. Lincoln, E. S. Malbon, F. J. Matera, R. C. Tannehill and W. S. Vorster included here are good examples, has proved valuable in highlighting the nature of the text as it now stands. By focusing attention on its overall literary effect on the reader[52] rather than on the complex traditio-historical process of which it is the product, it has brought a rich new dimension to Marcan studies, as the current output of literature in this field clearly attests.[53]

It would be impossible to review adequately and with justice the many recent publications on the Gospel of Mark, but having summarized some of the major developments in Marcan study, let us briefly comment on some of the major issues in the literary-critical analysis of the Gospel which have given rise to scholarly debate. There are four which might be highlighted, and they are interrelated. The first is the "orality versus textuality" debate or the question of the relation of Mark as written text to the oral tradition which preceded it (see G. Strecker, 1992; W. R. Telford, 1992). There is still a lack of certainty among scholars regarding the precise nature and reliability of the pre-Marcan tradition, the character of its tradents (apostles, disciples, teachers, prophets, story-tellers, the anonymous community?), the medium (or media?) of its transmission and the process which brought the Gospel itself into its present form. Classical form criticism proposed certain answers to these questions by claiming that the evangelist drew upon a lively oral tradition and, assuming a continuity between orality and textuality, posited a relatively linear development from oral tradition to written gospel. Discussion has revolved subsequently around the transmission process itself and its socio-historical matrix. In particular, dissent has been registered over the question whether pre-Marcan traditions were transmitted in a controlled or a fluid environment (as most form critics held), and if the latter whether the quest for the original or even an earlier form of the tradition is a legitimate one (cf. J. D. Crossan, 1983; C. Breytenbach, 1992).

It is now commonly accepted, in line with the premises of form criticism, that the Gospel of Mark does stand on the borderline of oral and written literature. The Gospel is stamped with the marks of oral structure and patterning, as already observed (cf. W. H. Kelber, 1979b, 1983; A. Stock, 1984; E. Best, 1989 – with reservations; J. Dewey, 1989). It used a combination of oral and written sources (cf. e.g. E. Brandenburger, 1984, on chapter 13, or P. Sellew, 1990, on chapter 4). It may even have been composed for and/or used in oral performace (cf. T. E. Boomershine, 1987; M. A. Beavis, 1989). A number of scholars, mainly European ones, have also continued to support form criticism's model of "aggregate growth" (cf., e.g. H.-J. Wrege, 1978, and his thesis of *Vorstrukturen*, pre-Gospel thematic patterns which, as collective entities, helped mould individual

14

traditions into corporate wholes, or J. Wanke's hypothesis, 1981, of a pre-Gospel synthesizing stage when originally independent dominical sayings were combined with "commentary" texts which served to interpret them). Where the transmission process is concerned, some have argued for the controlled environment of the master/disciple context (e.g. B. Gerhardsson, 1979, 1986, and his article in Stuhlmacher, 1982, and R. Riesner, 1982, 1984) rather than the fluidity of the free-floating folk tradition which is the more common form-critical position. The assumption of continuity between orality and textuality or between the oral tradition and the written gospel still underpins that traditional view, discussed already, which posits a direct or indirect link between Mark and the *Urgemeinde* (or primitive church) or between Mark and Peter (e.g. J. Ernst, 1980; M. Hengel, 1985).

Drawing on E. Güttgemanns (see n. 20), on modern oral studies (E. A. Havelock, A. B. Lord, W. J. Ong, et al.) which, despite form criticism, have been neglected in New Testament studies, and acknowledging his debt to scholars such as M. E. Boring (1982) and J. M. Robinson (1982), W. H. Kelber has challenged this assumption in a number of publications (e.g. 1979b, 1983, 1987a, 1987b, 1988), thereby sparking off a wide debate (see also n. 20). Kelber posits a more radical discontinuity between the oral and the written gospel, the latter reflecting a breakthrough from collectivity to genuine authorship in the Synoptic tradition. Specifically (and controversially), he argues that the Gospel embodies Mark's estrangement from the oral tradition and its tradents (disciples, prophets, the family of Jesus). Like Güttgemanns before him, he has also questioned the notion of an original oral form but his chief contribution lies in the articulation of the first key issue, one which has dominated discussion particularly in the last decade, viz. whether the process that led from oral tradition to gospel composition was an inevitable, collective and evolutionary one (as form critics have asserted) or whether the non-linear and multi-directional nature of the tradition requires us to posit gospel composition as the consequence of individual authorial decision adopting a specific genre (as redaction criticism and the newer literary criticism are increasingly suggesting; cf. e.g. M. A. Tolbert, 1989).

This brings us to the second interrelated issue to occupy scholars in the last thirty years, namely the *Gattung* or *genre* debate. This debate has focused on the question of the literary model(s) by which the author may have been influenced in the overall conception of his work.[54] Three main positions have emerged. One view is that Mark's Gospel is not a *nouveau genre* but one with parallels in Jewish literature (e.g. apocalyptic, wisdom literature or the Old Testament stories of the prophets) or the wider Hellenistic world. Attempts have been made to place Mark in particular within the framework of ancient historiography and to see the Gospel as an example of Graeco-Roman biography (e.g. C. H. Talbert, 1978; D. E. Aune, 1987). Of such, there were three main types: the "life" or *bios* (cf. Lucian's "Life" of the Cynic Demonax and H. Cancik, 1984), "memorabilia" or *apomnemoneumata* (cf. Xenophon's *Memorabilia* of Socrates and V. K. Robbins, 1984) and the "aretalogy".

This latter category, developed perhaps out of collections of miracle stories, presents the career of an impressive teacher, depicting him as a divine man with preternatural gifts, the gift of oratory, the power to work miracles, etc. and in some cases attributing to him a precocious childhood, a martyr's death and a subsequent apotheosis. The examples most often cited are Philostratus' *Life of Apollonius of Tyana*, Porphyry's *Life of Pythagoras* and Philo's *Life of Moses*. This claim was first advanced by C. W. Votaw in 1915[55] but has been developed by M. Hadas and M. Smith in their book, *Heroes and Gods* (New York, 1965), and in numerous articles.[56] In response, critics (most notably H. C. Kee),[57] have expressed doubts regarding the legitimacy of the term "aretalogy" for describing a definable literary type, and have pointed out that the extant "aretalogies" with the strongest claim to similarity are of post-Marcan date.

Links have also been made between Mark and Greek tragedy (e.g. D. O. Via, 1975; G. G. Bilezikian, 1977; B. Standaert, 1978; M. A. Beavis, 1989), the Gospel being conceived as a drama constructed according to the rules of ancient rhetoric. Because it appears less sophisticated, however, in comparison with all such elite Hellenistic works, a number of scholars prefer to locate the Gospel within the popular literary culture of the ancient Mediterranean world, and hence deem it more akin to the ancient novel (or romance), which often combined Greek drama and historiography (cf. e.g. the Alexander romance and M. Reiser in Cancik, 1984, and the erotic novel and M. A. Tolbert, 1989).

A second, and common, view is that Mark's Gospel, on the other hand, is a *nouveau genre* and would argue for its uniqueness. Many, indeed, would concur with the statement of W. Schneemelcher that "the genus 'gospel' (understood as a literary type) represents a form which we do not elsewhere meet with in ancient literature"[58] and of W. Barclay that "in Mark we have the oldest surviving example of a type of literature which was the invention of Christianity".[59] According to S. Schulz in this collection, Mark's chief significance resides in the fact that he was the first and only one to create a "Gospel" in the strict sense of the word,[60] although his highly original literary creation was to provide a structural model for many successors.

A third, modified position is that since there is no such thing as a literary genre which has no roots in antecedent literary types, the most we can say is that Mark's Gospel represents a new type of "evolved" literature[61] for which numerous "partial" antecedents in the ancient world can be suggested (e.g. "sayings" collections,[62] cycles of miracle stories,[63] the martyrology,[64] etc.). The innovative feature of the Marcan redactor was hence to provide an existing pre-Marcan *passion narrative* (a martyrology) with an *extended introduction* (comprising, among other things, such collections of miracle stories as had circulated about Jesus, together with a series of his sayings set frequently in controversy settings). This view of the Gospel's basic structure was first suggested by M. Kähler,[65] and has operated as a major premise for a number of subsequent studies. The particular reasons which motivated Mark to create this distinctive literary genre out of the disparate elements available to him have also been sought and will be discussed below.

The debate on literary antecedents, whole or partial, which may have acted as an overall model for Mark has been paralleled by a third major debate, the "sources" debate, one prompted by the continuing attempt by scholars to identify and isolate these disparate elements out of which the evangelist constructed his Gospel.[66] The nineteenth-century quest for specific written sources behind Mark, or at least of extensive connected cycles of pre-Marcan traditional material, has not been entirely abandoned. Under discussion, in the first place, has been the question whether some of the miracle material in Mark exhibits in its content and structure evidence of having been taken over from one or more specific and connected pre-Marcan sources. Attention has been drawn, for example, to the evidence of dual material (often a pointer to the employment of sources) in the section 4:35–8:26.

Here we find two remarkably similar feeding miracles (6:35–44 and 8:1–10), set alternately on Jewish and Gentile soil (?), as well as two sea miracles (4:35–52 and 6:45–52), two crossings of the lake (6:45 and 8:10), two disputes with the Pharisees (7:1–13 and 8:11–13). Common links between the miracle pericopae of this section, repetition and other suggestive patternings[67] have prompted several interesting theories.

L. E. Keck (1965), for example, suggests that Mark incorporated a single extended cycle of traditional material (recognizable in 3:7–12; 4:35–5:43; 6:31–52, 53–6) which portrays Jesus in the colours of the Hellenistic *theios anēr* or "divine man", in contradistinction to a second stream of Marcan miracle material which is "closely related to the Palestinian scene and the message of Jesus in its native setting" (350) and which portrays him as God's eschatological agent in defeating Satan, "the Strong One" (3:23–7). Keck's theory was persuasively rebutted by T. A. Burkill (1968), however, who demonstrated that the positive and negative distinguishing features of this alleged "divine man" cycle are paralleled in other Gospel pericopae outside of this block.

P. J. Achtemeier (1970, 1972) has argued for the incorporation of a *double* cycle of pre-Marcan miracle catenae with a "divine man" colouring (comprising a sea miracle, three healing miracles and a feeding miracle; 4:35–5:43 with 6:34–44, 53 and paralleled again in 6:45–51; 8:22–6; 7:24b–30, 32–7 and 8:1–10). These catenae, whose background is to be sought in Hellenistic-Jewish Moses traditions, originally formed part, he suggests, of a eucharistic liturgy celebrating the presence and status of Jesus as "an epiphanic figure along the lines of Moses, the *theios anēr* (1972: 212). While Achtemeier's source-critical analysis is very persuasive (all of the material accredited to the second of his alleged parallel cycles, for example, is curiously omitted by Luke, following Mark), his suggested *Sitz im Leben* for the pre-Marcan double cycle is too speculative to be convincing.

Another double cycle with a different configuration (comprising the pattern "feeding miracle – crossing of the lake – dispute with the Pharisees – discourse on bread") has also been mooted for 6:30–7:23 and 8:1–21.[68] The fact that this pattern is also found in the possibly independent John chapter 6 is suggestive, although the degree of Marcan redaction evident within these sections militates against a connected source hypothesis. R. M. Fowler (1981), for example, casts doubts on the existence of these pre-Gospel miracle cycles and argues that the repetitions evident in chapters 4–8 are to be attributed to the hand of the evangelist himself. While it is usual to regard the two feeding accounts as variants of a single core tradition (see e.g. S. Masuda, 1982; cf. also L. Schenke, 1983), Fowler claims that one element of the supposed doublet, the first feeding miracle (6:30–44), was in reality composed by Mark himself to act as "a backdrop for the traditional story (8:1–10), thereby controlling how the reader perceives the traditional story" (181). The narrative function of this doublet in relation to the author and his implied reader is also the subject of C. Focant's perceptive analysis (1992).

Source-critical analysis has, in the second place, focused on the controversy stories, taking up the question whether pericopae in such sections of the Gospel as 2:1–3:6; 7:1–23, 11–12, 14–16 display sufficient positive and negative distinguishing features as to suggest they derive from a non-Marcan source or sources. One such study is that of M. J. Cook, *Mark's Treatment of the Jewish Leaders* (1978). Building upon, but modifying, the previous work of M. Albertz, B. S. Easton and P. Winter, among others, Cook claims to be able to isolate, on the basis of leadership group designations, three specific written sources upon which the Marcan redactor drew for his accounts of the conflicts between Jesus and his opponents. The three sources postulated are: (1) an early Passion source, which featured chief priests, elders and scribes, and associated them with Jerusalem only; (2) a source which mentioned only scribes and again set them in Jerusalem; (3) a source which focused on Pharisees (and Herodians) only and was possibly set in a Galilean context. The theory is plausible, but its chief weakness lies in the fact that there are an insufficient number of factors outside of group titles to argue for the integrity or discreteness of these alleged more extensive sources.[69]

J. Dewey (1980), on the other hand, reached a different conclusion concerning "controversy" sources. Dewey argued that the literary structure of the section 2:1–3:6 was a product of Mark's redaction upon previously independent units of tradition and did not belong to a pre-Marcan source which he had incorporated. No pre-Marcan collections were similarly involved in chapters 11–12. The 1973 article included in this volume anticipates her full-length study.

The Interpretation of Mark

Continuing research in the 1980s has, if anything, left the matter unresolved. While J. G. D. Dunn (1984) adheres to 2:1–3:6 as a pre-Marcan unit, Dewey's influential rhetorical-critical study (1980) and that of W. Weiss (1989) from a form-critical perspective, have together cast some doubt on this supposition, as also on a pre-Marcan collection in chapters 11–12. Albertz's hypothesis that 11:27–33 and 12:13–37 were likewise a pre-Marcan collection has also been challenged by J.-G. Mudiso Mbâ Mundla (1984) and this result has been strengthened by a consensus among recent commentators (e.g. J. Gnilka, 1978–9; D. Lührmann, 1987; R. A. Guelich, 1989).[70]

The question of the use by Mark of "sayings" sources has similarly been raised (e.g. in 9:33–50 or 10). Similarities exist between some Marcan sayings and those attributed to the hypothetical sayings-source Q but a direct literary link is generally thought improbable (cf. R. Laufen, 1980).[71] Even among the scholars who argue for Marcan dependence upon Q (e.g. F. C. Grant, J. P. Brown, W. Schenk, J. Lambrecht), the nature of the parallels suggest that if Mark had used Q "it was from memory, and that a rather poor one".[72] The evangelist's sayings probably came to him for the most part from the oral tradition in free-floating form or in relatively small previously linked clusters,[73] which were employed by the community and adapted to its practical needs, as Kuhn (1971) suggested.

Three possible exceptions have been the subject of continuing research, and these are the longer teaching sections in Mark, the parable discourse in 4:1–34, the discipleship discourse or *Regelkompendium* in chapter 10 (cf. R. Busemann, 1983) and the eschatological discourse in chapter 13. Original documentary sources redacted by Mark may possibly have formed the basis for each of these, but to date no scholarly consensus has emerged about the necessary existence of such, far less on their putative reconstruction.

Where the parable discourse is concerned, there is still the general assumption (following Jeremias) of an underlying pre-Marcan collection, with 4:11–12 as an alien insertion (e.g. V. Parkin, 1986). P. Sellew (1990) has recently posited two partially overlapping sources, one oral (4:3–9, 26–9, 30–2) and the other written (4:14–20), which, with insertions (4:11–12, 21–5) were combined together into an edited whole. Following Dewey, however, G. Fay (1989) has argued for a seven-part concentric structure to 4:1–34, which, while not ruling out a pre-Marcan collection, militates against it.[74]

In the case of the eschatological discourse, the incorporation of pre-Marcan material is not in question but the extent and cohesiveness of the traditional elements does remain a matter of dispute.[75] One prominent view is that the discourse was built around the nucleus of an apocalypse (or apocalyptic "flysheet", pamphlet or tract) of independent origin, which had originally circulated in Jewish (cf. R. Bultmann), Jewish-Christian (cf. R. Pesch) or early Christian circles (cf. K. Grayston), either in the reign of the Emperor Caligula (37–41 C.E.) or at the time of the Romano-Jewish War (66–70 C.E.). This "little apocalypse" theory has a long ancestry, and was subjected to criticism by G. R. Beasley-Murray in his book *Jesus and the Future*, published in 1954. Beasley-Murray claimed, however (but in the days before redaction criticism), that the teaching of chapter 13 represented an authentic discourse of Jesus which began to circulate as a document within the first decade of the church's existence (c.f. D. Wenham, 1984).[76] J. Lambrecht's literary analysis (*Die Redaktion der Markus-Apocalypse*, 1967), on the other hand, made a powerful case for the composite nature of the discourse. Lambrecht recognized the evangelist's dependence on traditional elements (most notably Q and the Old Testament) but argues persuasively for the high degree of Marcan redactional activity evident throughout it, as well as for its links, in terms of style, structure and content, with the rest of the Gospel.

Arguments for a written source or *Vorlage* in chapter 13 have been based on the numerous discrepancies and ambiguities which exist in the passage, particularly in the attitude expressed towards apocalyptic. In a major recent study, E. Brandenburger (1984) opts for a combination of a written *Vorlage*, oral tradition and a redaction which used apocalyptic positively and not negatively. Other perspectives have been developing, however. K. Tagawa (1977) assessed the ambiguity in the discourse as a function not only of the interplay between tradition and redaction but also of the evangelist's personal ambivalence about apocalypticism, and Geddert's more recent holistic approach (1989) has added to this trend by claiming that these ambiguities were deliberately created by "a writer with a carefully considered and subtly communicated theological perspective" (18). Building on Brandenburger, J. Verheyden (1992) has now, however, posed the question of the need for a *Vorlage* and, in the article included in this collection, W. S. Vorster, in line with the increasingly popular literary approach to Mark, has called for more attention to be given to the narrative character of the discourse.

In pointing to the links between Mark 13 and prophetic and apocalyptic passages in the Greek Bible (particularly Daniel, Micah, Joel and Zechariah), J. Lambrecht also highlighted the literary and theological role of at least one indubitable literary source which the evangelist (as well as his tradition) has drawn upon, viz. the Old Testament. L. Hartman, too, the previous year (*Prophecy Interpreted*, 1966) had argued that Mark 13 was based on an exposition or meditation upon the book of Daniel, although his research, unlike Lambrecht's, was largely devoted to the tradition history of the discourse and involved a comparative study of a number of Jewish apocalyptic texts outside of the Old Testament. A number of other studies from the 1960s onwards have similarly contributed to our growing awareness of the extent to which the Marcan evangelist has used the Jewish scriptures in the service of his theology, or been influenced, consciously or unconsciously, by them.[77]

This influence has been seen particularly in the Marcan passion narrative,[78] an extended section of the Gospel (14–16) for which, it has long been claimed, the evangelist was dependent upon a documentary source. Even form-critical orthodoxy allowed this as an exception to its basic axiom that the tradition behind Mark was handed down in small, separate, self-contained and easily memorized units.[79] Although this view has been modified by the acknowledgement that Mark may have brought several originally isolated pericopae (e.g. the Anointing at Bethany, 14:3–9, or the Gethsemane story, 14:32–42) into connection with a smaller nucleus of connected tradition about Jesus' arrest, trial and crucifixion, the amount of redactional activity upon this pre-Synoptic report has generally been regarded as minimal when compared with the rest of the Gospel.

A move away from this position, nevertheless, has been in evidence. E. Linnemann (1970) produced a study which claimed that the Marcan passion narrative did not exist as a unified, coherent and consecutive whole in the pre-Marcan oral tradition but from beginning to end was composed of fragments of tradition. L. Schenke's analysis of 14:1–42 (*Studien zur Passionsgeschichte des Markus*, 1971) argued that this particular section of the narrative was a somewhat more elaborate redactional composition by the evangelist woven out of separate tradition units and acting as a kind of theological preface to the traditional account of the passion which followed.[80] Others have argued that even single pericopae like the Gethsemane story,[81] or the crucifixion narrative itself (cf. e.g. Schreiber, 1967: 22–82, and 1986), are likewise composite creations, woven out of more than one strand of tradition.

A challenge has been issued, moreover, even to this modified position by those scholars who would argue for an even greater compositional activity on the part of Mark. This can be seen, for example, in J. R. Donahue's study of the Sanhedrin trial (*Are You the Christ?*, 1973) which advanced the case for this pericope (14:53–65) to be considered a Marcan composition (albeit out of some disparate traditional elements) and one clearly influenced by the evangelist's theology (cf. also D. Juel, 1977). The volume of essays edited by W. Kelber (1976) went further and called into question, as Linnemann had done, the very existence of an independent and coherent pre-Marcan passion narrative. All seven of these essays by American scholars united in claiming that "virtually all major Marcan themes converge in 14–16" and that this section "constitutes a theologically inseparable and homogeneous part of the Gospel whole" (156f.). The literary and theological achievement of Mark was to compose an entire Gospel, not just 1–13, out of a multiplicity of disparate tradition units.

The passion narratives and the search for a pre-Marcan passion narrative in particular have continued to occupy scholarship in the 1980s, even though literary and synchronic approaches (see e.g. F. J. Matera, 1982, 1986; J. P. Heil, 1990; cf. D. Dormeyer, 1979) have also been in evidence. Despite the Kelber volume (1976) and the recent emphasis placed by B. L. Mack (1988) on the role of the evangelist in creating the passion story, the consensus is still in favour of a pre-Marcan passion narrative of some kind (though its parameters are disputed) and one possibly going back to the *Urgemeinde* (cf. R. Pesch, 1979a; R. Pesch, R. Kratz, 1979; T. A. Mohr, 1982; E. Trocmé, 1983). J. B. Green (1988) is the most recent comprehensive attempt to assess the case and comes out in favour.

Source criticism with its diachronic perspective is still an ongoing concern in Marcan studies, as is the search for the pre-

Marcan tradition. The trend in general, nevertheless, has been increasingly away from theories which posit the existence of written sources underlying Mark. It is more the *use* by Mark of his material rather than its *origin* which has been occupying scholarly attention in recent times. Where pre-Marcan collections are concerned, there would appear to be a general agreement still in favour of a collection of controversies (in 2:1–3:6 but not in 7:1–23 or 11–12), parables (in 4:1–34) and sayings (in 10). The issue is more divided in the case of miracles (4:35ff.) and the apocalypse (13), and generally against in the case of the prologue (1:2–15) and the so-called "day in Capernaum" (1:21–39). Where the "sources" debate is concerned, therefore, a majority of scholars would probably still endorse (with the passion narrative a qualified exception) the statement of W. G. Kümmel: "We cannot go beyond declaring that Mark is probably based on no extensive written sources, but that more likely the evangelist has woven together small collections of individual traditions and detailed bits of tradition into a more or less coherent presentation" (1975: 85).

It is in this "more or less", however, that the nub of another key issue lies, one upon which we have already commented in describing the newer literary criticism. The recent discussion of the passion narrative highlights the fourth, and arguably the most important, debate being conducted among Marcan scholars, viz. the "creativity" debate (cf. U. Luz, 1980). This centres on the question of the extent to which Mark was master of his material. On the one hand, there are those, following Bultmann (1968: 349f.), who would say that the evangelist was a conservative redactor exercising comparatively little creative influence on the tradition (e.g. R. Pesch, H. Riesenfeld, E. J. Pryke, E. Best). It was a growing conviction that this was the case which led Pesch, for example, to revise his earlier views on the tradition-redaction components of Mark 13.[82] Certain factors (kerygmatic, traditional, historical) would have exercised a controlling influence upon Marcan creativity, as Riesenfeld has argued.[83] When faced with a piece of tradition, he altered it as little as possible, beyond supplying notes of place, time and audience where these were missing, seams uniting the individual pericopae, and summary and transitional passages linking series of pericopae. This is the point of view expressed in E. Best's article here, "Mark's Preservation of the Tradition" (cf. also Best, 1979). Best asks us to

24

consider Mark not as an author but as "an artist creating a collage" and warns us against looking for a consistent or coherent theology from the evangelist "since he laid his theology over an existing theology, or theologies, in the tradition he received" (below, 163–4).

On the other hand, there are those (e.g. R. H. Stein, N. Petersen, R. C. Tannehill, W. H. Kelber, J. D. Crossan, F. Kermode, J. Dewey, N. Q. Hamilton, W. S. Vorster, J. Lambrecht,[84] B. L. Mack, M. A. Tolbert) who would claim with N. Perrin that Mark was a genuine author and not a scissors-and-paste editor. This view is not a new one but was advocated, for example, by A. Farrer, an early proponent of a literary-critical/theological approach to the Gospel.[85] The newer literary criticism would argue for a move away from the prevailing view which sees the Gospel as an edited collection of traditions with a theological perspective towards one which sees it as a genuine narration. N. Petersen, for example, has called attention to the literary evidence in the text which reveals its author as a bona fide narrator.[86] R. C. Tannehill, too, from a literary perspective, has argued that "Mark is a single, unified story because of its progressive narrative lines" (1979: 77). Two recent works by B. L. Mack (1988) and M. A. Tolbert (1989) have both emphasized the high degree of internal coherence which Mark has imposed on his materials. Others have argued for a considerable creation of material on the part of Mark (the three passion predictions, for example, according to Perrin [1967–8]; the didactic scenes of 8:14–21; 9:14–29 and 10:1–12, according to P. Sellew [1989]; the Gethsemane scene, according to Kelber [1972];[87] the resurrection narrative, according to Crossan or Hamilton[88]). Literary artifice and intentional symbolism have also been detected in two of the most enigmatic passages of the passion and resurrection narratives, the flight of the naked young man in 14:51–2 and his reappearance (?) in the Marcan ending.[89]

Whether we think of Mark, then, as a highly creative author/theologian or merely as a skilful (or even clumsy! – cf. J. C. Meagher, 1979) but conservative redactor, it remains for us to ask if the research to date has thrown light on the key concerns which governed his literary and theological enterprise. An emergent scholarly consensus would probably now identify the following themes, interests or motifs as of prime importance in determining the evangelist's purpose insofar as it can be gauged from his redactional activity:

(1) the *secrecy* motif and the writer's interest in the true but hidden *identity* of Jesus;

(2) an interest in the *passion* of Jesus (his suffering, death and resurrection) and its significance for Christology;

(3) an interest in the nature and coming of the *Kingdom of God* and in the question of Jesus' return as *Son of Man*;

(4) an interest in *Galilee*;

(5) his use of the term *"gospel"* (*euangelion*);

(6) an interest in *Gentiles* and the *Gentile mission*;

(7) an interest in *persecution, suffering* and *martyrdom* and the true nature of *discipleship*;

(8) his harsh treatment of the *Jewish leadership groups*, Jesus' *family* and especially his original *disciples*.

"A major aspect of the Marcan purpose is christological", N. Perrin tells us, and few would disagree.[90] The Gospel, as it now stands, invites the reader to view the Jesus of history (or of the tradition) in a certain light, and to respond in faith or even worship to the figure thus presented. But in what precise light does Mark intend Jesus to be seen? Scholars are divided on this issue.[91] Is the evangelist's purpose to depict Jesus primarily as a powerful wonder-worker and exorcist (cf. J. M. Robinson), as the teacher/prophet of the "gospel" whose (passion) kerygma is authenticated by his miracles (cf. E. Schweizer, et al.),[92] as the new Moses (cf. J. A. Ziesler),[93] as the promised Jewish Messiah (cf. W. Wrede),[94] or even more significantly as the incarnation or "epiphany" of God in human form, as K. Kertelge argues in the 1969 essay included here?[95]

This last view is representative of one popular school of thought which owes much to R. Bultmann. In an oft-repeated dictum, Bultmann defined the Marcan purpose as "the union of the Hellenistic kerygma about Christ, whose essential content consists of the Christ myth as we learn of it in Paul (esp. Phil. 2:6ff.; Rom. 3:24) with the tradition of the story of Jesus" (1968: 347f.). This position has been frequently espoused (cf. e.g. W. Marxsen, S. Schulz, J. Schreiber), although its critics point to the absence in the Gospel of any explicit attribution of pre-existence to Jesus by Mark, a point acknowledged by Bultmann himself.[96]

The Marcan Jesus, nevertheless, is a figure surrounded by an aura of mystery (cf. F. J. Matera, 1989) and the part played by the secrecy motif (at least at the literary level) in the fulfilment of the evangelist's christological purpose is now widely recognized.[97] By means of this motif, the reader is made a party to the secret of Jesus' true identity, as Mark perceives it. This secret is also shared and confessed by the supernatural world but withheld from the human characters in the Marcan story, with the exception of the Roman centurion at his cross, and perhaps also (but questionably) his disciples. In connection with the "secrecy" theme, scholarly attention has also focused on the import of the titles applied to Jesus in Mark, as well as on the overall relation and function (in respect of his christological presentation) of the miracle and controversy pericopae, the parable and eschatological discourses and the passion narrative.[98] Certain key pericopae, such as the Caesarea Philippi episode and the transfiguration have in particular been the subject of detailed study.[99]

Such investigations have highlighted the importance for Mark of two of the christological titles in particular which are found in the Gospel, the ascriptions "Son of God" and "Son of Man". These titles convey more than any others the real significance of Jesus, as Mark sees it, and disclose to the Marcan reader the very essence of the "secret" of his mission and identity. Over each, however, a question-mark still remains. What does Mark intend his first-century reader to infer about Jesus' true status by having him confessed as "Son of God" (cf. e.g. 1:11; 3:11; 9:7; 15:39), or by having him speak of himself as the "Son of Man" whose destiny it is to suffer, die and rise again (cf. e.g. 8:31; 9:31; 10:33–4)? The precise meaning and significance of these terms as employed by Mark is not clear and division among scholars is here again apparent.

Where the title "Son of God" is concerned, some would posit a Jewish background as decisive for its interpretation. As employed in this Gospel, according to D. Lührmann (1977), for example, it would indicate that Jesus stands in the tradition of the Jewish sage or suffering righteous man, God's loyal servant, as described in Isaiah or the Wisdom literature (cf. e.g. Isa. 42:1; 52:7; 53; Wisd. 2:12–20).[100] Others would view the term as a Jewish Messianic designation, a synonym for the royal Messiah or "eschatological king" (cf. H. C. Kee, J. R. Donahue, J. D. Kingsbury).[101] In both cases, the term would imply that Jesus was God's "Son", not in metaphysical terms but as the obedient human agent of the divine will.[102] On the other hand, positing a Hellenistic background as the chief determinant of its meaning, a number of scholars (cf. R. Bultmann, W. Marxsen, J. Schreiber, S. Schulz, K. Kertelge) would see in its Gospel usage the primary evidence of Mark's intention that Jesus be regarded as an epiphany of God in human form, a supernatural being or Hellenistic "divine man" (in contradistinction to Jewish Messianic or "Son of David" connotations).

It is this latter claim which was, until fairly recently, the stimulant to a vigorous debate. Reference has already been made to the importance of the miracle stories in Mark and to the views of those scholars (e.g. L. E. Keck, P. J. Achtemeier, N. Perrin) who detected in this material the imprint of a "divine man" Christology.[103] In presenting Jesus as a powerful and charismatic figure awakening numinous awe in his followers, able to calm storms or walk on water, to heal at a touch or raise from the dead, a mysterious being subject to metamorphosis or transfiguration, these traditions are said to reflect the influence of the "divine man" or *theios anēr* concept, a type encountered in or deemed to underlie stories associated with Hellenistic heroes such as Socrates, Apollonius of Tyana or Pythagoras.

Critics of this view, however, have denied the existence of the *theios anēr* as a unified category or definable concept in the ancient world[104] and have pointed to formative influences closer to home. These are taken to reside in the Old Testament and Jewish apocalyptic, with parallels between Jesus' alleged miracles and those attributed to Moses, Elijah and Elisha being cited instead.[105] Even were the case for a "divine man" Christology to be granted, it is not clear whether such a Christology can properly be described as distinctively Marcan (rather than being merely a feature of the Hellenistic traditions he has taken over) nor is it certain whether he himself approved or disapproved of the characterization of Jesus reflected therein.

Suspicions that the evangelist may not have been entirely happy with the tradition of Jesus as a wonder-worker and exorcist have been raised by his use of the second, and perhaps complementary, ascription, the "Son of Man". The origin, import and function of the "Son of Man" sayings in Mark, as well as their relation to the other christological titles, have been the subject of much discussion, although to date this has been largely inconclusive.[106]

These sayings have traditionally been divided into three categories. A first group depicts Jesus as a triumphant apocalyptic figure promising his future return (e.g. 8:38; 13:26; 14:62); a second as a charismatic figure proclaiming his present authority (e.g. 2:10; 2:28);[107] and a third as a suffering, rejected figure predicting his death and resurrection (e.g. 8:31; 9:31; 10:33–4). This third group, the passion predictions, has received particular attention. N. Perrin, as we have noted, regards them as redactional. Others would argue that they have been taken over from the tradition.[108] Whether traditional or redactional, however, few would doubt that these passion predictions lead us to the very heart of Marcan Christology and soteriology. Jesus the "Son of God" is at the same time, for Mark, the suffering, crucified and exalted "Son of Man".

Whatever the ambiguity, then, surrounding the precise meaning of these christological titles, there is nowadays a gathering consensus among Marcan scholars that the emphasis by the evangelist on the divine necessity of Jesus' suffering and death ("the way of the cross") represents a major thrust of his christological presentation. It was W. Wrede, in his highlighting of the "secrecy" motif, who first articulated, as we have seen, the case for a strong theological ("dogmatic") motivation at work in the composition of the Marcan Gospel. Wrede's contribution in this regard was often critically received, especially by Anglo-Saxon scholarship. "The farther we travel along the Wredestrasse, the clearer it becomes that it is the road to nowhere", was the judgement of T. W. Manson.[109] Subsequent scholarship has not borne this out. It is clear now that "the Wredestrasse has become the Hauptstrasse" (to borrow the title of N. Perrin's 1966 article). In modification of Wrede's thesis, however, it is now generally agreed that Mark has not imposed a Christology upon pre-Marcan traditions that have *no* christological stamp, but rather that he sought to *develop* or *counter*, by means of his own, the Christology already *implicit* in these various traditions.

One now common view is that by means of his passion emphasis or kerygma, the Marcan redactor is seeking to develop (cf. S. Schulz), qualify or oppose (cf. E. Schweizer, U. B. Müller, D.-A. Koch) traditions that portrayed Jesus in a *triumphalist* light, either as the wonder-working Hellenistic "divine man" (cf. R. Bultmann, J. Schreiber, H. D. Betz, T. J. Weeden) or as the victorious Jewish Messiah (cf. J. B. Tyson, 1961; C. B. Cousar,

1970), the Son of David[110] or the triumphantly returning apocalyptic Son of Man. In either case, such traditions gave insufficient significance to his death on the cross or, in the language of the debate, they promoted a "theologia gloriae" but lacked a "theologia crucis". The dispute among scholars, therefore, devolves once again upon the question concerning the precise nature of the Christology the evangelist is deemed to be promoting, and that which he is seeking to combat.

For example, S. Schulz, following Bultmann, argues that Mark has wedded a Hellenistic/Pauline kerygma about the crucified and risen Christ to Palestinian and Hellenistic Jesus traditions (cf. also now B. L. Mack, 1988). The miracle stories so incorporated, he claims, serve a positive function in the Gospel. They reflect his own Hellenistic "epiphany" Christology and, together with the passion emphasis and the secrecy motif, they present what is ultimately a "theologia gloriae", a theology whose subject is the incarnate Son of God, the *Deus praesens*, who lives, dies, is raised and exalted.[111]

In the course of the debate, it is now often said that the evangelist's theology has been formulated out of a concern for his own contemporary church situation (e.g. Lambrecht, 1973), and even that his presentation itself dramatizes christological disputes which were being waged within his community. A key contribution to this argument has been T. J. Weeden's *Mark – Traditions in Conflict* (1971), the gist of which is summarized in the article included here. Weeden claims that the Gospel was written in response to a christological conflict which was unsettling the Marcan community. The heretical Christology which Mark sought to combat was a "divine man" Christology which emphasized Jesus' power (and hence that of his followers) as a miracle-worker without a corresponding emphasis on the necessity of suffering and persecution which was equally the lot of the follower (as it had been of Jesus). Behind the "secrecy" motif (cf. Mark 9:9) lies a Marcan assertion that the true significance of Jesus can only be recognized, not in his miracles, but "sub specie crucis et resurrectionis". This conflict of christologies he dramatized by having the disciples represent the attitudes appropriate to the "divine man" perspective, and consequently showing them up as in error. For Weeden, unlike Schulz, the miracle stories serve a basically negative function in Mark's redactional scheme. They are taken over by him precisely to be qualified by his own "theologia crucis", an effect achieved by their juxtaposition with the passion narrative and its compelling picture of a suffering Messiah whose power is revealed in weakness.

Objections to Weeden's thesis have been raised.[112] It is not clear whether the miracle traditions incorporated and redacted by Mark do indeed serve to counteract a "divine man" view of Jesus or whether they in fact enhance it, as Schulz maintains. It is also somewhat curious that the original Jewish disciples, the representatives of the Jerusalem church, should be chosen as the exponents of a Hellenistic Christology opposed by the evangelist.[113] More plausible in this respect is J. B. Tyson's view that Mark, as the representative of Gentile Christianity, is attacking in the person of the twelve the royal Messiah/Son of David Christology of the original Jerusalem church, which claimed that Jesus was Messiah in spite of, not because of, his death and, in consequence of his resurrection, would shortly return in glory. By virtue of its historical links with Jesus, moreover, this primitive community, the *Urgemeinde*, also laid claim to spiritual authority over the nascent Gentile-Christian communities founded by hellenistic-Jewish missionaries like Paul.

The debate over the nature of Marcan soteriology and the extent to which a developed "theologia crucis", passion kerygma or atonement theology underlies the presentation (cf. Best, 1965) has naturally raised again the question of the influence of Paul on Mark. The classic case denying any direct influence was made in 1923 by M. Werner,[114] who argued that the Marcan Gospel was representative of a type of Gentile Christianity which was independent of Paul. Comparing the Gospel with the epistles, Werner noted that a number of specific Pauline concepts were on the whole lacking in Mark, while the resemblances between them were explicable as the product of beliefs which were common to, and widespread in, primitive Christianity. While various positions on this question have been adopted,[115] Werner's case has been influential.

The advent of redaction criticism, however, has opened up the possibility of a more discriminating analysis. W. Marxsen, for example, has criticized Werner for comparing Pauline thought with the Marcan Gospel in toto and not with the distinctive theological contribution of Mark to the pre-Marcan traditions it incorporates (as detected by redaction criticism).[116] Following

31

Bultmann, Schreiber and others, he too claims that "Mark ties together the two 'strands' of primitive Christian preaching: the Pauline kerygma and the (so-called) synoptic tradition" (216). Insufficient allowance has also been made for the differing ways in which each writer has chosen to express his kerygma, Paul in abstract theological terms and in the direct form of an epistle, Mark in the "visual" and narrative form of a Gospel. When due account is taken of this difference, Mark can be seen, says Marxsen, to have taken up "the Pauline fundamentals", a judgment in which he is increasingly supported as redaction-critical studies proceed.[117]

The Pauline epistles and the Marcan Gospel both stem from the primitive period of Christianity when Christian communities believed they were among mankind's final generation, and appeared to have that belief confirmed in the events which led up to the fall of Jerusalem. Both Mark and Paul were interested in the nature and advent of the Kingdom of God and in the question of the return of Jesus as world-ruler (though Paul himself did not use the ascription "Son of Man" of Jesus). The precise nature and significance of Marcan eschatology has been the subject of much discussion. Following analysis of the parable discourse as well as the other Marcan Kingdom sayings, some scholars would argue that the evangelist sees the promised Kingdom as having been already "realized" (cf. C. H. Dodd) in the person and mission of Jesus, or as having been at least "inaugurated" (cf. J. Jeremias) with his coming. Others, following A. Schweitzer, hold that Mark retains the primitive expectation of the Kingdom's coming as a future apocalyptic event. The structure of the Gospel itself is claimed to have been conceived along the lines of an "apocalyptic drama" (cf. N. Perrin).

Crucial to this debate has been scholarly assessment of the importance (or otherwise) within the structure of the Gospel of the eschatological discourse. Is it a "foreign body" (cf. R. Pesch) or an integral part of the evangelist's literary enterprise (cf. D.-A. Koch, T. J. Geddert)? While Marxsen has asserted that the parousia was of central importance for Mark, and Brandenburger that he has modified his sources to apply them to a new situation, others (e.g. E. Schweizer, 1969) would argue, among other things, on the basis of his redaction of this chapter (cf. e.g. 13:34–7), that it was of peripheral concern. By his insertion and alteration of this discourse, Mark, it is claimed, was actually seeking to tone down the apocalyptic enthusiasm of the 60s (cf. R. Pesch, 1968; C. B. Cousar, 1970). Contradicting any belief in imminent parousia, 13:10 in particular ("And the gospel must first be preached to all nations") indicates that the evangelist held at least a modified eschatological expectation, and it was this "Atempause" introduced into the apocalyptic scenario which was further to be developed by Luke into a salvation history scheme which would explain the delay of the parousia (cf. H. Conzelmann, 1959).

The importance attached by scholars to the eschatological discourse derives not only from the fact that it provides a clue to the writer's eschatological orientation, but also because it is seen as a pointer to the nature and situation of the Marcan community which is being addressed through the medium of Jesus' promises for the future. Two further such promises are found on Jesus' lips in 14:28 and 16:7. These inform the reader that Jesus will "go before" his disciples to "Galilee" where he is henceforth to be "seen". These verses have been interpreted in three main ways. While most scholars take them as representing the promise of an immediate post-resurrection appearance,[118] they could also have been understood by the Marcan reader as predicting Jesus' future parousia (e.g. W. Marxsen, following E. Lohmeyer, 1936; N. Q. Hamilton, 1965) or even his spiritual presence and leadership within the context of the community's post-Easter missionary activity (e.g. C. F. Evans [1954], following E. C. Hoskyns). Whichever view is taken, it is significant that the locale for this experience (as for much of Jesus' activity in Mark) is "Galilee" (not Jerusalem, as in Luke). According to W. Marxsen's study, *Mark the Evangelist* (1956; ET 1969), most of the references to "Galilee" throughout the Gospel have been inserted by the evangelist. The interest shown by Mark in "Galilee", then, may derive from the Gospel's historical setting, the community addressed being representative of a Galilean Christianity (cf. E. Lohmeyer, 1936) and one being literally summoned, at the time of the Romano-Jewish War, to await Jesus' parousia in Galilee (W. Marxsen). On the other hand, if, in keeping with its Gentile associations (cf. Isa. 9:1, Matt. 4:15 "Galilee of the Gentiles"), the references to "Galilee" betray a theological or symbolic intent on the part of Mark (e.g. J. Schreiber, W. H. Kelber), then further support is given to those who would interpret 14:28 or 16:7 in particular as in effect a Gentile mission prediction (cf. 13:10).[119]

If the theological nature of Marcan geography is being increasingly asserted,[120] then other features of the Gospel too, point to the Gentile-Christian orientation of the Marcan evangelist and his links (direct or indirect) with Paul or his kerygma. As with the "Galilee" references in Mark, Marxsen has demonstrated the redactional nature of occurrences of the word "gospel" (*euangelion*), a term associated principally with Paul and used by him to describe his proclamation of the crucified and exalted Christ. Whether Mark uses the term precisely in a Pauline sense is a matter of dispute. Marxsen (1969) thinks that "Paul's understanding is the presupposition for Mark's, though we need not assume direct dependence" (147). Others (e.g. G. Dautzenberg, D. Lührmann) question this and prefer to think that Mark meant by the expression the "good news" about the coming Kingdom rather than a proclamation or kerygma about the coming of the Christ of the hellenistic-Jewish Christ-myth.[121]

The particular nuances of Marcan usage aside, it is clear, nonetheless, that the author of this first Gospel had a particular interest in Gentiles, in Jew-Gentile relations, and in the Gentile mission, as did Paul. This is borne out by studies on the significance of the miracle pericopae for Mark and the Marcan community. Scholars have long argued for the symbolic significance of the feeding stories, for example, in the Gospel.[122] Recent studies such as those of Q. Quesnell and R. M. Fowler have drawn attention in general to the prominence of "food and eating" imagery in Mark.[123] The "giving of bread" motif is found in a number of pericopae (e.g. 2:26; 5:43; 6:37ff.; 7:27–8; 8:1ff., 14ff., etc.). Quesnell draws the conclusion that the two feeding miracles of 6:30–44 and 8:1–10 would have been understood by the Marcan reader as prefiguring the Christian eucharist. Others would press for a more general christological, universalistic and even ecclesiological significance (e.g. K. Kertelge), the stories implying that Jesus feeds man in general or the believer in particular with heavenly bread. Many have seen an ecumenical significance in the two parallel feedings, with bread being supplied by Jesus to both Jewish and Gentile crowds respectively (cf. e.g. N. A. Beck, 1981). Even were this not the case, and both feedings are assumed to occur on Gentile soil, as G. H. Boobyer contends,[124] then the Leitmotif of the whole section 6:30–8:21 is Jesus' dealings with the Gentiles and the lesson that "national and religious exclusivism must have no place in their conception of the scope of Christ's mission" (1953: 87). One or even both stories, then, prefigure the extension of the "gospel" to the Gentile world after Easter.

The influence of the post-Easter situation on the Gospel is also borne out by studies on the significance of the controversy pericopae for Mark and his community (cf. e.g. W. Thissen, 1976; A. J. Hultgren, 1979; W. Weiss, 1989). Throughout the Gospel, but especially in these passages, the hostile attitude of the evangelist to the Jews and the Jewish authorities is given literary and theological expression, as a number of recent studies have pointed out (cf. e.g. W. A. Johnson, 1989; E. S. Malbon, 1989; J. D. Kingsbury, 1990; cf. also C. Dahm, 1991). Through the medium of these pericopae, the Marcan reader is presented with a charismatic Gentile-Christian Jesus in conflict either with Judaism (T. L. Budesheim, 1971) or with Pharisaic-Jewish Christianity of an apocalyptic/nomistic kind (S. Schulz, 1961). According to Budesheim, these stories exalt Jesus over the Jewish tradition. On the basis of his authority or "pneumatic demon-stration" (*exousia*), he is the *theios anēr* par excellence of the tradition, and the initiator ultimately of the community's break with its Jewish roots. His disciples, too, are shown in dispute with Judaism (e.g. 9:14) and hence act as positive paradigms (*pace* Weeden) for the Marcan community.

The role of the disciple and the true nature of discipleship is a major theme for the evangelist, especially in the section 8:22–10:52. E. Best's ecclesiological study, *Following Jesus* (1981), has brought this out (see also Best, 1986), as has the work of E. Schweizer. The evangelist's interest in the persecution, suffering and martyrdom which followers of Jesus may expect (cf. e.g. 8:34ff.; 10:29–30) has led interpreters to suggest that the work may have been produced in order to offer encouragement to the Marcan community in the face of such persecution, or even martyrdom, for the sake of the Gospel. If so, the portrayal by the evangelist of Jesus' first disciples and their relation to him would have taken on an added dimension for the original readers.

When this portrayal is examined, however, as it has been in many studies to date,[125] what stands out is the harsh treatment which not only Jesus' opponents but his Jewish disciples and family, too, receive at the hands of the evangelist. Though the disciples are commissioned by Jesus, according to Mark, to spread his message and to exorcise demons, they are nevertheless revealed as being not only failures as exorcists themselves, but also as preventing others from acting as such in Jesus' name. While excluding others from Jesus' circle, they are at the same time depicted as seeking power and status for themselves. Shown to have been the privileged recipients of private instruction from Jesus himself, they are presented notwithstanding as unable to understand his teaching, as failing to recognize his true status as Son of God and even as positively misunderstanding the real nature of his mission (and its implications for discipleship).

The function of this harsh portrait has been interpreted in different ways and more often than not in accordance with the assumptions held by scholars as to the historical situation of the Marcan community. One popular view is what we may call the parenetic or pastoral view, an approach which is represented in the article by R. C. Tannehill included here, and adopted by the majority of scholars (including E. Lohmeyer, V. Taylor, E. Best, E. Schweizer, R. P. Martin, U. Luz, K.-G. Reploh, W. Bracht, D. J. Hawkin, C. Focant, E. S. Malbon; cf. also H. J. Klauck). This explanation suggests that the "misunderstanding" of the disciples is a literary and pedagogic device employed by Mark[126] to enable him to expand on, or clarify, aspects of Jesus' teaching which he considered important to his own community. The role of the disciples is hence to act as a foil to Jesus (E. Best). They represent prototypical Christians with whose weaknesses, lack of faith, miscomprehension and cowardice the readers are intended to identify (a "typology per contrarium", D. J. Hawkin) and thus be led to self-criticism. In addressing his followers in the text, the Marcan Jesus is in actuality speaking to the "church" or to the community (K.-G. Reploh, W. Bracht). In other respects, the Marcan disciples represent the "world" which, in its blindness, cannot or will not understand him in the light of a "theologia crucis", a world which refuses to accept a passion kerygma and which is disinclined to follow "the way of the cross" (E. Schweizer).

Not all scholars accept that a pastoral motive adequately explains the evangelist's portrayal of Jesus' original disciples and family. The treatment would often appear to go beyond that demanded simply by the author's parenetic or didactic interests. One of the twelve, for example, is addressed as "Satan" (8:33), another is described more than once as a traitor (3:19; 14:10, 17–21, 43). At points the disciples as well as Jesus' relatives are

described in the same terms as, or bracketed with, Jesus'
opponents, the "outsiders" (cf. e.g. 3:21–2, 31–5; 6:52 with 3:5 or
10:5; 8:17–18 with 4:11–12; 9:14, 18–19), and shown to be
obtuse, fearful, cowardly and lacking in faith. They frequently
display the opposite qualities of the true follower, with people
outside their circle often being presented in a better light.[127]
Changes made by Matthew and Luke to their Marcan source at
these points, moreover, may demonstrate their sensitivity to his
derogatory portrait of these (later) revered leaders.

Observations such as these have led to the view that there is
a polemical thrust to the Gospel which eclipses its pastoral
function (e.g. A. Kuby, J. Schreiber, J. B. Tyson, T. J. Weeden,
W. H. Kelber, E. Trocmé, J. D. Crossan, M. D. Goulder, M. A.
Tolbert). One school of thought sees Mark as speaking for a
Gentile-Christian community engaged in conflict with Jewish
Christianity or even with the Jerusalem church represented in the
person of Jesus' family and the twelve. Hence his attempt to
denigrate them. Behind this conflict may lie Gentile-Christian
resentment against the authority exercised by the *Urgemeinde*
(and hinted at in Paul's letters, especially Galatians). In the
opinion of some, the christological issue was uppermost, as we
have already seen, with Mark directing himself against the
spiritual blindness of those who espoused either a "divine-man"
christology (T. J. Weeden) or a royal Messiah/Son of David
christology (J. B. Tyson) without a recognition of the divine
necessity of Jesus' redemptive suffering and death on the cross.

Nowhere are the respective strengths of either pastoral or
polemical explanations more severely tested than in attempts to
make sense of the conclusion of the Gospel. On the one hand, the
promise of 14:28 reiterated in 16:7 is taken as evidence that the
author did not "hate the twelve" but had in mind their ultimate
post-Easter enlightenment or rehabilitation (see e.g. Catchpole,
1977). On the other hand it is curious that the Gospel is devoid of
any post-resurrection appearances to them (and hence lacks, one
notes, those scenes which directly commission them, as in the
other Gospels, to play a leadership role in the post-Easter
community). The women are merely instructed to tell his
disciples that he "goes before" them to Galilee where he is
henceforth to be "seen", although the message, the reader is told,
was not relayed (and therefore not received) "for they were
afraid".

It is not surprising, then, that the question of this enigmatic Marcan ending has been taken up frequently in recent discussion. Answers to a number of key questions have been sought. What was the origin, for example, of the evangelist's resurrection narrative (16:1–8)? Did the Gospel originally end at 16:8 with the discovery of the empty tomb, and if so, what was the function or significance of this conclusion in the light of the author's presentation throughout?

Scholars who see Mark as a conservative redactor claim that the empty tomb pericope was substantially taken over by him from the tradition, either as an independent pericope with its own original cultic function (L. Schenke),[128] or as previously linked with the pre-Marcan passion narrative (R. Pesch, 1974; see n. 82). Arguing for greater Marcan creativity, others would claim that the pericope is the evangelist's own composition (J. D. Crossan) and that it functions in the Gospel, in reality, as an *anti*-resurrection story, proclaiming to the reader that the earthly Jesus, having been translated to heaven, was not now present in the community but absent, although he would shortly be seen again in glory at his coming parousia in Galilee (N. Q. Hamilton).[129]

While a number of scholars would still adhere to the view that the Gospel originally extended beyond 16:8,[130] more and more are coming to the opinion that it was intended to end at 16:8,[131] and that it does so indeed, in literary terms, with dramatic appositeness. A number of the themes of importance to the evangelist converge in this final pericope. Representing the newer literary criticism, N. R. Petersen (1980), for example, asks whether the Marcan ending is satisfactory from a literary point of view, and concludes that it is. Textually generated expectations are satisfied when the narrative ending is considered in terms of the literary category of "closure".[132] While 16:8 appears to frustrate the expectation generated by 14:28 and 16:7, this climactic verse, he asserts, must be taken ironically (*pace* Weeden) and not literally. Mark 13 predicts events beyond 16:8 and indicates that the evangelist envisaged a role for the disciples in the post-Easter situation. Mark expects the reader, therefore, to supply for himself the meeting in "Galilee" which would reverse the disciples' ideological orientation. The dramatic juxtaposition of divine promise and human failure in these last two climactic verses (16:7 and 8) is also the theme of the perceptive article by

A. T. Lincoln (1989) included in our collection. Lincoln demonstrates that the promise-failure motif here not only coheres with the rest of Mark's narrative but is likely to be redactional.

Whether the disciples, in Marcan intention, are left ultimately in the dark or not may, in the final analysis, therefore, be a question for the literary critic. It may indeed be a question which only the discerning reader can decide, in supplying for himself or herself the ending. The Gospel's ending in some ways prompts the reader to return to its beginning, where, according to F. J. Matera's article (1988), Mark's essential themes are first presented.[133] One's view of the message of Mark (cf. M. D. Hooker, 1983) depends, however, on one's total reading of the text and on the conclusions drawn from the individual assessment and overall interpretation of the various features of the Gospel which have been discussed. That the Gospel should end with an enigma is not altogether surprising when one considers the enigmatic ethos it seeks to create throughout. In a celebrated dictum, M. Dibelius (1934: 230) described Mark's Gospel as a book of secret epiphanies. Despite intensive research, this Gospel, in scholarly terms, still withholds many secrets which have yet to be revealed. The overall purpose of the Gospel still eludes us, as does its *Sitz im Leben*. Current theories are inclined in the main to view the evangelist's main purpose as parenetic (cf. E. Best), kerygmatic (cf. E. Schweizer) or christological (cf. N. Perrin). Only a few voices have been raised in defence of a primarily historical intention (cf. e.g. J. Roloff).[134] Some recent work, on the contrary, has emphasized its mythopoeic function (cf. B. L. Mack, 1988), the formation of the Gospel itself being considered an originative moment in Christianity. A Marcan theology has yet to be written (although, if E. Best is right, this task may not be in the end either possible or appropriate). Arguments are voiced in support of a Palestinian provenance for Mark (cf. W. Marxsen, H. C. Kee, E. E. Ellis) or in favour of its having been written in Rome (cf. S. G. F. Brandon, M. Hengel, D. Senior), but many agree with R. P. Martin (n. 9) that it remains "a gospel in search of a life-setting" and that "the quest for the community of Mark still continues" (J. R. Donahue, 1982: 838).

Yet in the Gospel's own words "there is nothing hid, except to be made manifest, nor is anything secret, except to come to light" (4:22). The way forward for Marcan studies seems reasonably clear for the moment. Further research needs to be conducted on individual pericopae. On the hermeneutical front, more attention needs to be given to the methodological problems involved in analysing the text at its various levels and co-ordinating the results. In view of the variety of analytical tools and approaches at present available to and employed by the critics (source, form, tradition and redaction criticism, together now with the newer literary criticism and sociology) more comprehensive and systematic methodological procedures are called for. This is all the more important if synthetic constructions such as a Marcan theology are to be attempted. As the distinctiveness of this first Gospel emerges in sharper relief, further investigation needs to be conducted into its place in the theological history of early Christianity, building on the contributions already made on this subject by K. L. Schmidt, J. M. Robinson, W. Marxsen, S. Schulz, G. Dautzenberg and now B. L. Mack, among others.

The prospects for Marcan studies also appears bright, given the current interest in the Gospel and the significance attached to it in recent studies. Something of this interest, it is hoped, will be captured for the scholar and student alike in the essays here presented, a selection encompassing, it should be noted, a considerable diversity of opinion and approach. We began this survey by noting a traditional view that Mark's Gospel was unsophisticated and untheological. The literary explosion to which it has given rise, however, in the last thirty years, has surely chronicled the reversal of this judgment.

NOTES

1 For useful reviews of Marcan scholarship within this period, see e.g. R. S. Barbour, "Recent Study of the Gospel according to St. Mark", *ExpTim* 79 (1967–8) 324–9; H. D. Knigge (1968); H. C. Kee, "Mark as Redactor and Theologian: a Survey of some recent Marcan Studies", *JBL* 90 (1971) 333–6, and "Mark's Gospel in Recent Research", *Int* 32 (1978) 353–68; E. Schweizer, "Neuere Markus-Forschung in USA", *EvT* 33 (1973) 533–7, and "Towards a Christology of Mark?" in N. Dahl, Festschrift, *God's Christ and His People* (Oslo, 1977), ed. J. Jervell, W. A. Meeks, 29–42; C. L. Mitton, "Some Further Studies in St. Mark's Gospel", *ExpTim* 87 (1975–6) 297–301; N. Perrin (1976); R. Pesch (1979) 1–12; S. P. Kealey (1982); B. G. Powley, "Revisiting Mark", *Scripture Bulletin* 12 (1981) 40–5; R. Smith, "Thy Kingdom Come: Some Recent Work on Mark's Gospel", *CurrTheolMiss* 8 (1981) 371–6; K. Stock, "Methodenvielfalt. Studien zu Markus", *Biblica* 62 (1981) 562–82; P. Pokorny, "Das Markus-Evangelium. Ein Forschungsbericht" in *Aufstieg*

und Niedergang (Berlin/New York, 1985), ed. H. Temporini, W. Haase, II. 25. 3. 1969–2035; D. J. Harrington, "A Map of Books on Mark (1975–84)", *BTB* 15 (1985) 12–16; F. J. Matera (1987); L. W. Hurtado, "The Gospel of Mark in Recent Study", *Themelios* 14 (1989) 47–52; W. L. Lane, "The Present State of Markan Sudies", in J. H. Skilton (ed.), *The Gospels Today. A Guide to some Recent Developments* (New Testament Student, 6; Philadelphia, PA, 1990) 51–81; W. R. Telford (1990, 1992); J. Dewey, "Recent Studies on Mark", *Religious Studies Review* 17 (1991) 12–16; V. K. Robbins, "Text and Context in Recent Studies of the Gospel of Mark", ibid., 16–23. For bibliographies on Mark, see H. M. Humphrey (1981) and F. Neirynck (1992).

2 J. Lambrecht, "Redaction and Theology in Mk. IV", in M. Sabbe (1974); cited C. L. Mitton, op. cit., 297.

3 J. V. Bartlet (1922), 29; *gratia* P. J. Achtemeier (1980) 466.

4 Cf. Acts 12:12, 25; 13:5, 13; 15:37, 39; Col. 4:10; 2 Tim. 4:11; Philem. 24; 2 Pet. 5:13.

5 See Eusebius, *Ecclesiastical History* (Loeb Classical Library; Cambridge, Mass./London, 1926), ET K. Lake, III, xxxix, 14–16.

6 Cf. R. S. Barbour, op. cit., 324. For a defence of the Papias tradition and the Petrine connection, see e.g. H. E. W. Turner, "The Tradition of Mark's Dependence upon Peter", *ExpTim* 71 (1959–60) 260–3.

7 See e.g. the excellent article of K. Niederwimmer, "Johannes Markus und die Frage nach dem Verfasser des zweiten Evangeliums", *ZNW* 58 (1967) 172–88. Cf. also W. G. Kümmel (1975) 95–7.

8 See, however, P. Parker, "The Authorship of the Second Gospel", *Perspectives in Religious Studies* 5 (1978) 4–9. Parker notes that the information supplied by the New Testament itself about John Mark (which he takes at face value) acts against his traditional identification with the author. He confesses to have toyed with the notion of John, son of Zebedee, but opts in the end for the suggestion of J. Weiss (1903) that the author was an unknown Marcus, probably a dweller at Rome. "He evidently got caught up in the Judaizing controversy, where he was a strong partisan for the gentile side and grew highly impatient with the leadership of the twelve. For his book he drew on a primarily Galilean tradition. His own understanding of Judaism, and its scriptures and its holy city, was not robust" (9).

The question of the date, authorship and provenance of Mark's Gospel has also been the subject of several articles in the recent Festschrift for F. Neirynck. See E. Schweizer, "Markus, Begleiter des Petrus?", B. Orchard, "Mark and the Fusion of Traditions", E. E. Ellis, "The Date and Provenance of Mark's Gospel", and J. R. Donahue, "The Community of Mark's Gospel", in F. Neirynck, Festschrift, *The Four Gospels 1992* (3 volumes; Leuven, 1992), ed. F. Van Segbroeck, 2, 751–3, 779–800, 801–15 and 817–38 respectively. Cf. also J. Ernst (1980a) and D. Senior (1987).

9 Cf. R. P. Martin, "A Gospel in Search of a Life-Setting", *ExpTim* 80 (1968–9) 361–4.

10 H. C. Kee, n. 1 above (1978) 353.

11 Useful and more detailed surveys are given by R. P. Martin (1979) chapter 2, for example, and V. Taylor (1966) 1–25.

12 Cf. e.g. Irenaeus' justification for there being four Gospels in the church's canon (and only four). "For since there are four regions of the world in which we live, and four principal winds, and the church is as seed sown in the whole earth, and the Gospel is the pillar and ground of the church and the breath of life, it is natural that it should have four pillars, from all quarters breathing incorruption, and kindling men into life" (*Adv. Haer.*, III, xi, 8; cited R. H. Lightfoot, 1934, 1).

13 R. P. Martin (1979) 29f., points to the singular fact, for example, that the Apostolic Fathers and Apologists (in the second century) are reticent when it comes to actually quoting from Mark. The first commentary on the Gospel was not written until the fifth century, and its author, Victor of Antioch, complained that he could find no treatment of it comparable with expositions of Matthew and John.

14 *De Consensu Evangelistarum*, I, 2(4); cited V. Taylor (1966) 9. Taylor renders the term "*pedisequus*" as "lackey".

15 A leading proponent of Matthean priority and the so-called "Griesbach hypothesis" (i.e. the theory first suggested by J. J. Griesbach in 1789 that Mark is a secondary conflation of Matthew and Luke) is W. R. Farmer, *The Synoptic Problem: a Critical Analysis* (New York, 1964). Farmer gives a survey of the revival of interest in the Griesbach hypothesis and its strengths in his article, "Modern Developments of Griesbach's Hypothesis", *NTS* 23 (1976–7) 275–95. One piece of evidence cited is the doctoral dissertation of T. R. W. Longstaff, *Evidence of Conflation in Mark? A Study in the Synoptic Problem* (Society of Biblical Literature Diss. Ser. 28), published in 1977 (Missoula, Montana). Citing other examples of composite works, Longstaff concludes that Mark's Gospel exhibits many of the literary characteristics of conflation. For the hypothesis that Mark used the Gospels of Matthew and Luke as his sources, see also B. Orchard and H. Riley, *The Order of the Synoptics. Why Three Synoptic Gospels?* (Macon, GA, 1987) and H. Riley, *The Making of Mark. An Exploration* (Macon, GA, 1989). Weighed against the theory of Mark as mere conflator, however, must be the accumulating literary evidence revealing Mark as an author/theologian acting with considerable freedom upon the discrete oral traditions he has committed to writing.

Another recent attack on the Marcan hypothesis is H.-H. Stoldt's *History and Criticism of the Marcan Hypothesis* (Edinburgh, 1980), ET D. L. Niewyk, J. Riches. Stoldt has sought to expose the shaky grounds on which historically and logically the scholarly consensus on Marcan priority was reached, but he offers insufficient grounds to show that any alternative theory like the Griesbach hypothesis provides a more plausible explanation of the evidence, nor does he do adequate justice to the modern case in defence of the consensus.

Introduction

The continuing strength of the Marcan hypothesis and the Two Document theory has been largely borne out by the innumerable redaction-critical studies based on it which have appeared in recent years. The corresponding weakness of the hypothesis of Matthean priority is the failure to date by its adherents to provide a generally convincing redaction-critical theory for a Marcan abbreviation of Matthew.

That the Griesbach hypothesis, once dismissed, is at least gaining respectability, however, is shown by the openness to the whole question of Gospel relationships exhibited, for example, in a Colloquy devoted to the subject held at Trinity University, San Antonio, Texas, in 1977. A volume based on the proceedings of this Colloquy, *The Relationships among the Gospels: An Inter-disciplinary Dialogue*, ed. W. O. Walker, was published in 1978. Insights from other disciplines (the study of oral traditional literature, Classics, Judaic Studies, literary criticism) were brought to bear on the Synoptic Problem. In the words of the editor, while no conclusion was reached "there was significant, though by no means unanimous, agreement that the solution to the problem of Gospel relationships may be considerably more complex than most New Testament scholars have assumed" (op. cit., 9). For a useful collection of previously published articles on this question, see A. J. Bellinzoni (ed.), *The Two-Source Hypothesis: a Critical Appraisal* (Macon, GA, 1985), and, for the papers of the 1984 Jerusalem Symposium on the Synoptic Problem, see D. L. Dungan (ed.), *The Interrelations of the Gospels* (BETL 95; Leuven, 1990).

16 A classic defence of Marcan priority is still G. M. Styler's "The Priority of Mark", Excursus IV in C. F. D. Moule's *The Birth of the New Testament* (3rd ed.; London, 1981) 285–316. First published in 1962, it has been rewritten to take into account recent developments such as the revivial of the Griesbach hypothesis. See also J. Fitzmyer's essay, "The Priority of Mark and the 'Q' Source in Luke", in *Jesus and Man's Hope* (Pittsburgh, 1970), ed. D. G. Buttrick, 1, 131–70. For a critical assessment of the Griesbach hypothesis, see C. M. Tuckett, *The Revival of the Griesbach Hypothesis* (Cambridge, 1982).

17 For an account of these, see e.g. V. Taylor (1966) 67–77; E. Trocmé (1975) chapter 1. Although "Ur-Markus" or proto-Mark theories are no longer popular, similar hypotheses still continue to be advanced. In a variation of the Griesbach hypothesis, P. Rolland has argued that Matthew and Luke used two parallel Greek versions of a primitive Semitic Gospel, while Mark had access to both and harmonized them. See P. Rolland, "Les prédécesseurs de Marc. Les sources présynoptiques de Mk, II, 18–22 et parallèles", *RB* 89 (1982) 370–405; "Marc première harmonie évangélique?", *RB* 90 (1983) 23–79; "L'arrière-fond sémitique des évangiles synoptiques", *ETL* 60 (1984) 358–62; *Les Premiers Évangiles: un Nouveau Regard sur le Problème Synoptique* (Paris, 1984). For a critique, see F. Neirynck, "Les expressions doubles chez Marc et le problème synoptique", *ETL* 59 (1983) 303–30;

"L'arrière-fond sémitique des évangiles synoptiques. Réponse à P. Rolland", *ETL* 60 (1984) 363–6. Both responses are reprinted in F. Van Segbroeck (ed.), *Evangelica II* (Leuven, 1991) 293–320, 321–4.

One area to occupy scholars recently has been the interrelationship between canonical Gospels like the Gospel of Mark and the extra-canonical Gospels. J. D. Crossan, for example, maintains that two of these, viz. Papyrus Egerton 2 and the Secret Gospel of Mark were used by Mark and that he was also indebted to a passion-resurrection source contained in the Gospel of Peter. See *Four Other Gospels: Shadows on the Contours of Canon* (Minneapolis/Chicago/New York, 1985), and *The Cross that Spoke. The Origins of the Passion Narrative* (San Francisco, 1988). Cf. also H. Koester, "History and Development of Mark's Gospel (From Mark to Secret Mark and 'Canonical' Mark)", in B. Corley (ed.), *Colloquy on New Testament Studies. A Time for Reappraisal and Fresh Approaches* (Macon, GA, 1983) 35–57. For a critique of Crossan (1985), see W. R. Telford, *Theology* 89 (1986) 402–4. For further discussion, see e.g. F. Neirynck, "The Apocryphal Gospels and the Gospel of Mark", in J.-M. Sevrin (ed.), *The New Testament in Early Christianity* (Leuven, 1989) 123–75 = *Evangelica II* (Leuven, 1991) 715–72, and M. Smith, "Clement of Alexandria and Secret Mark: the Score at the End of the First Decade", *HTR* 75 (1982) 449–61.

18 For a detailed review of the way scholars have come to terms with Wrede and the so-called "Messianic Secret", see J. L. Blevins (1981), C. M. Tuckett (1983) and H. Räisänen (1990). For an astute theological and sociological assessment of the secrecy motif, see F. Watson (1985). Watson argues that the secrecy injunctions are an expression of a predestinarian outlook which reinforced the Marcan community's elitist position.

19 For a discussion of the valuable contribution made by form critics to Synoptic Studies (including Mark) between 1917 and 1930, see J. Schniewind, "Zur Synoptiker-Exegese", *TRu* 2 (1920) 129–89.

20 See e.g. the severe critique of form (and redaction) criticism's methodological foundations advanced by E. Güttgemanns, *Candid Questions Concerning Gospel Form Criticism* (Pittsburgh Theol. Mono. Ser. 26; Pittsburgh, 1979) ET W. G. Doty. Güttgemanns questions, for example, the form-critical assumption of a basic continuity between the oral and literary nature of the tradition. The unravelling of the history of the pre-literary tradition is accomplished, among other things, by the application of the form critic's knowledge of the "laws of oral transmission". These "laws", or better, "tendencies", deemed to govern the oral transmission of tradition were largely based, however, on observations and analysis of the literary sources. If the oral and literary processes of tradition are distinct, or even discontinous, then confidence in the possibility of a history of the pre-literary tradition is undermined. For responses to Güttgemanns, see e.g. W. G. Doty "Fundamental Questions about Literary-Critical Methodology: a Review Article", *JAAR* 40 (1972) 521–7; E. V. McKnight, *JBL* (1972) 554–7;

44

Introduction

F. Mussner, "Grenzen der Formgeschichte", *BZ* 15 (1971) 267–71; H. Thyen, "Positivismus in der Theologie und ein Weg zu seiner Überwindung?", *EvT* 31 (1971) 472–95.

This point was taken up in a perceptive and radical article by W. H. Kelber, "Mark and Oral Tradition", *Semeia* 16 (1979) 7–55, and subsequently in his book, *The Oral and the Written Gospel* (1983). Kelber argues for a discontinuity or tension between the literary process of which the Gospel of Mark is a product (its "textuality") and the oral tradition of which its author is deemed by form critics to be merely the transmitter. For responses to Kelber, see W. J. Ong, "Text as Interpretation: Mark and After", and T. J. Farrell, "Kelber's Breakthrough", in L. K. Silberman (ed.), *Orality, Aurality and Biblical Narrative* (Semeia 39; Decatur, GA, 1987) 7–26, 27–45 respectively; L. W. Hurtado (1990). See also C. Breytenbach, "Das Problem des Übergangs von mündlicher zu schriftlicher Überlieferung", *Neotestamentica* 20 (1986) 46–57, and G. Strecker, "Schriftlichkeit oder Mündlichkeit der synoptischen Tradition? Anmerkungen zur formgeschichtlichen Problematik", in F. Neirynck, Festschrift, *The Four Gospels 1992* (Leuven, 1992), ed. F. Van Segbroeck, 1, 159–72.

For a more recent, alternative and comprehensive form-critical treatment of all of the literature of the New Testament, see K. Berger, *Formgeschichte des Neuen Testaments* (Heidelberg, 1984), *Einführung in die Formgeschichte* (Tübingen, 1987) and his associated article, "Hellenistische Gattungen im Neuen Testament" in *Aufstieg und Niedergang*, ed. H. Temporini, W. Haase (Berlin/New York, 1984), II, 25, 2, 1031–432, 1831–85. Berger departs from classical form criticism in a number of ways, e.g. by employing ancient rhetorical categories for the classification of the forms, by disclaiming the possibility of reconstructing oral forms antecedent to written texts by using literary methods, and by disassociating questions of historicity and authenticity from the strictly form-critical enterprise. For a review and critique of Berger's work, see e.g. D. E. Aune in *CBQ* 48 (1986) 734–5 and F. Lentzen-Deis in *Biblica* 68 (1987) 279–82.

21 Miracle stories, for example, are recounted in a series (1:21–45; 4:35–5:43; 6:34–56; 7:24–8:26), controversy dialogues between Jesus and his opponents are grouped together in distinguishable sections (2:1–3:6; 7:1–23; 11:27–12:37), parables are clustered in the artificially constructed discourse of 4:1–34 and so on.

22 In a cautiously worded article, "The Framework of the Gospel Narrative", *ExpT* 43 (1931–2) 396–400, C. H. Dodd argued that Mark may have been guided in the chronological arrangement of his material by a brief historical outline of the ministry of Jesus (cf. Acts 10:37–41) which had come to him in the tradition. This article is reprinted in the author's *New Testament Studies* (Manchester, 1953), 1–11, and also in H. K. McArthur (ed.), *In Search of the Historical Jesus* (London, 1970) 109–18. Dodd's influential theory, espoused with less caution by his supporters, was persuasively countered by D. E.

Nineham in an article appearing in the Festschrift for R. H. Lightfoot in 1957 ("The Order of Events in Mark's Gospel – an Examination of Dr. Dodd's Hypothesis", *Studies in the Gospels*, Oxford, ed. D. E. Nineham, 223–39). See also E. Güttgemanns (n. 20) 311–18.

23 M. Dibelius, *Die Formgeschichte des Evangeliums* (Tübingen, 1919). The second edition (1933) was translated into English by B. L. Woolf with the title *From Tradition to Gospel* (London, 1934).

24 R. Bultmann, *Die Geschichte der synoptischen Tradition* (Göttingen, 1921). A translation from the second German edition (1931) was made by J. Marsh in 1963, and revised, with corrections and additions from the 1962 Supplement, in 1968.

25 This classification largely follows that of Bultmann. Dibelius' classification of traditional material into paradigms (the equivalent of Bultmann's "apophthegms", viz. sayings with a brief narrative setting, or V. Taylor's "pronouncement stories"), parenesis, *Novellen* (viz. miracle stories), legends and myths has in general not proved as helpful, although his highlighting of the role of preaching in the formation of the traditional forms has been influential.

26 For a list and a discussion of the forms that have been isolated in Mark's Gospel, see e.g. V. Taylor (1966) 78–89; E. Trocmé (1975) 34–68; H. C. Kee (1977) 10, 30–49.

27 Collections of material already existing before Mark took them over as "prestrung pearls" have been sought, for example, in the sections 2:1–3:6; 4:1–34; 4:35–6:52; 10:1–45. In an important study, H.-W. Kuhn (1971) was able to isolate relatively few, however, and in this respect his results were largely negative. For a review and assessment of form criticism and its developments from 1980 to the present, including the investigation of pre-Marcan collections, see Telford (1992) 690–705.

28 Not identical in substance is his *Das Geschichtsverständnis des Markus-Evangeliums*, published in 1956 (Zürich). The German version consists of the original, more fully documented version of chapters 2–5 of the English edition. Robinson's important monograph, *The Problem of History in Mark*, was reissued together with other Marcan studies in 1982. A German version of this also followed (Transl. K. Fröhlich, U. Berger; Munich, 1989).

29 A major criticism, admitted by himself and understandable given the infancy of the redaction-critical method at this time, is his failure to distinguish sharply enough between tradition and redaction in determining Marcan theology. For a critique of Robinson, see e.g. W. H. Harter, "The Historical Method of Mark", *USQR* 20 (1964–5) 21–38; E. Best (1965) 19–23; H.-D. Knigge (1968) 62–3. For Robinson's response to his critics, see "The Problem of History in Mark, Reconsidered", *USQR* 20 (1964–5) 131–47.

30 Bultmann (1968) 338–51, presents an illuminating analysis of the nature of Mark's not inconsiderable editorial activity on the traditional materials available to him. While stating it "a misconception to infer from Mark's

ordering of his material any conclusions about the chronology and development of the life of Jesus", however, he likewise judges it "false to point out, with very few exceptions, what Mark's leading ideas were" (349). "Mark is not sufficiently master of his material to be able to venture on a systematic construction himself" (350).

31 *Der Evangelist Markus. Studien zur Redaktionsgeschichte des Evangeliums* (Göttingen, 1956–9). ET 1969. For a useful review of Marxsen and of subsequent redaction-critical work on the Gospel, see J. Rohde, *Rediscovering the Teaching of the Evangelists* (London/Philadelphia, 1968), ET D. M. Barton.

32 See esp. *Mark the Evangelist*, 15–29. "The unity subsequently created by the evangelists – first of all by Mark – is something else again. It is a systematically constructed piece which cannot be understood as the "termination" of the anonymous transmission of material. The transmission leads rather to ultimate "fragmentation". The redaction, on the other hand, counteracts this natural development" (18).

33 R. H. Stein, "What is Redaktionsgeschichte?", *JBL* 88 (1969) 46.

34 E.g. 1:32–4; 3:7–12; 6:53–6. Two such studies are W. Egger's *Frohbotschaft und Lehre. Die Sammelberichte des Wirkens Jesu im Markusevangelium* (Frankfurt, 1976) and G. Van Oyen's *De Summaria in Marcus en de compositie van Mc 1,14–8,26* (Leuven, 1987). Of the importance of these passages, Egger states: "In the course of the work it has become evident, then, that the summary passages play a vital role in Mark's theological proclamation, in that they characterize the activity of Jesus as good news and teaching" (3). For an evaluation of Egger and Van Oyen, see J. Verheyden, "Mark 1, 32–4 and 6, 53–6: Tradition or Redaction?", *ETL* 64 (1988) 415–28. Cf. also C. W. Hedrick, "The Role of 'Summary Statements' in the Composition of the Gospel of Mark: a Dialog with Karl Schmidt and Norman Perrin", *NovT* 26 (1984) 289–311. Hedrick challenges Perrin's view that summary passages in conjunction with geographical shifts in the narrative mark out the basic divisions in the Gospel's literary structure.

35 See e.g. R. H. Stein (1970) or C. W. Hedrick (1987).

36 See his "Zur Erzählerkunst des Markus", *ZNW* 27 (1928) 193–8, for an early (but remarkably contemporary) essay on Marcan literary technique. Von Dobschütz highlights the author's skill in intercalating or dovetailing pericopae for literary effect (e.g. in 3:20–35; 5:21–43; 6:12–30; 11:11–25; 14:1–11, 53–72) or anticipating with redactional notices material that is to come (e.g. the "boat" pericopae 3:9; 4:1, 36ff.). For more recent discussion of the significance of Marcan intercalations, see e.g. J. R. Donahue (1973) 42, 58–63; W. R. Telford (1980) 15,48–9; J. R. Edwards (1989); G. Van Oyen (1992).

37 Turner's articles (1923–8) remain (despite his historicizing presuppositions) a classic analysis of Marcan style and linguistic usage.

38 *Untersuchungen zum Markus-Stil. Ein Beitrag zur stilistischen Durchar-beitung des Neuen Testaments* (Rome, 1937).

39 Cf. e.g. J. C. Doudna, *The Greek of the Gospel of Mark* (Philadelphia, 1961), who concludes that Mark's Greek, despite its unusual and "unclassical" features, stands within the development of the koine and need not be considered translation Greek from an Aramaic or Semitic original. Two studies in the 1980s have proved somewhat contradictory on the question of Semitic influence upon Mark's Greek. E. C. Maloney's investigation (1981) concluded that syntactical Semitic interference permeates every page of the Gospel, while M. Reiser (1984), using different documentary parallels, sees no evidence of syntactical or stylistic Semitisms. Cf. also P. Dschulnigg (1984).

40 See e.g. F. Neirynck (1972–88). Neirynck argues that the phenomenon of "duality" in Mark (repetition, pleonasms, duplicate expressions, double statements, doublets, synonymous expressions, etc.) is so widespread in the text as to constitute a characteristic feature of the author's style, a result which tells against the phenomenon being regarded as a source-critical (or even too stringently as a redaction-critical) criterion. Cf. also E. J. Pryke (1978). For a rigorous methodological analysis, which seeks to isolate those features of Mark's language, vocabulary and style which are characteristic of the evangelist and not his sources (and which is not committed to the Two-Document Hypothesis), see D. B. Peabody (1987).

41 See e.g. G. Theissen (1983) for an excellent analysis of the ways the evangelists composed their Gospels, and especially his description of the compositional techniques and connective devices employed by Mark, particularly in respect of his miracle traditions.

42 Cf. e.g. A. Kuby, "Zur Konzeption des Markus-Evangeliums", *ZNW* 49 (1958) 52–64. Kuby surveys the Gospel's overall structure pointing out the skill and artifice involved in the placement of the pericopae. A key, indeed programmatic, pericope is 8:22–6. The dominant conception of the Gospel is the incomprehension of the disciples regarding Jesus' Messiahship before 8:21 and their misconception of it thereafter. E. Schweizer also highlights as the overriding conception of Mark the blindness of the world vis-à-vis the manifestation of its Messiah, and the way of the cross (*der Leidensweg*) that true discipleship must follow. F. G. Lang, "Kompositionsanalyse des Markusevangeliums", *ZTK* 74 (1977) 1–24, argues that the symmetry and proportion shown by the Marcan scheme shows Mark as consciously arranging his material with ancient drama as his model. G. Rau (1985) follows Theissen's compositional analysis and sees in the Gospel the hand of an active redactor who has created an intentional and thematic representation of the beginning of the Christian mission initiated by Jesus. Two interesting suggestions have recently come from J. Dewey (1989) and R. Zwick (1989). Dewey claims that Mark is an oral narrative (for a more qualified view, see E. Best, 1989) and hence that oral compositional methods are to be discerned

within it. Composed for a listening audience, its easily visualized events appear not in logical order but in an endless chain of association based on the echo principle. Taking his analogy from filmic texts, Zwick, on the other hand, sees "montage" (as in cinematic narration – the production of a rapid succession of images to illustrate an association of ideas) as a clue to uncovering the literary and theological unity of Mark. In the most recent study, C. Minette de Tillesse argues that Mark's six-part structure (1:1–13 the prologue, and 3:7–6:6a; 6:6b–8:26; 8:27–10:52; 11:1–12:44; 13:1–16:8) is dictated by his understanding and response to the contemporary church situation and that his Gospel, therefore, and not that of Matthew (which was derived from it) should be considered the ecclesiastical Gospel *par excéllence*. Cf. also D. Blatherwick (1970–1); R. Butterworth (1972) cf. M. Smith (1981); D.-A. Koch, "Inhaltliche Gliederung und geographischer Aufriss im Markusevangelium", *NTS* 29 (1983) 145–66; A. Stock (1985a, 1985b); L. Schenke (1986); S. H. Smith (1989).

43 Cf. also H. Räisänen, *Die Parabeltheorie im Markusevangelium* (Helsinki, 1973), who posits four stages in the development of the parable discourse in 4:1–34. The substance of Räisänen's reconstruction is to be found in his recently published *The "Messianic Secret" in Mark* (Edinburgh, 1990). See also H. Weder, *Die Gleichnisse Jesu als Metaphern* (Göttingen, 1978) 99–135.

44 See e.g. W. J. Bennett, "The Gospel of Mark and Traditions about Jesus", *Encounter* (Indianapolis), 38 (1977) 1–11; J. D. McCaughey, "Literary Criticism and the Gospels – a Rumination", *Australian Biblical Review* 29 (1981) 16–25; F. Watson (1987); R. Morgan and J. Barton, *Biblical Interpretation* (Oxford, 1988), esp. chapter 7; S. D. Moore (1989).

For some recent illuminating studies of the biblical text from the point of view of the secular literary critic, see e.g. F. Kermode, "The Structures of Fiction", *Modern Language Notes* 84 (1969) 891–915, and *The Genesis of Secrecy. On the Interpretation of Narrative* (Cambridge, Mass./London, 1979). For responses to Kermode's approach to Mark, see e.g. H.-D. Betz, "Is Hermes the Hierophant, or is Christ?", *JR* 62 (1982) 178–85; M. A. Tolbert and J. G. Lawler, *Religious Studies Review* 8 (1982) 1–10; T. R. Wright, "Regenerating Fiction: The Gospel as Narrative", *Religious Studies* 20 (1984) 389–400. See also J. Licht, *Storytelling in the Bible* (Jerusalem, 1978); R. Alter, *The Art of Biblical Narrative* (New York, 1981); N. Frye, *The Great Code. The Bible and Literature* (London, 1982).

45 A revised version of Perrin (1971) appears in M. Sabbe (1974–88). For other works reflecting his approach and key positions, see Perrin (1966); (1967–8); "The Literary Gattung 'Gospel' – Some Observations", *ExpTim* 82 (1970–1) 4–7; "Towards an Interpretation of the Gospel of Mark" in H.-D. Betz (1971) 1–78 (cf. also E. C. Hobbs' critique of Perrin in this same volume, 79–91); also Perrin (1976). For general assessments of his work, see, for example, W. H. Kelber, "The Work of Norman Perrin: an Intellectual Pilgrimage', *JR* 62 (1984) 452–67, and W. O. Seal, "Norman Perrin and his 'School': Retracing a Pilgrimage", *JSNT* 20 (1984) 87–107.

46 For treatment of Mark as a narrative and the application of literary theory and perspectives to it, see e.g. W. Egger (1979); D. Rhoads (1982); A. Stock (1982); F. Hahn (1984); J. Drury (1987); W. H. Kelber (1987; 1988 – for a response to this article, see D. O. Via, "Irony as Hope in Mark's Gospel: a Response to Werner Kelber", *Semeia* 43 (1988) 21–7); C. Breytenbach (1989).

47 See e.g. L. Marin's structuralist analysis of the passion narrative in the Gospels, *The Semiotics of the Passion Narrative. Topics and Figures* (Pittsburgh, 1980), ET A. M. Johnson, Jnr., as well as O. Genest, *Le Christ de la Passion. Perspective structurale. Analyse de Marc 14,53–15,47, des parallèles bibliques et extra-bibliques* (Tournai/Montreal, 1978).

   A useful introduction to structuralism is D. Patte's *What is Structural Exegesis?* (Philadelphia, 1976). An exposition of the structuralist approach to the New Testament, with special reference to Mark, is also given by Via (1975). For a critical review of Via, and a defence of the historical method, see G. B. Caird in *JTS* 28 (1977) 544–7.

   Cf. also J. Delorme, "L'intégration des petites unités littéraires dans l'Évangile de Marc du point de vue de la sémiotique structurale", *NTS* 25 (1979) 469–91; J. Drury (1985); D. O. Via (1985); B. Van Iersel, "The Reader of Mark as Operator of a System of Connotations", *Semeia* 48 (1989) 83–114. For a critical evaluation of Malbon and Via, see M. A. Harris, "Structuralism, Hermeneutics and the Gospel of Mark", *Perspectives in Religious Studies* 15 (1988) 61–70. For a poststructuralist reading of Mark, see T. F. Berg, "Reading in/to Mark", *Semeia* 48 (1989) 187–206.

48 For useful discussions of the redaction-critical method, see J. Schreiber (1961) 154–5; Q. Quesnell (1969) 46–55; N. Perrin (1970); R. H. Stein, "The Proper Methodology for Ascertaining a Marcan Redaction History", *NovT* 13 (1971) 181–98; T. J. Weeden (1971) 1–19; C. M. Tuckett, *Reading the New Testament* (London, 1987) 116–35, and "Redaction Criticism" in R. J. Coggins, J. L. Houlden (eds.), *A Dictionary of Biblical Interpretation* (London/Philadelphia, 1990) 580–2.

49 See D. O. Via, Jnr. (1975) 71–8; Donahue in W. H. Kelber (1976) 15ff.; E. Güttgemanns, *Candid Questions*, passim.

50 See e.g. J. B. Muddiman, "The End of Markan Redaction Criticism?", Review Article, *ExpTim* 101 (1990) 307–9.

51 Cf. e.g. R. Alter, op. cit., 12ff., who, in a series of strictures, laments the fact that literary analysis of the Bible is still in its infancy, when compared with what he terms the "excavative" scholarship which has dominated biblical criticism for so long. For a critical evaluation of the methodological split in Marcan Studies occasioned by the literary approach, see Räisänen (1990) 1–37 and Telford (1992).

52 This emphasis is adopted as a hermeneutical principle by T. J. Weeden (1971) 11–19. Weeden argues that "the only way to interpret the Gospel as the author intended it is to read his work with the analytical eyes of a first-century reader" (11) and that to do so the modern reader needs to be guided

by a knowledge of the methods of literary interpretation inculcated in Hellenistic education. Cf. also R. C. Tannehill (1979) 59–95, whose analysis is devoted to the compositional techniques employed by the evangelist to influence his readers.

53 See e.g. the series of articles by W. H. Kelber, R. C. Tannehill, E. S. Malbon and J. Calloud in N. Petersen (1979). Excellent examples of the use of a literary-critical approach as a complement to a redaction-critical one are R. M. Fowler (1981), previously cited, and A. T. Lincoln (1989), included here. Cf. also W. H. Kelber (1976) and N. R. Petersen (1980, 1992). Helpful introductions to this field are W. A. Beardslee's *Literary Criticism of the New Testament* (Philadelphia, 1970), N. R. Petersen's *Literary Criticism for New Testament Critics* (Philadelphia, 1978) and S. D. Moore (1984). For a review of literary studies on Mark (1980–90), see W. R. Telford (1992).

54 For a sample of the discussion on this question, see e.g. N. Perrin (1970–1) n. 45 above; J. M. Robinson (1970); D. O. Via, Jnr. (1975) 78–103; H. C. Kee (1977) 17–30; E. Güttgemanns, *Candid Questions*, passim; C. H. Talbert (1978) and D. E. Aune's "The Problem of the Genre of the Gospels: A Critique of C. H. Talbert's *What is a Gospel?*", in R. T. France, D. Wenham (eds.), *Gospel Perspectives: Studies of History and Tradition in the Four Gospels* (Sheffield, 1981) 2, 9–60; R. A. Guelich, "The Gospel Genre", in P. Stuhlmacher (1982); W. S. Vorster, "Kerygma/History and the Gospel Genre", *NTS* 24 (1983) 87–95; articles by H. Cancik, M. Reiser and G. Lüderitz in H. Cancik (1984), D. Dormeyer, H. Frankemölle, "Evangelium als literarische Gattung und als theologischer Begriff; Tendenzen und Aufgaben der Evangelienforschung im 20. Jdt., mit einer Untersuchung des Markusevangeliums in seiner Verhältnis zur antiken Biographie", in H. Temporini, W. Haase (eds.), *Aufstieg und Niedergang der Römischen Welt* (Berlin/New York, 1984), II, 25, 2, 1543–1704; V. K. Robbins (1984); D. E. Aune (1987); D. Dormeyer (1987); F. J. Matera (1987) 75–85; M. Gerhart, J. G. Williams (eds.), *Genre, Narrativity, and Theology* (Semeia, 43; Atlanta, 1988); M. A. Tolbert (1989) chapter 4; A. Y. Collins (1990); W. H. Hare, "Genre Criticism and the Gospels", in J. H. Skilton (ed.), *The Gospels Today. A Guide to some Recent Developments* (Philadelphia, 1990).

55 C. W. Votaw, "The Gospels and Contemporary Biographies", *AJT* 19 (1915) 45–73, 217–49. These essays were reprinted in the Facet Book series as *The Gospels and Contemporary Biographies in the Greco-Roman World* (Philadelphia, 1970).

56 See e.g. M. Smith (1971). Cf. also H. Koester, "One Jesus and Four Gospels", *HTR* 61 (1968) 230–6.

57 Cf. H. C. Kee (1973).

58 W. Schneemelcher in *New Testament Apocrypha* (London, 1963), ed. E. Hennecke, Vol. 1, 76; for a classic essay on the place of the Gospels in the general field of ancient literature, see K. L. Schmidt, "Die Stellung der Evangelien in der allgemeinen Literaturgeschichte", in H. Gunkel (Fs.),

Eucharisterion (Göttingen, 1923), ed. H. Schmidt, 50–134. This essay has been reprinted in a collection of Schmidt's writings, *Neues Testament. Judentum. Kirche. Kleine Schriften* (Munich, 1981), ed. G. Sauter, 37–134.

59 *The First Three Gospels* (London, 1966) 150.

60 For a helpful discussion of the original and derived meanings of the term "Gospel", see W. Schneemelcher, op. cit., 1, 71ff. Cf. also D. Dormeyer, H. Frankemölle (n. 54) and D. Dormeyer (1987).

61 See M. J. Suggs, *Interpreter's Dictionary of the Bible* (Supplementary Volume; New York, 1976), ed. G. A. Buttrick, "Gospel, genre" ad loc. Such a view is held, for example, by A. Y. Collins (1990), for whom Mark is an "apocalyptic historical monograph", the evangelist having integrated the various genres of the Jesus tradition into an historical framework which was informed by his own eschatology.

62 Examples often cited are the sayings-source Q, or the "Sayings of the Sages" in Rabbinic tradition, or the collection of sayings/logia found in Gnostic texts like the Gospel of Thomas.

63 Examples often cited are those in the Graeco-Roman world depicting the exploits of deities, divine men or heroes or in the Old Testament those associated with Elijah and Elisha.

64 Accounts of the death, at the hands of the civil or religious authorities, of persons regarded as remarkable for their wisdom or exploits appear in the popular literature of this period. Cf. H. C. Kee (1977), 21–2, who issues a caution, however, against taking the Hellenistic martyrology as a model for Mark.

65 *The So-called Historical Jesus and the Historic, Biblical Christ* (Philadelphia, 1964), 80, n. 11.

66 For a succinct and critical review of the Marcan sources which have been posited, see H. C. Kee (1977) 30–49; E. Trocmé (1975) chapter 1 and W. R. Telford (1992).

67 The section 5:1–43, for example, has three miracles arranged in an apparently climactic series (an exorcism, a healing and a raising from the dead), the first (on Gentile soil) featuring a man, the other two (set on Jewish soil) connected with two women. Conversely, a second group of three healings (7:24–37 and 8:22–6), also commencing with an exorcism, describes Jesus' dealings (on Gentile soil) firstly with a woman and then with two men. W. H. Kelber (1974, chapter 3) makes much of such patterning but explains the textual phenomena in terms of a conscious selectivity and symbolic intent on the part of the evangelist.

68 Cf. N. Perrin, *The New Testament. An Introduction* (New York, 1974) 145–6.

69 For a review of Cook's book, see W. R. Telford in *JTS* 31 (1980–1) 154–62.

70 For other work on the controversy pericopae, see e.g. W. Thissen (1976); A. J. Hultgren (1979); J. Kiilunen (1985); H. Sariola (1990). On the specific theme of purity in Mark, see R. P. Booth (1986) and J. H. Neyrey (1986).

Introduction

71 W. G. Kümmel, *Introduction*, 70. Recent major commentaries (Pesch, Gnilka, Lührmann, Guelich) have been also generally in agreement. See also F. Neirynck, "Recent Developments in the Study of Q", in *Evangelica II* (Leuven, 1991), ed. F. Van Segbroeck, 409–64.

72 F. C. Grant, *The Gospels, their Origin, and their Growth* (London, 1959) 109. According to J. P. Brown, "Mark as Witness to an Edited Form of Q", *JBL* 80 (1961) 29–44, both Mark and Matthew used a revised version of Q. W. Schenk, "Der Einfluss der Logienquelle auf das Markusevangelium", *ZNW* 70 (1979) 141–65, claims the priority of the pre-Marcan tradition over Q (generally held to be the older witness) and argues that Mark knew Q but used it selectively. See also J. Lambrecht, "The Influence of Q on Mark 8:34–9:1", in J. Delobel (ed.), *Logia. Les Paroles de Jésus – The Sayings of Jesus. Mémorial Joseph Coppens* (Leuven, 1982).

73 Logia-sequences, linked by catchword connection, such as (all or part of) 9:33–50 (see H. Fleddermann, 1981) or 11:22–5 (see W. R. Telford, 1980, 49–59, and S. E. Dowd, 1988) are often cited. For discussion of this latter passage in connection with Mark's teaching on faith and prayer, see M. A. Beavis, "Mark's Teaching on Faith", *BTB* 16 (1986) 139–42 and S. Hre Kio, "A Prayer Framework in Mark 11", *Bible Translator* 37 (1986) 323–8.

74 For the extensive bibliography on this passage, see J. Lambrecht, op. cit., 269, n. 1 (cited above, n. 2). Cf. also C. E. B. Cranfield, "St. Mark 4:1–34", *SJT* 4 (1951) 398, n. 2; E. Best, "Mark's Use of the Twelve", *ZNW* 69 (1978) 16, n. 31. For a survey of research, see H. Räisänen (1990) 76–87, and M. A. Beavis (1989) 69–86. For a sample of the discussion, see in addition to the Lambrecht article, W. Marxsen (1955) 255–71; J. Jeremias, *The Parables of Jesus* (3rd ed.; London, 1972), ET S. H. Hooke, 13–18, 77–9, 149–51; E. Schweizer in Tuckett (1983); H. Räisänen (n. 43) passim; W. H. Kelber (1974) chapter 2; C. E. Carlston, *The Parables of the Triple Tradition* (Philadelphia, 1975) chapter 5; H. Weder (n. 43); M. Boucher (1977); G. Sellin (1983); J. Marcus (1986).

Nothing illustrates better the difficulties in separating tradition from redaction in 4:1–34 than the lack of consensus in particular over the origin of the logion 4:11–12 with its statement concerning the purpose of Jesus' parabolic teaching. While most scholars would agree that 4:11–12 is a redactional insertion, some view it as a genuine, if misplaced, saying of Jesus (e.g. Jeremias), others as post-dominical but taken from Mark's tradition or *Vorlage* (e.g. Schweizer, Carlston), others still as a redactional construction reflecting the evangelist's own conception of the function of the parables (e.g. Marxsen, Lambrecht and now Räisänen). Beavis (1989) has contended for 4:11–12 as not only Marcan but programmatic for the Gospel. For a review of Beavis, see W. R. Telford in *Epworth Review* 18 (1991) 98–9. For a reader-response approach to the logion, which sees it as an example of Mark's intentional narrative opacity and irony, see also Fowler's article here included.

75 In addition to the literature already cited, see R. Bultmann (1968) 125; K. Grayston (1973–4); W. H. Kelber (1974) chapter 6. In an article, "Markus 13", in J. Lambrecht (ed.), *L'Apocalypse johannique et l'Apocalyptique*
    dans le Nouveau Testament (Louvain/Gembloux, 1980) 355–68, R. Pesch, revising some of the views presented in his earlier work (1968), claims that Mark inserted into his inherited passion narrative, after 13:1–2, a separate Jewish-Christian apocalypse which had addressed itself to the community's eschatological concern aroused by the Romano-Jewish War. This apocalypse, he speculates, might be the oracle cited by Eusebius which led to the flight of Judaeo-Christians from Jerusalem to Pella. Pesch's new position is both summarized and criticized by F. Neirynck in the same volume (369–401).

76 For second thoughts on his earlier work on Mark 13, see G. R. Beasley-Murray (1983). Employing a rigorous source criticism, D. Wenham has attempted to reconstruct a pre-Synoptic eschatological discourse. A. Y. Collins (1992), on the other hand, does not find arguments for such a written source compelling, although she does think it likely that Mark drew on oral tradition. The possibility that such tradition may go back to Jesus, moreover, should not be ruled out.

77 See e.g. S. Schulz (1961); A. Suhl (1965); H. C. Kee (1975) as well as (1977) 45–9; H.-J. Steichele, *Der leidende Sohn Gottes. Eine Untersuchung einiger alttestamentlicher Motive in der Christologie des Markusevangeliums* (Regensburg, 1980); C. P. März (1980); W. R. Telford (1980) chapter 5; W. S. Vorster (1981); J. D. Derrett (1985).

78 See e.g. C. Maurer, "Knecht Gottes und Sohn Gottes im Passionsbericht des Markusevangeliums", *ZTK* 50 (1953) 1–38 (reprinted in Limbeck, 1981, an anthology of previously published articles on the Synoptic passion accounts), who argues for the influence in particular of Isa. 53, at both the Marcan and pre-Marcan levels, in shaping the image of Jesus in terms of deutero-Isaiah's "Suffering Servant". Cf. also C. F. Evans, *Explorations in Theology* (London, 1977), 2, 7ff.; J. Oswald (1979); J. Ernst (1980b); J. D. Crossan, *The Cross that Spoke. The Origins of the Passion Narrative* (San Francisco, 1988); V. K. Robbins (1992).

79 Cf. R. Bultmann (1968) 262–84. For a review of subsequent research, see J. Ernst (1980b) and M. L. Soards (1985). Soards' useful article (published in expanded form in R. E. Brown's *The Death of the Messiah*, 1994) offers some sobering methodological caveats in respect of the weaknesses of the tradition-historical criteria employed in some reconstructions of the source. M. Ruhland (1987) has suggested that a primitive apocalyptic *Warnschrift* (comprising Peter's denial and related material) was the germinative core for the pre-Marcan passion narrative, but her reconstruction exemplifies some of these weaknesses, especially her over-use of the criterion of (in)coherence in separating source from redaction. For a critical review of Ruhland, see W. R. Telford in *JTS* 40 (1989) 182–5. Crossan's hypothesis (n. 78) that a core

version of the Gospel of Peter was the source for all of the intracanonical Gospels has been criticized by F. Neirynck (n. 17).

The relation of the empty tomb story (16:1–8) to the pre-Marcan passion narrative has also generated some discussion but again some contradictory estimates. While H. Paulsen (1980) has argued for the redactional nature of 16:7 (and hence for a pre-Marcan form of the story which was probably joined to the passion narrative by the evangelist), F. Neirynck (1980) notes that it was no longer possible to speak of a consensus with respect to the secondary character of 16:7 and hence of the composite nature of 16:1–8. For other work on the passion narrative itself see, in addition to the literature already cited, E. Linnemann (1970); D. Dormeyer (1974, 1979).

80 For a critique of Schenke, see D. Dormeyer (1974) 302–17.

81 See e.g. K. G. Kuhn, "Jesus in Gethsemane", *EvT* 12 (1952–3) 260–85 (reprinted in Limbeck, 1981); R. S. Barbour (1969–70); W. Mohn, "Gethsemane (Mark 14:32–42), *ZNW* 64 (1973) 194–208; D. M. Stanley, *Jesus in Gethsemane* (New York, 1980). Cf. also R. Feldmeier (1987).

82 Vide supra, n. 75. Cf. also R. Pesch, "Der Schluss der vormarkinische Passionsgeschichte und des Markusevangeliums: Mark 15:42–16:8", in M. Sabbe (1974–88), and "Anfang des Evangeliums Jesu Christi. Eine Studie zum Prolog des Markusevangeliums (Mark 1:1–15)" in H. Schlier, Festschrift, *Die Zeit Jesu* (Freiburg i. Br., 1970), ed. G. Bornkamm, K. Rahner, and reprinted in Pesch (1979b).

83 See H. Riesenfeld, "Tradition und Redaktion im Markusevangelium", in *Neutestamentliche Studien für Rudolf Bultmann* (Berlin, 1954), reprinted in Pesch (1979b); also E. R. Martinez, "The Identity of Jesus in Mark", *Communio* 1 (1974) 323–42 and H. Räisänen (1990) chapter 1.

84 Cf. e.g. "That Mark radically *rewrote* his sources has often caused shock to us. He definitely is not the conservative redactor he was thought to be" (J. Lambrecht in M. Sabbe, 1974, 304).

85 Cf. A. Farrer (1951) and (1954). Farrer is noted for his ingenious highlighting of patterns in the composition of the Gospel and their alleged symbolic function.

86 See N. R. Petersen, *Semeia* (1978). In arguing that Mark should be read as a narrative rather than a redaction, Petersen points to the systematic rhetoric pervading the text in its entirety, and the consistent "point of view" adopted by its author. The evangelist, he notes, uses throughout the third person of the "omniscient" and "intrinsic" narrator. He is present in every scene and knows even the inmost thoughts of Jesus as well as the other actors in his narrative (cf. 2:1–12). Whether, of course, the narrative is true or fiction, he adds, is a historical rather than a literary problem.

87 "Mark is not merely the redactor, but to a high degree the creator and composer of the Gethsemane story" (176).

88 See J. D. Crossan, "Empty Tomb and Absent Lord (Mark 16:1–8)", in W. H. Kelber (1976); N. Q. Hamilton (1965).

89 Few verses in the New Testament reveal more the hermeneutical orientation of scholars (either historical or literary) than their attempts to interpret 14:51–52! At one end of the spectrum are proposals which would identify this young man as a thinly disguised John Mark of Jerusalem. At the other end are a number of interpretations which would invest the young man with christological or baptismal significance. For a fascinating review of such interpretations, see e.g. F. Neirynck, "La Fuite du Jeune Homme en Mc 14, 51–2", *ETL* 55 (1979) 43–66, and (from a literary perspective) F. Kermode (1979) chapter 3; cf. also his article, "The Structures of Fiction", *Modern Language Notes*, 84 (1969) 891–915.

The Old Testament has often been suggested as the underlying catalyst for this curious datum (cf. e.g. Amos 2:16). An intriguing article by H. Waetjen, for example, "The Ending of Mark and the Gospel's Shift in Eschatology", *Annual of the Swedish Theological Institute*, 4 (1965) 114–31, suggested a link between 14:51–2, 16:5 and the Joseph story (cf. Gen. 39:11–12; 41:39–43). "As a Joseph figure, the youth gives expression to the destiny of Jesus. The latter is unjustly apprehended, put to death and buried in a tomb. But like Joseph he is raised up, exalted and enthroned as God's viceregent" (120).

90 See, however, E. Trocmé (1973). Basing his claims on his own "Ur-Markus" hypothesis, Trocmé contends that Mark had merely synthesized the various images of Jesus in the traditions he took over, and that he had done so with a pastoral rather than a strong christological purpose in mind. None of the christological titles in Mark is used as a vehicle for the evangelist's own christology, and no unified "Messianic Secret" motif exists.

91 For a review of recent discussion on Marcan christology, see E. Schweizer (1977), n. 1 above, J. R. Donahue (1978) and M. E. Boring (1984).

92 See e.g. E. Schweizer (1962); K.-G. Reploh (1969); R. H. Stein (1970); U. B. Müller, "Die christologische Absicht des Markusevangeliums und die Verklärungsgeschichte", *ZNW* 64 (1973) 159–93; P. J. Achtemeier (1980). Cf. also M. Smith, "Forms, Motives and Omissions in Mark's Account of the Teaching of Jesus", in M. S. Enslin, Festschrift, *Understanding the Sacred Text* (Valley Forge, Pa., 1972), ed. J. Reumann, 155–64.

93 "The Transfiguration Story and the Markan Soteriology", *ExpTim* 81 (1969–70) 263–8.

94 Cf. "For nothing is more obvious than that Mark understood the miracles as manifestations of the Messiah" (1971: 17).

95 See also his monograph (1970) already cited. From a different perspective, E. R. Martinez (n. 83) also argues for the miracles as theophanies in the Marcan presentation.

96 "The only essential element of the Christ myth not yet adopted by Mark is the pre-existence of Jesus. The dogmatic idea clearly does not lend itself so easily to a presentation of the life of Jesus; John was the first who was able to use it in this way" (1968: 349). For a critique of Bultmann's position, see e.g. P. Vielhauer (1964).

97 See e.g. T. A. Burkill (1972) chapter 1; G. Strecker, E. Schweizer and U. Luz in Tuckett (1983). See also n. 18.

98 On the significance of the miracle stories for Mark, for example, cf. K. Kertelge (1970) and D.-A. Koch (1975) already cited; on the function of the controversy pericopae cf. T. L. Budesheim, (1971); P. von der Osten-Sacken, "Streitgespräch und Parabel als Formen markinischer Christologie", in H. Conzelmann, Festschrift, *Jesus Christus in Historie und Theologie* (Tübingen, 1975), ed. G. Strecker, 375–94; on the relation of the eschatological discourse to the rest of the Gospel (esp. 8:27–9:1), see D.-A. Koch, "Zum Verhältnis von Christologie und Eschatologie im Markusevangelium", in the Conzelmann Festschrift, 395–408; on the passion narrative and its christological thrust, see W. H. Kelber (1972).

99 Cf. e.g. R. Bultmann (1967); E. Haenchen (1963); E. Dinkler (1971); M. Horstmann (1973); J. Lambrecht (1973); U. B. Müller (see n. 92); J. A. Ziesler (see n. 93); H. Klein (1987).

100 The influence of this "suffering wise man" motif at the earliest levels of the passion tradition has also been detected by J. R. Donahue (1973) and C. Maurer (n. 78).

101 See e.g. H. C. Kee (1972); J. R. Donahue, "Temple, Trial and Royal Christology", in W. H. Kelber (1976); J. D. Kingsbury, "The 'Divine Man' as the Key to Mark's Christology – the End of an Era?", *Int* 35 (1981) 243–57. An interesting thesis is that of P. Vielhauer (1964) who detects an enthronement scheme similar to ancient Egyptian kingship ritual underlying the Marcan christological presentation. For Mark, Jesus has been enthroned as the eschatological king. The Gospel's key Baptism, Transfiguration and Crucifixion scenes witness in turn to the three-fold stages of Adoption (by God), Proclamation (to his disciples) and Acclamation (by the Gentile centurion). See also H. Weihnacht, *Die Menschwerdung des Sohnes Gottes im Markusevangelium* (1972).

102 See e.g. L. S. Hay, "The Son-of-God Christology in Mark", *Journal of Bible and Religion* 32 (1964) 106–14. Hay also gives a helpful review of the various ways "Son of God" has been interpreted. Cf. also C. R. Kazmierski (1979), who claims that Mark's Son-of-God Christology rested firmly on the foundations of the traditions that he had received and which he employed in the service of his community's missionary proclamation, and H.-J. Steichele (n. 77) who brings Mark's use of the term into connection with Old Testament and Jewish concepts.

103 An article frequently quoted in the debate was that by H. D. Betz (1968). Betz sought to identify a "divine man" christology underlying the Synoptic Gospels and John, and argued that this christology, present in the miracle tradition, underwent transformations in the hands of the individual evangelists. Cf. also P. J. Achtemeier, "Gospel Miracle Material and the Divine Man", *Int* 26 (1972) 173–97.

104 Cf. e.g. D. L. Tiede, *The Charismatic Figure as Miracle-Worker* (Missoula, Mont., 1972); C. Holladay, *"Theios Aner" in Hellenistic Judaism: A Critique of the Use of this Category in New Testament Christology* (Missoula, Mont., 1977). An important result of Holladay's study in particular is his denial of the claim that Hellenistic Judaism depicted its Old Testament worthies as "divine men" and so prepared the way for Jesus to be thought of in such terms. For a critical review of Holladay's book, see W. R. Telford, *JTS* 30 (1979) 246–52. Cf. J. D. Kingsbury (n. 101).

105 See e.g. O. Betz (1972); H. C. Kee (1973).

106 For a detailed treatment of this subject, see e.g. M. D. Hooker (1967). For contrasting positions cf. H. E. Tödt, *The Son of Man in the Synoptic Tradition* (London, 1965) and B. Lindars, *Jesus, Son of Man* (London, 1983).

107 For a discussion of these verses, see e.g. L. S. Hay, "The Son of Man in Mark 2:10 and 2:28", *JBL* 89 (1970) 69–75; C. Tuckett, "The Present Son of Man", *JSNT* 14 (1982) 58–81.

108 Cf. e.g. G. Strecker (1968). Strecker thinks that 8:31 is based at least on pre-Marcan tradition, with 9:31 and 10:33–4 being modelled subsequently on it. See also C. K. Barrett, *Jesus and the Gospel Tradition* (London, 1967).

109 T. W. Manson in C. H. Dodd, Festschrift, *The Background of the New Testament and its Eschatology* (Cambridge, 1954), ed. D. Daube, W. D. Davies, 216; cf. N. Perrin (1966) 296.

110 For a discussion of the title "Son of David" in Mark with particular reference to the Bartimaeus story, see V. K. Robbins (1973). Arguing for the christological significance of this pericope, Robbins claims that Mark has not rejected the "Son of David" concept but instead has christianized it by linking it with the Christian healing tradition. For a contrary view, see E. S. Johnson (1978). Also C. Burger, *Jesus als Davidssohn* (Göttingen, 1970).

111 For a critique of Schulz, see e.g. D.-A. Koch (1975) 175–9.

112 E.g. E. Schweizer, "Neuere Markus-Forschung in USA", *EvT* 33 (1973) 533–7; W. L. Lane, "Theois Aner Christology and the Gospel of Mark" in R. Longenecker, M. C. Tenney (eds.), *New Dimensions in New Testament Study* (Grand Rapids, 1974) 144–61.

113 This point, of course, touches upon a key issue in New Testament Christology, viz. our assumptions about the priority of christological traditions. While many scholars (e.g. H. C. Kee, R. H. Fuller, O. Betz) would argue for the primitiveness of those Christologies which disclose their links with an Old Testament, Jewish or apocalyptic background (e.g. Jesus as eschatological prophet or apocalyptic Son of Man), some (e.g. M. Smith, H. D. Betz) would nevertheless claim such primitiveness (especially in the light of the radical hellenization of Palestine) for a "divine man" Christology (Jesus as wonder-worker) with the subsequent overlays of Jewish apocalypticism, "suffering servant" Christology, "Logos" Christology, etc. a product of later reflection on Jesus' death and a belief in his resurrection.

Introduction

114 M. Werner, *Der Einfluss paulinischer Theologie im Markusevangelium* (Giessen, 1923).

115 Fenton (1957) reviews these and argues himself for the presence in Mark of six themes which are paralleled in the Pauline Epistles.

116 "Till now, a comparison of Mark with Paul was *bound* to encounter difficulties, since it was not *Mark* who was compared with Paul, but rather the material Mark transmitted. After detailed investigation, Werner, e.g. asserted that 'any influence of Pauline theology upon the Gospel of Mark is entirely out of the question'. But this judgement probably relates to the fact that Werner never compares the evangelist but only the tradition he presented" (W. Marxsen, 1969: 213).

117 Cf. e.g. F. G. Lang, "Sola Gratia im Markusevangelium. Die Soteriologie des Markus nach 9, 14–29" (Tübingen/Göttingen, 1976), ed. J. Friedrich, et al., 321–37. The section of the Gospel 8:27–10:52 is often taken as an important window into Mark's "theologia crucis". Lang argues that two pericopae in particular (9:14–29 and 10:17–31) reflect the Pauline emphasis on salvation by God's grace alone which is to be received in faith by the individual. For an analysis of the distinctiveness of the Marcan and Pauline soteriology, see also U. Luz, "Theologia crucis als Mitte der Theologie im Neuen Testament", *EvT* 34 (1974) 116–41. For a different perspective, see W. Schenk, "Sekundäre Jesuanisierungen von primären Paulus-Aussagen bei Markus", in F. Neirynck, Festschrift, *The Four Gospels 1992* (Leuven, 1992; 3 Vols.), 2, 877–904.

118 See e.g. R. H. Stein, "A Short Note on Mark XIV.28 and XVI.7", *NTS* 20 (1973–4) 445–52.

119 Cf. e.g. G. H. Boobyer (1952–3), following R. H. Lightfoot (1950), 116 (cf. also, however, Lightfoot [1938], 61–5, 73–7); M. Karnetzski, "Die Galiläische Redaktion im Marusevangelium", *ZNW* 52 (1961) 238–72.

120 A significant article is that by F. G. Lang, "Über Sidon mitten ins Gebiet der Dekapolis: Geographie und Theologie in Markus 7,31", *Zeitschrift des deutschen Palästina-Vereins* 94 (1978) 156–60. Lang argues that the route Jesus is described as following in 7:31 is implausible geographically and hence historically, and that it has been theologically conceived, therefore, by Mark. The three stories of 7:21–8:10 which are connected by means of this journey have, moreover, a theological unity in that they are concerned with the question of Gentile-Jew relations and the Gentile mission. By placing these stories in the context of an elaborate journey by Jesus throughout the Gentile regions to the north and east of Galilee, Jesus is shown as blazing a trail in the Gentile area which the church was later to follow. D. Blatherwick (1970–1) sees symbolic significance also in the many lake-crossings described in Mark. "The lake ceases to be merely an area of water but symbolizes the fringes of Jewish society and the dividing line between Jew and Gentile" (187). Cf. also W. H. Kelber (1974) chapter 3, and the structuralist treatments of Marcan geography by B. Van Iersel (1983), J. Drury (1985) and E. S. Malbon (1979, 1982, 1984, 1986a) referred to above (p. 11 and n. 47).

121 Cf. G. Dautzenberg (1976). Mark, according to Dautzenberg, stands in a stream that is closer to the primitive Palestine-Jewish tradition than to a Hellenistic-Jewish one. Similarly, D. Lührmann (1977), who thinks that the Marcan usage goes back to Isa. 52:7 and not (as Paul) to the Hellenistic ruler-cult.

122 Cf. e.g. A. Farrer (1951), esp. chapter 13.

123 See Q. Quesnell (1969), esp. chapters 6, 7; R. M. Fowler (1981) 132ff.

124 See G. H. Boobyer (1952) and (1953).

125 See e.g. E. Schweizer already cited; A. Kuby (n. 42); J. Schreiber (1961); J. B. Tyson (1961); T. J. Weeden (1968) and (1971); K.-G. Reploh (1969); E. Best (1970), (1975–6), (1976–7), (1978a) and (1978b); D. J. Hawkin (1972); W. H. Kelber (1972) and (1974); G. Schmahl, "Die Berufung der Zwölf im Markusevangelium", *TTZ* 81 (1972) 203–13, and (1974); C. Focant, "L'Incompréhension des Disciples dans le Deuxième Évangile", *RB* 82 (1975) 161–85; K. Stock (1975); E. Trocmé (1975) chapter 2; W. Bracht, "Jüngerschaft und Nachfolge. Zur Gemeindesituation im Markusevangelium", in J. Hainz (ed.), *Kirche im Werden* (Munich, 1976) 143–65; P. S. Minear (1978); W. H. Kelber (1979a); H. J. Klauck (1982); J. R. Donahue (1983); J. Scott, "Story and Discipleship in Mark's Gospel", *Friends Quarterly* (Ashford, UK) 23 (1985) 583–94; E. S. Malbon (1986); T. E. Boomershine (1987); C. C. Black (1988, 1989); J. D. Kingsbury (1989); M. R. Thompson (1989); M. D. Goulder (1992). On the family of Jesus in Mark, see also E. Grässer (1969–70); J. D. Crossan (1973, 1978); J. Lambrecht (1974).

126 This does not, of course, rule out the possibility that the twelve were already regarded in somewhat of a bad light in the tradition Mark took over, as E. Best maintains, and that the evangelist has "worked up" this tradition for his own pastoral or parenetic purposes. Nor does it necessarily imply that the "blindness" motif is entirely redactional in nature or uniform in function, as C. Focant cautions us against assuming.

127 P. S. Minear (1972), for example, draws attention to the very significant role which Mark assigns to the "crowd" (*ochlos*) in the Gospel. With the exception of 14:43 and 15:8, 11, 15 (where a separate group is in view), they respond positively to Jesus and his message and represent, therefore, a continuing audience of committed believers, a "kind of primitive laity" (J. A. Baird), with whom the laymen in the Marcan community would identify.

128 L. Schenke (1969) argues that, formerly separate from 15:42–7, the Empty Tomb tradition reflected in 16:1–8 was originally an aetiological cult-legend which was designed to explain the origin of a rite celebrated by the primitive Jerusalem community, viz. an annual procession at Easter to the empty grave of Jesus.

129 Vide supra, n. 88. Cf. also H. Waetjen (n. 89). For a critique of Hamilton and Waetjen, see e.g. E. Schweizer (1977), n. 1 above.

130 A traditional view holds that this original ending was either lost, mutilated or suppressed, with various secondary endings having been supplied in the subsequent transmission of the text. For a discussion of those textual endings

and the manuscript evidence, see K. Aland, "Der Schluss des Markusevangeliums", in M. Sabbe (1974–88), and H. Hug, *La Finale de l'Évangile de
Marc. Marc 16:9–20* (Paris, 1979). Hug presents the evidence that the longer
ending of Mark was not written by the evangelist and assigns it to the second
third of the second century. According to E. Linnemann, however, "Der
(weidergefundene) Markusschluss", *ZTK* 66 (1969–70) 255–87, the original
conclusion consisted of 16:15–20 of the now longer Marcan ending together
with what Matthew has reproduced in 28:16–17. Cf. also W. Schmithals, "Der
Markusschluss, die Verklärungsgeschichte und die Aussendung der Zwölf",
ZTK 69 (1972) 379–411. While agreeing with Linnemann that the original
Marcan conclusion included 16:15–20, Schmithals also contends that the
evangelist's source for the resurrection narrative comprised an appearance to
Peter, which he transposed to 9:2ff. as the transfiguration story (cf.
R. Bultmann) and an appearance to the twelve which he also transposed to a
pre-Easter context in 3:13–19. For a critique of Linnemann, see K. Aland, "Der
wiedergefundene Markusschluss?", *ZTK* 67 (1970) 3–13, and J. K. Elliott,
"The Text and Language of the Endings to Mark's Gospel", *TZ* 27 (1971)
255–62. Reference may also be made to H.-W. Bartsch's "Der Schluss des
Markus-Evangeliums", *TZ* 27 (1971) 241–54. Bartsch argues that the real
question of the Marcan ending should be considered a tradition-critical
problem, rather than a text-critical one.

131 Cf. W. G. Kümmel (1975) 100. For a detailed discussion of the Marcan ending,
see also T. J. Weeden (1971) chapters 4, 5.

132 For a similar judgment, see F. Kermode (n. 89) 901ff. and (1979) 65ff.; T. E.
Boomershine (1981); T. E. Boomershine, G. L. Bartholomew (1981) and J. L.
Magness (1986).

133 For a review of suggested aims for Mark in the context of his own analysis of
the Gospel's introduction, see L. E. Keck (1965–6).

134 J. Roloff (1969) argues that Mark intended to record past events rather than
merely to subordinate or develop his traditions under the influence of a
kerygmatic, existential or theological concern. Post-Easter Christology has
not obliterated the historical Jesus, he claims, for the secrecy motif employed
by Mark reflects his attempt to preserve the distinction between past and
present, between pre- and post-Easter faith. For a similar view, see E. E.
Lemcio (1986).

Cf. also K. Schubert, "Kritik der Bibelkritik. Dargestellt an Hand des
Markusberichtes von Verhör Jesu vor dem Synedrion", in M. Limbeck (1981)
(reprinted from *Wort und Wahrheit* 27 (1972) 421–34). In a study attempting to
uncover historical data in the Marcan account of the trial of Jesus, Schubert
makes an appeal to scholars not to abandon the search for history as a result of a
hermeneutical programme which today emphasizes more and more the literary
process, and which views the biblical texts as witnesses only to the faith of
Christians and not to the events which inspired that faith. Such a position, of
course, begs many questions, for the recovery of historical data from faith-
inspired texts should at least begin (even if it should not end) with literary
analysis.

1

Mark's Theological Achievement *

EDUARD SCHWEIZER

Thirty years after the death of Jesus the gospel had reached most of the countries surrounding the Mediterranean. A period of Spirit-inspired "enthusiasm" was followed by theological con-solidation. Whereas the piety of the hellenistic church had stressed Jesus' exaltation as Lord over all powers, and so connected his pre-existence and his incarnation, Paul had taken up an aspect of Jewish-Christian proclamation and seen the true centre of Christianity in the crucifixion and resurrection of Jesus. This provided the basis for the Christian's freedom from law, sin and death, but in contrast to all charismatic enthusiasm he continued to emphasize that the consummation, i.e. the visible victory over sin and death, could be expected only at the parousia. A decade later, when Mark wrote his Gospel, the battle over freedom from the law was won. The progress of the law-free gospel through the world, which Paul in particular had promoted, could no longer be stopped. The demise of a narrow Jewish Christianity was already apparent. In the wide world outside, Colossians, Ephesians, the hymn in 1 Tim. 3:16 and the post-Pauline doxology at the end of Romans show how the triumphal march of the gospel into the gentile world was understood as the decisive eschatological revelation of God's eternally hidden mystery. The Church had to be recalled from its all too pneumatic

* First published in *EvT* 24 (1964) 337–55, and republished in the author's *Beiträge zur Theologie des NT* (Zurich: Zwingli Verlag, 1970). Translated by R. Morgan. A shorter version appeared in *NTS* 10 (1963–4) 421–32 entitled "Mark's Contribution to the Quest of the Historical Jesus".

talk of the Cosmocrator who had already overcome all principalities and powers – recalled to earth and to sober reality, and above all to the task of mission, in which the Exalted One intended to exercise his sovereignty over the world.[1] The Spirit-filled enthusiasts behaved as though there were no more death, so that the already deified Christian had no further need of a future resurrection. They understood the victory over sin to mean that all earthly behaviour was unimportant, whereas here in Mark, following Paul, the Church was called to the task of witness to all the world, and if necessary to suffer and die for its testimony. Paul became the symbol of this exalted Lord's will to establish his sovereignty over all the world in and through the suffering and dying of his messengers. In the weakness, defeat, even the destruction of his followers he established his world dominion in power, and only those who were given the new eyes of faith to see through suffering and dying the Lord who was victorious throughout the world could understand what was happening here.

But the question remained what all this had to do with Jesus of Nazareth. He was, after all, a long way removed from the new churches outside Palestine. Only a few Christians knew that peculiar corner of the Roman empire where his history and that of the Old Testament was located, and there were many reports circulating about that peculiar people with their odd customs and superstitious practices. So there was a danger of Jesus becoming a mere symbol or empty cipher, merely signifying freedom from superstitious observance of the law and incomprehensible cultic practices, the overcoming of death or victory over the demons.[2] Why not equally well Attis or Hermes? One could see on the horizon a kerygma theology that had lost all its roots in history and could equally well be attached to Hermes as to Jesus. The gnostic threat had arrived.

I *The Gospel*

In this situation Mark wrote his Gospel. The fact that he wrote it at all is the most astonishing point. There existed collected sayings of hellenistic itinerant philosophers, connected to a few biographical notes. But Mark has reversed this: the story of Jesus was scarcely any precedent for that in the Church prior to Mark. There were creeds and hymns which clearly centred on what had happened to Jesus. But apart from the crucifixion they did not include the life of the earthly Jesus; only the framework of this life, which gave it its theological dimension – pre-existence and incarnation, resurrection and ascent. There were also a few miracle stories which had in some cases already been joined together into small cycles of tradition,[3] and there was an outline of the passion narrative, as is already presupposed and partially reproduced in the liturgy at 1 Cor. 11:23. But essentially it was at most sayings of the earthly Jesus that had been collected. Catechetical needs and so on had caused these, too, to be combined into collections linked by catchwords. There was probably a larger collection of sayings corresponding to part of what we normally call Q, prior to Mark. And there was also probably a collection of controversy dialogues, and a short outline of an apocalypse with the sequence: revolution, world war, famine, plague, persecution, earthquake, cosmic collapse.[4]

In view of all this it comes as a complete surprise when Mark decides to narrate essentially only what happened to Jesus and what, through him, God caused to happen to mankind. Broadly speaking, he simply strings events together: what God does in Jesus, and what Jesus does for mankind. Even more astonishing is the amount of space he sets aside for the passion narrative – and a passion narrative that dispenses with any transfiguring splendour. It has only one real model: the Old Testament. This is in the first place the story of all that God caused to happen to Israel. It, therefore, has figures like Moses or Jonah whose real significance lies not in what they said but in what happened to them. Precisely because Mark elsewhere hardly ever makes use of so-called scriptural proofs, the superscription for the whole Gospel is all the more astonishing. It says that Mark wants to present not the words and deeds of Jesus but the gospel of Jesus Christ (the Son of God), and that in it God's history with Israel, as the prophets announced it, has come to fulfilment.[5] Therein consists the properly theological achievement of Mark, and we must reflect on what has happened here. Has Mark gone back to a theology of history which sees history as such, or a special salvation history within the whole of history, as the direct revelation of God?

II *The terminology of the Marcan redaction*

The methodological difficulty consists in distinguishing between tradition and Mark's own theological interpretation. Whereas the material used by Matthew and Luke is largely known, in Mark this has to be worked out by literary analysis. But I think there is an approach which strangely enough has hardly been used at all. It is possible to pick out a number of words which occur only, or almost only, in passages where Mark is evidently at work as an editor, that is above all, in the short links between individual pericopae or in brief summaries.[6] We shall look at these first.

Mark twice uses *kērussein* ("to proclaim") to designate the Baptist's activity, three times for Jesus, and twice each for the twelve[7] and the world-wide Church. The content of this proclamation is characterized by two terms that have come to Mark from the tradition. It is a call to *metanoia* ("repentance") and so is *euangelion* ("gospel"), or message of salvation. It is striking that these two important concepts are again distributed between the Baptist, Jesus and the twelve or the world-wide Church. Mark thus shows how strongly he is rooted in the theological tradition of the post-Pauline Church. Even Paul sees the cosmic significance of the Gospel consisting in its permeating the world in the mission of the Church, within which he valued the testimony rendered by his churches very highly. He, too, likes to connect gospel and cosmos or Gentiles or similar expressions: Rom. 1:8f., 15f.; 10:16–18; 15:16–20. This is more clearly the case after Paul: Rom. 16:25f.; Col. 1:5, 23: Eph. 3:6; cf. 1 Tim. 3:16. Eschatological salvation consists first of all in the Gospel breaking through the boundaries of Palestine and Judaism in the Church's proclamation, and becoming world-wide, so that all nations are called and brought into salvation. What the connection of the terms "proclaim", "repentance", "gospel" in Mark suggests is confirmed by the construction of his writing.

Oddly enough, the picture is quite different with the equally typical Marcan terms *didaskein* ("to teach") and *didachē* ("teaching") which occur twenty times and refer exclusively to Jesus.[8] Within the kerygma's larger period of salvation Jesus and his teaching thus occupy a special place. The reaction to this teaching of Jesus is four times expressed as *exeplēssonto* ("they were amazed") – which is also said once of his miraculous activity. The situation is similar with *thambeisthai* ("to fear"). Expressions with *holos* ("whole") or *pas* ("all"), describing the impact of Jesus on all the world,[9] the whole people, etc. are also often found in redactional sections. They can describe, too, the impact of the Baptist's proclamation on "all Judea" and "all Jerusalem", or the preaching of the Gospel to "all nations".

So the period of Jesus is marked out within the proclamation of salvation from the Baptist to the world-wide gentile church, as the period of Jesus' teaching. But the vital point is that the content of this teaching is generally not given at all,[10] or only summarized very briefly or illustrated by a single example.[11] What Mark is concerned with is only the fact that this teaching was done with authority (1:22, 27),[12] and that is shown by paralleling it with Jesus' deeds of power[13] and by the world's astonishment at his teaching (6:2; 11:18). Matthew understands it quite differently when he places Mark 1:22 at the end of the Sermon on the Mount, and so bases Jesus' authority on an appeal to the content of his teaching (Matt. 7:28f.). For Mark, by contrast, it is not this content – what can be handed down and repeated – which is decisive. So it is emphatically not the "historical Jesus", who can perhaps still be reconstructed, that he preaches, not the *didaskalos* ("teacher").[14] What he reports cannot be verified, cannot be transmitted into our day by historians, cannot be reconstructed. Mark proclaims what can only be understood by faith: that in Jesus' teaching God himself has broken into this world.

That is confirmed by a third group of purely redactional terms: *parabolē* ("parable"), *kat' idian* ("privately"), *ou sunienai* ("not to understand"),[15] *kardia pepōrōmenē* ("heart hardened"), *ginōskein* ("to know"),[16] and also *suzētein* ("to question", "to seek")[17] and *diastellein* ("to charge").[18] They all clearly describe the fact of the world's not understanding, which Jesus confronts with his parabolic speech and his private instruction. Jesus' speaking in parables is thus for Mark not simply a more or less chance choice of form. These illustrations are neither a pedagogical tool nor are they optional. On the contrary, pure communication of facts can be taken over and handed on without active participation. But the pictorial saying challenges the hearer, because it can only be understood by someone who opens himself personally to the speaker, as the pictorial language of love shows.[19] For that reason parabolic speech withholds the meaning from those who do not allow their hardened hearts to be opened in existential confrontation with the one who addresses them. That is why for Mark all talk of God is ultimately pictorial, and for that very reason binding. That marks the limits of all demythologizing.[20]

We must now investigate these three areas: the world-wide proclamation, Jesus' teaching with authority, and the parabolic speech, within the construction of the Gospel.

III *Prologue and first part: Jesus' authority over demons, sin and law, and the blindness of the Pharisees*

Even the superscription in 1:1 makes clear from the outset, through the typically Marcan term "gospel", and perhaps too by the title "Son of God", what this writing is to be concerned with. This becomes even clearer from the Old Testament quotations in vv. 2f. Since Mark scarcely ever elsewhere refers back to the Old Testament this is all the more emphatic in calling all that follows fulfilment of the whole previous history of God. 1:4–8 marks the start of the period of salvation in which the kerygma causes astonishment throughout the world. So *kērussein* ("to proclaim") and the success indicated by "all Judaea" come immediately next to the Old Testament quotations, whereas the traditional description of the Baptist is not taken up until v. 6. Jesus appears for the first time in 1:9–13 and is at once described in the terms in which he has to be understood. This scene in which Jesus' divine sonship is central is dominated entirely by God, the Son, the Spirit, Satan and angels.[21] That makes it clear from the outset that the Gospel is not concerned with the "historical" Jesus but with the event in which God's world is breaking into the world of men. Jesus is indeed historical, and that without any qualification, but what most matters about him is what can only be proclaimed, only spoken, not proved, nor verified nor historically transmitted, what in Mark's report has neither eye-witnesses nor hearers. The prologue ends with the arrest of the Baptist which with its *paradothēnai* ("to be handed over") may already hint at the fate of Jesus himself.

The first part begins with a summary (1:14f.) and the call of the disciples (1:16–20). The summary shows by its catchwords *kērussein*, *euangelion*, *metanoiein* how Jesus steps into the kerygma's period of salvation and continues the activity of the Baptist, only that now the fulfilment of time and the nearness of God's Kingdom are pronounced. The call of the disciples introduces the concept of discipleship. Jesus passes along the

68

shore and "sees" Simon and Andrew. This seeing by Jesus, which includes calling, recurs repeatedly (1:16, 19; 2:14; 10:21; cf. 5:32; 10:23, 27). It embodies God's reaching out for mankind, which requires no prior conditions. Those who are here the first to be called have not even heard Jesus' preaching. They are involved in their daily work. That is how things begin when people follow Jesus, because his call was stronger than they themselves and their interests.

1:21–45 contains material depicting Jesus' teaching and healing with authority. So teaching and doing miracles stand in parallel from the outset. Jesus' deeds are never understood here as an expression of his compassion or love. They demonstrate God's holy wrath that breaks out in Jesus against the power of the adversary (1:41,[22] 43; similarly 3:5; cf. 8:12). They demonstrate, too, the authority of one who as conqueror of the demons frees the world of them (1:24; similarly 5:7–9, 15, etc.). And they show that the supernatural world knows about the secret of Jesus' person (1:24; 3:11; 5:7). Although these deeds of power are often told crudely, like hellenistic *theios anēr* ("divine man") ideas, they are not understood as giving grounds for faith. On the contrary, in a way that has long perplexed historical critical research it is emphasized here that these miracles cannot be handed on. The silence commands (1:44, etc.) are in effect prohibitions against handing on the historical Jesus. Neither supernatural voices (1:34) nor the miracles desired by the people (1:37) nor the narration of his deeds of power (1:45) are any help. Only the underivable and unverifiable testimony of the evangelist that here – in this historical person and his actions – God himself truly confronts mankind, can say what is happening here. That is why they are preceded by the superscription in 1:1–3, the prologue in the "heavenly dimension" and the report of the call to discipleship. Without these a purely historical report of what happened here would inevitably be misleading.

That is confirmed by a recognition that for Mark, Jesus' teaching with authority is even more important than the miracles. These can only depict the dimension in which that takes place. So he is happy to take them over. But even the vocabulary statistics show that Mark's real interest is in Jesus' *teaching* with authority. Thus in 1:27 even the first major miracle of exorcism leads to the question, "What is this? A new *teaching*, with authority!"

69

The second block of tradition that Mark takes over is a collection of controversy stories. They are introduced with the sentence, "and he was speaking" (RSV "preaching") "the word to them", which we shall find repeated at crucial points, and by a scene which describe Jesus' incredible success (2:1f.). They show Jesus' victory over sin and law. Entirely without theological reflection, Mark here comes close to Paul who likewise interprets Jesus' victory over the powers as victory over sin and law (Gal. 4:3, 8–10). That this is for Mark the decisive point is clear from the redactional conclusion to the whole section which for the first time registers the hardening and reports the Pharisees' decision to destroy him. Overcoming the law, which will open the Gospel to Gentiles, at once brings the cross into view (3:5f.).[23] The world's blindness to God's revelation becomes visible first of all in the Pharisees.

IV   Second Part: Jesus' parable discourse and the blindness of the world

Just like the first part, the second begins with a summary that describes Jesus' saving activity and success, and with the call of the twelve disciples (3:7–19). We see here that the supernatural world of demons also knows about the secret of Jesus being the Son of God, which God has communicated to Jesus at his baptism (3:11). The next section is an excellent example of Marcan redaction. The parallels in Matt. 12:22–9 and Luke 11:14–20 show that Mark has put what is for him the decisive v. 23, that basically establishes the start of Jesus' parable discourse, into an already existing firm context. This is confirmed by the strictly speaking impossible, but typically Marcan, expression, "and he called them to him". Mark has presumably broken off the original opening, the exorcism of Luke 11:14 (cf. Matt. 12:22f.), in order to put v. 21 there instead: the hardening of his own family who say he is crazy. In the tradition the exorcism is followed by the reproach that Jesus drives out demons by Beelzebul, as Matt. 12:24 = Luke 11:15 shows. Evidently Jesus answers in the earliest stage of the tradition, "If I cast out demons by Beelzebul, by whom do your sons cast them out?" (Matt. 12:27 = Luke 11:19), which is followed by the saying about the finger of God which shows that in Jesus, God's Kingdom has already broken in. Mark, on the other hand, has only taken up the sayings about the Kingdom

70

divided against itself and the strong man bound, which do not speak of Beelzebul but Satan.[24] So although it plays no further part in his account he has taken over the catchword Beelzebul, but reshaped it in a typical way. In his account the scribes from Jerusalem, i.e. from the centre of the Jewish leadership, explain, "He is possessed by Beelzebul". So they are completely parallel to the hardened relations (RSV "friends") of Jesus who explain, "He is beside himself". The redactional note in v. 23 that Jesus began to speak in parables follows on this double hardening in vv. 21 and 22. The framework at the end of the pericope corresponds to this: in v. 30 Mark relates the saying about the unforgiveable sin explicitly to the hardening of the scribes in v. 22, and in vv. 31–5 he contrasts the true family of Jesus, which hears his word and does the will of God, with the hardened family of v. 21.[25] So according to Mark the parable discourse is the response to the world being hardened, from the closest relations of Jesus to the leaders of Israel. In 4:1 Mark takes up the tradition that he has already introduced at the beginning of his second part (3:9) to depict Jesus' incredible success. The boat was out of place there since Jesus was only healing, but Mark postponed Jesus' teaching in parables in order to include first, parallel to his first part, the call of the disciples and then his basic theological judgement on the phenomenon of speaking in parables. Chapter 4 then presents Jesus' speaking in parables, and whatever stands behind it in the tradition 4:10–12 shows that Mark saw this as a matter of principle: "everything is in parables" (v. 10). "He did not speak to them without a parable" (4:34). Everything that Jesus has to say is *mystērion* (a "mystery" or "secret", 4:11) as regards its significance, incomprehensible for mankind.[26] Only God himself can disclose to mankind the meaning of the parables: "to you has been given the mystery" (RSV "secret") "of the kingdom of God". Without God's "giving" there is no *ginōskein* ("knowing"). The catch-word "mystery" found at Rom. 16:25, Col. 1:26f., 2:2; Eph. 3:3f., 9; 6:16; 1 Tim. 3:16[27] thus appears here, too, and shows what larger context Mark is to be set in. That was no longer understood by Matthew and Luke when they changed the singular, *to mystērion*, which describes the mystery of revelation itself, namely the word of the cross, into a plural and so find all kinds of individual mysteries behind the parables, which are then unveiled in allegorical interpretation. It is true that Mark also takes over this interpretation of the first parable from the

71

tradition. But that does not fulfil the *dedotai* ("it is given") of 4:11. It is not the case that for Mark one would have to attach only one interpretation. The tradition of the historical Jesus could provide that. It could, without ado, offer the resolution of the puzzle, and then one would only have to wonder why Jesus did not himself provide it at once and for everyone. One would have to ask why he talked in parables at all instead of at once providing the solution to the puzzle. For Mark, however, the disciple of Jesus needs something quite different from the historical Jesus. He needs the Jesus who speaks to him today, i.e. the Exalted One. As at Rom. 1:18ff. and John 15:22, so too at Mark 4:12, it is the event of revelation, the Gospel itself, which has to reveal the blindness of mankind and so bring the world under God's judgement. So then it becomes plain that only God's grace itself can rescue mankind from his judgement. This is what is described when Mark again and again has Jesus take his disciples on one side *kat' idian* ("privately").[28] That not even this will remove their failure to understand will be shown by Mark in his third section. At this point the expression "he spoke the word to them" appears a second time, but now with the addition "with many (such) parables" (4:33). Thus Mark signals how important this fact is.

In 4:36 the "other boats" which now play no further role show that this comes from the tradition and that the story which follows was connected with 4:1 prior to Mark.[29] It thus probably followed the parable of the sower originally, since in the present composition of Mark, Jesus has already left the boat at 4:10. So Mark simply follows his tradition when he inserts the story of the crossing the lake in a storm and the healing of the Gadarene on the other shore at this point. The same may be true of 5:21–43, though the story perhaps also fits in the context because Jesus here too takes aside three chosen people (5:37, 40) and, by raising Jairus' daughter, allows them to become witnesses of his deepest secret. At any rate, Part 2 closes exactly like Part 1 with Jesus being rejected (6:1–4). Only it is now no longer the Pharisees but his own countrymen. The blinding is heightened.

V   *Part 3: Hope for the Gentiles and the blindness of the disciples*

As in Parts 1 and 2, Mark again begins with a summary of Jesus' healing and teaching ministry, though admittedly a very short one

72

(6:5f., i.e. 6:6b), which is followed by the sending out of the twelve (6:7–13). Since their return is connected with that (6:30) Mark inserts a story to fill the gap, as is his custom.[30] He chooses the death of the Baptist which hints at what will befall Jesus himself. What follows is again an example of Marcan redaction. In almost Johannine manner the traditions of the miraculous feeding are used to demonstrate the total blindness of the world and the miracle of divine revelation. As John 6 shows, feeding, crossing the lake, and the demand for a sign were already connected in the tradition. Mark clearly knew this tradition in two forms, and so can doubly underline his interest. Perhaps the position of this story shortly before Peter's confession also comes from the tradition (John 6:68f.)

Mark 6:34 is typical. The saying about Jesus' compassion referred originally to the bodily hunger of the people, as 8:2 still shows. Mark refers it afresh to spiritual hunger and has Jesus answer in the Marcan formula, "and he began to teach them many things". In the concluding phrase after the two miracles we hear in Marcan terminology but thoroughly Johannine meaning about their not understanding "concerning the loaves", and the hardening of their hearts. So what was said at 3:5 about the Pharisees is now true of the disciples (6:52). The fact that according to the summary in 6:53–6 the whole crowd wants to see signs of healing does not alter the increasing blindness of the world one bit.[31]

But what does this consist in? Rather like 2:1–3:6, only now far more explicitly, Mark points to the question of the law in chapter 7.[32] The true blindness of the world consists in neither the Pharisees and scribes (as Mark likes to add redactionally) nor the disciples (7:17f.) understanding the very simple statement that what God wants is not external observance of the cult but the religion of the heart. This is one of Mark's few large discourses, which shows how important this problem is to him. Granted that Mark no longer has to argue the question theologically, as Paul had to – 7:15 is too simple for that – all he can see in holding on to the law is the incomprehensible blindness of a world that closes itself to God. So it is here in this pasage that the first Gentile appears. We see from the Syrophoenician woman what true faith is (7:24–31). Then comes the healing of the deaf-mute, whose ear and mouth Jesus miraculously opens, parallel to the healing of the blind man in the second version, symbolically introducing Jesus' self-revelation at Caesarea Philippi. So the gentile world emerges

73

for the first time between Jesus' fundamental rejection of the way of the law and his miracle that opens the ear of the deaf and the mouth of the dumb and so fulfils the eschatological prophecy of Isa. 35:5.

The second version of the feeding sharpens the opposition to it considerably. The sequence – feeding, crossing the lake, demand for a sign – comes from the tradition. But then comes a section which surpasses even John (8:14–21).[33] The Old Testament saying that, at 4:12, characterizes the lostness of those "outside" is now applied to the twelve. "Having eyes you do not see, and having ears you do not hear". Still they do not understand that Jesus is speaking of spiritual not natural bread, their heart is so hardened (8:17). Nothing less than a divine miracle can open their eyes, as the story that follows about the miraculous healing of the blind man indicates. As Part 1 ended with the blindness of the Pharisees and Part 2 with the blindness of Jesus' fellow-citizens, so Part 3 ends with the blindness of the disciples themselves. But, the figure of the Syrophoenician woman and the healing of the deaf-mute in fulfilment of Isa. 35 already showed a glimmer on the horizon. Here, too, what is said about the total hardening of the world is not the last word. The miracle performed on the blind man points forward to what is to come.

VI *Part 4: The revelation event in uncoded speech*

At this point comes Peter's confession, forming in a way the watershed in Jesus' ministry. Admittedly Peter with his orthodox messianic confession has not yet even reached the stage of the demons who at 3:11 and 5:7[34] have already formulated the secret of Jesus far more correctly. Jesus' only answer is, for that reason also, the command to silence. But then follows the revelation: the Son of Man will suffer and die. It is introduced by the redactional phrase which describes Jesus' teaching that separates him from the general event of the kerygma: "And he began to teach them", and it is closed by the typical statement, "And he spoke the word" (8:32).[35] But now it says, "And he spoke the word plainly". So this is also the only passage where the content of the *didaskein* ("to teach") is really given its full weight. Jesus here abandons the parabolic language of 4:33 and speaks directly. So what happens here is humanly speaking quite impossible. God, truly God, who passes all understanding, cannot be conceived in human terms,

God who can be spoken of to humans only in parables, becomes clear, public word and so confronts mankind. And this word describes a suffering and dying. But that means: the word must become flesh in the body of the Crucified One. In no other way can he reach the hearts of men and women.

But teaching on its own is no help either. What follows shows that precisely this uncoded speech is totally misunderstood, even by Peter who has just made his confession of Christ. Again we see the infinite difference between God and man. There is no bridging here. There are only *ta tou theou*, "the words of God", and *ta tōn anthrōpōn*, "the human world". And even the first of Jesus' disciples belongs to the latter, not the former. The radical Johannine separation between the above and below, spirit and flesh, logos and cosmos, God and Satan, is once again surpassed. That is how well Mark knows that not even Jesus' word of revelation in its most direct form, as it might be passed on as word of the historical Jesus, is any help. So what beyond this is necessary?

The next verse speaks of discipleship.[36] That was the first thing we heard about immediately after the prologue. Even there it was already clear that discipleship always involves Jesus himself having precedence beyond compare, and making this discipleship possible by going on ahead. He has already proclaimed God's Kingdom and he overpowers these men with his electing look. The complete initiative of Jesus was clearest at 2:14 where the call of the tax-collector was placed between the statement of Jesus' authority to forgive sins and the meal with sinners. The latter point underlines the fact that this call of one who is outside the community is not to be seen as a unique case.[37] That nothing but Jesus' creative act and the giving of his own authority makes such disclipleship possible was again repeated at the start of Parts 2 and 3 (3:13f.; 6:7). That discipleship does not mean freedom from all doubt had already been made clear. The redactional *suzētein* ("to question, seek") shows on the contrary that Jesus forces both opponents and disciples to ask questions. The disciples' question, "Who is he?" (4:41), shows that God is at work among them, whereas the people of Nazareth with their correct information, "He is the carpenter, the son of Mary and brother of Joses and Judas and Simon" (6:3) only show their unbelief, and even Peter, with his even more correct "You are Christ" understands nothing of Jesus' way. So, too, to repeat everything that Jesus says is not yet faith, and not all following is discipleship (cf. 1:37f.; 6:1f.; 8:13). Concretely as God's election takes place, it aims to be equally concrete in the life of the person who is elected.

All that now becomes clear. In this part *akolouthein* ("to follow") is no longer used in a general sense. Now Jesus' way to the cross is set clearly before mankind's following, as is plain not only from the saying about taking up one's cross, but also from Mark's redactional link in 8:34a. Only in following is that discipleship possible in which one becomes free from oneself, finds one's true life in no longer having to worry tensely about one's own life, and is able to find it truly in self-abandonment and self-giving (8:35).

Jesus' public declaration is followed by that of God in the transfiguration. What up to now God has said only to his Son (1:11) is now said to the three chosen ones and directs them to Jesus' teaching (9:7). In the preceding verse Mark inserts a note about the disciples' total lack of understanding. It is taken from 14:40 which is the only place it has a point. Again it is clear that only a divine miracle can disclose to mankind the mystery of Jesus.

This Part 4 is also controlled by the three-fold statement of the suffering of the Son of Man (8:31; 9:31; 10:32–4),[38] three times followed by the disciples' total misunderstanding (8:32f.; 9:32–4; 10:35–7) and echoed three times in the call to discipleship (8:34ff.; 9:35ff.; 10:38ff.). The material placed in between shows broadly what genuine discipleship is, especially the story of the rich man which climaxes in the saying that what is impossible with men is possible with God, and thus forms a transition to the promise of divine reward for the disciples' following (10:27–31). But Mark seems here to be simply using up material he has not yet utilized. Only in the last third is his redactional hand again visible. The section begins, "And they were on the road, going up to Jerusalem" (10:32), and ends, ". . . and he followed him on the way" (10:52). It is the blind man whose eyes have been opened by Jesus' miraculous deed. The divine miracle creates discipleship "on the way". After that there is only the passion itself to relate.

VII Part 5: The way of suffering of the Son of Man

The sequence of events is fixed. The debate with Pharisees, Sadducees and scribes has clearly to lead on up to Jerusalem. The apocalyptic discourse is naturally placed at the end of Jesus' activity.[39] That makes the passages where Mark's redaction emerges all the more interesting. The most difficult to judge is the apocalyptic discourse in chapter 13. Its importance for Mark is shown by its prominent position and great length. That is confirmed by 8:38; 9:1, and probably also by 14:62 where, as in 8:27–32, the Christ title is taken up positively, but immediately interpreted by the Son of Man title. Since now the suffering of the Son of Man is already under way, only his exaltation and parousia are proclaimed here, as at 8:38.[40] The question is simply what is meant by this. The thesis that Mark expected the parousia in Galilee in the immediate future[41] seems to me to break down because all the passion announcements, and also 9:9f.; 12:18ff. have only the resurrection of Jesus in view. 8:38 is plainly intended to underline the urgency of discipleship. But also in chapter 13 there are not only the frequently recurring observations of Mark himself to consider, but also the concluding parables which call for watchfulness.[42] Even if the references to endurance in persecution at vv. 9–13 comes from the tradition, the necessity of the Gospel being proclaimed in all the world (v. 10) is a Marcan insertion.[43] The reference to the Jewish War was also probably in the tradition; the formulation in vv. 14–18 certainly does not mean the exodus of the community to Pella or Galilee, and vv. 21–3 seems to separate these events from the eschaton. Finally, Mark has connected 14:62 with Peter's denial, so this has probably to be understood in the same way as 8:38. The expectation of the coming Son of Man certainly underlines the seriousness of the decision to be a disciple, and the whole arrangement of the Gospel proves that Mark reckons with an intervening period in which the kerygma goes on to all nations and in which through following Jesus people are to participate in the eschatological revelation of God.

For Mark it is the revelation to the Gentiles that is decisive. We begin with 11:17f. The passage teems with Marcan terminology. Again Jesus is described as teaching (*didaskein*), this being the first time in Jerusalem. Again it is said that "all the multitude was astonished at his teaching" (*didachē*). As at 3:6 in the beginning, so now once again the decision is made to destroy him, and this represents the definitive rejection by the Jewish authorities. The cleansing of the Temple precedes this, and Mark sees it as destroying in principle the Temple business, since Jesus separates himself sharply from the *hymeis* ("you"): "But *you* have made of it a den of robbers!" But God intended it to be not a house for the Jewish cult, but a house of prayer *for all nations* (*pasin tois ethnesin*). It is not the obedient observance of the commandments, which only a small group of legal rigorists could keep, that God demands; he opens himself to the worship of all nations, without the law. This pericope is framed by the cursing of the fig-tree and the fulfilment of the curse.[44] Israel's precedence is at an end. Exactly as at 3:6, the decision to destroy Jesus follows his abolition of the law. So the statement about the end of the law and the revelation for all nations is surrounded by Jesus' way of suffering which even his disciples do not yet understand. The cross is the end of the law and the beginning of the Gentile mission.[45]

The next passage is 12:9. The parable of the wicked husbandmen has just shown that Israel's behaviour was not obedience but rebellion, and the conclusion in v. 9 shows the transfer of salvation to the Gentiles. Mark's redactional note in v. 12 says again that the parable is not aimed at the nation but is aimed at the authorities in Israel who are listed at 11:27. They again respond by trying to arrest Jesus.

At 13:10 Mark has presumably inserted the statement about the world-wide proclamation of the Gospel to the Gentiles (*ethnē*).[46] In a similar way to the Pauline and post-Pauline passages already mentioned the penetration of the world in the Church's mission is understood as eschatological event. It is clear that the saying stands in some tension with the apocalyptic expectation of the imminent end. Mark solves the problem with his *prōton* ("first"). But that does show that for him history is no longer merely a preliminary sign of the end but has become God's path to his goal.[47] It has kept its apocalyptic character.

The last passage is linked with the crucifixion itself. The mockers take up Jesus' saying about the destruction of the Temple and scoff at him because it has not been fulfilled (15:29f.); but at the hour of his death the veil of the Temple is rent from top to bottom, and the Gentile in charge of the execution breaks out in the cry, "Truly this man was God's Son",[48] thus taking up the title which is particularly characteristic of this second Gospel. The first to recognize what has taken place here are not the theologians and Jewish church leaders but the Gentile, the secular man who stands where it is impossible to keep one's hands clean and is up to his neck in the dirty and responsible questions of human politics, and even has to carry out executions.

So the title "Son of God" occurs once more, at the end of the Gospel. It has been communicated by God to the Son at 1:11 as an inner-divine secret; knowledge of it was betrayed by the demons at 3:11 and 5:7; it was then revealed by God to the three disciples after Jesus had proclaimed the secret of his suffering *parrhēsią* ("plainly"); and finally Jesus took it up in the affirmative at the interrogation before the high priest but at the same time interpreted by the Son of Man title. And now the first person to use the title in a confession is a Gentile.

This last Part 5 also is packed full of disciples' failure. The Last Supper is embedded between the pointer to Judas' betrayal (14:19–21) and that to the flight of all the disciples and Peter's denial (14:26–31). This is, in fact, the sole content of Mark's farewell discourses. Last Supper is viaticum for those who are tempted and who deny. It is followed by the sleeping and the flight of the disciples in Gethsemane (14:37–50), Peter's denial, which Mark was probably the first to combine with a night trial in order to underline the contrast between the Lord's fidelity and the disciple's lack of it (14:53–72)[49] and finally the unbelief of the women at the empty tomb (16:8).

So then it is true of the disciples, too, that in the most radical sense there is but one who saves them. So it is not so simple to separate world and Church, godless and faithful. One can only experience the divine miracle. Part 4 began at 8:31, 34 with the proclamation of Jesus' path of suffering and that was followed by the call to discipleship. It concluded with Jesus' miraculous opening of blind eyes and with a follower "on the way" up to Jerusalem (10:52).

This sequence is now followed here too. Mark has the announcement of Judas' betrayal and the disciples' flight followed by the promise that Jesus after his resurrection will go before them (14:28). And when the suffering was complete what follows is not only the centurion's confession under the cross, but the appearance too, of the women who had "followed after" Jesus, had served him in Galilee, and had come up with him to Jerusalem (15:41). They will be the first witnesses of the empty tomb. On Easter morning they will be told by the angel himself that the Living One is no longer among the dead. The disciples who have fled, in particular Peter who has denied Jesus, are once again given the promise that the Risen One is going before them to Galilee and that they will see him there if they go there after him (16:6f.). Thus is fulfilled what was announced back at 9:9, in the appearance of the Risen One in Galilee, which after all probably formed the original ending,[50] and in the disciples following (as in John 21:19–22): the revelation of God, his way in the world.

So Mark is the Gospel of the amazing, incomprehensible condescension and love of God which in Jesus seeks the world. But the world is so blinded that it cannot recognize him although he does everything to help it find him. So the world has to become flesh, God has to give himself over completely into solidarity with mankind, and that in the radical way that Mark depicts it in his report of Jesus' crucifixion, a report that is shatteringly naked and sober. Here is the hiddenness of God at its most radical: "My God, my God, why hast thou forsaken me?". "And he uttered a loud cry and died". That can be believed and understood only in discipleship. The disciple thus enters into relationship with God and follows in the steps of Jesus in the same incarnated way that God meets him. This fundamental hiddenness of God, which is disclosed only to the follower, is intended by Mark's messianic secret which he introduces four times with his characteristic world *diastellesthai* ("to charge"). But that the miracle of discipleship has really happened and that God's revelation will reach its goal, a Gentile, a few women, and a half-believing onlooker who buries Jesus are the sign. These, but especially the disciples, whom despite all their denials Jesus precedes to Galilee,[51] point to the miracle of the coming community which the Risen One himself will call into life and send out into the world.

ADDENDUM[52]

This is how the author now sees the construction of Mark.

I   1:1–13 The beginning: time of salvation fulfilled (1–8) and prologue in heaven (9–13).

II   1:14–3:6 Jesus' authority and the blindness of the Pharisees.

a   1:14f. Transitional section: summary.

b   1:16–20 Call of the disciples.

    A 1:21–45 Authority over demons and sickness.

    B 2:1–3:5 Authority over sin and law.

c   3:6 Rejection of Jesus by the Pharisees.

III 3:7–6:6a Jesus' work in parables and signs, and the blindness of the world.

a 3:7–12 Transitional section: summary.

b 3:13–19 Choice of the twelve disciples.

A 3:20–4:34 Jesus' parables discourse.

B 4:35–5:43 Jesus' miraculous deeds.

c 6:1–6a Rejection of Jesus by his fellow-citizens.

IV 6:6b–8:21 Jesus' work extending to the Gentiles, and the blindness of the disciples.

a 6:6b Transitional section: summary.

b 6:7–13 Sending of the disciples.

A 6:14–31 Death of John, return of the disciples.

B 6:32–56 and 8:1–13 Jesus' authority to do miracles and men's demand for a sign.

c 7 Promise for Gentiles.

c 8:14–21 Rejection of Jesus by the disciples.

V 8:22–10:52 Jesus' revelation in uncoded speech and the discipleship of the disciples.

a 8:22–6 Transitional section: opening blind eyes – *Bethsaida*.

b 8:27–32a The suffering of the Son of Man – *Caesarea Philippi*.

c 8:32b–9:1 Disciples' misunderstanding and the call to discipleship.

A 9:2–8 Transfiguration – *the high mountain*.

B 9:9–13 Elijah and the suffering Son of Man.

c 9:14–29 The faith question.

b 9:30–32 The suffering of the Son of Man – *Galilee (Capernaum)*.

c 9:33–50 Disciples' misunderstanding and call to discipleship.

A 10:1–12 Marriage – *Judea and Transjordan*.

B 10:13–16 Children.

c 10:17–31 Riches.

b 10:32–34 The suffering of the Son of Man: *Road to Jerusalem*.

c 10:35–45 Disciples' misunderstanding and call to discipleship.

10:46–52 Transitional section: opening blind eyes and discipleship – *Jericho*.

VI 11:1–16:8 Suffering and resurrection of the Son of Man.

11:1–13:37 Public debate and instruction of disciples about the end – *Jerusalem*.

14:1–16:8 Suffering of Jesus and resurrection.

NOTES

1 Cf. E. Schweizer, *The Church as the Body of Christ* (Richmond: John Knox/London: SPCK, 1964) 65–9; F. Hahn, *Mission in the New Testament* (London: SCM, 1963) 143–52.

2 It is probably even more important that Jesus was widely understood as simply a miracle-worker. This was the real difficulty for Mark – not, as Wrede thought, an originally "unmessianic" life of Jesus. Cf. Schweizer in Tuckett (1983) 73, n. 33, and *Comm.*, 358.

3 Cf. John 6:1–21, 30, 66–71 with Mark 6:45–52 and 8:1–11, 27–33.

4 It appears in Rev. 6 as in Mark 13 if we exclude there the sections on world mission and the Jewish War, together with the warnings to the community. Cf. E. Schweizer, "Der Menschensohn", *ZNW* 50 (1959) 189, n. 12 = *Neotestamentica* (Zurich, 1963) 59, n. 12. And *Comm.* 264f.

5 On Mark 1:1–6 cf. Schweizer (1962) 37, n. 2 = *Neotestamentica* 94, n. 10.

6 Ibid., 35–42 = 93–100. Also J. Schreiber, *Die Markuspassion* (1969) 40ff.

7 6:12 gives precedence to proclamation, even though v. 7 speaks only of power over demons (cf. v. 13).

8 Apart from 6:30, where it takes second place and is in a different verbal form from elsewhere.

9 *Thambeisthai* ("to be amazed") at his teaching (1:27), his words (10:24), his progress to Jerusalem (10:32). It is different with *ekthambeisthai*. On *pas ho* ("all the"), *holos ho* ("the whole") cf. also Hahn (n. 1) 71.

10 1:22; 6:2. It is clear there that all that matters is whether when this teaching takes place God's presence is believed or denied.

11 11:17; 4:2; and 12:35, 38.

12 The disciples on the other hand are given authority to cast out demons (3:15; 6:7), cf. the not yet redactional 2:10; 11:28–33; 13:34.

13 *therapeuein* ("to heal") is said redactionally of Jesus (1:34; 3:10; 6:5), but also of the disciples (6:13), and is already in the tradition (3:2, probably). Also redactional are *arrōstoi* ("sick") (6:5, 13), *kakōs echontes* ("sick") (1:32, 34; 6:15; but cf. 2:17).

14 This word is absent in redactional passages, as is *didaskalia* ("teaching") (Prof. G. McLean Gilmour).

15 *idios* ("his own") occurs only in this formula and only in redactional sections. 4:34 too is, as codices A and D show, presumably not an exception. The comparison of 4:3, 10 with 7:14, 17 is interesting. It shows how the schema of a call to all the nation followed by an instruction of the disciples is especially typical of Mark. Cf. also the frequently redactional *palin* ("again") that designates Jesus' struggle on behalf of mankind (e.g. 4:1; 7:14; 10:1, 24, 32; 11:27).

16 *ginōskein* ("to know") is the special recognition of the disciples at 4:(11)13, of Jesus at 5:29; 8:17, the knowledge of the world that wants to avoid Jesus at 5:43; 7:24; 9:30. (It is different for the first time at 12:12, cf. n. 24.) But the

word is also found in the tradition at 6:38; 13:28f., 15:10, 15. Cf. also *noein* ("to perceive"), *agnoein* ("not to understand"). *epiginōskein* ("to perceive") is ambiguous.

17 Of all (1:27), the Pharisees (8:11), the Sadducees (12:28), the disciples (9:10). Cf. 9:14, 16 where it is perhaps traditional.

18 Sharpening the messianic secret at 5:43; 7:36 (twice); 9:9. Otherwise only in the also typically redactional passage 8:15.

19 Cf. E. Jüngel, *Paulus und Jesus* (1962) 135ff.

20 On this, see also E. Jüngel's and my essay on the historical Jesus in *EvT* 8 (1964) 403–43, and further what is said below on Mark 8:32a. When Mark designates the saying about the suffering, dying and rising of the Son of Man as open speech in contrast to the speaking in parables, he nevertheless at once makes clear that especially these events can only be understood in the act of discipleship. But that means: 1. Not until the events of the crucifixion and resurrection is the centre set up from which Jesus can be understood at all. So that must always be stated. Its significance can only be understood by one who is already a disciple, but it can be paraphrased. Thus far "mythological language" is inescapable. 2. But merely to take over this kind of picture is no help. In that sense one must always demand that account be given of what this "mythological language" is getting at. It has to be made clear that its meaning is ultimately clear only to discipleship.

21 Whether the position of *huios mou* ("my son") at 1:11, which is different from the Septuagint, was first rearranged and given its present reference by Mark, or whether it already existed in this form in the tradition, we do not know. At any rate it is strongly emphasized by the change. Cf. Vielhauer (1964).

22 We should very probably read *orgistheis* ("angered") as Burkill (1963) 38 does. *splagchnizesthai* ("to have compassion") is taken up by Mark only from the tradition (cf. below on 6:34; 8:2) and used once on the lips of a suppliant. Cf. by contrast Matt. 9:36; 20:34; Luke 7:13.

23 Cf. S. Schulz (1961) 193–7.

24 The first saying was certainly, and the second presumably, in Q. Whether both Mattthew and Luke inserted the first saying here, only because in Mark it followed directly upon the reproach against Jesus, and so simultaneously reconciled to it Q, or whether it was inserted between Matt. 12:24 and 27 at an earlier stage and so was already available to Mark, can no longer be decided with certainty. Mark has to come back to the cause of the dispute in v. 30 in an observation which is rather loosely tacked on. But, of course, I think that Mark had access to the tradition which is found in a more original form in Q. Whether he had access to Q itself is very questionable and disputed.

25 For more detail, see Schweizer (1962) 39f. (*Neotestamentica* 97f.).

26 It is only once said that all understood the *parabolē* (12:12), but this leads only to hardening and judgement. Cf. on this A. M. Ambrozic, "Mark's Concept of the Parable", *CBQ* 29 (1967) 220–7.

27 On Qumran see K. G. Kuhn, "Der Epheserbrief im Lichte der Qumran-texte", *NTS* 7 (1960–1) 336.

28 "All true knowledge of God begins with the knowledge of the hiddenness of God", K. Barth, *Church Dogmatics* II/1, 183, also quoted by G. von Rad, *Theology of the Old Testament* II 377. For analysis of this (vv. 10–12 as a transition already reshaped at the pre-Marcan stage; v. 13 as Marcan) cf. E. Schweizer in Tuckett (1983) 67–9.

29 At least the motif of teaching in the boat comes from the tradition; cf. above, on 3:9.

30 Cf. 5:25–34; also 3:22–30 above; 11:15–19 below.

31 Cf. G. Friedrich, "Die beiden Erzählungen von der Speisung in Mark 6:31–44; 8:1–9", *TZ* 20 (1964) 10ff.

32 At 2:1 also this follows a demonstration of Jesus' authority by miracle (1:21–45).

33 Was 8:15 the conclusion of 8:11–13 in the tradition? For signs of Marcan redaction see n. 16 and n. 18. Cf. Schweizer in Tuckett (1983) 69, and J. Mánek "Mark VIII 14–21", *NovT* 7 (1964) 10–14.

34 I think it likely that Mark himself has replaced the original title (cf. 1:24 and on that E. Schweizer, "Er wird Nazoräer heissen", in Jeremias Festschrift (1960) 91f. and *Neotestamentica* 52f.) with the Son of God title (as certainly happened at John 6:69 in b, sy^c), since he can no longer go back behind 3:11.

35 Lohmeyer (*Comm.*) on this passage felt the difficulty of this little statement so acutely that he tried taking the infinite reading in k, thus making the Risen One the subject of the *lalein parrhēsią* ("to speak openly").

36 Admittedly John 12:24–6 shows that in essence the connection was probably traditional even before Mark. 3:23 (see above) proves that Mark can also insert notes like 34a into an already existing context. Luke 12:4, 8, 41 and similar passages are also worth comparing. On the motif of Jesus' path to suffering, and on the discipleship of the disciples cf. also J. Schreiber (1961) 160, 167f., 175f., and E. Haenchen (1963) 91ff.

37 *ekolouthoun* ("they followed") in 2:15 presumably refers to the tax-collectors.

38 Cf. Strecker (1968).

39 Cf. H. Conzelmann (1959) 211f., who brings in Q and *Didache* as further examples. The localization on the Mount of Olives is probably Marcan redaction.

40 In its Marcan context the saying certainly refers to the parousia even if it may originally once have described only the exaltation.

41 For discussion with Marxsen (1969) 83ff. and 151ff. cf. Conzelmann (1959) 215f. and Hahn (n. 1) 114, n. 1 and 116, n. 2. For further literature, see Schweizer (1962). It is highly unlikely that a community which certainly knew about resurrection appearances could ever have understood 16:7 in any other way. Though I understand the construction of the Gospel very much as Hahn does (who, of course, I could only read subsequently), I remain doubtful about

seeing chapter 13 as central because it is hardly referred to in the rest of the Gospel.

42 Cf. Conzelmann (1959) 217ff. In the present form of the chapter it is the doorkeeper's watching that is most strongly emphasized, whereas v. 34 was originally intended to depict general present-day behaviour in view of the coming judgement. Cf. J. Jeremias, *The Parables of Jesus* (London: SCM Press, 1963) 53ff. Also Schweizer (1969) 117.

43 Like Hahn (n. 1) 71–4 I consider *kērussein* ("to proclaim") and *euangelion* ("gospel") to be fixed formulae. The connection between them is not original and could be also determined by the specifically Marcan distinction between the Church's *kērussein* ("proclaiming") and Jesus' *didaskein* ("teaching"). I am not so sure whether the postponing of the parousia present in 13:10 is really pre-Marcan. But Hahn is right that the evangelist especially emphasizes the proclamation of the Gospel. On Mark's use of *euangelion* ("gospel") cf. F. Mussner in the Rahner Festschrift, vol. 1 (1964).

44 11:20f. and 22 were probably already joined prior to Mark, as Luke 17:6 shows. See now Hahn (n. 1) 36ff. and 114f. Still, the reference to *pistis* ("faith") is very welcome to Mark. Cf. also the discussion about *pistis* in v. 32.

45 At 14:8f. a reference to Jesus' death and to the world-wide proclamation are placed together. Further observations on this in Hahn (n. 1) 112ff.

46 Cf. Marxsen (1969) 125f. Mark perhaps had access to a formulation such as Matt. 10:18. 13:27 is also comparable in subject-matter (Boobyer, 1952–3: 340).

47 It is, therefore, now the false teachers who proclaim the direct imminence of the parousia (13:5f.). What is demanded of the community by contrast is watching and enduring, if necessary also suffering (13:21–3, 32–7). (Conzelmann, 1959: 215, 217–21).

48 Not a "man of God"; cf. my article *huios* ("son") in *TDNT* viii. 379, n. 323.

49 Cf. P. Winter, *On the Trial of Jesus* (1961) 23f. and E. Linnemann (1970).

50 Matthew may still to some extent show what the Marcan ending looked like. The appearance of Jesus to the women would be expected on the basis of Mark 16:8, but not on the basis of Matt. 28:8. Matt. 28:18, which Matthew changed by using his typical word *proselthōn* ("come"), proves that 28:6ff. was originally a purely heavenly appearance. Without this accommodation to the later church view this perspective would not have been enough. Is that why the original Marcan ending disappeared? N. Q. Hamilton (1965) believes that Mark 16:1–8 is a Marcan construction. This doubt about the historicity of the appearances (Mark 16:7) seems to me unreasonable in view of 1 Cor. 15:5–8 and the assurance given by Paul in 1 Cor. 15:11. Paul met with Peter and others in Jerusalem at the latest 5–8 years after Easter, and for years he had Jerusalem people accompanying him (Acts 4:36; 12:25; 13:2; 13; 15:38; 1 Cor. 9:6; Philem. 24, etc.). How are we to understand these appearances is, of course, another matter.

51 On the Galilee question, see W. Schmithals, *Paul and James* (1963 ET 1965) 33f.

52 Added in the reprint of this essay in *Das Markus-Evangelium*, ed. R. Pesch (Darmstadt: Wissenschaftliche Buchgesellschaft, 1979). Based on the 14th (1975) German ed. of Schweizer's *Commentary*, with a few additions due to Perrin (1971). For discussion with more recent views, see Schweizer (1977).

ADDITION IN 1970 REPRINT

S. Schulz, *Die Stunde der Botschaft* (1967) takes an almost diametrically opposed view (esp. 46–79). I gladly admit that I understated the extent to which Mark takes up in large numbers the miracles available to him in the tradition, even though he corrects them theologically by the way he builds them into his Gospel (so, too, Schulz, 71ff.). They, too, can become revelations of the power of God, though only for a disciple of Jesus. I do not deny, either, that all kinds of ideas of an almost physical power dwelling in Jesus are also present. But I do deny that this makes Jesus into a "God-man" (*theios anēr*, "divine man"). Firstly, it is very doubtful whether any such idea existed before the second century C.E. It may be that miracle stories about Old Testament men of God, which contained legendary elements but never thought of them as supernatural beings (Schulz, 70f.), along with all kinds of oriental magic, were more important than late Greek "divine men". At any rate 2 Kings 13:21 is more striking even than Mark 3:10; 5:25ff.; 6:56 (Schulz, 70f.). Further, Paul can evidently unite (the apostle's) "signs and wonders and deeds of power" in Rom. 15:19; 2 Cor. 12:12 even with his theology of the cross. Above all, consider how Mark inserts the miracles of his proclamation (very different from Paul's) of Jesus' (and his disciples') way of the cross. The construction of the Gospel shows that the miracles serve only as a foil for the three-fold rejection of Jesus (above, p. 52 end of section 5). I see now from *BZ* (1959) 298, that H. Schlier understands 1:16–3:6; 3:7–6:6a; 6:6b–8:26 almost exactly as I do. But this does not mean that Jesus' "whole life becomes a demonstration of unstoppable deeds of strength" (Schulz, 73). They stop at 8:26. 9:14–29 is a treatment of faith and unbelief (vv. 18f., 23f., 28); on 10:46–52, see above, p. 54 end of section 6. The parallels 11:1–4 and 14:12–16 and the apocalyptic signs at the death of Jesus are not deeds of strength performed by Jesus and are also balanced by the Gethsemane scene. The three-fold announcement of the passion starting with 8:31 is not "monotonously" intended to emphasize the supernatural know-

86

ledge of Jesus but rather the failure of the disciples and the call to discipleship (cf. end of section 6). Peter's messianic confession seems to me not simply to mark the end of the disciples' not understanding (start of section 6, against Schulz, 61f.). Finally, the institution of sacraments, the relativizing of Torah, and the application to Jesus of Old Testament quotations referring to God (common in Paul) were at any rate not created by Mark, and his "mythic" thought does not reach the level of Paul's (pre-existence) – (Schulz, 52–4, 57f.). See also n. 50 in this essay. Also Schweizer in Tuckett (1983) 71, n. 8; 72, n. 26. So against Schulz, 151, what he calls "the most important evidence for Mark's conception of the messianic secret", namely 4:11f. is probably not Marcan. (On the question of Galilee, see Schweizer in Tuckett (1983) 71f., n. 17). So while I do not find Paul's theology of the cross in Mark, neither do I find in the miracles a theology of glory which surpasses even that of John (Schulz, 77f.).

2

*The Heresy that Necessitated Mark's Gospel**

THEODORE J. WEEDEN

Recently two significant developments have taken place in Marcan research: (1) a recognition of a Marcan polemic against the disciples[1] and (2) an identification of two opposing Christologies within the Gospel – one, a hellenistic *theios anēr* ("divine man") Christology inherent in a large section of Marcan material and the other, Mark's own suffering Christology presented in his *theologica crucis* (theology of the cross).[2] It is my opinion that an intrinsic relationship exists between these motifs which, when examined, points to a heresy that threatened the Marcan community and necessitated the creation of the Gospel. To support this thesis we must first examine Mark's treatment of the disciples.

The derogatory fashion in which the disciples are cast in the Marcan drama has usually been attributed to the evangelist's accurate reporting of the facts or explained as the unfortunate by-product of the evangelist's broader theological motif (the messianic secret). However, the recent recognition of a Marcan polemic against the disciples casts an entirely new light upon Mark's presentation of the disciples. The pervasiveness and devastating thoroughness of this polemic can be fully comprehended only when one examines it through Mark's schema of the three successive and progressively worsening stages in the relationship between Jesus and the disciples.[3]

* First published in *ZNW* 59 (1968) 145–58.

The first such stage occurs in the first half of the Gospel (1:16–8:26) and is characterized by the disciples' strange inability to perceive who Jesus is. Despite the continuous manifestation of Jesus' messiahship before the disciples in countless healings, exorcisms, and nature miracles, they remain amazingly obtuse in the face of their involvement in the messianic drama. Not even in their own miraculous activity to which they are commissioned (3:15; 6:7) and in which they are successful (6:13) do the disciples appear to detect their relationship to Jesus and his true identity. In fact, this unbelievable imperceptiveness of the disciples, rather than diminishing, appears to increase and become more persistent as the narrative unfolds (4:10–13, 38–41; 6:52; 7:17; 8:4, 14–21). It is particularly astonishing when one realizes that throughout Mark the disciples enjoy a special and privileged position before Jesus (1:16–20; 3:13ff.; 4:11; 6:7–12, 30–43; 8:1–10) which is open to no one else. Yet, ironically, those far less acquainted and associated with Jesus appear to respond to him with more perceptive insights than do the disciples themselves.[4]

With 8:27ff., however, a sudden change takes place in Mark's rendering of the disciples' capacity for discernment. Peter experiences a great revelation: Jesus is the Christ (8:29). This sudden burst of insight occurs inexplicably as the previous imperceptivity persisted. In 8:21 the disciples appear just as dense and unenlightened as they were in the earlier portions of the Gospel. Up to 8:29 there is no indication that they have any awareness of Jesus' identity. In fact, they often appear blind to the capabilities of Jesus which others have discerned. Yet suddenly in 8:29, Peter, the spokesman for the disciples, makes a confession that suggests the disciples are now as keenly perceptive as they were imperceptive before.

Any assumption, however, that by this confession the disciples have received a complete understanding of Jesus is soon dispelled by the presentation of the disciples in the last half of the Gospel. With the interchange between Peter and Jesus after the confession (8:30–3) the understanding of the disciples shifts from imperceptivity to misconception. It now becomes evident that, while identifying Jesus as the Christ, the disciples are not able to understand the type of messiahship Jesus claims for himself (8:31–3; 9:30–2; 10:32–4). Whatever Peter's concept of messiahship is, it is not Jesus' concept of suffering Messiah. He and his colleagues are unable to understand or accept the concept of suffering Messiah or the commitment to suffering discipleship which is demanded of disciples of a suffering Messiah (9:33–5; 10:23–31, 35–43).

The final stage in Jesus' relationship to the disciples is inaugurated in 14:10ff. with Judas' plans to betray Jesus. The disciples no longer just misunderstand Jesus. Now they totally reject him. That this is true of all the disciples and not just of the traditional villain, Judas, is substantiated by the episode in Gethsemane and the incident in the courtyard of the high priest. In Gethsemane Peter, James and John remain completely oblivious and apathetic toward the distress and apprehension which have seized Jesus. Implored by Jesus to support him by watching and praying, the three confidants respond by falling asleep (14:32–42). Subsequently Judas delivers him over to his enemies (14:43–6) and the rest forsake and abandon him (14:50). Then as the final *coup de grâce*, upon the condemnation of the Sanhedrin, and despite his swearing to the contrary (14:29–31), Peter completely renounces Jesus, adamantly denying that he ever knew him (14:66–72).

This evolution in the disciples' relationship to Jesus from imperceptivity (1:16–8:26) to misconception (8:27–14:9) to rejection (14:10–72) is no accidental development, nor is is is intended to be an objective presentation of the actual historical relationship which existed between Jesus and his disciples. It is a carefully formulated polemical device created by the evangelist to disgrace and debunk the disciples. But why – and for what reason?

It is my opinion that the answer lies at the heart of a christological dispute raging in Mark's community, a dispute which had reached such a critical point that Mark felt he could settle it only by dramatizing the two sides through his presentation of the interaction between Jesus and the disciples. Thus, Jesus represents one point of view and the disciples the other. If the points of view can be identified, the dispute is revealed and the need for the polemic explained.

There is no particular problem in identifying Jesus' christological position. It is well spelled out in the passion predictions and the passion narrative. Authentic messiahship is suffering messiahship which culminates in the crucifixion. It is not easy, however, to identify the position of the disciples. The first mention of their christological position is found in 8:27–33 where Peter recognizes Jesus as the Messiah. Precisely what the nature of the messiahship Peter acclaims is, is not stated explicitly by the evangelist. Negatively, one can be certain that by Messiah Peter and the disciples did not understand a suffering messiahship. Positively, the content of the Marcan disciples' understanding is more difficult to ascertain. At first glance the material prior to 8:29 sheds no light on Peter's sudden revelation. Yet the inability to recognize clues which point to the conceptual basis for such a revelation may be the fault of the contemporary reader.

It is difficult to read Mark without bringing to it consciously or unconsciously an awareness of the other Gospels and the rest of the New Testament literature which, by virtue of our knowledge of this material, must colour, or not in some cases distort, any reading or interpretation of Mark. One cannot assume that the first readers of Mark had the benefit of the full breadth of the Christian tradition which the non-Marcan material of Matthew, Luke and John offers contemporary scholarship. I believe a more accurate interpretation, less subject to error, occurs when Mark is approached, as far as possible, in the way the first reader approached it: without preconceived knowledge of its contents and without the prejudicial knowledge of the other Gospels.

If the Gospel is so read, when the reader arrives at the point of Peter's confession, he has no recourse but to assume that whatever insights dawned upon Peter must have grown out of a recognition of the nature of Jesus revealed to the disciples (and to the reader) prior to the confession. What then is this picture of Jesus revealed to the reader? It was stated that recent Marcan research has argued that a large section of the Marcan material comes from a Jesus tradition characterized by a hellenistic *theios anēr* Christology which stands in opposition to Mark's own suffering Christology focused in a *theologia crucis*. There can be little doubt which of these christological positions gets the attention prior to the Petrine confession. Waving the red flag of *theios anēr* Christology, as he does, by introducing Jesus as the Son of God, saturating the first half of his Gospel with wonder-working activities of Jesus, and interspersing his own summaries on this *theios anēr* activity (1:32ff.; 3:7ff.; 6:53ff.),[5] Mark intends the reader to draw the only conclusion possible; Peter makes a confession to a *theios anēr* Christ.[6] In fact, if 1:1–8:29 were the only extant section of the Gospel a reader possessed, he would be forced to believe that from the Marcan perspective the only authentic understanding of Jesus is as a *theios anēr* Messiah. Of course, we know from 8:30 on, when Mark presents his *theologia crucis*, that the former is not the Marcan viewpoint at all. But without previous knowledge of the last half of the Gospel, what other conclusion could a reader draw with regard to 1:1–8:29 except that Jesus is a *theios anēr* Christ and that it was this revelation that came finally to the Marcan Peter?[7]

If one is to suggest that Peter and the disciples hold to a *theios anēr* Christology, then the corollary must follow: their orientation toward discipleship must also be *theios anēr* directed. Evidence for this can be found in a number of places. First of all, in line with the *theios anēr* picture of Jesus in the first half of the Gospel, the disciples are commissioned by the *theios anēr* with the *exousia* ("authority") of the *theios anēr* to exorcise demons and heal the sick (3:14f.; 6:7, 13).[8] Second, in conjunction with this image of Jesus the disciples also became custodians of the type of secret teaching (4:10–12, 33f.; 7:17ff.) which a *theios anēr* imparts only to his confidants.[9] In the third place, evidence of the disciples' *theios anēr* attitude towards discipleship becomes particularly glaring when the episodes of the controversy over who is the greatest disciple (9:33–7), the unwillingness of the disciples to recognize Christians who do not imitate them (9:38–41),[10] the disciples' rejection of children (10:13–16),[11] and the request of James and John for honoured positions (10:35–45), are viewed over against the suffering discipleship Jesus advocates and when they are compared with Georgi's description of the *theioi andres* at Corinth who thrive on the sense of their self-exaltation, seek personal glory and honour in the acclaim of their admirers, and relish comparing themselves with each other, each seeking to prove his superiority over the other.[12] Viewed against Jesus' call for suffering discipleship (8:34–7; 9:35–7, 42; 10:13–16, 23–31, 42–5; 13:9–13) and his importuning for the disciples' understanding of suffering messiahship (8:31; 9:30f.; 10:32–4), the disciple's apparent contempt for such humiliation (8:32; 14:66–71) and their brandishing of their own self-importance and superiority over others (9:38ff.; 10:35ff.) stand in stark relief to Jesus' position and forcefully argue that in line with their *theios anēr* Christology, Mark has purposely presented the disciples as advocates of a *theios anēr* discipleship.

The foregoing analysis leads to the conclusion that Mark has cast the disciples as advocates of a *theios anēr* Christology which is pitted against the suffering messiahship of Jesus. Since there is no historical basis for a dispute of this nature having taken place between Jesus and the disciples, the only conclusion possible is that the *Sitz im Leben* for this dispute is Mark's own community and that Mark has intentionally staged the dispute in his Gospel using the disciples to play the role of his opponents and presenting Jesus as the advocate of the evangelist's own position. But, one might ask, what other evidence is there in the Gospel to support this description of the Marcan *Sitz im Leben*?

Mark 13 provides such support. Unlike the rest of the Gospel, in which the focus is primarily on the events in Jesus' life, in chapter 13 the attention is centred primarily on the post-Easter life of the early community. If Mark were going to give insight into his own community, though he might express it elsewhere through his redactional treatment of his "life-of-Jesus" material, he could express it more easily and in more transparent fashion in material whose chronological reference falls within the time of his own community.

Ever since Weizsaecker and Pfleiderer, exegetes have generally agreed that Mark 13 is a composite of basically two kinds of material: one (vv. 7–8, 14–20, 24–7) which is described as a Jewish-Christian apocalyptic core and the other (vv. 5–6, 9–13, 21–3, 28–37), different in mood and intention, which is traced to the early Christian community and which has been interjected in or appended to the apocalyptic core by a Christian editor.[13] Recent scholarship, imputing to the evangelist a greater amount of literary creativity than earlier exegetes would admit, argues that Mark was this editor.[14] It follows logically then that the Marcan mind is best reflected in the material (13:5–6, 9–13, 21–3, 28–37) which he has appended to or interjected in his apocalyptic source.

A quick perusal of this interjected or appended material produces the following general observations.

1. For whatever reason, the evangelist's interjection or appending of vv. 5–6, 9–13, 21–3, 28–37 softens the apocalyptic tone and obstructs the purpose and thrust of his apocalyptic source (7–8, 14–20, 24–7).

2. The occurrence of *blepō* ("see") in the imperative mood, a Marcan key word,[15] in each of the four sections of this editorial material (vv. 5, 9, 23, 33) emphatically indicates that the evangelist is primarily interested in the reader focusing his attention on the subject-matter of these sections and reinforces the conclusion that

one can best discover the Marcan *Sitz im Leben* in chapter 13 through an analysis of vv. 5–6, 9–13, 21–3 and 28–37.

3.   Verses 5–6 and 21–3 deal with the same subject-matter, so-called messianic pretenders who lead the community astray. The first reference to these "pretenders", vv. 5–6, has been placed at the beginning of the historical, "this-world" unfolding of the end-time events, and the second reference to such "pretenders", vv. 21–3, has been placed at the conclusion of this world's history and prior to the final cosmic-supernatural events.[16]

4.   Verses 9–13 and 28–37 convey broadly the same message: admonition to faithful perseverance during the absence of the exalted Lord from his community until the end when he will be united with them.[17]

With regard to point three, Keck insists that 13:5–6 and 21–3 are crucial for Mark's interest. He theorizes that these "pretenders" are Christians claiming to represent the "real" Christ.[18] If this is true, could such references to "pretenders" in Mark 13 be in reality Mark's identification of his opponents, who are represented by the disciples in the rest of the Gospel? In my opinion 13:22 is a particularly illuminating verse at which to begin the search for the answer to this question. 13:22 reads "False Christs and false prophets will arise and show signs and wonders, to lead astray, if possible, the elect". The combination of the two terms, *sēmeion* ("sign") and *teras* ("wonder") occurs sixteen times in the New Testament, fourteen times outside the Synoptics.[19] Nine of these instances are found in Acts (2:19, 22, 43; 4:30; 5:12; 6:8; 7:36; 14:3; 15:12). Ernst Haenchen has already pointed out for us Luke's interest in the *theios anēr* concept of Christian existence, turning Mark's *theologia crucis* into a *theologia gloriae* and presenting Jesus and Paul and the other apostles as *theioi andres*.[20] It is apparent that the combination of *sēmeion* and *teras*, occurring in the Lucan context exclusively with reference to the activity of *theioi andres*, serves almost as a *terminus technicus* for Luke's description of *theios anēr* activity.[21] To these nine instances of the *theios anēr* connotation of the terms one can also add John 4:48, where a *theios anēr* story from the evangelist's signs source has not been fully reworked,[22] and 2 Cor. 12:12, where Paul is involved in a debate with his *theios anēr* opponents over the characteristics of apostleship.[23] Thus the evidence strongly suggests that the use of the terms in combination in the

New Testament, and as they appear in Mark, signifies a reference to *theios anēr* activity.[24] The descriptive clause, "they will do signs and wonders", pinpoints the "false Christs" and "false prophets" of 13:22 as *theioi andres*.[25]

It would be helpful if one could identify more specifically what relationship the terms "false Christs" and "false prophets" have to the description of "signs and wonders" and thereby more sharply define the profile of the people Mark is attacking. Unfortunately a study of these titles in the New Testament does not provide a great deal more information. *Pseudochristos* ("false Christ") appears nowhere else in the New Testament, save for the Matthean parallel to the Marcan passage. If the term is understood to be a reference to the antichrist, the closest parallels are 1 John 2:18, 22; 4:3; and 2 John 7 where the term *antichristos* ("anti-Christ") is used to denote the Docetic heretics of the community. With regard to the term *pseudoprophētēs*, G. Friedrich claims it cannot be identified as a *terminus technicus* for any one group throughout the New Testament.[26] It may be, as Keck suggests, that these terms as they appear in Mark are no more than symbolic references to those who promulgate a false Christology.[27] It may be that they are nothing more than invectives which Mark hurls at his opponents. However, in view of Dieter Georgi's description of the *theios anēr* opponents at Corinth, there may be an intrinsic relationship between the titles "false Christs" and "false prophets" and the *theios anēr* activity attributed to them. According to Georgi, the Pauline *theios anēr* opponents believe that Christ was a great *theios anēr* and that he becomes existentially and fully manifested in the life of the community through the *theios anēr* activity of his *theios anēr* followers. In a real sense the exalted Lord is revealed and embodied in their *theios anēr* activity. If this is the character of *theios anēr* thought in the hellenistic world, that a revered *theios anēr* became existentially manifested in the *theios anēr* activity of his future followers, then it is understandable how such followers would claim that they are the contemporary manifestation of that *theios anēr*.[28] It would be easy to see how someone opposed to such a christological position would look upon such people as impostors and call them "false Christs" and "false prophets". Such an interpretation of the terms "false Christs" and "false prophets" would also explain the warning in 13:21, "And then if any one says to you, 'Look, here is the Christ!' or 'Look, there he is!' do not believe it", a warning obviously against *theioi andres* who are confusing those unfamiliar with the *theios anēr* position into thinking that they (*theioi andres*) are indeed the eschatological exalted Lord returning to his elect in the end time.

Turning to the description of the opponents in 13:6, one runs into the problem of the interpretation of "Many will come in my name, saying, 'I am he!'". Scholars are divided over whether "in my name" refers to the members of the Christian community or generally to any one in that day who made messianic claims. Based on the study of Hans Bietenhard and the usage of the expression "in my name" in the New Testament[29] the only conclusion is that the "many" of 13:6 are Christians claiming "I am he".[30] If this is true, how could a Christian be so audacious as to use such a christological expression? This phenomenon is not so strange in the Christian community when one recalls the nature of some pneumatic experiences. In the height of the pneumatic ecstasy it would be no problem for certain Christian spiritualists to sense such complete union with the Divine that they felt they could speak for Christ and become the vehicle for the exalted Lord's communication to others. To the uninitiated, unable to understand such spiritual excesses and experiences of union, the claims of such pneumatics might easily be misunderstood as meaning that they were claiming to be Christ himself.

If, as has been suggested, 13:6 is a reference to certain pneumatics and 13:22 is a reference to *theioi andres*, are the two descriptions compatible, and do they complement each other in detailing the profile of the adversaries Mark refers to in chapter 13? Dieter Georgi's study of the heretics in 2 Corinthians provides an affirmative answer. He has described them as *theioi andres* making extravagant pneumatic claims for themselves.[31] Georgi's identification of the Corinthian heretics is not unlike the Marcan description of the subversives in chapter 13 and conforms to the type of heresy concluded to be behind the Marcan portrayal of the disciples.

If this is the nature of the Marcan heresy, why is it that it causes such a threat to the Marcan community? In regard to this 13:9–13 and 28–37 offer important clues. Based on his exegesis of these verses Conzelmann asserts that the Marcan community is eschatologically oriented, anxiously awaiting the eschaton (13:28–37), and caught in the throes of the *Zwischenzeit*, a time between the resurrection and the long-awaited parousia, a time when the exalted Lord is absent (13:9–13). Caught in the suffering of the *Zwischenzeit* (13:9–13) with neither the historical Jesus nor the future Son of Man to turn to, the community has become dismayed and disillusioned over the inexplicable and unbearable delay of the parousia and is at the point of losing its faith.[32] When the crisis in the community is so perceived, one can understand how devastating would be the arrival of Christians who claimed, contrary to the community's faith, that the exalted Lord was present in their lives, that Jesus must be seen as a great *theios anēr*, not a suffering servant, and that authentic Christian existence finds meaning and fulfilment not in the humiliation of suffering servanthood (8:34f.; 10:43f.; 13:9–13), but in the pneumatic glory of *theios anēr* existence. In such a crisis it would be easy for members of Mark's community, because of their despair, to succumb to this new teaching and even, because of their misunderstanding of pneumatic experiences, to think that those who used christological terms (13:6) in the ecstasy of their experiences were claiming to be the returning Christ.

In all likelihood the Marcan heretics claimed that their position went back to the disciples themselves. Against such a formidable claim Mark's only recourse in his attempt to save the faith of his community was to call upon a higher authority than the disciples – Jesus! Thus he enacts the dispute raging in his community by staging it before the reader in the conflict between Jesus and the disciples. In the creation of this polemic he was forced to deal with the material of his opponents' tradition in which Jesus is pictured as a great *theios anēr*. He does this by placing most of their material in the first half of the Gospel prior to the Petrine confession.[33] Then when Peter (the opponents) makes his confession to a Messiah of the *theios anēr* type, Mark (through Jesus) claims that the only authentic characteristic of messiahship is that of suffering, a suffering and humiliation which lead to the cross. To think otherwise, to persist in holding that one must see Jesus' messiahship from the *theios anēr* point of view is satanic, the position of men rather than God (8:32f.).

Having said this in the attempt to contrast sharply the positions of Mark and his opponents, one must not conclude that what is being argued is that Mark was totally opposed to the presentation of Jesus as a miracle worker. The very fact that he presents this picture at all in his Gospel, though it is for polemical reasons, indicates that such a presentation was not completely offensive to him. It may be that Mark gave no more meaning to this miracle-working activity of Jesus than to suggest that the power of Satan had come to an end and that the eschatological age had dawned in Jesus. It may be that as Paul was forced to concede certain things to his enemies at Corinth (2 Cor. 11:21a–12:6), so also to stage his argument against the *theios anēr* position of his opponents Mark had to make certain concessions to their position in order to unmask it and save the faith of his community. In any case it must be emphatically stated that no matter what proclivity Mark had toward Jesus' being pictured as a *theios anēr* he did not consider this characterization to be that attribute of Jesus which made him the Messiah.

Finally, granted that Mark constructed his attack on the false Christology and discipleship as described above one might still legitimately ask whether this would effectively silence his opponents. Could not the heretics counter Mark's assault by claiming that Mark's position is really in error, at its best confused and distorted, because he had not been privileged to receive the final and complete revelation, the authentic and authorized interpretation of Jesus' messiahship and Christian discipleship, which can come, according to the heretics, only in the pneumatic experiences of the exalted Lord's self-revelation to his community of believers – revelation which the heretics claim they have received in their pneumatic experiences and demonstrated in their powerful deeds but revelation which Mark cannot claim for himself because of his insistence that the exalted Lord is absent from his community of believers and will not return until the final cosmic-supernatural event occurs? In other words, despite the fact that Mark plays his historical Jesus over against them, could not they successfully counter by playing their own grandiose past-present exalted Jesus, manifested through their own deeds, over against Mark's suffering Jesus – anaemic by comparison – and thus outwit him? What is the standard, the constant, that is operative in the pre-resurrection life of Jesus and the post-resurrection life of the Church that will assure Mark's community that his presentation of the historical Jesus and the call to suffering discipleship is accurate and authoritative and can never be altered by any subsequent experiences or claims of manifestation? To what final authority can he appeal that will successfully squelch any such counter-attack by his opponents?

The most obvious answer is the way in which Mark creates chapter 13 as *vaticinium ex eventu* (prophecy after the event) thus giving credibility to his own tradition by not only having the historical Jesus of this tradition forecast the events of the period of the Church and the emergence of the false Christology and discipleship of the Marcan opponents (13:6, 22), but also by having this same Jesus assert that he, as exalted Lord, will remain absent from the Church until history has fully run its course. Yet the most cogent and convincing argument Mark provides for the authenticity of his position is found in two verses of 13:9–13.

In 13:10 the Church is admonished: "And the gospel must first be preached to all nations". In view of Marxsen's comprehensive study of the word "gospel" in Mark, the clause "the gospel must be proclaimed" takes on very profound meaning. Marxsen (1970: 128–36) argues persuasively that for Mark the term "gospel" is but an amplification of the phrase "for my sake" and that in Mark's mind Jesus and the gospel are synonymous. Jesus himself is the entire content of the gospel which he preaches. Thus the Marcan Jesus calls for belief in the Jesus (the gospel) which Jesus preaches through the Marcan narrative. There can be no other authentic Jesus (gospel) but the Jesus (gospel) which Jesus preaches through the Marcan narrative. This is the gospel (the Jesus) for which one is to witness (13:9), which one is to preach to all nations (13:10) and for which one will win the emnity of relatives and the hatred of all (13:12f.). For the Marcan opponents to preach another Jesus or gospel is for them to preach a false gospel and false Christ.

In 13:11 the text reads: "And when they bring you to trial and deliver you up, do not be anxious beforehand what you are to say; but say whatever is given you in that hour, for it is not you who speak, but the Holy Spirit". Here again Marxsen (1970: 129) offers a valuable insight: "It is, of course, in a real sense not quite the persecuted who preach Jesus is here, rather the preaching content is given to them by the Holy Spirit". When one reflects upon the Marcan understanding of the role of the Holy Spirit this insight takes on profound significance in understanding Mark's defense against any rebuttal by his opponents. Mark understands the Holy Spirit in the Old Testament sense as symbolic of God's action in Jesus and in those who are possessed by it. In Mark the Holy Spirit not only authorizes one to speak and act for God but also controls what is said and done in the name of God. In 1:10 the Spirit is bestowed upon Jesus in baptism, the guarantee that

100

Jesus is an authorized emissary of God (1:11) who speaks for God and therefore must be listened to (9:7). The Spirit, however, does not authenticate one's credentials; it also manifests complete control over the individual who has received it and directs his whole course of action (1:12).[34] In Mark, then, the Holy Spirit not only authorizes one to speak and act for God but also controls what is said and done in the name of God.

The Holy Spirit, therefore, provides the final court of appeal upon which Mark rests his case for the authenticity of his position and the fallacy of his opponents'. In Mark's argument it is the Holy Spirit that provides the authentic continuity between the pre-resurrected time of the historical Jesus and the post-resurrected period of the Church. The same Holy Spirit that was bestowed upon Jesus, that directed Jesus' life, that made sure he was the right kind of Messiah (a suffering Messiah), also directs the proper confession of the Christian to this same Messiah (13:11). Thus there can be no disagreement, no discontinuity, no false preaching, no distortion of the true gospel, if the speaker allows the Holy Spirit to do the witnessing and preaching for him. The Holy Spirit guarantees the uniformity in witness between the suffering Christology and discipleship Jesus preached and the suffering Christology and discipleship which members of Mark's community are existentially called upon to believe and affirm. The same Spirit directs and empowers the Jesus of history and the faithful of Mark's community.

Mark has successfully combated his opponents, supported his position and discredited theirs, a position discredited because it was not guided by the Holy Spirit. The forebears of this position, the disciples, according to Mark, neither responded to the Spirit-directed Jesus (8:30–2) nor were they responsive on occasions when the Spirit could have guided them (14:38).[35] They submitted to the things of the flesh of man and not to the things of God (8:32f.; 14:38ff.), and thus as they were ashamed of and rejected Jesus during his lifetime (14:43–5, 50, 66–71), and as their successors, the Marcan opponents, rejected this same Jesus in the life of the Church, so Jesus will be ashamed of all of them when he comes as the exalted Lord in power and glory (8:38f.; 13:26).

NOTES

1 See Johannes Schreiber (1961); particularly Joseph Tyson (1961); and perhaps Leander Keck (1965), implicitly.

2 See Johannes Schreiber (1961); Ulrich Luz in Tuckett (1983); Eduard Schweizer in Tuckett (1983); James M. Robinson, "The Recent Debate on the 'New Quest' ", *Journal of Biblical Research*, 30 (1962) 203f.; Keck (1965); Philipp Vielhauer (1964).

3 In the following discussion I am dependent for many insights into the first two stages in this relationship on Alfred Kuby's article, "Zur Konzeption des Markus-Evangeliums", *ZNW* 49 (1958) 52–64.

4 Compare the response of the "outsiders" to Jesus and his supernatural powers (1:32–4, 35–8, 40–5; 2:1–12; 3:7–12; 5:1–20, 21–43; 6:53–6; 7:24–30; 8:22–6) to that of the disciples (particularly at 5:28–31; 8:4, 14–21, where they apparently have failed to comprehend the supernatural capacity exhibited in the two feedings, 6:30–44; 8:1–10). That this obtuse character of the disciples is a distinctively Marcan motif is substantiated by Matthew's and Luke's deletion (Matthew deletes Mark 4:13; 5:29–31; and Luke deletes Mark 4:13 and the entire section in which Mark 6:52; 7:17; 8:4, 14–21 occur) and Matthew's alteration (Matt. 14:33; 16:11–12 according to the respective Marcan passages) of the Marcan text in favour of a better picture of the disciples' acumen.

5 Keck (1965) claims that 3:7–12; 4:35–5:43; 6:31–56; 8:1–21 represent a block of material from a *theios anēr* ("divine man") tradition which is characterized by "boat" and "touching" motifs and which the evangelist has worked into his narrative.

6 Luz (1983) 85 states that the disciples recognize Jesus on the basis of his miraculous power; and Kuby (1958: 58) claims that Peter expected confirmation of his confession from Jesus through some miraculous deed.

7 Traditionally the assumption has been that Peter made a confession to a Messiah in the royal image of David, but such a conclusion is drawn without consideration of all the facts. First, such an understanding is not explicitly stated or implied by the disciples. Second, such a conclusion might be drawn if the evangelist were primarily concerned with the original historical account of Peter's confession which could have been a confession to Davidic messiahship. But with the possibility that the evangelist is no longer concerned with the facts of A.D. 30 but rather with the specific problems of his own community in the late sixties (see following discussion) the content of the confession can be understood only in view of the evangelist's own situation, not in terms of whatever content may have been behind a confession made originally in A.D. 30 – if such a confession was made then.

8 Cf. L. Bieler, ΘΕΙΟΣ ANHP, 80f., and particularly Dieter Georgi, *Die Gegner des Paulus im 2. Korintherbrief*, 210, 214.

9 See Bieler, 97; James M. Robinson (1957) 80; Georgi, op. cit., 252–73, where Georgi speaks of the secret tradition of the *theioi andres* in Corinth.

10 The crux of the problem in 9:38–41 is not that the exorcist is a non-Christian performing an exorcism in the name of Christ, but that he is a Christian exorcist who is not a part of the disciples' group. Cf. Johannes Weiss (1903) 257ff.; A. Loisy (1912) 277ff.; and Rudolf Bultmann (1963) 25.

11 There is a material relationship between 10:13–16 and 9:36f. In 10:13ff. as in 9:36f., children serve as examples to emphasize further the essential Christian quality of humility (cf. commentaries), a quality which stands in stark relief to the disciples' concern for self-exaltation and refusal to receive those of lowly position (19:13–16). The seriousness of the disagreement between the disciples and Jesus in 10:13ff. has been reduced in Matthew and Luke by their deletion of *ēganaktēsen* ("he was indignant") (10:14).

12 Op. cit., 220–34, 296ff.

13 See G. R. Beasley-Murray (1954) for a history of the exegesis of the chapter. See also W. G. Kümmel, *Promise and Fulfillment*, 98–104 for a recent discussion of the material.

14 Willi Marxsen (1970) 151ff.; Hans Conzelmann (1959); L. Keck (1965–6) 365ff.

15 *Blepō* ("see") in the imperative mood is apparently a Marcan keyword as consultation with a concordance shows, and the tendency of Matthew and Luke to omit it or substitute *prosechō* ("beware") (Matt. 10:17; 16:6; Luke 12:1; 20:46) underscores. Matthew and Luke render *blepō* in their parallels to Mark 13 only in 13:5.

16 This Marcan division of events between the inner-historical and the transcendental-supernatural in chapter 13 is expounded by Conzelmann (1959).

17 Conzelmann (1959) 211 argues persuasively that for Mark and his community the exalted Lord is absent. He bases his conclusion on the fact that the exalted Lord plays no role in chapter 13. There is no suggestion that he is present to help those who witness in his behalf. All that is present to guide the believer is Jesus' word (13:31) and the Holy Spirit, who alone is the active intercessor in the life of the Church (13:11).

18 (1965–6) 364f.

19 The synoptic occurrences are Mark 13:22 and its Matthean parallel (24:24).

20 E. Haenchen, *The Acts of the Apostles*, 91, 113, 118, 123f.

21 See Georgi, op. cit., 216f. for his discussion of Moses as a *theios anēr* in Acts 7:20f., where this combination of terms is used to describe the exodus (7:36). The addition of *sēmeia* to the Joel prophecy in Acts 2:19 appears to be Luke's attempt to provide a proof-text for *theios anēr* activity before the eschaton and during the protracted history of the Church.

22 R. Bultmann, *The Gospel of John*, 207.

23 Georgi, op. cit., 231.

24 Three occurrences of the combination in the New Testament (Rom. 15:19; 2 Thess. 2:19; Heb. 2:4), not discussed at this point, do not suggest any reason to

103

raise doubt as to the conclusion drawn. *Did.* 16:4 contains the combination of terms in a context similar to both 2 Thess. 2:9 and Mark 13:22.

25 Additional support for this view is suggested by Luke's deletion of Mark 13:21–3. Luke, recognizing an obvious opposition and threat to his own *theios anēr* proclivity, deleted the material.

26 G. Friedrich, "*prophētes*: Prophets and Prophecies in the NT", *TDNT* vi, 855f.

27 Keck (1965–6) 366.

28 Georgi, op cit., 288–300, particularly 292f. Georgi asserts that the Pauline opponents blurred, if not completely obliterated, the distinction between the historical Jesus and the post-resurrection exalted Lord. Ignoring the clear-cut break (the crucifixion) between the historical Jesus and the resurrected Lord, the opponents of Paul conceived of the power and manifestation of Jesus as continuing to manifest itself without a break and without loss of continuity in their own *theios anēr* activity.

29 "*onoma*", *TDNT* v. 271. Bietenhard's study does not suggest any possibility that "in my name", used christologically, could designate anyone who stands in opposition to the spirit and will of Christ or who stand outside of the Christian community.

30 The term *egō eimi* ("I am") has been recognized for some time as an identification for the deity and in the Christian community as a specific identification for Christ. See E. Stauffer, *ego*, *TDNT* ii, 352f.

31 Op. cit.. 224, 227ff., 232, 293–9.

32 See Conzelmann, 210–12.

33 Luz, in Tuckett (1983) 84, in pointing out that the wonder history predominates in the first half of the Gospel but is absent in the second half, contends that the two exceptions to this schema (9:14–29; 10:46–52) should not be viewed as wonder stories as such but as illustrations of the disciples' relation to Jesus and the following of Jesus. It is not correct, however, to suggest that Mark has removed all *theios anēr* traits of Jesus in the last half of the Gospel. Certainly these traits are present in the transfiguration (Georgi, op. cit., 215f.), in 9:14–29; 10:46–52, in the Palm Sunday experience, and perhaps in certain aspects of the passion narrative. But it is certainly accurate to say that these traits have been reduced to a low key, if not neutralized entirely, by the strong emphasis upon Jesus' messianic commitment to suffering servanthood.

34 See Eduard Schweizer, "*pneuma*" *TDNT* vi, 396–401; James M. Robinson (1959) 29ff.

35 With regard to 14:38, Schweizer, op. cit., 396 states that the phrase "the spirit indeed is willing but the flesh is weak" is not a reference to hellenistic psychology. *pneuma* ("spirit") in this verse refers not to man but to God, the Holy Spirit.

3

The Epiphany of Jesus in the Gospel (Mark) *

KARL KERTELGE

The historical standpoint of Mark can be approximately, though
not exactly, determined by interpreting his Gospel. Mark writes
at a time when the gentile mission has become self-evident. The
Pauline missionary proclamation is presupposed. Mark combines
in his Gospel different earlier attempts at a kerygmatic presentation of Jesus' activity. The composition of the Gospel cannot
therefore be placed too early, certainly not in the first decades
after the death of Jesus. Since chapter 13 probably "shows traces
of the threatening nearness of the Jewish war" (Kümmel, 1973:
98), Mark's Gospel is probably to be dated, with the majority of
exegetes, around c.e. 70.[1]

Early Church tradition names as author the Mark who
according to the testimony of Papias was the "interpreter of
Peter" (cf. 1 Pet. 5:13), probably to be identified with the John
Mark of Acts 12:12, 25; 13:5, 13; 15:37–9, though he was more a
pupil of Paul (cf. also Philem. 24; Col. 4:10; 2 Tim. 4:11).[2] These
divergent testimonies compel caution about being any more
precise about their relationship.

Mark is writing for Greek-speaking Christians, but still
preserves the semitic linguistic peculiarities of his largely Palestinian sources or material. The gentile mission is presupposed.
Mark wants to combine the passion and the resurrection kerygma

* First published in *Gestalt und Anspruch des Neuen Testaments*, ed. J. Schreiner
(Würzburg: Echter-Verlag, 1969) 153–72. Translated by R. Morgan.

which corresponds especially to Pauline theology, with the traditions of Jesus' miracle working which point to the Galilean-Syrian border region.[3] This suggests that Mark himself belonged to the hellenistic Christianity of the Syrian communities, e.g. Antioch (cf. Gal. 2:11). That would explain the sharp accentuation of the Jewish leaders as Jesus' opponents.

I   *"Gospel" as Mark's Theme*

In early Christianity the word "gospel" was used for the oral proclamation of Jesus Christ.[4] Paul designated the missionary preaching and hence his own proclamation of Jesus the Crucified and Risen One, "gospel" (Rom. 1:1–4, etc.). In Rom. 2:16, Paul can even speak of "my gospel" (cf. Gal. 1:11; 2:2). The word "gospel" only became used as the title of a book, i.e. the first four books of the New Testament in the course of the second century (Justin, *Apology* I, 66), in the period of the formation of the canon. That, of course, also obscured the characteristic differences between the four "Gospels". For the name "gospel" does not suit the four Gospels to the same extent. It properly and primarily applies only to Mark, who begins his presentation with the words: "Beginning of the gospel of Jesus Christ, the Son of God".[5] The step from what had until then been an orally proclaimed gospel, to the written word of the Gospel, deserves consideration. This tradition can be observed incipiently as early as Paul. In 1 Cor. 15:1–5 he communicates the gospel outline, so to speak, in the form of the confession handed down in tradition. But Paul was not in his letters trying to write a "Gospel", and does not use the word of his writings. That is an essential difference between Paul and Mark. Faith for Paul is directed to the living gospel and its saving power (cf. Rom. 1:16). Whereas here its "object", to which it must be related, is apparently the written word about Jesus Christ as well.

We do, of course, have to draw attention here to the range of meaning in the concept "gospel", evident in Mark itself. Mark 1:1 speaks of the "beginning of the gospel", which clearly refers to the report about the Baptist (1:2–8) as the beginning of his book, whereas at 1:14f. Jesus himself appears in a programmatic statement as a proclaimer of the "gospel" with his call to "repent and believe in the gospel". In this passage Jesus himself speaks of the gospel as the object to be believed in. That corresponds to the character of the early Christian missionary proclamation found in its early New Testament form in Paul. Later on the author of the Gospel of John has Jesus say directly, "Believe in me" (John 14:1). Mark also probably means believe in Jesus with his challenge to believe in 1:15, since in Mark's Gospel, Jesus himself is present as its real content.

Mark thus takes up the keyword "gospel" from early Christian missionary language. But he unfolds its content in a new and unusual way by depicting the path of the earthly Jesus from his baptism by John through his ministry in Galilee up to his passion, his death on the cross and his resurrection in Jerusalem.

II   *How the earliest Gospel was composed*

Mark has taken up earlier traditions which were not originally formed and transmitted as "gospel". These were, roughly speaking, narratives about Jesus (and also about John the Baptist: 1:2–8; 6:17–29) and speeches or rather sayings of Jesus. "Gospel" in the original sense meant, as we saw, the message of Jesus' saving act which found its proper expression in his death and resurrection. We can assume that this was Mark's view too. Since the majority of the traditions that he has taken up into his Gospel were certainly not passion and resurrection texts the question arises whether Mark has interpreted his traditions in the sense of "gospel", or whether the traditional meaning of "gospel" has been exploded by being enriched with other kinds of material, above all traditions about the earthly activity of Jesus, and has been changed into a first sketch of a connected story of Jesus. The attempt to answer this question needs the help of redaction criticism. But first we must look at the individual traditions available to the evangelist.

(*a*) *Form criticism.*   The basic question of form criticism to the earliest Gospel is this: Where does the material which Mark has mostly got from the tradition come from, and what are the original "life-settings" of these individual traditions?

Form-critical questioning, which has exercised New Testament scholarship since the First World War is associated above all with the names of Rudolf Bultmann (1968) and Martin Dibelius (1934).

Dibelius distinguished individual traditions in the Gospels by their external formal characteristics and derived them in part from the preaching of the early Christian Church and in part from the inventiveness of story-tellers and creators of legends. In opposition to Dibelius' "constructive" method Bultmann applied a contrary method: he separated the gospel materials from their context and tried by his "analytic" method to reach their smallest individual units. He judged these smallest units, distinguished by their literary form, to be the earliest stage of tradition. The history of the tradition, he thought, followed on from these by its own rules. But Bultmann largely overlooked the actual situations of the early Christian communities in which the traditions were developed and by which they were much influenced. Dibelius on the other hand placed too much reliance on how far the sociological conditions which he postulated as influencing the gospel tradition could be known. This is where the limitations of the form-critical method become visible. But it can be said that with its help the emergence of the pre-Marcan tradition can in broad outline be approximately charted, down to the stage of its final redaction by the evangelist.

For the most part Mark is *narrative material*. The passion narrative (chapters 14 and 15) represents the largest connected portion of tradition. Alongside this the miracle stories take up a considerable space. Altogether they total 156 verses, as against 119 verses of passion narrative. That does not, of course, settle the theological relationship of these two groups of material, as the evangelist sees it. The two groups are very different in their content and their form. The *passion narrative* reads like a historical report with a clear temporal sequence and internal logic. The miracle stories are quite different. They are connected by no necessary time sequence. Even the individual stories lack much sign of historical reporting. Each of them has its own temporal sequence and a kind of inner logic. But it is clear in each report of a miracle that they are not interested in this sequence of events as such, but in the person of Jesus. Each aims in its own way to say who Jesus is rather than who meets Jesus. In the passion narrative, by contrast, the central point is what Jesus has done (for us). It depicts the path Jesus has trod. That Jesus' path was the way of suffering, Mark has seen even before the passion narrative proper begins. He has indicated that throughout Jesus' miraculous activity, and so has connected that period editorially with the passion (see below).

Even in the passion narrative, the largest connected piece of tradition in Mark's Gospel, there are traces of a gradual enriching of the story by individual smaller units.

One such case of an originally independent unit inserted secondarily into its passion context is the "anointing at Bethany" (14:3–9).[6] How easy it is to lift it out of its Marcan context (14:1f. fits 14:10f.) can be seen from Luke who omits this story from his passion narrative and includes a doublet of it earlier (the sinner at the meal: Luke 7:36–50). This story shows neatly how the tradition grew at the pre-Marcan stage. The oldest layer, which may well go back to historical memory, presumably ended at this point: "The poor you have always with you . . . me you have not always" (Mark 14:7). In this form the tradition spoke originally of the irreplaceable significance of Jesus' presence, as it does in a similar way in the saying about the bridegroom (2:19). Jesus and his presence are what matters most. Over against the parallel construction of the two parts of the verse (14:7) quoted above, the words "and whenever you will, you can do good to them" sound like an insertion. A later hander on of the tradition may, in fact, have added these words in order to secure a reference to "charity", i.e. a practical concern of the Church, in this context. The insertion indicates a paraenetic application of the story in early Christian sermons. Originally it proclaimed only the eschatological character of the time of Jesus, as in Q, for example Matt. 11:4–6 = Luke 7:22f., and Matt. 13:16f. = Luke 10:23f.

However, on account of the words "but you will not always have me", this verse, and so the whole story, could be interpreted with reference to the imminent death of Jesus. That is how the subsequent tradition understood our narrative, interpreting the reported anointing by the addition of v. 8b which refers to Jesus' burial. Finally Mark has inserted the gradually growing tradition into the context of his passion narrative and connected it to this with v. 9. He thus emphasizes that what the woman has done is significant not in itself, but only in connection with the passion, which for him is the kernel of the Gospel. That in this context the post-Easter proclamation "in the whole world" comes into view clearly betrays the later standpoint of the evangelist who can look back to the beginnings of a "world mission".

In a similar way, though not always so easily, further units of narrative can be lifted out of their passion context and identified as traditions which were at first independent of Jesus' passion. It is probable that the pericope of the Last Supper had a more independent significance of its own in the earliest tradition. At any rate the parallel in 1 Cor. 11:23–7 shows clearly enough that this tradition was at first used in early Christian celebrations of the Lord's supper, and that in the context of a memorial of Jesus' passion, as is plain from the note in 1 Cor. 11:23: "The Lord Jesus, on the night when he was betrayed . . ."

But the passion report resists radical dissolution into its smallest units. For the following elements can with some certainty be recognized as original: Jesus' arrest, the trial before the Sanhedrin, the condemnation by Pontius Pilate, and finally the crucifixion.[7] This outline corresponds to the passion prophecy at Mark 10:33f. which can be assumed to be pre-Marcan in origin, coming probably from the Jewish-Christian community in Palestine (the mention of "Gentiles" is to be noted). But since this kind of short report – similar to the pre-Pauline tradition contained in 1 Cor. 15:3–5 – shows credal characteristics, we may confidently assume that both the basic outline of the passion narrative and its later expansion by the tradition are shaped by the credal confession of the suffering and death of Jesus "for us". This formula is frequent in Paul (Rom. 5:8; 8:31f., 34; 1 Cor. 15:3, etc.) but admittedly occurs only twice in Mark (on Jesus' lips as "for many"), at 10:45 and 14:24. But the whole passion narrative is full of allusions to the Old Testament – actual citations are rarer – so here especially the efforts of the earliest Christian communities to interpret the death of Jesus theologically are reflected.

The miracle stories in Mark have undergone a quite different development. They too, were from the outset controlled by early Christian confession of Jesus. That is sufficiently clear from their frequent use of the different christological titles, such as "Kyrios" (5:19, 7:28), "Teacher" or "Master" (4:38; 5:35; 9:17; 10:51), "Son of God" (3:11; 5:7), "The Holy One of God" (1:24), "Son of Man" (2:10). The acclamations at the end of the miracle stories also serve the direct or indirect confession of Jesus, as at 1:27; 2:12; 4:41, etc. But Mark's miracle stories are not so peculiar to him as his passion narrative is. They have their various models in the Old Testament (e.g. the raisings by Elijah and Elisha), and above all in the hellenistic milieu of early Christianity. There are not only occasional parallel motifs common to hellenistic and early Christian miracle stories but even extensive agreements in the style and construction of these narratives (cf. Bultmann, 1968: 209–44 on this). One cannot of course speak of a direct dependence and borrowing of early Christian miracle stories from the quite different realm of lives of hellenistic "divine men". But consideration of the formal parallels should prevent one from overestimating the extent to which the gospel traditions are historical reports.

Closer observation reveals that not all the miracle stories in Mark are structured in the same way. In noting different forms of miracle narratives we are less interested in distinguishing between healing miracles and so-called nature miracles than in certain differences of form which betray different uses of the narratives in the life of the communities which transmitted them. For example, in the report of the healing of the lame man (2:1–12) the central point is not so much the miracle as the question of Jesus' authority to forgive sins. And again in the healing of the withered hand on the Sabbath (3:1–6), an answer is being given to the Sabbath conflict between Christians and Jews. In contrast to most of the other miracle stories of the Gospel we speak here not merely of "miracle stories" but of "apophthegmatic narratives". The point in these cases is a saying of Jesus or his word and deed together. In such stories the early Christian community found answers in Jesus' word to their own questions. But even those miracle stories told without a saying of Jesus attached were not handed on by the first Christians merely out of a delight in telling stories. They too, aimed to tell of Jesus and his significance in order to interest non-believers in him or to depict the picture of Jesus for believers in a perspective determined by faith. Above all the significance of the miracle stories for missionary practice and for theology should not be overlooked. This is where the explanation of, for example, the conclusion to the healing of the Gadarene demoniac (5:18–20) lies. It is clearly secondary in terms of the history of the tradition but is still pre-Marcan. It reflects the beginnings of the gentile mission in the Decapolis.[8]

Alongside the narrative material the speeches and sayings of Jesus in Mark are very modest in scope. Apart from the parables chapter (4:1–34) and the Marcan apocalypse (chapter 13) and to some extent the instruction in 7:1–23 this Gospel contains no large discourses, only individual pieces of debate, parables and sayings of Jesus.

The basic outline of the *parables chapter* (chapter 4) is probably a small pre-Marcan collection of parables (4:3–9, 26–9, 30–2). Even in Mark it is still apparent that who the hearers are remains quite vague in these parable passages. They have a common theme – a sower or seed. Prior to Mark they seem to have been only loosely hung together by a kind of catch-word connection. On the other hand the doubtless secondary "interpretation" of the parable of the sower in vv. 13–20, introduced by v. 10, was quite early transmitted together with the parable of 4:3–9. The sayings in 4:21–5 which make contact with the sayings material of Q have been inserted in the collection of parables by the evangelist. He must in particular be credited with vv. 11f. and 33f. which characterize his understanding of the parables. The extent of the pre-Marcan parable source cannot be established with any certainty.[9] But this chapter shows by its rather arbitrary changes of addressee (crowd and disciples) where these can be ascertained at all, and by the change of different forms of Jesus' speech (parable,[10] instruction, allegorical interpretation, sayings and short similitudes), that the early Christian tradition operated with small units. These were connected with one another under different perspectives, but above all for purposes of community catechesis.

The *apocalyptic discourse of Jesus* about the "End" in chapter 13 is again not a unity, from a form-critical point of view. Without going into a detailed analysis[11] we may note the combination of primarily prophetic-apocalyptic sayings (prophecies), which are broadly related to Old Testament and Jewish ideas and motifs, with warnings directed against apocalyptic enthusiasm. The latter are probably due largely to Mark's redaction, whereas the typically apocalyptic sayings which may stem largely from a pre-Christian Jewish apocalypse, are probably a pre-Marcan collection of prophecies, the emergence of which is best explained in terms of early Christian expectation of Jesus' imminent return.

From the remaining tradition of Jesus' sayings in Mark we may pick out finally the *controversy and didactic sayings*. This type has already been touched on above in connection with our treatment of the "apopthegmatic miracle stories". The two pericopae which belong here, 2:1–12 and 3:1–6 form the beginning and the end of a larger collection of "controversy dialogues" between Jesus and his opponents. This collection also was probably available to the evangelist as a collection. We see in the individual pieces of this collection the interest of the community who collected them in the sayings of Jesus which might contribute to the solution of its practical problems, such as the question of fasting and keeping the

Sabbath. The stereotyped labelling of Jesus' opponents as "Pharisees" or "scribes" or both (3:6 and 12:13 mention the puzzling "Herodians" too) should probably not be explained as simply memory of the events of Jesus' life, but reflects early Christian experience of Jewish opposition and also the different positions represented within the early Palestinian church. So the circumstances and regularly recurring form of debate, known also from rabbinic disputes (occasion, sometimes a question, reply – usually in the form of a counter-question) are scarcely to be derived from the life of Jesus himself. The answers of Jesus are more likely to be original, but they may well have originated in a variety of different contexts. 7:1–23, the dispute about "clean and unclean" is a good example of how a controversy saying was enriched and enlarged by further sayings of Jesus – evidently on account of the relevance of this topic for the Jewish Christianity of the time. Finally, the demand for a sign (8:11–13), the question of authority (11:27–33), the Pharisees' question about taxes (12:13–17), the Sadducees' question about the resurrection (12:18–27), and the question about David's son (12:35–7) are clearly controversy sayings. Between these last five controversy sayings, which again go back to a pre-Marcan collection, stands a single didactic saying which has no polemical purpose, namely the question of the greatest commandment (12:28–34).

(*b*) *Redaction criticism.* This form-critical survey of the traditional material used by Mark has already shown that there was movement towards collecting the Jesus tradition even before Mark, and that he could take these over in his more comprehensive work. Without pursuing these collections and their pre-Marcan redaction any further, even up to the question whether the evangelist used an *Ur-Markus* document, we shall now try briefly to see and understand the most important adjustments made by the final redactor who is known to us as Mark to the traditional material he had collected.

The first thing to recall again is that Mark means to write a "Gospel" and not as it were a "life of Jesus". The content of the Gospel is God's saving act in Jesus Christ, especially in his death and his resurrection. That explains the significance of the passion narrative in Mark. In its external form it is a report, in its real content and intention it is kerygma. That is Mark's intention: to speak of Jesus not only as a figure in the past, but also as the "Son of Man" who is decisive for the present and future of believers. His suffering and death are the key to his work. One can, therefore, not deny that Martin Kähler's often-quoted saying about the Gospels being "passion narratives with extended introductions"[12] has a measure of truth with respect to Mark. Even though Mark 1–13 has a certain significance of its own, it can still be shown that the thread of the passion narrative has been extended back by Mark into the preceding chapters of his Gospel. The passion narrative is introduced as early as the entry of Jesus into Jerusalem (11:1–10). This extension is served also by the passion announcement in 10:33f. which has already been twice given by Mark, at 8:31 and 9:31. The controversy debates which follow (chapters 11–12) concern "how they might destroy him" (11:18). This intention of Jesus' opponents is clear as early as 3:6 at the end of the first collection of controversy debates, so that even the activity of Jesus in Galilee becomes a path to the passion.

From these last-mentioned passages it is already apparent that the evangelist's redactional activity consists above all in a particular arrangement of the traditional material and in placing some theological accents. Mark is happy to take over quite large collections of material already shaped in the tradition. That is true of the passion narrative, the apocalypse (chapter 13), for a part of the parables (4:3–32), the two collections of controversy material (2:1–3:6 and 11:27–12:37) and for parts of the miracles tradition (1:23–31[34] and 4:35–5:42).

Although Mark evidently sets no store by exactness in the historical sequence of individual events, he is not arbitrary in the way he joins pieces of tradition together. His kerygmatic intention controls his editorial redactional activity. Admittedly the evangelist's theological purpose is not always equally clear throughout his Gospel. That accounts for the partly divergent judgements about Mark in recent redaction criticism.[13] Mark's theological accents are not evenly spread throughout his traditional material. But it is debatable whether this stems solely from the alleged inability of the earliest evangelist who was not completely in control of his material or whether the observable "inconsistency" in his way of working does not rather correspond to an overall conception which does not harmonize tensions in the tradition because they are used for the theological interpretation.

The main accent which Mark places is the secrecy motif by which he builds into the public ministry of Jesus a retarding element, so that until his passion Jesus in his preaching and miracle working remains the hidden "Son of Man", not understood by any, even his disciples.

III *The theological conception of Mark*

If we accept the view that Mark is writing a "Gospel" and not really a "life of Jesus", we must now ask about the theological ideas which have controlled the composition of his work. Whereas the "form-critical school" wanted on the whole to restrict the evangelist's achievement to his activity as a collector, it is now more strongly emphasized through redaction-critical investigations that Mark's collecting and editing was controlled by a theological conception.[14] The main theological lines in the earliest Gospel which yield a unitary total conception of Jesus' activity can now be indicated.

(*a*) *The "secret epiphanies" of Jesus.* If we want to evaluate Mark's work theologically we have to begin from the observation that he had a great variety of traditional materials. He had to bring these into a coherent kerygmatic total picture of Jesus' ministry. Above all the tradition's material about the earthly Jesus had now to be connected with the basic early Christian gospel data, the message of Jesus' death and resurrection. This could happen in two ways:

1. The tradition of Jesus' sayings and deeds are prefaced to the passion report and understood as a report of the life of Jesus. The passion would then become the final part of a life of Jesus.

2. The teaching of Jesus and his miracles are still placed before the passion, but now interpreted with reference to the suffering and death of Jesus. Our earlier observations on the passion announcements and the early decision of Jesus' opponents to put him to death have already made it clear that Mark chose the second option. He understands not only the passion narrative but also the whole Jesus tradition as kerygma.[15]

Mark will, of course, have been aware that his sequence of events gives the impression of a connected history. That may well be his intention, too. Mark does not deny the individual parts of the story of Jesus. On the contrary, he wants to witness to their true significance. But that means that he is concerned with the historical course of events only insofar as this temporal sequence continuously and ever anew reveals and unfolds the story of Jesus and its claim upon mankind. Mark's temporal sequence of events is not a history of Jesus Christ that is intelligible in itself, with its own continuity proceeding to a successful outcome. In the developing failure of Jesus and his claim down to his death the story is revealed as willed and directed by God, and not intelligible from the sequence of events alone. Actually Mark shows Jesus in the individual events as a thoroughly successful and thronged teacher and miracle-worker who, however, remains in all his activity not understood, and through all his success finally fails – incomprehensibly in human terms. It is only comprehensible as God's will. Even the most clearly drawn line in the representation of Jesus' successful activity, the conquest of the powers opposed to God through the Kingdom of God which he proclaims still remains as a whole veiled in the failure of the disciples and crowds who accompany him to understand. The story of Jesus is seen to have succeeded only at Easter.[16]

In the light of Mark's view of history the whole life and work of the earthly Jesus appear in a characteristic way broken. Jesus acts, he preaches and performs miracles. But his true significance is not recognized. Indeed, he does not even want to be known. This fracture, which runs right through Mark's account of Jesus' public ministry, is, of course, only visible in the interpretation of the evangelist. How far it was already present in the traditions available to the evangelist and even in the life of the historical Jesus himself, cannot be discussed here. At any rate Mark knew he was justified in strongly emphasizing this aspect as he interpreted his tradition. This was intended to present and explain the peculiar tension that existed between the historical Jesus, whose public activity led finally to death on the cross, and the claim that he was Son of God, here in his earthly activity, though it was only recognized and confessed after his death. The death of Jesus is thus made the event of the Son of God's most extreme hiddenness and at the same time of his revelation. To show how the tension between hiddenness and revelation determines the whole of Jesus' activity, Mark makes use of three different but connected motifs: the commands to silence which he imposes on the demons and those healed, the secret instruction he gives to the disciples, i.e. to "those inside" in contrast to "those outside" (4:11) in the parables discourse,[17] and the repeated failure of the disciples to understand Jesus' word and work (6:52; 8:17–21). Mark's theological aim can here be briefly explained from the significance of the silence commands.

According to 1:34 and 3:11f. Jesus drives out many demons, but does "not allow them to speak, since they knew him" (1:34). The demons call him by his name, "Son of God" (3:12), or "The holy one of God" (1:24), or "Son of the most high God" (5:7). Why does Jesus want to prevent his true identity as "Son of God" from being revealed? The answer to this is given by the evangelist at 3:12, so that "they [the demons] should not make him known". So Jesus wants to remain hidden in his public activity, by his own intention and corresponding to the divine plan of salvation. It is, apparently, important to the evangelist, however, that he cannot in fact remain hidden. How much store Mark sets on this discrepancy between Jesus' wanting to remain hidden and the fact that he cannot remain hidden is especially clear in some of the healings. Jesus commands the healed leper, "See that you say nothing to anyone" (1:44). And immediately we read, "But he [the healed man] went out and began to talk freely about it, and to spread the news, so that he [Jesus] could no longer openly enter a town, but was out in the country, and people came to him from every quarter" (1:45). This breaking of the silence command is not simply reported as a fact. In it the intention of the evangelist finds expression. It is similar when the deaf-mute is healed. Jesus takes him aside and heals him. Then it says, "And he charged them to tell no one; but the more he charged them, the more zealously they proclaimed it" (7:36). In both passages the word "proclaim" occurs. This shows the real intention of the evangelist. Jesus and his true significance should and must be proclaimed. And the evangelist, of course, has his readers in view as he uses this technical language of proclamation (kerygma!). The stories handed down continue now the same proclamation that Jesus set in motion then. Admittedly proclamation should not really have taken place then, according to Jesus' wishes; his true nature should not yet have been revealed. But the evangelist saw in this breaking of the silence commands and the spread of his reputation the fact that Jesus could not remain hidden. We may, therefore, speak of Mark's indirect revelations, or in M. Dibelius' phrase, of Jesus' "secret epiphanies" (1934: 297).

One might be inclined to explain Jesus' wanting to remain hidden in psychological ways, as has often been attempted. On this view Jesus will have feared that his messiahship might have been misunderstood in his lifetime in a political sense. This might explain the time set for keeping the secret until "the Son of man should have risen from the dead" (9:9). Whether such considerations did, in fact, feature in the life of the historical Jesus cannot be decided on a basis of Mark alone. It at any rate remains psychologically inexplicable how, for example, a girl raised from the dead, like Jairus' daughter, could remain hidden, as Jesus wishes as 5:43. But Mark's intention is clear from these notes and from the consistent thrust of his Gospel: Jesus is during his earthly activity the hidden Messiah (Wrede) – for Mark "Messiah" has the same meaning as "Son of God" and "Son of Man". The true significance of Jesus is only understood from the perspective of his resurrection.

(*b*) *Jesus' path, followed by the disciples.*   In Mark the story of Jesus takes place essentially on two stages: in Galilee and Jerusalem. In Galilee, Jesus appears proclaiming and performing miracles (chapters 1–9); in Jerusalem, he suffers and dies (chapters 11–15). Chapter 10 is transitional. In Mark the teaching reported in this chapter (and the healing of a blind man, vv. 46–52), takes place on the way from Galilee to Jerusalem. This rough division into two geographical spheres has a deeper meaning.

Even at the historical level Galilee and Jerusalem were fundamentally different at the time of Jesus. It is true that Galilee was inhabited, like Jerusalem, by people belonging to the Jewish nation, holding themselves obligated to the same "law of Moses". But Jerusalem is their religious and national centre, whereas Galilee lies more on the periphery of Jewish territory – and that holds for Jewish consciousness too. Galilee is surrounded by gentile territory and penetrated by gentile immigration. Jews counted it as "Galilee of the Gentiles", whereas Jerusalem was the stronghold of orthodox Judaism, closed to all desacralizing gentile influences.

It is, therefore, no coincidence that Jesus begins his work in Galilee and there achieves his first successes, even if they did not last. The people in Galilee are quite open to Jesus' activity. Jesus is not closed to Gentiles, even though Mark does not record a clear gentile mission. In contrast to this, Jerusalem becomes the symbol of ultimate hardening against Jesus. There he dies. Of course, this sketch of Galilee and Jerusalem corresponds only to the broad outline of Mark. For there is in Galilee too, a failure to understand what Jesus is doing. The hardening in his native town Nazareth does not fall far short of that in Jerusalem. The first plot to kill him is hatched by his opponents in Galilee (3:6). And conversely there is messianic jubilation over Jesus at the entry into Jerusalem. In Jerusalem too, "all the multitude was astonished at his teaching" (11:18). But this does not affect where Mark has placed the theological accents.

From Galilee and through Galilee, Jesus' path leads to Jerusalem, to suffering and dying. That is the path that Jesus treads by God's plan, and on which he does his work. Jerusalem thus becomes the high point of his activity. In that he finally (humanly speaking) fails and dies there, his work achieves its proper fulfilment. Beneath the cross the Roman centurion, a Gentile, cries out: "Truly this man was a son of God" (15:39), and so provides the response of believing humanity evoked by Jesus' activity. But Jerusalem now becomes *the* place at which the previously hidden nature of Jesus is revealed in his resurrection.[18] From this point the gospel of Jesus Christ should be spread in all the world, and that through his *disciples,* who for a long time not understanding him (8:32–4; 9:32; 10:32) had followed on the path towards Jerusalem. In a more fundamental sense the disciples were called to follow Jesus in discipleship and according to 8:34f.; 10:39; 40–5, that meant into discipleship of a suffering Lord who was laying down his life. Only through the experiences of suffering discipleship would they understand Jesus in his true significance. In this sense Jesus' repeated instructions to his disciples on the road through Galilee become a schooling introducing some understanding of his whole work of salvation, though admittedly this does not during the earthly ministry of Jesus attain its goal. *Peter's confession* at 8:29 is a big exception to the disciples' lack of understanding. It represents in the evangelist's composition a boundary division between Jesus' activity in Galilee and the beginning of the passion in Jerusalem rather than a historically and psychologically comprehensible success of Jesus' activity, at least with respect to his disciples. One may perhaps see in Peter's confession a parallel to the confession of the gentile centurion at the cross. The first comes at the end of the Galilean period, the last at the end of the passion narrative. It also makes clear that the consistent failure of the disciples to understand during the period of the earthly Jesus was not without hope. Even before the centurion at the cross, representing the

119

whole gentile world, made his Christ-confession, the first of Jesus' disciples had to have uttered the confession of the believers or disciples from Israel. One thinks here of the Pauline principle: "To the Jews first, then also to the Gentiles" (Rom. 1:16; 2:9f.).

(c) *Easter.* Mark's Gospel closes with the Easter report, 16:1–8. This conclusion is unsatisfying in that it tells the story of the empty tomb, but does not provide any appearance of the Risen One.[19] Admittedly this judgement is conditioned by our knowledge of the other Gospels. On the other hand, this historically and psychologically unsatisfying conclusion seems to correspond to the evangelist's deeper intention.

For Mark the whole activity of Jesus can only be understood from the perspective of its end. And this end is the final, valid and unsurpassable revelation of God in Jesus. But that means that for Mark's outline it is not the passion and death of Jesus which constitute God's last word on the history of Jesus, but his resurrection. This, however, takes the resurrection of Jesus out of a simple historicizing perspective. Mark does see the resurrection of Jesus as a unique event, but he also sees it especially as the actual event of revelation, i.e. the disclosure of the life of Jesus for all mankind. It is only from the perspective of Easter that the earthly life of Jesus is understood at all. But that does not make it superseded or superfluous. The earthly Jesus has and retains for Mark an irreplaceable historical significance. This significance is none other than that of the Risen One.

This means, however, that the *gospel* is precisely the message of the Risen One, or – better – of the identity of the earthly Jesus with the Risen One. "Gospel" and "Easter" are admittedly not quite equated by Mark, for Easter still exists (16:1–8) as a "part" of the gospel. But they are so closely and indissolubly related to one another that Easter appears as what makes the gospel theologically possible. The gospel, which is now proclaimed in all the world, lives from Easter.

IV   *"Gospel" as Epiphany of Jesus*

The Gospel which Mark writes is thus not simply the sum total of the individual traditions he has collected. His Gospel is shaped from two points: from the tradition about the earthly Jesus and from the perspective of Easter. Easter here is not merely

information handed on, as it is rather testified to as early as 1 Cor.
15:3–5. That would make Mark's Gospel merely the result of two
different traditions. And we would have to ask why the Easter
story comes so incomparably short alongside the story of Jesus'
ministry, passion and death, whereas the later Gospels clearly had
access to further Easter traditions. For Mark, Easter is rather the
actual goal of his Gospel. Everything that the evangelist has been
able to report about Jesus, points to Easter. And conversely the
whole public ministry of the earthly Jesus is so shaped that Easter
is now reflected in the story of Jesus. The content of the Gospel is
Jesus, and admittedly paradoxically, the earthly Jesus as the Risen
One.

This is the key to Mark's secrecy motif. Mark intends it to
support the proclamation of Jesus who is already the Christ
during his ministry on earth, but as such before Easter is still
misjudged and misunderstood. As the risen Christ, however,
Jesus is now present and public in the proclaimed gospel. And
there the gospel of Jesus written down by Mark actually achieves
the meaning intended by the evangelist: In the Gospel, and that
means also in the proclaimed word of Jesus' ministry on earth, he
himself is present as the risen Christ. In this verbal form he is now
bringing salvation to the world through the proclamation received
in faith. The epiphany of Jesus which at the time of his earthly
activity could only be a hidden one, comes now in the public
proclamation of the gospel. Mark dared to fix this in a new way
and expanded form in writing, though entirely for the sake of
assisting the living proclamation of Jesus. Mark is primarily
concerned with the proclamation of the gospel.

Summary

Mark created with his Gospel a new literary genre. "Gospel" is
the binding proclamation of Jesus Christ. The individual traditions about the earthly Jesus that Mark has assembled find their
true meaning in the theme "gospel". The pieces of tradition
brought into his Gospel are in the first part above all miracle
stories, controversy and didactic dialogues and parables, and
in the second part (from 8:27) alongside a few teachings
and controversies and the parable of the wicked husbandmen
(12:1–12) above all, the apocalyptic discourses (chapter 13) and
the passion narrative. The individual traditions, in themselves

examples of the earthly ministry of Jesus, now seen from the point of view of the Gospel, form a connected story: the story of Jesus Christ, the Son of God in human form. Mark depicts in the Gospel the path of Jesus from his baptism by John to his death and his resurrection. This path is characterized by two main parts: public ministry in Galilee (and surroundings); suffering, dying and resurrection in Jerusalem. Jesus' path is not understood by his disciples, much less by his opponents and the people that accompany him. Mark gives his readers a clue to interpreting Jesus. In his earthly ministry he could not be known as who he really was because he himself only wanted to be understood as the Risen One, i.e. as God's Son made manifest through the resurrection. The Gospel composed from the perspective of Easter thus becomes the medium of the epiphany of God's son, Jesus, who is subsequently at work beyond his earthly history in the world of proclamation.

NOTES

1 W. Marxsen, *Introduction to the New Testament* (ET Oxford: Blackwell/ Philadephia: Fortress, 1968; German, 1964) dates it between 67 and 69.

2 K. H. Schelkle, *Das Neue Testament* (Kevelaer, 1966) 60 points out the credibility of the author's name: "Mark was not one of the twelve apostles and was not an important name in the New Testament. Would not a free composing legend have chosen someone more significant?"

3 R. Bultmann (1968) 347 designates Mark's purpose as "the union of the Hellenistic kerygma about Christ, whose essential content consists of the Christ myth as we learn of it in Paul (esp. Phil. 2:6ff.; Rom. 3:24) with the tradition of the story of Jesus". But Mark seems no more interested in a mythical narrative than Paul. His story of the earthly Jesus moves towards the passion and resurrection. Like Paul, Mark emphasizes the decisive importance of the passion and resurrection kerygma.

4 Cf. G. Friedrich, "Evangelion" in *TDNT* ii. 721–37, 735; K. H. Schelkle (n. 2) 39ff.; F. Mussner, " 'Evangelium' und 'Mitte des Evangeliums' ", in Festschrift K. Rahner I (1964).

5 This view is considered especially by W. Marxsen (1969) 11–135. Cf. also his *Introduction* (n. 1) 138; J. Schmid, *Comm.* 14f.; E. Schweizer, *Comm.* 23f., 30.

6 J. Schmid, *Comm.* 253; E. Schweizer, *Comm.* 288ff.

7 Cf. E. Lohse, *History of the Suffering and Death of Jesus Christ* (Philadelphia: Fortress, 1967) 14. (German, 1964).

8 Cf. E. Lohmeyer, *Comm.* 98f. The significance of the place names in the miracle stories for the study of early Christian history is established esp. by G. Schille, *Die urchristliche Wundertradition* (Stuttgart, 1967), though Schille over-hastily draws from his observations far-reaching consequences for the historical problem of the miracle tradition and the beginnings of the Church.

9 A good overview of the very different reconstruction of the pre-Marcan parable source is given by J. Gnilka, *Die Verstockung Israels. Isaias 6:9–10 in der Theologie der Synoptiker* (Munich, 1961) 53–7.

10 On the distinction between *Parabel* and *Gleichnis*, see e.g. J. Schmid, *Comm.* 88.

11 For the details, cf. J. Lambrecht (1967); R. Pesch (1968).

12 M. Kähler, *The so-called Historical Jesus and the Historic Biblical Christ* (Philadelphia: Fortress, 1964) 80. (German, 1896²)

13 See above all W. Marxsen (1969); J. Gnilka (n. 9); A. Suhl (1965); J. Schreiber (1967).

14 Cf. H. Conzelmann, *Outline of the Theology of the New Testament* (London: SCM/New York; Harper & Row, 1969) 98, 140ff. Bultmann, by contrast, still does without a presentation of the theology of the synoptic evangelists. In his view only the conceptual spelling out of the kerygma in Paul and John can properly be designated theology in the New Testament. Similarly, Schmid, *Comm.* 11, while allowing the "other gospels" particular theological tendencies, does not accept this in the same way of Mark. Schweizer by contrast (*Comm.* 380) speaks unambiguously of Mark's "theological achievement".

15 The kerygmatic intention of the evangelist is especially stressed by I. Hermann, *Comm.* (Düsseldorf, 1965 & 1967) (Die Welt der Bibel).

16 On the Gospels' understanding of history, cf. esp. W. Trilling. *Fragen zur Geschichtlichkeit Jesu* (Düsseldorf, 1966).

17 On Mark's "parable theory" cf. esp. J. Gnilka (n. 9) 23–86.

18 The further mention of Galilee in the Easter report 16:1–8 (v. 7), corresponding to the prophecy in 14:28, again shows Mark's disposition of his work between Galilee and Jerusalem. Lohmeyer (1936) and W. Marxsen (1969) 102–16 have proposed different solutions to the problem of the significance of the journey of the Risen One to Galilee. Lohmeyer finds the basis of Mark's account in there being "two early churches" alongside one another, a Galilean and a Jerusalem one. Marxsen interprets the event envisaged at 16:7 as referring to the parousia expected shortly in Galilee. This is, however, opposed by a passage like 13:10: "And the gospel must first be preached to all nations".

19 The Marcan ending (16:9–20) added later by someone else seeks to remedy this deficiency by a summarizing report drawn from parts of the later Gospels. On the problem of the Marcan ending cf. J. Schmid, *Comm.* 313–16.

.

4

The Christology of Mark *

A Study in Methodology

NORMAN PERRIN

Contemporary scholarly investigation of the Synoptic Gospels is dominated by redaction criticism (*Redaktionsgeschichte*),[1] the key to which is the ability to distinguish material used by the evangelist and the literary activity of the evangelist in editing, to determine the theology of the evangelist. The conclusion is that one can do this by observing his literary activity in redaction and composition. In the cases of Matthew and Luke[2] this has worked well, because we have a firm basis to work on as we observe their use of Mark and of the sayings source Q.[3] In the past several years we have had real breakthroughs in our understanding of the theology of these two evangelists, and redaction critics have established a firm basis for work in this area.[4] But in the case of the Gospel of Mark we have had no such basis for our work, and as yet we have had no such breakthrough in connection with the theology of the second evangelist (Mark).

The problem in connection with Mark is one of method. Redaction criticism in this case is possible only to a limited extent, and it needs to be supplemented by other critical methods. As yet there is no scholarly consensus with regard to what particular blend of methods should be used in a historical investigation of the Gospel of Mark and the theology of the second evangelist. It

---

* This slightly revised version of "The Christology of Mark. A Study in Methodology" (*JR* 51 [1971] 173–87) was published in M. Sabbe (ed.), *L'Évangile selon Marc. Tradition et Rédaction* (Leuven: University Press, 1974) 471–85.

is the purpose of this chapter to suggest such a blend and then to attempt to demonstrate the possibility inherent in the particular approach suggested by carrying out a sample investigation of an aspect of the theology of the evangelist, namely his Christology.

One aspect of our approach to the Gospel of Mark must be that of redaction criticism itself. Despite the difficulties inherent in the fact that we have none of Mark's sources, we must make a serious attempt to separate tradition from redaction and to determine the literary activity of the evangelist. The main thrust of contemporary work on Mark is along these lines, and there are several ways of attempting to isolate Marcan redaction. One is to use the literary factors of vocabulary and style. Examples of this approach would include the work of Eduard Schweizer and his pupil, Ulrich Luz,[5] or of Erich Grässer or Johannes Schreiber.[6] Another way is to pay careful attention to particular Marcan concerns, such as the messianic secret, the geographical location Galilee (which in Mark has a more-than-geographical reference) or the use of Son of Man. A recent example of this approach is Étienne Trocmé (1975) with its chapters "The Aversions displayed by the Evangelist" and "The Causes defended by Mark". A third way is to pay careful attention to Marcan compositional techniques: the use of intercalation, the fondness for three-fold units, the practice of using related stories as parentheses to enclose a major unit, and so on. Ernst Lohmeyer in Germany and R. H. Lightfoot in England pioneered this approach during the 1930s, and it still remains a feature of the work of English scholars.[7] A fourth way is to attempt to isolate definite units of pre-Marcan tradition and then to observe Mark's use of these units. L. E. Keck did this with a cycle of miracle stories and its introduction,[8] and I attempted it with the Son of Man Christology (1967–8). In these and still other ways scholars attempt to identify Marcan redaction of tradition and to proceed along the currently well-established lines of *Redaktionsgeschichte*. But a major fact about Mark's Gospel is that it is a new creation – there was nothing like it before in early Christian literary history – and this leads to a second line of approach to the Gospel: the search for a model.

Prior to the writing of Mark there was no extended narrative Gospel. There were connected units of tradition – a passion narrative, cycles of miracle stories, collections of sayings, collections of parables, an apocalyptic discourse, perhaps short collections of stories with a geographical centre such as Capernaum or the Sea of Galilee, and so on – but no connected narrative beginning with John the Baptist and ending with the passion and/or resurrection (depending upon one's views of the current ending of the Gospel at 16:8). So Mark was creating a new literary genre, and the question is: "What does the literary form he creates tell us about his purpose in writing?" Or, to put it another way, "What literary model is he following?" In the days when the Gospel of Mark was regarded as fundamentally a life of Jesus or a chronicle of the ministry of Jesus, this question did not arise, but with the widespread acceptance of the fact that the Gospel is neither a life nor a chronicle it does arise, and today it is being strenuously debated. The most widely accepted view is that Mark's Gospel is "a passion narrative with an extended introduction" (Martin Kähler), and many contemporary interpretations of the Gospel proceed from this premise. This view does justice to Mark's theology of the cross, but it seems not to do justice to his eschatology. Another view being pressed at the moment is that Mark's Gospel is fundamentally an aretalogy, having grown out of a cycle of stories presenting Jesus as a divine man.[9] In conscious opposition to this latter view, Howard Kee is arguing that Mark is to be understood in apocalyptic terms,[10] a view which I would support. This debate is only just getting underway, but it clearly is important. Our interpretation of Mark will depend very much upon any decision we make as to the model he is following – as to his purpose in writing as this is revealed in the literary form he is creating or imitating.

A consideration of the literary form of the Gospel of Mark leads to a third aspect of our approach to the work: an approach via the insights of general literary criticism. The Gospel of Mark, is after all, a literary text, and it should therefore be interpreted according to the canons of literary criticism. We should observe such things as the movement of the "plot", the roles of the protagonists – especially perhaps Peter and the disciples – the literary structure of the total work, and so on. The evangelist Mark may not be an author in the conscious and sophisticated sense of a William Shakespeare, Henry Fielding or James Joyce, but he is an author, he has written a literary work, and he must be treated from the standpoint of literary criticism.

It is my contention that each of these three avenues of approach to the evangelist Mark and his Gospel must be explored, and the three approaches must be held in tension with one another. No one of them is the key to the whole, but together they offer us the opportunity to come close to Mark and his theology as redaction criticism has brought us to Matthew and Luke and their theologies.[11] As a *Probe*, I turn to the question of the Christology of Mark.

A consideration of the Christology of Mark can begin with a literary point: the importance to the Gospel of 14:53–71, the trial before the Sanhedrin and the denial by Peter. Here many of the themes which play a major role in the Gospel as a whole, reach a climax. In v. 62, the messianic secret is unveiled, and in Peter's denial both the theme of the disciples' "hardness of heart" and Peter's role as leader of the disciples reach a tragic climax which Aristotle would have recognized. From a literary standpoint these scenes are climactic of what has gone before and preparatory of what is to come after – the account of the crucifixion.

We can reinforce the importance of these scenes to Mark by observing the amount of Marcan literary activity in them. The trial scene (vv. 55–65) is intercalated between references to Peter in the *aulē* (vv. 53–4), a Marcan composition technique, and itself bears strong evidence of Marcan vocabulary and style.[12]

From the standpoint of Christology, the trial scene offers an important point. In v. 61, Jesus is addressed as Christ and Son of God: in the verse he accepts these designations and immediately interprets them by means of a use of Son of Man: "Are you the Christ, the Son of the Blessed?" (61). And Jesus said, "I am; and you will see the Son of Man sitting at the right hand of Power, and coming with the clouds of heaven" (62).

A very similar thing happens at Caesarea Philippi. Now the Caesarea Philippi pericope (Mark 8:27–9:1) is also very important from the standpoint of a literary critical approach to the Gospel of Mark. As lives of Jesus without number testify, it is the watershed of Mark's literary composition. Furthermore, it also shows strong evidence of Marcan literary activity.[13] At Caesarea Philippi, Jesus is confessed as the Christ. He implicitly accepts this confession (not explicitly as in 14:62 because according to Mark's literary device it is not yet time for the messianic secret to be unveiled) and immediately goes on to interpret the designation in terms of a use of Son of Man: Peter answered, "You are the Christ" (29). And he began to teach them that the Son of Man must suffer (31). At two key points in his literary composition, therefore, Mark has

Jesus interpret and give content to the titles Christ and Son of God by using Son of Man.

Thus far, we have approached the Christology of Mark by considering literary points – the role of the trial and denial and of the Caesarea Philippi pericope in the plot of the Gospel as a whole – and reinforcing those by considering the redaction critical point of Marcan literary activity in those pericopes. In other words, we have used the third and the first of the approaches advocated at the beginning of this chapter. Now we will turn to the second: a consideration of the model Mark might be following and of what this will tell us of his purpose in writing. In this regard we have to admit at once that the discussion has not yet reached the point of a consensus as to the model for the Gospel as a whole, and therefore of an agreement as to Mark's overall purpose in writing. But although we have no agreed model for the Gospel as a whole, scholarship does recognize models – and hence purposes – for certain aspects or parts of it. In particular it would be agreed that Mark inherits and uses the model of the synoptic tradition itself. From its earliest days the Palestinian church used the form of sayings of Jesus and stories about him in preaching, in paraenesis, in controversy and apologetic. A Son of Man saying exhorting to penitence, wisdom-type teaching to instruct in the essential preparation for the coming, controversies between the early believers and their Jewish brethren in the form of stories about Jesus and Pharisees, apologetic for the cross in the form of Jesus showing its divine necessity from the Scriptures, all this and more is Mark's heritage and most immediate model. So we can say with confidence that the Gospel of Mark is in part *didactic narrative*. The form is a narrative of the ministry of Jesus, but the concerns are those of Mark and his church, and the purpose is directly to exhort, instruct and inform Mark's readers.

Thus far, we can go by general agreement, but we can go one step farther because there would also be general agreement that a major aspect of the Marcan purpose is christological; he is concerned with correcting a false Christology prevalent in his church and to teach both a true Christology and its consequences for Christian discipleship. I have discussed this matter at some length elsewhere,[14] and therefore I may here simply assert the fact that Mark is concerned with correcting a false Christology, the point I argued earlier, and go on to make some further points in more detail.

An analysis of the literary structure of the Gospel reveals the importance of the three passion prediction units (8:31–9:1; 9:30–7; 10:32–45). Each has exactly the same structure (prediction-misunderstanding-teaching), and each is a form of an interpretation of Peter's confession. The fact that there are three of them is certainly due to Mark's concern for three-fold repetition. As has often been noted they are part of the basic structure of the section of the Gospel (8:27–10:45)) in which Mark presents his *theologia crucis* (theology of the cross). In these interpretations of Peter's confession, Mark is presenting his own passion-oriented Christology, using Son of Man, and then drawing out its consequences for Christian discipleship: in the first, the necessary preparedness Jesus exhibited; in the second, the necessity of servanthood; in the third, the climactic presentation of servanthood culminating in the ransom saying. At no point in the Gospel, except for the discourse in chapter 13, is Mark so clearly addressing and exhorting his own readers. The dynamic use of the form of sayings and stories of Jesus in the synoptic tradition has here become a literary convention, a convention which Mark establishes, develops and adheres to strictly. The disciples set the stage by asking the questions or voicing the tendencies or opinions (and these are the questions, tendencies and opinions present in Mark's church) and Jesus exhorts and teaches. So far as Christology is concerned, Peter confesses Jesus as the Christ but then exhibits a false understanding of the meaning of that confession, in all of which he is representing Mark's church. The true Christology is then expressed by Jesus using Son of Man, and, adhering to the convention, Son of Man is never found in Mark except on the lips of Jesus.[15] There is one possible exception to this, Mark 2:10. The abrupt change of subject and the tautologous repetition of the command to the paralytic indicate that the Son of Man saying may be an aside addressed by the evangelist to his readers. See n. 21 below. So a consideration of a possible model for an aspect of Mark's Gospel and of an aspect of his overall purpose leads us to a point already recognized: Mark uses Son of Man to correct and give content to a christological confession of Jesus as the Christ.

We can reach a similar point with regard to Son of God if we concentrate upon the first of our recommended approaches to the Gospel, the separation of redaction from tradition and the careful observation of the use made of tradition. Since Karl Ludwig

Schmidt's epoch-making investigation (1919), it has been generally recognized that Mark 3:7–12 is a Marcan *Sammelbericht* (redactional summary) and hence, more recently, that it, together with other summaries, is of great importance to a redaction critical investigation of Mark.[16] Mark 3:7–12 was further studied by Leander E. Keck,[17] who showed that it introduces a cycle of miracle stories in which Jesus is portrayed as a hellenistic *theios anēr* (3:7–12; 4:35–5:43; 6:31–52; 6:53–6) and that Mark is concerned with playing down and correcting this understanding of Christology, as can be seen both from his redaction of the introduction and from his redaction of the cycle of stories themselves (especially the introduction of the secrecy motif). The outlook of the original tradition was that of Jesus as a *theios anēr*, and Mark's own understanding of the Son of God category is sufficiently different from these stories to enable us to infer that he took them into his Gospel partly because they allowed him to present the divine sonship during Jesus' lifetime and partly because he wanted "to check and counterbalance this way of understanding Jesus' life and work".[18] Thus, on the basis of a redaction critical investigation, Keck reached a conclusion similar to that which we have reached on other grounds.

I am moving toward the point of claiming that the Christology of Mark may best be approached by assuming that he uses "Christ" and "Son of God" to establish rapport with his readers and then deliberately reinterprets and gives conceptual content to these titles by a use of "Son of Man", a designation which is not, properly speaking, a christological title but which to all intents and purposes becomes one as Mark uses it. Let me now approach this matter from the viewpoint of observing the occurrence of these three titles in Mark, paying special attention to their place in the literary structure of the Gospel and to their relation with one another.

"Christ" is to be found in Mark at 1:1; 8:29; 9:41; 12:35; 13:21; 14:61; 15:32. From the viewpoint of literary structure three of these seven occurrences are comparatively unimportant: 9:41 with its paraenetic use of "you are Christ's"; 13:21, a reference to false Christs in the apocalyptic discourse;[19] and 15:32, the mocking at the cross. A fourth, 12:35 where Christ is not the Son of David, is more difficult. It may that Mark is here correcting a Son of David Christology as elsewhere he corrects Christologies associated with Christ and Son of God, but I must admit that as yet I have no firm opinion with regard to the function of the Son of David pericope in the Gospel of Mark. But the remaining three are all at key points in the Gospel: 1:1 is the superscription defining the whole work as "the gospel of Jesus Christ"; 8:29 is the confession at Caesarea Philippi; and 14:61 is the high priest's question at the trial. In 1:1 the title is associated with Son of God in some textual traditions; in 8:29 and 14:61 it is immediately interpreted by a use of Son of Man.

In connection with my contention that Mark is concerned with correcting a false Christology prevalent in the Church of his day, one should note how many of these references are to a false use of "Christ"; 8:29 (an immediate correction by a use of Son of Man); 13:21 (the false Christs); 14:61 (an immediate reinterpretation using Son of Man); 15:32 (the mocking). Although Mark clearly intends the title to represent the full and proper Christian confession, especially in the central Caesarea Philippi pericope, in his Gospel there is no correct human christological confession of Jesus until we come to the centurion in 15:39. The centurion uses Son of God which is the most important title so far as Mark is concerned as he addresses his readers, as we shall see immediately below. Although it is not the one by means of which he expresses his own Christology. He could not use it for that purpose because it could never have been made to bear the range of meaning he intended to fuse into his own Christology. The correct confession by the centurion is possible because by 15:39 the literary process of correcting the Christology held by Mark's readers is complete, having been completed by Jesus' response to the high priest's question at the trial.

"Son of God" (or its equivalent) is to be found in Mark six or seven times, always at places which are important to the Gospel as a whole. According to some textual traditions it is part of the superscriptions in 1:1.[20] Then it occurs at each of the places in the Gospel where cosmic phenomena (heavens opening, or the like) indicate a revelatory moment according to the conventions of the first century C.E.: 1:11, the baptism; 9:7, the transfiguration. Then it occurs twice on the lips of demons, creatures whose supernatural origin would indicate supernatural knowledge in the world in which Mark lived and for which he wrote: 3:11 (in a redactional summary); 5:7. Finally it is linked with "Christ" in the high priest's question, 14:61, and in 15:39 it is the confession of the centurion in what is clearly for Mark a climactic moment.

132

It can be seen that neither "Christ" nor "Son of God" is especially frequent in Mark, but that the former is found at key moments in the narrative and that every occurrence of the latter is significant. "Son of Man" occurs much more frequently than either, a total of fourteen times: 2:10; 2:28; 8:31; 8:38; 9:9; 9:12; 9:31; 10:33; 10:45; 13:26; 14:21 (twice); 14:41; 14:62. The sheer frequency of occurrence of this title indicates its importance for Mark; but at the same time it presents problems to the interpreter for the fact is that the usage does not immediately appear to be homogeneous. A comparatively crude division is that into three: present authority, 2:10; 2:28; apocalyptic 8:38; 13:26; 14:62; suffering, 9:12; 10:45; 14:21 (twice); 14:41; 8:31; 9:31; 10:33. But that leaves one unaccounted for, 9:9, and the third group is not really a group at all. To say the very least, the predictions, 8:31; 9:31; 10:33, have to be separated from the rest as having an internal cohesiveness of their own. At the same time it is possible to account for each occurrence in terms of inherited tradition, Marcan development of that tradition, and creation of new tradition, and by doing this to reach the heart of the Christology of Mark. To this task we now turn.

We will begin with 9:9, the redactional command to secrecy "until the Son of Man be risen from the dead". It would be generally acknowledged that this is Marcan redaction and, equally, that it is important to an understanding of the secret and of the Marcan purpose altogether. In the Gospel of Mark the transfiguration is proleptic of the parousia, and this saying directs Mark's readers to the post-resurrection pre-parousia situation in which they stand and to which Mark is directing the teaching he puts on the lips of Jesus. That the saying uses Son of Man is due in part to the fact that it is Mark's own designation of Jesus and also probably in part to the proximity of the predictions of the passion and resurrection. In any case, the saying is readily explicable and understandable as a Marcan hint to his readers as to his own understanding of his purpose in writing.

Let us take next the two references to the Son of Man's authority on earth in the present of the ministry of Jesus, "the Son of Man has authority on earth to forgive sins" (2:10), and "the Son of Man is Lord even of the Sabbath" (2:28). I have argued elsewhere that these represent a particularly Marcan development of a tendency at work in the synoptic traditions,[21] and I would repeat them here. Only in Mark and in dependence on Mark is *exousia* used of the earthly ministry of Jesus in the Synoptic Gospels, and from a literary standpoint these two references to the Son of Man stand dramatically in the section of the Gospel in which the authority of Jesus in word and deed is being thematically presented (1:16–3:6). There are no further references to the Son of Man until it begins to play its dominant role in the central interpretative section of the Gospel (8:27–10:45). The movement toward the view of Jesus' earthly ministry as already exhibiting his full authority is to be found in the synoptic tradition, for example, Matt. 8:9 par., but it is Mark who first takes the step of using *exousia* of that earthly ministry and linking it with Son of Man. Moreover, there is real literary artistry in the two uses of Son of Man in the first major section of the Gospel which are followed by two uses of Son of God in the second (3:11 and 5:7 in the section 3:7–6:6a). The two are thereby established as equivalent designations for Jesus in his full authority, and the way is prepared for the interpretation of the latter in terms of the former which is a fundamental part of Mark's christological concern. The use of Son of Man in 2:10 and 2:28 therefore fits smoothly into Mark's overall concern.

The three uses of Son of Man in an apocalyptic context in Mark, 8:38; 13:26; 14:62, present no problems. I have discussed them all at some length elsewhere,[22] and may simply reiterate the conclusion that 8:38 is a Marcan redaction of a "sentence of holy law" (Käsemann) like that now found in Luke 12:8f. par. 13:26 is an early Christian apocalyptic promise, and 14:62 a product of early Christian midrash-pesher use of the Old Testament.[23] What we have here is the use by Mark of early Christian tradition: 8:38 juxtaposes with 8:31 in the Caesarea Philippi pericope, and so provides the basis for the full development of Mark's Son of Man Christology in 8:27–10:45, a point to which we shall be returning; 13:26 sounds a keynote in the apocalyptic discourse by means of which Mark seeks to prepare his readers directly for the requirements of their pre-parousia situation; and 14:62 is the climactic element in Mark's christological statement, fittingly so since it comes in the trial scene which is a climax of Mark's literary activity, as I argued above. For his own purposes Mark is here mining and using elements from the early and well-established apocalyptic Son of Man Christology of the Church.

The real problems arise in connection with the remaining sayings: 9:12b; 10:45; 14:21, 41; and the predictions 8:31; 9:31;

10:33–4. But the problems here lie in the area of determining the element of Marcan literary activity in the composition of these sayings; their use in the overall literary structure of the Gospel fits the pattern of the Marcan use of Son of Man which I would claim is beginning to emerge.

1.   9:12b, where the Son of Man *polla pathē kai exoudenēthē* ("must suffer many things, and be set at nought") shatters the tight-knit structure of 9:9–13 so obviously that many commentators have argued that it is a post-Marcan gloss that crept early into the text of the Gospel, and I can only agree. It can, and indeed must, be ignored so far as the use of Son of Man by Mark is concerned.

2.   10:45 is a saying with a complex history. In the first place Mark probably inherited it in a eucharistic setting, for the parallel section in Luke (22:24–7) does have such a setting, and it is clear that Mark has extensively rearranged his traditional material, especially in the carefully constructed central section of his Gospel, 8:22–10:52. Further, Lohse has argued convincingly that both Mark 10:45 and the "I am among you as one who serves" of Luke 22:27 have independent histories in the tradition of the Church, the former in a more semitic and the latter in a more hellenistic area.[24] If that is the case then the question is which is the more original, the form using Son of Man or that using the first person singular. In general it can be shown that Luke 22:24–7 with its concern for church order is somewhat later than Mark 10:42–5,[25] and in any case where we have tradition in both a more semitic and a more hellenistic form the probability is that the former is earlier than the latter, since the Church did, in fact, begin as a sect within Palestinian Judaism and move into the hellenistic world by means of a hellenistic Jewish-Christian mission. So the balance of probability is that the Son of Man is the more original and that the I-saying was formed from it. In that case the original saying was in some form as, "The Son of Man came not to be served but to serve" and as such stands close to the saying, "The Son of Man came to seek and to save the lost" (Luke 19:10, cf. Matt. 19:11). Is it perhaps possible that both these sayings have a common point of origin in a moment of solemn reflection at a very early Christian Eucharist? Be that as it may, the verbal parallel with Luke 22:27 and the sense parallel with Luke 19:10 indicate that at one time Mark 10:45a existed as a

complete saying and that the ransom clause was added as a gloss.[26] This glossing certainly took place in the semitic language area of the tradition of the Church and very probably in a eucharistic setting. Mark 10:45b has a strongly semitic cast, and it and the eucharistic word (Mark 14:24) are the only allusions to Isa. 53 that can be definitely located in the semitic language area of the tradition of the Church. It is very probable, therefore, that they have a common original setting.

I have discussed the origin of Mark 10:45 at some length because of its intrinsic interest. But for our immediate purpose the origin of the saying is less important than the use to which Mark puts it, and that is clear enough. He uses it to climax the three-fold teaching on discipleship in the passion prediction units and in this way to link that teaching decisively to the Son of Man Christology which for him is its essential basis.

3.   In 14:21, 41 we have an apologetic use of Son of Man with the verb *paradidonai* whereby the passion of Jesus is summarized by the verb, which means "to betray", "deliver up", and the stress is on the divine necessity for the passion. The link between Son of Man and the verb *paradidonai* in connection with the passion is pre-Marcan,[27] and in that sense Mark 14:21, 41 are traditional, whatever the actual history of the Gethsemane material may be in the synoptic tradition and in Mark's Gospel. As they stand, these Son of Man sayings are Marcan echoes of traditional early Christian passion apologetic. All passion narratives in the New Testament are saturated with such notes, including Mark's.

4.   The real problem with regard to Marcan composition is presented by the predictions of the passion and resurrection, 8:31; 9:31; 10:33–4. The three most recent discussions of this matter, all from an avowedly redaction-critical standpoint, show a steady progression toward recognition of Marcan literary activity: H. E. Tödt thought all three were traditional; Ferdinand Hahn that the first and second were, the third being Marcan; and Georg Strecker that the first was, the second and third being Marcan.[28] It is my personal conviction that all three have been composed by Mark, who has mined their constituent parts from the *(para)didonai* tradition and the passion apologetic of earliest Christianity.[29] Be that as it may, the use of the predictions by Mark is not in dispute. He uses them to develop the passion-oriented element of his own Christology and to form the basis for the consequent teaching on

the essential nature of discipleship which follows each of them in the stereotyped pattern of the three passion-prediction units (8:36–9:1; 9:30–7; 10:32–45).

The position with regard to the Son of Man Christology in the tradition prior to Mark and the Marcan use of that tradition now becomes clear. Prior to Mark there are three uses of Son of Man in the tradition: use in an apocalyptic context, use in reflection upon the significance of the ministry of Jesus, probably in a eucharistic setting, and use with *(para)didonai* in apologetic for the passion. From these beginnings Mark develops the three-fold emphasis which is characteristic of his Gospel – apocalyptic, authority in the present, suffering – and all the references to Son of Man in the Gospel become explicable on the basis of this hypothesis of inherited tradition and Marcan development of it. Beyond this, an approach to the Gospel along the three avenues of redaction criticism, the question of model or purpose, and general literary criticism shows that Mark is using Son of Man to express his own Christology; that he uses Christ and Son of God to estabish rapport with his readers, and Son of Man to interpret and give content to those titles. It is not the claim of this chapter that these conclusions are new. On the contrary, they would generally be accepted by the world of scholarship, but it is the claim of the chapter that the fact that they can be reached by the approach suggested validates that approach and suggests a similar approach to other aspects of the Marcan theology and purpose.

NOTES

1 J. Rohde, *Rediscovering the Teaching of the Evangelists*, ET D. M. Barton (London/Philadelphia, 1969); N. Perrin (1970).

2 I am using the names Matthew, Luke and Mark to designate both the Gospel and evangelist concerned, adding further definition only where necessary to avoid confusion or for emphasis. This usage is for convenience only and is not intended to make any statement about the traditional authorship of the Gospels.

3 Redaction critics uniformly accept the two-source hypothesis of the Synoptic Gospels and regard the successful results of their work as an added substantiation of it.

4 Both J. Rohde and N. Perrin review this work in the books mentioned in n. 1 above. Unfortunately there is as yet no full-scale presentation in English of the

theology of Matthew and Luke as we now understand it in the light of the work of the redaction critics. Tragically, H. Conzelmann, the leading redaction critic to work on Luke and the author of the breakthrough in connection with his Gospel, has treated the matter most inadequately in his recently published *Outline of the Theology of the New Testament*, ET J. Bowden (London/New York, 1969).

5 E. Schweizer (1962); and U. Luz, in Tuckett (1983).

6 E. Grässer (1969–70); J. Schreiber (1961 and 1967).

7 E. Lohmeyer (1937); R. H. Lightfoot (1934, 1937 and 1950). Two recent works by English scholars embodying this approach are: T. A. Burkill (1963); and D. E. Nineham (1968).

8 L. E. Keck (1965).

9 Morton Smith (1971); cf. M. Hadas and M. Smith, *Heroes and Gods: Spiritual Biographies in Antiquity* (New York, 1965).

10 H. C. Kee (1973); cf. *Jesus in History* (New York, 1970) 104–47.

11 It goes without saying that considerations of model/purpose and of literary criticism will be helpful in the case of Matthew and Luke also. But their model is Mark, so even here their redaction of Mark will be the indispensable key.

12 John Donahue, S.J. (1973) has presented the following evidence of Marcan literary activity in the narrative: (1) the use of the impersonal third person plural in introductory sentences with Jesus as the object of a verb in the same context; *kai* ("and") parataxis; compound of *erchomai* ("I come"); the historic present; use of *pas* ("all") or *holos* ("whole") to universalize a scene (twenty instances of this in Mark): (2) sentence with the order *kai* ("and")-participle-subject; tautologous repetition of key words or phrases as in vv. 56, 59 (forty-seven instances of this in Mark) as "a Marcan insertion technique" (Donahue's own discovery); and more.

13 The parallelism between 8:31ff.; 9:31ff.; 10:32ff. (passion prediction-misunderstanding-teaching) shows that everything in the pericope after v. 31 is Marcan. Moreover the passion prediction itself is Marcan composition (as I shall argue later in this paper), and the teaching in vv. 8:34–9:1 has been heavily edited and in part actually composed by Mark (N. Perrin, 1970: 44–51).

14 (1970) 53–6. Cf. T. J. Weeden in this volume.

15 This is important in the context of the fact that nowhere in the Gospels is Son of Man found except on the lips of Jesus (for one possible exception, see n. 21 below); a fact from which it is often argued that Jesus did use the term as a self-designation, and the tradition has remained true to him in this regard. The fact does, however, admit of an alternative explanation, admittedly more complex. In the first place Son of Man is not a christological title. It is rather a designation for Jesus in his apocalyptic authority, derived from Dan. 7 and then used in the paradox of the necessity for his passion ("The Son of Man goes as it is written of him . . . is betrayed" [Mark 14:21]). It is never used confessionally and it tended not to survive the movement of the Church into the Greek-speaking world (in the formula-like 1 Thess. 1:10, Jesus is expected

from heaven as Son of God, not Son of Man. In the hellenized version of Mark 10:45 found in 1 Tim. 2:5, it is not the Son of Man but "the man Christ Jesus" who gave himself as a ransom for all). In the synoptic tradition before Mark, all the sayings are in the form of words of Jesus, including the Son of Man sayings. Mark develops the use of Son of Man very extensively, as we shall argue below, but he has the convention of restricting it, the true Christology, to the lips of Jesus. Luke never uses the expression except in dependence upon a source, and the additional uses by Matthew and John are not extensive enough to break the conventions of the synoptic tradition and of Mark, especially in view of the total absence of any confessional use of Son of Man as a christological title. So it is possible to account for the evidence in the Gospels without recourse to the hypothesis that Jesus used the expression as a self-designation in a way more meaningful than in an idiomatic expression such as "the Son of Man came eating and drinking", where it seems to be simply a circumlocution whereby the speaker refers to himself (N. Perrin, "The Son of Man in the Synoptic Tradition", *Biblical Research* 13 [1968] esp. 12).

16 A student of mine investigated the summaries from the viewpoint of Mark's Christology: V. Robbins, *The Christology of Mark* (Ph.D. diss., University of Chicago Divinity School, 1969).

17 L. E. Keck (1965); cf. V. Robbins, 77–103, where Keck's insights are taken up and developed further.

18 L. E. Keck (1965) 358; Paul Achtemeier (1970 and 1972). He argues for a rather different analysis of the pre-Marcan material, seeing two cycles of stories (catenae), as does Keck, but claiming that they are symmetrical, with each including a sea miracle, three healings, and a feeding. Catena I is Mark 4:35–5:43; 6:34–44, 53; and Catena II is Mark 6:45–51; 8:22–6; 7:24b–30, 33–7; 8:1–10. I find myself in agreement with many of Achtemeier's observations, but I have three reservations about his division. In the first place such symmetry is itself suspicious. Then, second, the second group of three healings (the blind man at Bethsaida, the Syrophoenician woman, and the deaf-mute, 8:22–6; 7:24b–30; 7:32–7) is not homogeneous. The first and third exhibit a common concern for healing techniques, but the second has the same aura of healing by fiat that is characteristic of Achtemeier's Catena I (the Gerasene demoniac, the women with the haemorrhage, Jairus' daughter, 5:1–20; 5:25–34; 5:21–3; 35–43). Last, Keck's argument about the relationship between a pre-Marcan version of 3:7–12 and its relationship with the subsequent cycle of stories is an important factor. Publication of the remaining parts of Achtemeier's study may change the situation, but at the moment I am personally inclined to stay with Keck's analysis and conclusion, except that I would add the Syrophoenician woman to his cycle of miracle stories originally presenting Jesus as a *theios anēr* and now being reinterpreted by Mark.

19 Even if this reference should be of real significance for an understanding of the historical occasion for the writing of Mark, it is not a significant reference in terms of the Marcan Christology. That the reference is of real significance for

the historical understanding of Mark has been strongly argued by Werner H. Kelber (1974).

20 In view of the importance of this title in Mark, one is tempted to say that if it was not part of the original superscription it should have been, and the scribe who first added it was Marcan in purpose if not in name!

21 See Perrin, 1967–8. The point that 2:10 is Marcan can now be strengthened by two further observations. The first of these is the anacoluthon which makes the Son of Man reference read very like a comment by the evangelist addressing his readers, rather as he does in 13:14. Prof. J. A. Fitzmyer suggested to me verbally that this may be one instance where Son of Man is not on the lips of Jesus in the Gospel. The second is that the tautological repetition of the command to the paralytic may indicate that we have here an example of the Marcan insertion technique identified by J. Donahue (n. 12 above).

22 N. Perrin, *Rediscovering the Teaching of Jesus* (London/New York, 1967) 185–91, 173–85.

23 This last conclusion receives strong support in Matthew Black on such a use of the Old Testament by early Christians in the development of Kyrios, Son of God, and Son of Man Christologies. *NTS* 18 (1971) 1–14.

24 E. Lohse, *Märtyrer und Gottesknecht*, 1955, 185–6.

25 F. H. Borsch, *The Christian and Gnostic Son of Man* (London/Naperville, Ill., 1970) 23–6, with references to earlier literature.

26 H. E. Tödt, *The Son of Man in the Synoptic Tradition*. ET D. M. Barton (London/Philadelphia, 1965) 202–11. The ransom clause actually comes from a well-defined tradition in the early Church in which (*para*)*didonai* is used of the passion. I have isolated and discussed that tradition in "The use of (*para*)*didonai* in Connection with the Passion of Jesus in the New Testament", in E. Lohse (ed.), *Der Ruf Jesu und die Antwort der Gemeinde* (Göttingen, 1970).

27 For the justification of this and subsequent statements about the use of (*para*)*didonai* in the tradition, see the article mentioned in n. 26 above.

28 H. E. Tödt, 152–221; F. Hahn, *The Titles of Jesus in Christology* (London, 1969) 37–42; G. Strecker (1968).

29 (1) The verbal parallelism of the last part of the predictions indicates a common origin; (2) there is no known *Sitz im Leben* for them as units apart from their present *Sitz in Evangelium des Markus* (setting in the Gospel of Mark) and (3) there is evidence for the prior existence of their separate parts in the tradition of the Church.

5

The Literary Structure of the Controversy Stories in Mark 2:1–3:6*

JOANNA DEWEY

It has long been agreed that the five controversy stories of Mark 2:1–3:6 – the healing of the paralytic, the eating with tax-collectors and sinners, the question about fasting, plucking grain on the Sabbath, and the man with the withered hand – constitute a collection of conflict stories compiled either by Mark or by some earlier collector.[1] These five stories have not merely been collected in one place because of similarities in form and content but have been constructed in such a way as to form a single literary unit with a tight and well-worked out concentric or chiastic structure: A, B, C, B', A' (Mark 2:1–12, 13–17, 18–22, 23–8; 3:1–6). If these pericopes do indeed constitute a coherent *literary* unit, recognized by Mark as such, then a consideration of the literary structure will aid in understanding the individual elements within the collection and its meaning and place in the over-all structure of the Gospel of Mark. First, the chiastic structure of the five stories will be established using formal, linguistic, and content criteria. Then the question of whether the structure is Marcan or pre-Marcan will be considered.

* First published in *JBL* 92 (1973) 394–401.

I

To begin with, the author of the Gospel intended 2:1–3:6 to be viewed as a literary unit or sub-unit within his Gospel. He set the section into a frame. The first chapter of Mark ends with Jesus healing the leper, and the leper spreading the news "so that Jesus could no longer openly enter a town, but was out in the country; and people came to him from every quarter" (1:45b). Chapter 2 opens with a complete break: "And when he returned to Capernaum" (2:1). The first thing Mark has Jesus do, after not being able openly to enter a city, is to enter a city. But Mark 3:7 picks up again right where 1:45 left off: "Jesus withdrew with his disciples to the sea, and a great multitude from Galilee followed; also from Judea and Jerusalem and Idumea, and from beyond the Jordan and from about Tyre and Sidon, a great multitude, hearing all that he did, came to him" (3:7–8). Jesus once again is outside the cities, and people are coming to him from every quarter; the places are now specifically named. The evangelist has blocked off the controversy section by means of a frame.

The five pericopae appear to be combined in a chiastic pattern according to content: A, the healing of the paralytic, contains a healing of the resurrection type; B, the eating with tax-collectors and sinners, concerns eating; C, the question about fasting, fasting; B', plucking grain on the Sabbath, eating again; and A', the man with the withered hand, contains another miracle of the resurrection type. The chiastic pattern is also to be seen in details of form and language.

The first and fifth stories, A and A', are constructed along parallel lines. They begin with virtually identical introductions: A: *kai eiselthōn palin eis*, "and having entered again into" (2:1) and A': *kai eisēlthen palin eis*, "and he entered again into" (3:1). Both occur indoors: in one case a house, in the other a synagogue.

Both stories have the same form: a controversy apophthegm imbedded into a healing miracle.[2] This is a mixed form and relatively uncommon.[3] The miracles are both of the resurrection type, not exorcisms; the paralytic and the withered hand are each restored. The verb *egeirō* is used three times in the story of the paralytic, and once in the parallel story of the withered hand in the rather odd expression *egeire eis to meson*, "get up to the middle" (3:3), which serves to bring the verb into the story.

142

In both stories the controversy apophthegm is imbedded into the miracle and set off from it by means of the repetition of Jesus' address to the man being healed: *legei tǭ paralytikǭ* in Mark 2:5 and 10; *legei tǭ anthrōpǭ* in Mark 3:3 and 5. In neither story do the opponents of Jesus openly state their opposition: in the first, A, Jesus knows that they debate in their *hearts*; in the last, A', Jesus is grieved at their hardness of *heart*. These are the first uses of *kardia* in the Gospel,[4] and the term is not used again until 6:52 where it is the disciples' hearts which are hardened. In both A and A', Jesus responds to unspoken opposition with a counter-question in good rabbinic controversy style: "Which is easier to say ... 'Your sins are forgiven'; or to say, 'Rise, take up your pallet and walk'?" (2:9), and "Is it lawful on the Sabbath to do good or to do harm?" (3:4).

Then, by means of Jesus' speaking again to the one being healed, stories A and A' revert to the miracle form. The miracle is completed, and the reaction of the onlookers described: "The impression the miracle creates on the crowd".[5] The content of the reactions is not parallel but antithetical; to the healing of the paralytic, "So that they were all amazed and glorified God, saying 'We never saw anything like this!'" (2:12); to the healing of the withered hand, "The Pharisees went out, and immediately held counsel with the Herodians against him, how to destroy him" (3:6). The reaction in 3:6 is hostile, not admiring, but it seems nonetheless to fill the slot in the miracle form of the response of the audience.

Thus A, the healing of the paralytic, and A', the restoration of the withered hand, are constructed in a parallel manner as shown by form, by content, and by assorted linguistic details. I would propose that 3:1–6 has been composed by Mark in order to balance the story of the paralytic and to complete the Sabbath controversy pattern (see below).[6] The parallelism of structure, in any case, seems beyond accident.

The middle three pericopae, B, eating with tax-collectors, C, fasting, B', plucking grain on the Sabbath, contain several features which set them off from A and A'. None contains a miracle and all contain wisdom sayings or proverbs. In A and A' the cast of characters consists of Jesus, opponents, and the sick man. In B, C and B' the cast consists of Jesus, opponents and disciples. In all three, either Jesus or his disciples are questioned about their behaviour; Jesus does not take the initative.

The setting of B and B' within the over-all structure of the controversy section is somewhat more complex, since not only are they parallel in structure to each other, but B is set in relation to A, and B' to A'. Story A, the healing of the paralytic, deals with the issue of forgiveness of sins. Story B, the eating with tax-collectors, has to do with Jesus' association with sinners. The two stories are joined by the catch-words *hamartia* ("sin") and *hamartōloi* ("sinners").[7]

B' and A', on the other hand, are both concerned with the Sabbath law. In B' the Pharisees ask why the disciples do what is not lawful on the Sabbath (2:24); in A' "they" are watching to see if Jesus will heal on the Sabbath (3:2), and Jesus asks if it is lawful on the Sabbath to do good or evil (3:4). The last two controversies are joined by the catch-words *tois sabbasin* ("on the sabbath") and *exestin* ("it is lawful").

Though in content B points back to A (the subject of sin), and B' ahead to A' (Sabbath law), in structure and form B is parallel to B'. Story B opens with Jesus out of doors, beside the sea calling Levi from his tax office, calling a sinner who is in the middle of sinning (2:13–14). It closes with a proverb, "Those who are well have no need of a physician, but those who are sick", followed immediately by the implied christological saying, "I came not to call the righteous, but sinners" (2:17).

Story B' similarly begins out of doors, in the fields, with the disciples breaking the Sabbath law by plucking grain (2:23). It ends with the proverb, "The sabbath was made for man, not man for the sabbath", followed immediately by the christological saying, "So the Son of man is lord also of the sabbath" (2:27–8). The content in B and B' is different, but the structure or form is the same. In both cases the final proverb and saying justify the initital action.

The central sections of B and B', however, are concerned *not* with sinners or Sabbath, but both are concerned with *eating*. In B, Jesus enters a house (as story A took place in a house) and eats with tax-collectors and sinners (2:15–16). The verb *esthiō* ("eat") is used twice in the present tense. In B', Jesus refers to the scriptural incident of David entering the house of God (as A' takes place in a synagogue), eating the bread of his presence and giving it also to "those with him" (2:25–6). *Esthiō* is used twice in the aorist. In story B, Jesus and his disciples eat with tax-collectors, something not lawful in light of the rabbinic laws of ritual cleanliness.[8] In B' David and his followers ate that which was lawful *only* for priests to eat (Mark 2:26).

In story B, the eating is an integral part of the pericope; Jesus is questioned on his behaviour in eating with tax-collectors and sinners. Yet the response, "I came not to call the righteous, but sinners" (v. 17b), may refer not merely to the call to table fellowship[9] but to the call of Levi in v. 14. The relevance of the example of David's action to the breaking of Sabbath laws in story B' is debatable,[10] and the story reads more smoothly without the insertion of vv. 25–6. I suggest, therefore, that Mark (or an earlier collector) has inserted this Old Testament reference into B'[11] because of its parallelism in content to story B, Jesus' eating with sinners, in order to balance his chiastic structure. And in the light of the chiasm, David's action may justify not so much the breaking of the Sabbath law but Jesus' behaviour in story B. David broke the law when he had need (*chreian eschen*, v. 25); Jesus asserted that it was the sick who need a physician (*chreian echousin*, v. 17).

The literary interrelationships and correlations of the first two and the last two stories seem sufficiently numerous and precise to establish that Mark 2:1–3:6 is a well-worked-out deliberate chiastic structure. This leaves C, the question about fasting, as the middle section of the structure by definition. Story C is set apart from the pattern of the other stories. Each of the other four stories has an explicit setting; C is completely without any indication of setting. In the other four, the opponents are named; in Story C they are not specified.[12]

C itself consists of three separate units: vv. 18–19, a controversy apophthegm about fasting, with Jesus' response, in effect that it was a time for joy, not fasting; v. 20, the christological allegorization of the "bridegroom" and the justification of the fasting practice of the early Church;[13] and vv. 21–2, two apparently unattached sayings on the incompatability of the old and new, which in their present context justify the new over against the old. The restatement of the apophthegm counter-question, "Can the sons of the bridechamber fast while the bridegroom is with them?" into the statement, "As long as they have the bridegroom with them they are not able to fast" (2:19), may have been done in order to produce a double saying to balance the two new-old sayings,[14] with v. 20, the allusion to Jesus' death, in between. The pattern: double saying, allusion to the crucifixion,[15] double saying, in itself seems quite probable. But then the whole of v. 18, contrasting the fasting practices of the disciples of John and of the Pharisees with the disciples of Jesus, would balance the phrase "new wine in new skins" (v. 22c). The phrase, however, is not parallel in form to v. 18 and is also of doubtful textual validity. Story C does not appear to be, as one might like, a precise chiastic structure within itself, set within the larger chiastic structure.

In terms of content, C fits very well as the centre of the chiastic stucture. It is concerned with fasting, set between B and B' which are concerned with eating. Verse 20, with its allusion to the crucifixion, is the centre not only of C but of the entire controversy section. It is set over against the two outside stories, A and A', with their "resurrection" type healings. According to Nils Lund's laws of chiastic structure, there is often a "shift at the centre" where an antithetic idea is introduced.[16] The death of Jesus is alluded to for the first time here. Also according to Lund, identical ideas are often distributed in the extremes and centre of a chiastic system:[17] so here the extremes and centre are concerned with death-resurrection (the verbs *egeirō* in A and A' and *apairō* in C) while the remainder of the system is concerned primarily with eating-fasting-eating.

Along with the chiastic structure of the five sub-units, there exists also a linear development of hostility in the opponents from silent criticism to the questioning of Jesus' disciples, to the questioning of Jesus himself, to watching him, finally to plotting to destroy him. The opponents are designated in order as the scribes, the scribes of the Pharisees, the Pharisees, and finally the Pharisees with the Herodians. The attack of the opponents becomes increasingly overt in the sequence of stories. This may be a deliberate literary device used to lend a time-sense, a sense of progression, to an otherwise content-structured unit.

Thus the five controversy stories of Mark 2:1–3:6 form a tightly-constructed literary unit, predominantly chiastic in principle: the first two stories have to do with sin; the last two with the Sabbath law; the first and last stories deal with resurrection-type healings; the second and fourth with eating; and the middle one with fasting and crucifixion. This pattern is seen not only in content, but in details of structure, form and language.

It would appear, furthermore, that the overall chiastic structure of Mark 2:1–3:6 has influenced the form of the individual pericopae within the section. The story of the man with the withered hand (A', Mark 3:1–6) may have received its precise form so that it would parallel A, the healing of the paralytic. The incident of David eating the showbread (2:25–6) may have been added not to fill out the pericope in which it is placed, but to balance another pericope altogether. The fact that stories B and B' each end with a proverb followed by a christological saying may not be the result of the independent development of each pericope but the result of the literary activity of the redactor setting the two pericopae in relation to each other, adding or deleting material as necessary.[18] The settings, in a house in stories A and B, in a house of God and a synagogue in B' and A', are not necessarily ideal settings produced by the community for each saying, but may in part be the invention of the evangelist creating a literary whole out of separate incidents. The compiler of Mark 2:1–3:6 appears to have been more than a redactor, indeed a genuine author. If the form of individual pericopae has indeed been influenced by the incorporation of the pericopae into a larger literary structure, then to determine the form criticism and history of tradition of a pericope, one needs to consider not only the isolated pericope but also its setting in larger literary units.

II

Such a structure as found in Mark 2:1–3:6 does not occur by accident. Either Mark worked out the literary structure himself, or the entire section virtually as it now stands was created by some earlier writer or collector, and Mark incorporated the unit as a whole. On literary and theological grounds it would seem that the present structure is due to Mark. This does not, of course, exclude the idea that Mark was using earlier tradition or even an earlier collection of traditions to construct his section.

As a writer, Mark often "sandwiched" blocks of material.[19] The setting off of material by means of a frame seems a natural extension of Mark's "sandwiching" technique. Therefore, the framework around 2:1–3:6 is quite as likely to indicate a Marcan construction as to indicate insertion of an already extant block of tradition. That Mark was sufficiently master of his material to create a fairly elaborate chiastic pattern has been shown by Lafontaine's and Beernaert's chiastic literary analysis of Mark

147

8:27–9:13,[20] a section whose construction is generally agreed to be Marcan.[21]

Albert Vanhoye in his study of the passion narratives in the Synoptics[22] demonstrates that it is Mark's habit to underline contrasts, a literary device used for a theological purpose. "Mark is not afraid to stun us; rather, he seeks to do so. He brings out contrasts, he underscores the paradox: the Cross is scandalous, it nonetheless reveals the Son of God".[23] The controversy section as a whole also emphasizes contrasts: eating/joy versus fasting/mourning; resurrection versus crucifixion. Viewed in this manner, the allusion to the crucifixion does not come surprisingly early in the Marcan scheme,[24] but it is for Mark a suitable literary climax. Theologically also, it is consonant with Mark's emphasis on the theology of the cross. Jesus' ministry is shown to be under the shadow of the cross from the beginning.

The controversy section fits naturally into the structure of Mark's Gospel. Mark, after he showed the enthusiastic response of the crowds to Jesus in chapter 1, then demonstrated the hostility that these actions of Jesus aroused, which eventually resulted in his death. The conclusion in Mark 3:6, "the Pharisees went out and immediately held counsel with the Herodians against him, how to destroy him", serves not only as a conclusion to the story of the withered hand, but also to the entire controversy section. To *this* result Jesus' actions lead.

Thus Mark employed the conflict stories theologically to place Jesus' life in the context of his death, and he used them in his narrative construction to show how Jesus' death historically was to come about. The controversy section appears to fit in with Mark's literary technique and with his theology; indeed, it is a good example of both.

The one fact not accounted for by the assumption of a Marcan construction from previously independent units of tradition is the occurrence of the title Son of Man[25] in stories A and B'. The title is not used in the suffering-eschatological sense that Mark employs from 8:31 on.[26] Nor does its double use fit into Mark's literary pattern, as the allusion to the crucifixion does. The double appearance of the title implies that Mark is reworking a previous collection of conflict stories.

Heinz-Wolfgang Kuhn in his recent study of earlier collections used by Mark arrives at the same result via the methods of form criticism, especially the determination of the *Sitz im Leben* in the community. He concludes that there was an earlier collection of four units: the healing of the paralytic, the eating with the tax collectors (without vv. 13–14), the question about fasting, and the plucking of grain on the Sabbath without its Old Testament reference.[27] Since all four concern Jewish praxis and are settled by appeals to christological arguments,[28] they serve the needs of the community against Jewish Christians who accept the full power of the earthly Son of Man.[29] Verse 28, "the Son of man is lord *also* of the sabbath", concludes the entire collection, referring to the Son of Man's authority to forgive sins in the first story.[30]

Kuhn interprets Mark's insertions of the Old Testament reference (2:25–6) and the story of the withered hand (3:1–5) as a re-inclusion of Jewish-type arguments,[31] the insertion of the call of Levi (2:13–14) and the conclusion in 3:6 as evidence of Mark's historicizing tendency.[32] The earlier collection explains the appearance of the title Son of Man and also the "too early hints of Jesus about his death" in v. 20.[33]

Kuhn's reconstruction of the earlier collection with its explanation of the occurrence of the title Son of Man in Mark's controversy section is admirable. However, his explanation for the Marcan expansions are inadequate. More probably, Mark has reworked the material in order to create his chiastic literary structure, which in turn brings out his meaning. Further, v. 20, the allusion to the crucifixion, is not a leftover from earlier tradition but the centre of Mark's literary structure and the heart of his message: Jesus's life is to be seen as the way of the cross.

Mark was a writer of considerable literary skill, if not of elegant Greek; it is only by paying attention to the literary structure he created that we can hope to interpret his Gospel properly. Moreover, since the literary structure has in part determined the shape of the individual pericopae, it is also necessary to consider it when studying the form or tradition-history of an individual pericope.

NOTES

1 Martin Albertz, *Die synoptischen Streitgespräche* (Berlin: Trowitzsch und Sohn, 1919) 5–16; Martin Dibelius (1934) 219; Vincent Taylor (1966) 91–2.

2 Contrary to the opinion of Rudolf Bultmann (1963) 12, 209, who views Mark 3:1–5 as an "organically complete apophthegm" not utilizing the style of a miracle story.

3 Bultmann (1963) 209.

4 Used twice in the first story.

5 Bultmann (1963) 225.

6 Cf. Rudolf Grob, *Einführung in das Markus-Evangelium* (Zürich: Zeingli, 1965) 38–9.

7 Johannes Sundwall, *Die Zusammensetzung des Markusevangeliums* (Acta academiae aboensis humaniora IX:2; Abo: Abo Akademi, 1934) 15.

8 If a tax-collector even enters a house, all that is in the house becomes unclean, not merely what he has touched (Mishnah, *Tohoroth* 7:6).

9 Bultmann (1963) 18.

10 David Daube, *The New Testament and Rabbinic Judaism* (London: Athlone, 1956) 67–71.

11 The prevailing view has been that vv. 27–8 were added to vv. 23–6 (Bultmann, 1963, 16–17; Taylor [1966] 218). Recently, Arland J. Hultgren ("The Formation of the Sabbath Pericope in Mark 2:23–28", *JBL* 91 [1972] 38–43), and Heinz-Wolfgang Kuhn (1971) 74–7 have argued that vv. 25–6 are an insertion into an earlier unit consisting of vv. 23–4, 27 (28).

12 The verbs *erchontai* and *legousin* in v. 18b are best understood as impersonal plurals, meaning in effect, "Jesus was asked". See C. H. Turner (1924) 378–9.

13 These two units appear already merged in the *Gospel of Thomas*, logion 104. The last unit appears as logion 47.

14 The restatement is not necessary to establish the allegory, the bridegroom = Christ, since both Matthew and Luke drop the restatement but keep the allegory (Matt. 9:15; Luke 5:34–5).

15 Crucifixion, of course, is not explicitly mentioned. The much milder verb *apairō* ("take away") is used here and in the parallels, Matt. 9:15 and Luke 5:35, its only occurrences in the New Testament.

16 *Chiasmus in the New Testament* (Chapel Hill: University of North Carolina, 1942).

17 Ibid.

18 For instance, there has been considerable debate as to whether Mark 2:27–8 is a unit, and if not, which verse was added later. See Hultgren, "The Sabbath Pericope", 38–43. One must also consider the possibility that Mark has added one or the other saying in order to balance the proverb-christological saying in v. 17. Or perhaps, more probably, Mark may have added v. 17b in order to balance v. 28 and to tie the incident of eating with sinners to the call of Levi in v. 14.

19 E.g., Mark 3:20–35; 5:22–43; 6:7–30; 11:12–25; 14:53–72.

20 René Lafontaine and Pierre Mourlon Beernaert, "Essai sur la Structure de Marc, 8:27–9:13", *Revue des Sciences Religieuses* 57 (1969) 543–61. For the use of chiasm in oral and written literature, see Charles H. Lohr, "Oral Techniques in the Gospel of Matthew", *CBQ* 23 (1961) 424–7.

21 Dibelius, *Tradition*, 230; Taylor, *St. Mark*, 98; Sherman E. Johnson (1972) 147, 154, 159; Ernst Haenchen (1963) 81–109; Norman Perrin (1970) 66.

22 *Structure and Theology of the Accounts of the Passion in the Synoptic Gospels* (Collegeville, Minnesota: The Liturgical Press, 1967).

23 Ibid., 8–9.

24 Albertz, *Streitgespräche*, 5; Taylor (1966) 211–12.

25 *If* it is to be considered a title in this section; see Lewis S. Hay, "The Son of Man in Mark 2:10 and 2:28", *JBL* 89 (1970) 69–75. For two interpretations which understand the use of Son of Man in 2:10 and 2:28 as part of Mark's own theology, see Norman Perrin, "The Creative Use of the Son of Man Traditions by Mark", *USQR* 23 (1968) 360–1; John H. Elliott, "Man and the Son of Man in the Gospel according to Mark", *Humane Gesellschaft* (ed. Trutz Rendtorff and Arthur Rich; Zürich: Zwingli, 1970) 50–8.

26 Another of the arguments of Albertz (*Streitgespräche*, 5) for a pre-Marcan collection.

27 Kuhn (1971) 74, 86, 87.

28 Ibid., 82, 83.

29 Ibid., 73, 81, 83–5, 96.

30 Ibid., 29.

31 Ibid., 74, 77, 86.

32 Ibid., 86, 87, 223.

33 Ibid., 87.

151

6

Mark's Preservation of the Tradition *

ERNEST BEST

Formgeschichte in isolating pre-Marcan material had little or no
interest in the Marcan residue and set it aside; *Redaktionsgeschichte*
has fastened on to this residue and made it the starting-point for
our knowledge of Mark's literary and theological work. Now that
we understand the latter more adequately it is perhaps time to look
back at the material which came to Mark in the tradition and ask
what he did to this material as he used it in his Gospel. We shall not
be concerned with the seams with which he unites incidents or with
the order in which he places them or with the summaries which he
writes but with what happened internally to the various pericopae
as he incorporated them into the larger whole he was creating. We
know that when Matthew and Luke took over the material from
Mark they regularly adapted it to their needs; Matthew in
particular consistently abbreviated it. Can we in any way trace
what Mark did to the tradition which he had received? How far did
he conserve it unchanged, apart from providing it with a linking
introduction to the rest of his Gospel? How far did he adapt or
mould it? What control did he exercise over it? Obviously it is
much more difficult to answer this question in the case of Mark
than it is for Matthew and Luke, but we must make some attempt.
We can only do this by examining individual passages and as we do
so the nature of the problem will itself become clearer.

* First published in M. Sabbe (ed.) *L'Évangile selon Marc. Tradition et Rédaction.*
Leuven: University Press (1974) 21–34.

153

Before we take up the material it is necessary to speculate briefly about the way in which words are used in the handing on of oral material. Any *raconteur* can probably observe what happens in his own retelling of stories. Within any material which is in the course of transmission there are constants and variables. The material cannot be handed on without using the constants, e.g. it is impossible to tell the parable of the sower without referring to seed and, if there is only one word for this, this is a constant. These constants are of less importance than the variables when we seek to determine what has happened to material in transmission. Variables are of many kinds. There are simple variables like synonyms, e.g. *meta* ("with") and *syn* ("with"). Here a person will normally use his own favourite word though he may have heard the other when he was given the material. With these simple variables it is only to be expected that many Marcan characteristic words would appear within pericopae. This may not be so in the case of more complex variables, e.g. *pneuma akatharton* ("unclean spirit") and *daimonion* ("demon"). Of particular interest for our purposes is the use of titles. When in Britain a man becomes ennobled and takes a title different from his original name (e.g. the British Prime Minister Disraeli became Lord Beaconsfield) some people may continue to refer to him by his earlier name and when they retell an anecdote in which he was referred to by his title they will change to the name. This suggests that when within a pericope of Mark we find a variable which has not been brought into line with Mark's normal usage we may be witnessing the preservation of pre-Marcan tradition. With this in mind we shall examine some individual Marcan passages.

I *Inconsistent use of titles of Jesus*

(*a*) 1:24. Both Matthew and Luke vary the christological titles of Mark,[1] and *a priori* this would seem a place where change would take place easily. In 1:24 the demon addresses Jesus as *ho hagios tou theou* ("the Holy One of God"). Commentators have difficulty in explaining the relevance and meaning of this title.[2] Mark's normal title of confession is *ho uios tou theou* ("the Son of God").[3] In the summary of 3:11f. where Mark is composing freely and can choose the title he wishes, he puts this latter title on the lips of the demons. If there is no clear and satisfactory explanation for the title of 1:24 within its Marcan context (and it may have had a clear meaning in an earlier stage of the tradition) then it is simplest to conclude that Mark found it in his source and did not alter it to the title which would have been more appropriate to his theology. In other words it is a variable which he has preserved. Interestingly Mark never puts the title "Son of God" on the lips of Jesus;[4] although it is the title of his preference it is always a confessional title; the title Jesus uses of himself in Mark is "Son of Man";[5] this itself is probably another instance of the preservation of tradition.

(*b*) In 10:47, 48 blind Bartimaeus addresses Jesus as *huie David* ("Son of David") and in 10:51 he calls him *rabbouni* ("Master"). Commentators again vary in their explanations of the significance of the first of these two titles in their Marcan context.[6] "Son of God" would have been the natural title for Mark to use. The story is found at one of the major turning points in the Gospel, at the conclusion of the central section 8:27–10:45 in which the way of the cross and the training of the disciples are expounded. It balances the story of the blind man (8:22–6) who receives his sight in two stages; Bartimaeus truly sees and at once follows Jesus. We would therefore expect him to confess Jesus as "Son of God", the true title used by God (1:11; 9:7) of Jesus, or, possibly, "Son of Man" which has been consistently used of the suffering of Jesus in this central sections, though always by Jesus and not on the lips of others. If it is argued that the Davidic title is appropriate because of the immediately succeeding entry into Jerusalem this must be allowed, yet in view of the position of the pericope in the total structure of the Gospel it is difficult to see, if another title had been originally present and a change had been made by Mark, how that change would have been made to "Son of David" rather than "Son of God". If changes were being made why was *rabbouni* permitted to remain? The Davidic title with its strong Jewish and even war-like overtones would hardly have been suitable in a gentile Roman Church, particularly in or after a time of persecution. Moreover, the title "Christ" (8:29) which is closely related has already been seen to be a misleading title, for in 8:31 it had to be reinterpreted and "Son of Man" is used in the reinterpretation;[7] in 12:35–7 the theology underlying its use is shown to be less important than the *kyrios* theology. Mark therefore preserves the title "Son of David" from his materials.[8] The semitic form of *rabbouni* almost certainly implies it belongs to the tradition; it can hardly have seemed to Mark's readers and hearers the most appropriate term with which to address Jesus when seeking the miraculous restoration of sight. *Ho didaskalos* ("the teacher") is used by the father of the epileptic boy in approaching Jesus (9:17) and often in Mark it appears to carry a sense of authority as did the teaching of Jesus (1:22, 27). Mark has, however, not changed the traditional term *rabbouni* to this, though it is a frequent term in the Gospel and often used editorially.[9]

(c) Probably the distinction between Jesus and the Son of Man which is found in 8:38 belongs to this category of the preservation of christological titles. Since Mark himself identifies Jesus and the Son of Man it would have been much simpler and would have produced a much crisper and better balanced logion if he had changed "Son of Man" to the first person pronoun. The appearance of the title "Son of Man" in 2:10, 28 falls too early according to the generally accepted view that Mark only uses this title after Peter's confession, and probably arises from Mark's desire to use at this point an existing collection of controversy stories.[10]

II *Inconsistent or superfluous information*

(a) 10:28. It is generally agreed that 10:17–31 is a Marcan compilation.[11] In v. 28 Peter says, "We have abandoned everything", and Jesus replies that those who have left house, family and farm will receive a hundred-fold compensation. But Peter was a fisherman and if Mark had really wished to accommodate the logion to its present position in the Gospel he ought to have added among the list of items which men might forsake some allusion to fishing-boats or fishing-nets. He has thus not adapted the logion to its present context though an easy addition would have enabled him to do so.

But there is a second matter in relation to this passage. Had Peter in fact left house and family as this implies and as 1:16–18 probably does also? In 1:29 we find that Peter still maintains a home to which he goes back and 3:9; 4:1, 36 show that the disciples as a whole still have a boat at their disposal. Both the absolute nature of 10:28 and its exclusion of any reference to fishing probably derive from the passage of an original logion through the tradition which reshaped it in terms of the community to which at any time it was addressed; Mark has probably used it in the form in which it circulated in his community, without modifying it to suit the context of his Gospel.

(*b*) There is more which merits our attention in 1:16–20. We have an unusual word for fishing, *amphiballein* ("to cast") which Mark explains with one of his typical parentheses (introduced by *gar* ["for"][12]) "for they were fishermen". *amphiballein* ("cast") is a word with many meanings[13] and to an audience not accustomed to the different methods of fishing would not normally suggest that Peter and Andrew were fishermen. Hence Mark's explanatory parenthesis; but it would have been easier to substitute for *amphiballein* a more generally accepted word for fishing, e.g. *halieuein* ("to fish").[14] Mark, in other words, has not changed the existing word in the tradition but explained it. We do have another word related to fishing, *diktua* ("nets"), in v. 19 but since it cannot be misunderstood it requires no explanation. There is one other possible instance of Mark's respect for the tradition in this passage: his reference to James and John leaving their father with the *misthōtai* ("hired servants"). Commentators again offer many interpretations. The *misthōtai*, may be mentioned to show the love of James and John for their father in that they did not leave him alone (Schlatter, Grundmann), or to show how much James and John were giving up in leaving a family wealthy enough to employ others (Wohlenberg, Loisy), "or does it add to the pathos – he (their father) is now left entirely at the mercy of 'hirelings'? . . . can it be that the contrast is here between the apostles, who answer Jesus' call, and the 'hirelings', who are held back by mercenary considerations?" (Nineham). The difficulty of commentators in finding an acceptable explanation of the significance of the word for Mark may suggest that it had none; Mark used it because it was already present in the tradition.

(*c*) 10:35 contains the superfluous detail that James and John are the sons of Zebedee; this has already been given in 1:19 and 3:17. What has happened here is that Mark has taken up a new incident, which when it was an isolated pericope required this information so that the scene might be adequately set, and he has failed to omit the detail when he incorporated it into the larger whole of the Gospel where it is unnecessary.

(*d*) 11:16 "and he would not allow anyone to carry anything through the Temple". This clause disappears in Matthew and

Luke. It fits into a Jewish situation and therefore is probably pre-Marcan.[15] It does not fit into the emphasis Mark himself lays on the cleansing of the Temple, i.e. judgement on Judaism and the admission of the Gentiles.[16] It is another case of the preservation of unnecessary detail.

III *Unmodified tradition*

(*a*) 8:31; 9:31; 10:33f.[17] The kernel of these three predictions appears to be a piece of unmodified tradition. There is the use of *apokteinein* ("to kill") rather than of *stauroun* ("to crucify"); we should expect the latter: (1) because Mark uses it throughout the passion narrative (15:13, 14, 15, etc.); (2) because *stauroun* would give a more correct prophecy of what was to happen; (3) because 8:34 with its reference to "taking up the cross and following Jesus" in Mark's mind certainly links the fate of the disciple to the fate of Jesus. More important than this is the retention by Mark of "after three days"; it may be that according to semitic time reckoning where a portion of a day is counted as a whole day this would be in no way different from "on the third day"; but normally in Greek our phrase would not have the same precision as the other or necessarily imply resurrection on Sunday morning after a death on Friday afternoon. Matthew and Luke have both altered Mark's phrase to "on the third day" (Matt. 16:21; 17:23; 20:19; Luke 9:22; 18:33). This latter is found more widely in the New Testament[18] and became the standard Christian phrase; we find it indeed appearing in written form in 1 Cor. 15:4 earlier than Mark's phrase; and 1 Cor. 15:4 is itself older than Paul's letter. Thus Mark retains an old formula although it would not be as immediately apparent in meaning as the formula which eventually became standard.[19]

(*b*) 9:35. 9:33–37 bears clear evidence of Mark's redaction. Probably most if not all of vv. 33, 34 come from his hand;[20] 9:30–2 gives the second prediction of the passion; vv. 33–4 are a connecting link; vv. 35–7 are probably largely traditional material. In v. 31 the passion prediction is made to the disciples; v. 33 implies that it is the disciples who go with Jesus to Capernaum and enter a house and who are asked about the subject of their conversation on the way; v. 35 then says that Jesus sat down and summoned the twelve. Unless we assume that Mark is here deliberately distinguishing between other disciples and the twelve, and in the present context this is most improbable, we must conclude that in bringing in at this point a brief pericope from the tradition Mark has carried over with it its introduction, for the disciples are already present.[21] Reploh, however, suggests that all the references to the twelve in Mark are editorial.[22] If this is so in the present instance it would have been much easier for Mark to introduce the reference to the twelve at either v. 31a, where he refers to the disciples, or at v. 33 where there is a neutral third person plural (both v. 31a and v. 33 come from Mark). In v. 35a *phōneō* ("call") is a non-Marcan word, he uses *proskaleō* ("call") and he prefers "and he said to them" to "and he says";[23] ("sitting") *kathisas* to teach is not otherwise emphasized by Mark; only in 4:1 and 13:3 does a reference to sitting go with authoritative teaching and in each case *kathēmai* ("I am seated") and not *kathizo* ("I sit") is used; but regularly Mark depicts Jesus as teaching without any allusion to his being seated.[24] We assume so often that he rewrote the introductions to the pericopae which he used that it may be surprising to find him retain one where it could easily have been modified.

IV   *Unnecessary or irrelevant logia*

There are a number of logia sequences whose connection at their commencement is clear and relevant but within which the final logia are both difficult in themselves and difficult to relate to their Marcan context.

(*a*) 9:35–50.[25] It is easy to trace the verbal connections which hold this sequence together: *onoma* ("name") (vv. 37, 38, 39, 41); *paidion mikrōn* ("little children") (vv. 37, 42); *skandalizein* ("to cause to stumble") (vv. 42–7); *pyr* ("fire") (vv. 43, 48, 49); *halas* ("salt") (vv. 49, 50). These verbal connections suggest oral transmission and, therefore, almost certainly imply pre-Marcan tradition.[26] Verses 49, 50 have proved almost impossible to interpret with any degree of certainty both in themselves and in relation to their Marcan context; the final clause "and be at peace with one another" may possibly refer back to the dispute about greatness in v. 34 and have been added by Mark[27] or it may have originally belonged and been the reason why Mark utilized the intervening irrelevant and incomprehensible logia. In either case Mark has included sayings which are unnecessary or irrelevant to the development of his discussion. It is conceivable that Mark and his community both understood what the sayings about salt and fire meant and saw their relevance, but this seems very unlikely. What is much more probable is that Mark has this sequence of logia; the initial logia and possibly the very last were very relevant and rather than divide the sequence he retained all of it.

(*b*) 11:22–5.[28] Around 11:15–19, the cleansing of the Temple, Mark has set according to his regular redactional method the story of the cursing of the fig-tree. Probably in the pre-Marcan tradition the fig-tree stood as part of a pericope whose point was Jesus' *dynamis* ("power")[29] with the addendum, already attached to it in the tradition, that a disciple could have the same power through prayer.[30] Mark now gives the fig-tree incident an entirely different meaning through its association with the cleansing of the Temple but he does not omit the accompanying logia about prayer. In their present position they do not fit into the larger context and commentators struggle to explain them in it.[31] (We might say that wherever we see the commentators in confusion this is a sign of the preservation of tradition). It is, therefore, most unlikely that Mark gathered together a set of independent logia about prayer (v. 25 has even a different theme from vv. 22–4) and set them in his Gospel at this point,[32] but they appear here because they were attached already to the piece of tradition about the fig-tree which he did want to use.

(*c*) 4:21–5 falls into almost the same pattern but here the most difficult saying is not the final (v. 25) but the penultimate (v. 24). It is generally held that vv. 21–5 were not part of the complex of parables which Mark obtained from the tradition,[33] but did they exist as a unit prior to Mark or did he bring together here a number of isolated logia? Jeremias has argued strongly that v. 21 and v. 22 first came together and that v. 24 and v. 25 came together independently and that these two units were joined to form more or less our present vv. 21–5 and only after this did Mark use the section.[34] On the other hand v. 23 is probably Marcan and v. 24a may be also. "And he said to them" might suggest that Mark is here introducing new material[35] but this same phrase is also used in v. 13 to rejoin the interpretation of the sower parable to the parable itself after a Marcan insertion, although in the pre-Marcan tradition parable and interpretation were already joined. Mark may then have inserted vv. 23, 24a into the original unit of vv. 21, 22, 24b, 25 and rejoined the group with the aid of the phrase. Verses 21, 22 are easily seen to be relevant to the Marcan context either as another parable[36] or as related to the parable context (the light which is given in the parables is not for hiding),[37] or, more generally, as suggesting that Jesus or the Kingdom of God or the word is not to be hidden.[38] Verse 25a may fit in with this in the sense that whoever has received revelation or light will receive more; but v. 25b, "he who has no revelation will lose it", is much more difficult to fit in. Probably v. 25 comes from a popular proverb – the rich grow richer while the poor become poorer – of which the first half is apparently appropriate to the richness which is light but the second is not since those who have no light, who are outside the Church (cf. v 11 *hoi exō* ["those outside"], cannot be deprived of what they do not have. But the difficulties with v. 24 are even greater than with v. 25b. The comment of Taylor is typical, "The significance of the saying in Mark is obscure".[39] In its Q form (Matt. 7:2 = Luke 6:38) it is more appropriate to its context.[40] Thus, again we appear to have a sequence of sayings of which the first were important for Mark but the others inappropriate yet were retained in order not to destroy the existing unity. It is, however, just possible that Mark himself added vv. 24, 25 which already existed as a unit to vv. 21, 22 which also was already a unit. He will then have joined them because he wishes to use v. 25a. The difficulty about v. 24 still remains; he must have brought it in, though it is hardly relevant, because he wished to use the later saying.

Perhaps some of the pre-Marcan collections may have been used in the same way by Mark: he desired one or more incidents and so used the whole. H.-W. Kuhn[41] argues that 10:1–45 embodies a pre-Marcan complex of which Mark certainly wanted 10:35–45; he used 10:17–23, 25 correcting it so as to universalize it from a discussion of the disciple's attitude to "wealth" to discipleship in general; he then retained 10:1–12 which has really little relevance to his argument at this point, and which is difficult to reconcile with the total context. Perhaps the same is true of 2:1–3:6.[42] Earlier critics pointed out that the references to the death of Jesus (2:20; 3:6), to the Pharisees and Herodians (3:6), and to the Son of Man (2:10, 28) fall too early in the "history" of the life of Jesus, but these earlier critics do not seem to have speculated on what this had to say about Mark's methods. It would take a longer analysis than is now possible to discuss which parts of this collection are relevant here to his redactional purposes and which are present only because he has retained an existing collection.

V Unncessary retention of names

In a number of places Mark has preserved names without apparent reason, though from time to time commentators have attempted to derive meaning, sometimes most esoteric meaning, from them. Levi's name is retained in 2:13f. though Levi is not mentioned among the twelve in 3:16ff. (Matthew corrects this); the names of the brothers of Jesus in 6:3, though these can have been of little interest to a Roman audience; the name Jairus (5:22), again of little interest to a Roman audience; Bartimaeus (10:46), whose name is translated but not in the way in which Mark normally explains Aramaic words *ho estin* ("which is"),[43] implying that both name and explanation go back before Mark. It is often stated by commentators[44] that the names of Alexander and Rufus whose father Simon of Cyrene carried the cross of Jesus (15:21) are given because Rufus was later well-known in Rome and a cross-reference is made to Rom. 16:13; but Romans 16 may not have been written to Rome and Mark may be doing nothing other than preserving names which have come to him in the tradition (this is not to say that at some point in the transmission of the tradition the names may not have been important).

In this paper we have dealt only with particular passages and not with the contradictions which many scholars find between the "suffering" Christology of Mark and the *theios anēr* ("divine man") Christology of his material,[45] which if true would reinforce our conclusions.

Conclusions

1. The evidence adduced is not exhaustive; no systematic attempt was made to look for examples, but those which turned up in the course of other work on Mark were noted. Anyone who works at Mark will be able to produce other examples. Naturally also any particular example will be disputed. It is, therefore, the cumulative effect which is important. There may indeed be evidence to be produced on the other side. This paper is only an

attempt to draw attention to something which appears to have been neglected.

2.   Faced with a piece of tradition Mark altered it internally as little as possible. If, as *Formgeschichte* has shown, notes of time, space and audience were missing then he felt himself free to set those pericopae which now lacked context in new contexts, but even where it would have suited his purpose to do so he has not altered their content nor has he abbreviated them by omitting logia which were irrelevant or even meaningless in the context he has given them. It is perhaps fair to say that in this respect he was more careful than Matthew or Luke.

3.   Redaction critics argue that Mark was a genuine author and not a scissors-and-paste editor. This requires more careful definition. In the way in which he has placed the tradition in his total context, supplying audience, place, time and sequence and in the summaries he has written he has been quite obviously creative. But in the way in which he has preserved the material which existed before him he has been conservative. Perhaps we should think not of an author but of an artist creating a collage.

4.   Mark appears to have had a positive respect for the material which he used; this is not to say that he was attempting to write "history", or that he possessed the journalist's ideal – facts are sacred, comment is free – or that he was positively attempting to preserve for the future what lay before him. We are only saying how it appears he actually did his work. It would suggest that he did not create incidents to illustrate general trends; as if we were to suppose Mark believed Jesus was an exorcist but since all stories of exorcism had disappeared he therefore created some to portray Jesus as exorcist. That is not the way he worked. His positive attitude to the tradition is also seen in his retention of material, as in the logia-sequences, which plays no useful part in his Gospel. Does this mean that somewhere or other he has managed to work in all the traditions which he knew? Does it imply that he did not know Q?

5.   If Mark has preserved material which does not fully correspond to the view which he himself holds then are we at liberty to speak of a theology of the Gospel of Mark? Must we not rather speak of Mark's theology? If a valid distinction can be drawn between these two then it may be that we should not look

163

for a coherent and consistent theology in the Gospel but be prepared to find unevenness since he laid his theology over an existing theology, or theologies, in the tradition he received.[46]

6. We must be careful not to press our argument too far. It would be illegitimate to conclude that all those who handed on oral tradition had the same attitude to it as Mark. Our results, therefore, do not permit us in any way to conclude that in the oral period the material was conserved accurately, and naturally therefore it does not enable us to make a judgement on the "historicity" of the material Mark preserved. But equally it does not allow us to argue from "picturesque" details in Mark to an eye-witness, e.g. Peter, who gave Mark the facts. We can say nothing about Mark's source or sources but only refer to what Mark did with what he received from them.

NOTES

1 E.g. both Matthew and Luke introduce the title *kyrios* ("Lord") where it does not appear in Mark (Matt. 8:25; 17:4, 15; 20:31; Luke 5:12; 18:41; 22:61); Matthew alters Peter's confession (16:16). For fuller details, see E. Best (1965) 160f. I would now disagree with my tentative suggestion there that it is probable that Mark would have altered the titles in the material as it came to him.

2 E.g. O. Procksch, *TDNT* i. 102 refers it to the Holy Spirit; T. Ling, *The Significance of Satan* (London, 1961) 14 takes it as in contrast to *akathartos* ("unclean"); V. Taylor (1966) 174f. traces its use to the Old Testament and suggests it has messianic significance (it expresses "the sense of the presence of a supernatural person"); Lohmeyer gives it a more cultic connotation; F. Hahn, *The Titles of Jesus in Christology* (London, 1969) 231ff. takes it to refer to "an eschatological prophet"; E. Schweizer (1970) 52 connects it with Nazareth or Nazarene through Judg. 13:7; 16:17 (LXX).

3 1:1; 3:11f.; 5:7; 9:7; 15:39. Jesus is confessed in this way by God in 1:11, 9:7; by the demons in 3:11f.; 5:7; and by the Gentile centurion in 15:39.

4 Although the absolute "Son" appears in 12:6 and 13:32.

5 Cf. J. Barr, "Christ in Gospel and Creed", *SJT* 8 (1955) 225–37 (at 229).

6 It would be more true to say that the commentators say very little about the meaning of the title for Mark at this point; they devote their attention to its significance for the primitive Church. Their failure to relate it to Mark's view of Jesus, other than to say that Mark accepts the Davidic sonship of Jesus, is an indication of its unimportance for him. In 7:28 the Syrophoenician woman appeals to Jesus as *kyrie* ("Lord", "sir"); in the storm at sea the disciples use *didaskale* ("teacher"); but normally Jesus takes the initiative in healing and

there is no address. It is also possible that the use of the title in a "public" scene conflicts with Mark's conception of the messianic secret (cf. T. A. Burkhill, 1963: 188f.).

7 Cf. similar alterations in 14:62 from 14:61 and in 13:26 from 13:21. On the inadequacy of "Christ" as a title for Mark, see R. H. Lightfoot (1950) 35f. Even if Mark uses the "Son of Man" suffering-sayings because he wishes to introduce the concept of suffering the point remains that on both occasions he has retained the title which existed in the tradition.

8 Probably the retention of the title "King of the Jews" throughout the passion narrative (15:2, 9, 12, 18, 26) is related to this; here Mark is certainly preserving tradition, but it would have been very difficult for him to change it since it was so essential a part of the story (cf. the title on the cross), a constant rather than a variable; thus its conservation is less significant.

9 *Rabbi* is used three times by Mark; at 9:5 in the middle of the transfiguration story where another title would seem more appropriate to the action of the story, unless the "ignorance" of Peter is being emphasized; at 11:21 again by Peter when he discovers Jesus has performed a miracle; at 14:45 it is Judas' salutation at the betrayal and we would hardly expect Mark to have placed a stronger title on the lips of Judas. The equivalent Greek title, *didaskalos*, is used within stories by disciples at 4:38; 14:14; by non-disciples at 5:35; 9:17; 10:20; 12:32; it is used in the initial address of stories, where it is most probably Marcan, by disciples at 9:38; 13:1; and by non-disciples at 10:17 (10:17 is undoubtedly difficult, as Matthew's rewriting of it shows, and may represent the tradition as Mark received it; if the address is Marcan it is probably derived from v. 20); 12:14 (here the title is appropriate in view of the context); 12:19. All this suggests that though Mark received the title from the tradition he also inserted it at other places; there is nothing to suggest that he altered other titles to this title. In Mark, Jesus occupies a position of authority as teacher and is often referred to as teaching though in comparison with the other Gospels little of his teaching is given. Cf. E. Trocmé (1975) 142f.; E. Schweizer (1962), in (1963) 93ff.

10 Cf. H.-W. Kuhn (1971) 53–99.

11 Cf. N. Walter, "Zur Analyse von Mc. 10:17–31", *ZNW* 53 (1962) 206–18; S. Légasse, "Jésus a-t-il annoncé la Conversion finale d'Israel? A propos de Marc x:23–27", *NTS* 10 (1964) 480–7; E. Best, "Uncomfortable Words VII: The Camel and Needle's Eye (Mark 10:25)", *ExpTim* 82 (1970–1) 83–9, and fuller references therein; cf. also H.-W. Kuhn (1971) 146ff.

12 Cf. 2:15; 6:14; 7:3f.; 11:13; cf. C. H. Turner (1925) 145–56.

13 See Liddell and Scott, *A Greek-English Lexicon* (ed. H. S. Jones and R. McKenzie), Oxford, 1951, *s.v.*

14 Cf. Lucian, *Piscator* 47ff.

15 "The prohibition implies a respect for the holiness of the Temple, and is thoroughly Jewish in spirit" (V. Taylor, 1966: 463).

16 Cf. E. Best (1965) 83f.

17 Mark may not have received all three of these passages from the tradition but may have created two of them out of the one which did come to him; if so, his respect for the tradition is more obvious. I cannot accept the argument of N. Perrin (1971) above 125–40, that he created all three.

18 Cf. Luke 13:32; 24:7, 21, 46; Acts 10:40; 1 Cor. 15:4; the "three days" tradition appears also to be found in the logia of Matt. 12:40; 27:63. On the origin and meaning of the two traditions, see G. von Rad and G. Delling, *TDNT* ii. 948–50; F. Nötscher, "Zur Auferstehung nach drei Tagen", *Biblica* 35 (1954) 313–19; J. B. Bauer, "Drei Tage", *Biblica* 39 (1958) 354–8; J. Dupont, "Ressuscité 'Le Troisième Jour'", *Biblica* 40 (1959) 742–61; G. M. Landes, "The Three Days and Three Nights' Motif in Jonah 2:1", *JBL* 86 (1957) 446–50; N. Walker, "After Three Days", *NovT* 4 (1960) 261–2; H. K. McArthur, "On the Third Day", *NTS* 18 (1971–2) 81–6.

19 There is some evidence in Josephus for the equivalence of "after three days" and "on the third day" (e.g. *Ant*. 7:280f.) but the LXX of Hos. 6:2 shows that they would normally be distinguished. J. Schreiber (1976) 103ff. contests the view that "after three days" is pre-Marcan.

20 In v.33 "in the house" and "in the way" are obviously Marcan; references to Capernaum appear in Mark only in material introducing pericopae (Luke omits it here and Matthew transfers it earlier to 17:24); *ēlthon* ("they came") is probably also part of the machinery Mark uses to show Jesus' journey to Jerusalem as a journey to the cross; the question of v. 33 disappears in both Matthew and Luke; v. 34 can hardly stand by itself without v. 33 and if a reference to the dispute about "greatness" which it contains was in the tradition, then Mark has rewritten it extensively; more probably Mark created this verse. Cf. K.G. Reploh (1969) 140ff.; D. E. Nineham (1968) 251; S. Légasse, *Jésus et L'Enfant* 23ff.

21 Cf. V. Taylor, D. E. Nineham, E. Schweizer, W. L. Knox, *The Sources of the Synoptic Gospels*, I (Cambridge, 1953) 21ff.; S. Légasse, op. cit., 24. E. Haenchen, *Der Weg Jesu*, ad loc. suggests that Mark added vv. 36f. We note that the use of the rare word *enagkalizesthai* ("take into one's arms") which occurs again only in 10:16. But if Mark composed vv. 36f. then v. 37 is not the proper conclusion to the implied question of v. 34; 10:15 would be much better. If vv. 36f. did not belong in this sequence prior to Mark then the use of the catchword *onoma* ("name") is upset in the passage.

22 Op. cit., 141.

23 Cf. H.-W. Kuhn, op. cit., 130f.

24 The *kai* ("and") is probably, as so often, his introductory link.

25 E. W. Bundy, *Jesus and the First Three Gospels* (Cambridge, Mass., 1955) suggests that vv. 38–40 are a Marcan insertion into an existing section, since they are dialogue in the middle section of logia and v. 37 joins easily to v. 41. But it is hard to see why Mark should insert these verses here and they contain the catchword *onoma* ("name"). Even if they are a Marcan insertion this does not affect the conclusion we draw about the later portions of vv. 35–50.

26 The most recent challenge to this comes from H.-W. Kuhn (1971) 32ff. following on R. Schnackenburg, "Markus 9:33–50", in *Synoptische Studien, Festschrift* A. Wikenhauser (Munich, 1953) 184–206 (unfortunately this was not available to me). He argues: *a*) Mark joins sayings and incidents by catchwords; *b*) Mark joins sayings together using *gar* ("for") even when there is no logical connection; *c*) the tradition in Matt. 10:40–2 shows that v. 37 and v. 41 were already linked and therefore Mark inserted vv. 38–40. He allows that the three "church-rules" of vv. 37, 41f. may have been a unit prior to Mark; Mark joined these to vv. 43–8 for they have no real connection other than through "catchwords"; v. 49 may have already been joined to vv. 43–8 prior to Mark but v. 50b is a comment of Mark relating the whole back to vv. 33f. Against this we may argue: *a*) That Mark uses "catchwords" on occasions does not prove that he necessarily was the first to use them here; they were widely used and could have been in the pre-existing tradition. As Kuhn himself shows (129) the root *speirein* ("to sow") was the link in the original collection of the three parables (4:3–9, 26–9, 31–2). *b*) Mark uses *gar* no more often than do the other evangelists and admittedly does join together sayings with it. We find it here at vv. 34, 39, 40, 41, 49. But Mark also uses *gar* regularly in narrative to hold together material which was already united in the pre-Marcan tradition, e.g. 6:18, 20; 8:34 and 8:35 were already a unit in the tradition as Matt. 10:38f. shows (cf. John 12:23–6); either they already had a *gar* which Mark preserved, which shows *gar* is not necessarily a sign of his hand, or he added *gar* which shows he used it with logia which were already united. In chapter 4 *gar* is used to join together vv. 21 and 22 and vv. 24 and 25, but we would hold that these were already joined in the tradition (cf. M. Thrall, *Greek Particles in the New Testament* [Leiden, 1962] 41ff.). *c*) There appear to be good grounds for seeing at least in vv. 38, 39, 42, 45, 48 a connected Aramaic substratum indicating a pre-Marcan union of these verses, cf. M. Black, *An Aramaic Approach to the Gospels and Acts* (3rd ed. Oxford, 1967) 169–71; cf. also 218–22. *d*) The real difficulty lies in seeing what was the purpose of Mark's redaction, if indeed he was responsible, in bringing together these sections; it is possible to see a connection between the closing clause of v. 50 "be at peace with one another" and vv. 33f. but not in regard to most of the rest of the material, in particular vv. 49, 50a. Kuhn supplies no redactional justification; commentators have always had great difficulty with these verses; lacking such justification we cannot accept Kuhn's view.

27 It was a piece of floating tradition, cf. 1 Thess, 5:13; Hermas, *Vis*. III, 9, 10.

28 There are again verbal links: "faith", "to believe", "to pray".

29 Cf. V. Taylor (1966) 458.

30 Taylor's remark that "with 21 the narrative element in the story ends; it appears to have been introduced for the sake of the saying which follow in 23–5" (466a) would be true of the tradition but not as he thinks of Mark's usage. But even v. 25 does not relate to the theme of *dynamis*; it must have been a part of the catechetical tradition on prayer.

31 E. Lohmeyer simply says: "the sayings here have hardly anything in common with the situation depicted".

The Interpretation of Mark

32 Contrast D. E. Nineham (298) who considers vv. 22–5 to have been added by Mark himself; even if Nineham is correct we would hold that these already existed as a unit prior to Mark and that, therefore, v. 25 really has little to do with vv. 22–4. The sayings certainly were found in other catechetical contexts; cf. Matt.17:20 and Luke 17:6 with Mark 11:23, and Matt. 6:14 with Mark 11:25, cf. also *Gos. Thom.* 48, 106. The Lucan form of v. 23 (Luke 17:6) shows that a connection between a tree and faith already existed apart from Mark 11 and this connection probably, therefore, predates Mark (so E. Schweizer).

33 So V. Taylor, E. Schweizer, E. Haenchen, E. Linnemann, *Parables of Jesus* (London, 1966) 180; J. Jeremias, *The Parables of Jesus* (London, 1963), 14, n. 1 and 91; W. Marxsen (1955) 262; R. H. Lightfoot (1935) 35f.; H.-W. Kuhn (1971) 130ff.

34 J. Jeremias, (1963) 90–2. There may again be catchwords; *modios* ("bushel"), *metron-eō* ("measure") (J. Jeremias, R. Bultmann (1963) 325ff.; E. Schweizer, D. E. Nineham).

35 This view has been sustained most recently by H.-W. Kuhn (1971) 130f. who apparently allows that vv. 21f. and vv. 24b, 25 were pre-Marcan formations. K.G. Reploh (1969) seems to go further and suggest that Mark found all four logia distinct from one another and brought them together.

36 Cf. J. Jeremias (1963) 91f.

37 E.g. E. Schweizer.

38 E.g. V. Taylor, D. E. Nineham, M.-J. Lagrange, E. Hoskyns and F. N. Davey, *The Riddle of the New Testament* (London, 1931) 129f. For Swete the light is the word and the lampstand the hearers who would defeat the purpose of the word if they put it under the "measure" or the "bed".

39 Cf. A. E. J. Rawlinson, D. E. Nineham, etc. It is this very obscurity which argues against the view that Mark collected the saying and added it to v. 25. K.G. Reploh (1969) 68f, notes the difficulty but does nothing to counter it. If Mark brought all these sayings together then a satisfactory redactional process must be offered as a supporting argument. This has never been done.

40 In Mark v. 25a links relatively easily to the last clause of v. 24 and this may explain why in some other previous context v. 25 was joined as an explanatory comment to v. 24.

41 (1971) 146–90.

42 H.-W. Kuhn (1971) 53–99 does not allow that 3:1–6 was part of the original collection.

43 Mark has thus not even brought this into line with his normal convention.

44 So V. Taylor, D. E. Nineham, etc.

45 E.g. L. E. Keck (1965); U. Luz in Tuckett (1983); T. J. Weeden in this volume.

46 One reviewer of my book (1965) waxed caustic because I had pointed out an inconsistency of this nature, viz. that the reference to Satan in the interpretation of the sower parable conflicted with the view that I had argued Mark held about Satan. The reviewer was prepared to dismiss the whole argument of the book on this alone. Quite apart from the wrong idea of proof which such a dismissal implies, it shows that the reviewer had not really understood the problem of determining Mark's theology.

7

The Disciples in Mark:
The Function of a Narrative Role*

ROBERT C. TANNEHILL

Norman Perrin has argued that, since the "evangelists are
genuinely authors", it is necessary to develop a "general literary
criticism" of the Synoptic Gospels and Acts which will borrow
perspectives from non-biblical literary studies.[1] This general
literary criticism must include, according to Perrin, "a concern for
the composition and structure" of these writings and "a concern
for protagonists and plot".[2] The following study is an attempt to
respond to Perrin's challenge. It will show that close attention to
the composition of the Marcan narrative can guide us to a better
understanding of the disciples' role in Mark. It will discuss the
function of the disciples in the implicit dialogue between author
and reader. It will also point to some resources in non-biblical
literary studies which may help us to understand these matters.

Redaction criticism has not fully recognized the importance of
studying the composition of each Gospel. Primary attention is
often given to the study of additions and changes made by an
evangelist in using his source material. In the study of Mark this
easily leads to dubious speculations, since the source material can
only be inferred indirectly. Furthermore, additions and changes
to source material do not in themselves reveal the concerns and
emphases of the author. The question of what is emphasized in a
writing is logically separate from the question of the origin of
material within it. An addition or change by an author may reflect

---

* First published in *JR* 57 (1977), 386–405.

only a passing concern of minor importance. The composition of the writing as a whole must indicate to us that a greater concern is involved. On the other hand, an author may quote material without change but shape his writing to show that this material is centrally important and has a significance both greater and other than it may have had in previous tradition. The study of modification of the tradition can provide suggestions of possible concerns of the author. We can only specify the nature and inportance of these concerns by studying the composition of the writing and the function of the modified material within it.[3]

This point has not been completely ignored in previous redaction-critical work. For instance, the possible thematic relations between the modification of tradition in a text and other material in the Gospel have been considered. The outline of a Gospel has also been a subject of frequent study. This usually results in a topical outline with neat divisions. Such an outline may be appropriate to a well-constructed essay, but it is not necessarily appropriate to a narrative. There are special aspects of *narrative* composition which biblical scholars will continue to ignore if there is not greater awareness of how stories are told and how they communicate. In the following discussion I will suggest some ways in which we can begin to do justice to the fact that Mark is a narrative.

Fortunately, a wide range of resources outside biblical studies can help us to develop a better understanding of narrative composition and communication. Among these are discussions of the novel. Some readers may be disturbed by my appeal to discussions of fiction, especially the novel, in the interpretation of Mark. It is proper to be cautious at this point. Certainly not all features of the modern novel can be found in Mark or in other ancient narratives.[4] Nor would I want to call Mark "fiction". However, there are qualities which all narratives share and further qualities which various narratives may share, even when some make use of historical fact, if the author has a strong, creative role.[5] Because of the importance of the novel in modern literature, qualities of narrative are often discussed in terms of the novel. With proper caution the biblical scholar can learn from this discussion.

We sometimes forget that a story represents a narrator's choice. Because we are familiar with certain stories and story types, the story seems obvious and necessary. However, just as the writing of history involves interpretation, so does telling a story. This is true both of stories which have a factual foundation and those which do not. Even when it reports actual events, a story represents a narrator's choice, for few events of our world are important enough to be remembered in story. The narrator also chooses how to tell the story. This choice will reflect the narrator's selective emphasis and values, and the story's composition helps to communicate the narrator's emphasis and evaluation to the reader. There are more ways of telling a story than we usually realize. The narrator chooses the way which fits his purpose or limits his purpose to the narrative forms at his disposal, and so his purposes are mirrored by his stories.

I

One helpful approach to Mark is the study of narrative roles.[6] I will confine myself to the role of the disciples in Mark, although study of other narrative figures and groups would probably be fruitful.[7] While recent scholarship has recognized that there are remarkable features to the treatment of the disciples in Mark, there has been little agreement on the significance of the author's handling of this group. We will see whether consideration of the role of the disciples in the Marcan narrative can bring greater clarity.

The author of Mark narrates a single, unified story. While the story's unity results primarily from the persistence of a single central figure, Jesus, a group of companions, or "disciples", appears early in the Gospel and plays a continuing role. To be sure, in different scenes the focus of attention may expand to a large group of "those around" Jesus (3:34; 4:10) or contract to the twelve or an individual among the twelve, but there are some common characteristics which define the group, despite its varying size.[8] It consists of those who have responded positively to Jesus and his message and are bound to Jesus in a continuing bond. While those healed by Jesus may or may not have a continuing relationship with him, the "disciples", those who "follow" Jesus, do have such a continuing relationship. Because there is continuity of persons and characteristics, we can also observe developments. When, in reading a story, we encounter the same person or group more than once, it is right to ask if the relationship between the scenes enriches our understanding of the characters. Certain scenes reinforce what we already know about a character or group, other scenes reveal new characteristics, still others indicate significant shifts and developments. The meaning of each scene is enriched if we can understand it in relationship to all the other scenes. In the story each scene then becomes part of a significant development that moves toward an end. Below we will try to discover whether the scenes in which the disciples have important roles fit together into a unity with significant development. The author will enable us to follow this development, not by describing developing states of mind from the inside, but by narrating significant words and actions which indicate a shifting relation to Jesus.

In reading a text we are continually seeking to establish connections among the parts of what we read. Possible connections are multiple and some authors may seek to hold open many of these possibilities so as to engage the active imagination of the reader.[9] Our imaginations are more active in reading stories than we realize. The brief scenes in the Synoptic Gospels are like pen and ink sketches in which an artist, with only a few strokes, has suggested some forms, relying on the viewer to fill in the rest with his imagination. Reduction of shapes to a few lines is also a means of emphasis, and the selective emphasis of the artist may help us to see the subject in a new way. This is also true of the succinct narrative scenes in the Synoptic Gospels. In our study of Mark we must pay special attention to the way that narrative composition indicates emphasis and suggests negative or positive evaluation of the actions of the disciples. Here we are dealing with what we might call narrative rhetoric.[10] This narrative rhetoric reveals the standpoint of the author, or, more cautiously, the "implied author", that is, the author insofar as he is immanent in the work.[11] The rhetoric of a story also reflects, by anticipation, a dialogue between author and reader. Writing a story, although it may involve persons and events quite distinct from the world of the author and reader, is, nevertheless, communication between author and reader.[12] At various points the author's reasons for narrating this story for a group of readers may become especially apparent. Furthermore, the author has a view of his readers and anticipates how they will respond to his story. Therefore, not only the standpoint of the author but also the standpoint of the reader (in the view of the author) may find indirect expression in the story.

The "implied author" of Mark communicates and recommends his norms and values to the reader by the way in which he narrates the disciples' story. Selective emphasis and control of evaluation of persons and events are indications of this communication with the reader. Selective emphasis establishes what we might call narrative hypotaxis, the subordination and super-ordination of narrative elements. Certain story elements are made to serve other elements, as the author focuses the reader's attention on what is important to the author.[13] For instance, in Mark certain aspects of the story are emphasized by repetition.[14] This includes repetition of elements in a single scene (Peter denies Jesus three times), repetition of statements in a single scene (Jesus repeatedly announces his coming passion), and narration of similar, though consecutive, events (Jesus feeds a multitude twice, followed in both cases by a boat scene which reveals the disciples' lack of understanding). The use of repetition for emphasis is clear from the fact that the most detailed and emphatic instance is placed last, that is, the series forms a climax.[15] We will see below that the aspects of the story emphasized by repetition commonly express evaluation of the disciples' behaviour.

A story may arouse expectation of an event and then report the realization or non-realization of our expectations. This not only emphasizes through repetition (our attention is drawn to the event before it happens and again as it happens) but also involves the reader through his interest in the outcome of events. The reader may be involved in several different ways. There may be elements of the narrative which are puzzling, causing the reader to look forward to further enlightenment. The reason for Jesus' commands to silence may constitute such a puzzle in the first half of Mark.[16] Or the reader may anticipate several clear but mutually elusive outcomes. Or the reader may be fairly certain as to how the story will turn out but still be emotionally involved through fear or hope as he anticipates the outcome for important persons in the narrative. Jesus' announcements of his passion and his prediction of the disciples' behaviour in 14:27–31 leave little uncertainty, but they can awaken fearful anticipation. Thus the selective use of prospect and retrospect in a story indicates emphasis by the "implied author". The material emphasized in this way is likely to also contain evaluation.

A further indication of emphasis is the selective use of dialogue and dramatic scenes. The use of dialogue in a dramatic scene involves the expansion of the amount of space in a writing given to a segment of time in the story, compared to the alternative possibility of presenting an event or series of events in a brief summary. Thus dialogue in a dramatic scene emphasizes, while summary narration of events gives them a subordinate position.[17] Of course, the author of Mark may have inherited many of the scenes in his Gospel from previous tradition and may have included some with little modification. Still, he chose to include this material and the emphases contained within it, whether he was fully conscious of what he was doing or not. These choices also reflect the "implied author".

Emphasis and evaluation are closely related, for much of what is emphasized in a story also has negative or positive value, and the emphasis helps to communicate the evaluation. Where the evaluating voice of the implied author is especially clear, we may speak of "reliable commentary". While such commentary is often made by the narrator of a story, it need not be confined to him, for "the author is present in every speech given by any character who had conferred upon him, in whatever manner, the badge of reliability".[18] In the Gospel of Mark it is obvious that Jesus wears the badge of reliability and authority. The most important evaluative commentary in Mark is given by Jesus. We are expected to judge the words and actions of others in the light of the words and actions of Jesus. Our surest guide to the implied author's evaluation of the disciples is to follow the shifting relationship between Jesus and the disciples, noting where they are in concord and where they are not. The viewpoint of the implied author merges with that of Jesus in Mark, since the author has given him the role of chief commentator. If the evaluation of the disciples which emerges by tracing their relation to Jesus appears to be worked out with considerable care, as I believe it is, this evaluation reflects a major concern of the implied author. While the relationship between the disciples and Jesus is the primary basis for judgement of the disciples' behaviour, the relations between the disciples and other figures of the story are also important. If the story suggests a similarity between the disciples and Jesus' opponents, this implies a negative judgement of the disciples. If certain minor characters in the narrative do what the disciples should but do not do, the contrast increases our sense of the disciples' failure. Noting the relations of similarity and contrast, of support and opposition, between the disciples

174

and others in the narrative will help us to understand the disciples' story as shaped by the author.

The implied author's evaluation of the events and persons in this narrative is very important in the communication between author and reader. This evaluation, insofar at it is an accurate reflection of the implied author's perspective rather than a view which will later be rejected or modified, is being recommended to the reader. This indirect recommendation may reflect the author's perception of the reader's situation and needs. The author's communication with his readers is aided by the fact that, just as we constantly evaluate events and persons in everyday life, so we constantly evaluate the events and persons in stories. The author does his part by shaping and guiding our evaluation. Whatever we judge to be positive attracts us; whatever seems negative repels us. These forces of attraction and repulsion, controlled by evaluation embedded in the narrative, guide us in experimenting with life roles. A character role in a story to which we are attracted becomes a possibility for our own lives, perhaps only for a brief holiday during the reading of the story, perhaps in a more serious way leading to changes in our behaviour and basic self-understanding. Noting the similarity between aspects of our own lives and negative aspects of story characters might also lead us to change. There is a natural connection between story and our experience of life, according to Stephen Crites, for human experience has a "narrative quality".[19] If experience is incipient narrative, it is not surprising that stories may react upon and "shape in the most profound way the inner story of experience".[20]

While any positive qualities of story characters will attract, a reader will identify most easily and immediately with characters who seem to share the reader's situation. Assuming that the majority of the first readers of the Gospel were Christians, they would relate most easily and immediately to characters in the story who respond positively to Jesus. The disciples, including the twelve, are the primary continuing characters who, at least at first, seem to respond in this way and to share this essential quality of the Christian reader's self-understanding.[21] I believe that the author of Mark anticipated this response by his readers. He composed his story so as to make use of this initial tendency to identify with the disciples in order to speak indirectly to the reader through the disciples' story. In doing so, he first reinforces the positive view of the disciples which he anticipates from his readers, thus strengthening the tendency to identify with them. Then he reveals the inadequacy of the disciples' response to Jesus, presents the disciples in conflict with Jesus on important issues, and finally shows the disciples as disastrous failures. The surprisingly negative development of the disciples' story requires the reader to distance himself from them and their behaviour. But something of the initial identification remains, for there are similarities between the problems of the disciples and problems which the first readers faced. This tension between identification and repulsion can lead the sensitive reader beyond a naively positive view of himself to self-criticism and repentance. The composition of Mark strongly suggests that the author, by the way in which he tells the disciples' story, intended to awaken his readers to their failures as disciples and call them to repentence. Allowing at first the comfortable assumption that Jesus and his disciples (and with them the Christian reader) are basically in concord, the story reveals points of essential conflict. The reader is left with a choice, a choice represented by the differing ways of Jesus and the disciples. In the light of what Jesus demands, this choice is not easy.

The view I am proposing conflicts with interpretations of Mark which assume that the disciples' difficulties arise from the fact that the passion and resurrection of Jesus, which are essential for true Christian faith, have not yet taken place. Since the Christian reader of Mark can look back on the passion and resurrection, he does not share the disciples' problems. This, I think, is a misreading of Mark's story. Beginning in 8:31 Jesus clearly announces his coming passion and resurrection, and the author of Mark brings out the disciples' reaction with care. The passion of Jesus, in its Marcan meaning, is not a solution to problems of discipleship but presents the problem in its sharpest form. Following the crucified Jesus means taking up the cross oneself (8:34). It also means becoming slave of all (10:44). These are not demands that disappear after Easter (see the prediction of suffering in 13:9–13) nor do they suddenly become easy to fulfill. Even in the first half of the Gospel the blindness of the disciples is associated with fear, lack of trust, and anxious self-concern (see 4:40–1; 6:49–52; 8:14–18), problems which do not disappear in the post-Easter Church. Nor does the message of the resurrection guarantee a faithful response. The disciples heard this message from Jesus beginning at 8:31, yet failed to follow him, and an indication of further failure by Jesus' followers (16:8) comes immediately after the resurrection message at the tomb. The decision of the author to write a Gospel, including the story of the first disciples, rests on the assumption that there are essential similarities between the situation of these disciples and the situation of the early Church, so that, in telling a story about the past, the author can also speak to his present.

The view I am proposing also conflicts with interpretations which regard the strikingly negative treatment of the disciples in Mark as an indication of polemic against a particular group in the Church, a group from which the author sharply distinguishes himself and against which he is warning his readers. One version of this interpretation is carefully developed by Theodore J. Weeden.[22] Such a view cannot explain the positive aspects of the Marcan portrayal of the disciples. In 1:16–20; 3:13–19; and 6:7–13 we learn that Jesus called members of the twelve and that the twelve were appointed by Jesus' own choice (stressed in 3:13) to share in his work and authority. If we assume a polemical situation, material pointing to the authority of the author's enemies and linking this authority to Jesus should be minimized or omitted. However, it is not. To say that it is Jesus as *theios anēr*, that is, the Jesus of Mark's opponents, who bestows his authority on the disciples[23] simply enlarges the problem. If Mark attempted to polemicize by first presenting his opponents' Jesus and then his own view of Jesus, both as parts of one continuous story, he surely failed. The unity of a story leads the reader to regard persons in it as unified characters. Change of character must be justified in the story. In this case the author Mark would have to make unmistakably clear that Jesus himself has been converted to a different viewpoint and that what Jesus says about himself in 8:31ff. means the rejection of what he said and did earlier. The author does not do this.

Jesus' statement in 4:11–12 also conflicts with Weeden's thesis, and attributing these verses to tradition[24] does not solve the problem, for this is precisely the kind of tradition the author could not afford to include in a polemical situation. Furthermore, 14:27–8 and 16:7 indicate, through authoritative speakers (Jesus and the messenger at the tomb), the intention of restoring the broken relationship between Jesus and the disciples. Even if the reconciliation is temporarily frustrated (see 16:8), it remains the

177

intention of Jesus (and the author). Weeden correctly notes the importance of Mark 13 as a clue to the post-Easter situation of the Church as the authors sees it.[25] However, he fails to note that the warnings and exhortations of Mark 13 are addressed to Peter, James, John and Andrew, representatives, supposedly, of the enemy group. The setting which the author gives to this discourse assumes the identity or continuity of these four disciples with the Church which must suffer and preach the Gospel, of which Jesus speaks in Mark 13. Because Weeden's hypothesis of polemic against opponents does not seem to be adequate, we should consider further the hypothesis that the author has undertaken the more subtle task of speaking through story to his friends about the glory of their calling and the grave dangers of failure to which they are largely blind.

The implied author of Mark shapes a story which encourages the reader to associate himself with the disciples. This may begin with a simple identification, assumed by author and reader, of the disciples with Christians of the time of the writing. However, the relation between the disciples and the Christian reader does not remain simple. As the portrait of the disciples becomes clearly negative, the tendency to identify is countered by the necessity of negative evaluation. A tension develops between these two attitudes, with the reader caught in the middle. The degree to which the one attitude or the other is encouraged by the text varies in the different parts of the Gospel and from scene to scene within the parts. Initial identification is encouraged by positive evaluation of the disciples in the early part of Mark. Identification is encouraged later in the Gospel by the similarity between the problems faced by the disciples and the problems faced by the Gospel's first readers (and, perhaps, by later Christian readers also). But as the inadequacies of the disciples' response to Jesus become increasingly clear, the reader must distance himself from the disciples and begin to seek another way. The identification of the reader with the disciples does not prevent this but contributes to the existential seriousness of the new search. The more clearly the reader sees that the disciples represent himself, the more clearly the necessary rejection of the disciples' behaviour becomes a negation of one's past self. The recognition of the disciples' failure and the search for an alternative way become a search for the new self who can follow Jesus faithfully as a disciple.

Wolfgang Iser's discussion of the role of "negation" in the novel offers a helpful parallel.

> Though the novel deals with social and historical norms, this does not mean that it simply reproduces contemporary values . . . [In the novel norms] are set in a new context which changes their function, insofar as they no longer act as social regulations but as the subject of a discussion which, more often than not, ends in a questioning rather than a confirmation of their validity. This is frequently brought about by the varying degrees of negation with which the norms are set up in their fictional context – a negation which impels the reader to seek a positive counter-balance elsewhere than in the world immediately familiar to him. The challenge implicit in the negation is, of course, offered first and foremost to those whose familiar world is made up of the norms that have been negated. These, the readers of the novel, are then forced to take an active part in the composition of the novel's meaning, which revolves round a basic divergence from the familiar.[26]

For instance, a novel may present an appealing character, endowed with the qualities generally approved, who, in spite of or because of those qualities, comes to a bad end. The novel will often not state the alternative qualities or choices which would have led to a happier result. But the negativity in the story induces the reader to ponder what went wrong and imagine an alternative. Thus negation of the expected encourages "the reader's production of the meaning of the text",[27] which requires the reader's active participation. It can also lead to a fresh perspective on one's past assumptions and values. The strong negative aspect of the disciples' story in Mark functions in a similar way, moving the reader to ponder how those called by Jesus could go so far astray and what is required if he is to escape similar failure.

In important ways Jesus represents the positive alternative to the failure of the disciples. He not only calls the disciples to save their lives by losing them and to be servants, but he follows this way himself. Presenting the positive alternative within the story may seem to remove the necessity for the reader to imagine the "positive counter-balance", decreasing the reader's active role, so prized by Iser. However, closer study of the alternative to which the author points will show that it is far from a cut-and-dried answer to what is true and right. In 8:31–10:45, and again in 14:1–16:8, the central symbol of the death and resurrection of Jesus is related in successive scenes to different aspects of the life of the disciple. The repeated use of this symbol as a key element in dramatic scenes, with new and expanding meaning for the disciple, suggests that it is an "expanding symbol", with a depth of meaning not easily exhausted.[28] Furthermore, the continuing challenge of this expanding symbol to our basic assumptions about life comes to expression in the repeated use of paradox (8:35; 9:35; 10:43–4; see also 10:31).[29] Paradox, a conflict in language, reminds the reader that the positive alternative indicated by the author persistently conflicts with what people assume is right and reasonable. So the positive alternative remains a mystery and a challenge.

II

We will now consider aspects of the Gospel's composition which indicate selective emphasis and guide the reader's response to the disciples. We must note the principal episodes in the disciples' story from the first to the last chapter of Mark, although the scope of the material will prevent detailed discussion. Our study will reveal a development presented with considerable care, indicating that we are dealing with a major concern of the author.

Immediately after Jesus begins his preaching, the author of Mark tells of the call of four disciples who will later take their place among the twelve (1:16–20). Jesus' command to follow him establishes a norm by which the reader can judge the behaviour of the disciples. At this point the response fits the command. Later in the story Jesus will again call for followers (8:34), but the subsequent narrative (especially chapter 14) will demonstrate the disciples' failure. The positive relation between Jesus and the disciples is emphasized and developed in two further scenes in the early chapters of Mark which centre on the intended role of Jesus' closest associates. In 3:13–19 we are told that Jesus selected twelve for a special relationship and responsibility. The twelve receive their position by Jesus' own choice (emphasized in 3:13). This position involves being "with" Jesus in close association and sharing in the work of preaching and exorcism which Jesus himself has been doing (compare 3:14–15 with 1:38–9). There is only one negative note, a reference to Judas' betrayal (3:19). The appointment of the twelve is obviously linked to 6:7–13 (see 6:30), where the twelve are actually sent out on the mission previously mentioned. They both preach and cast out demons, that is, they follow Jesus' instructions. Opposition is predicted, but there is no indication that this causes the twelve to fail in their mission. Thus, the author of Mark distributes three connected verses through the first six chapters of his Gospel, scenes which indicate, on the one hand, what Jesus commanded the twelve to do (establishing a norm by which they can be judged), and, on the other, the obedient response of the twelve. This series of three scenes presents the twelve positively. They have a special status and a special task, which, on one occasion at least, they fulfill. There is special emphasis on the close relation of the disciples with Jesus and the similarity of their role to his.[30]

This positive evaluation of the twelve in the early chapters of Mark is reinforced by other texts which refer to the disciples or "those around" Jesus. In 2:14–28 not only Jesus but the disciples face the criticism of the scribes and Pharisees, while Jesus defends both himself and them. In these controversies Jesus and the disciples stand together against the opposition of the scribes and Pharisees. This is no longer so clearly the case in the controversy in 7:1–23, as 7:17–19 indicate. In 3:20–35 the opposition of the scribes to Jesus is emphasized strongly and their attitude is associated with that of Jesus' family. This becomes the basis for some very positive statements about Jesus' followers. In 3:31–5 "those around" Jesus contrasted with his natural family.[31] Those around Jesus are his true mother and brothers (another way of stressing close association with Jesus). The phrase "those around him" is then carried over to 4:10, and the twelve are explicitly associated with this group. In the statement of Jesus which follows, a sharp contrast is made between the disciples and the outsiders: the mystery of the Kingdom is given to those around Jesus, but those outside do not see or understand. This is very positive evaluation of the disciples in authoritative commentary by Jesus, emphasized by contrast with the position of others. Whether the author wrote 4:11–12 himself or received these verses from previous tradition, they inevitabley shape the view of the disciples which his writing presents. They must have some place within the purposes of the author if he was as concerned with his presentation of the disciples as he seems to be elsewhere. If the author were engaged in polemic against a group of heretics represented by the disciples, these words would be counter-productive. They could and would be used by the opponents to support their own case. However, these words would be useful to the author if (1) he really believes that this is what Jesus intended and intends, that the mystery of the Kingdom be revealed to the disciples and the Church, and (2) he is not conducting a polemical argument against recognized opponents but doing something more subtle: involving his readers in a story in which they will first recognize themselves and the positive qualities of their own self-image and then be led to self-criticism.[32]

In the material mentioned so far, the author goes out of his way to make the disciples attractive figures, both by stressing their close association with Jesus and by contrasting them sharply with negative groups. The first part of Mark's Gospel encourages the reader to have high expectations for the disciples and to associate himself with them. If we think in terms of consistent but static doctrine, there may seem to be a conflict between this positive view of the disciples and other material in Mark. If we think in terms of narrative development, however, we have the common story technique of encouraging the reader to contemplate one possibility so that he will feel more sharply the opposite development when it arrives. Jesus' authoritative statement about the disciples in 4:11–12 will serve as a norm by which the author will measure the disciples' failure (see 8:17–18).

When we look back at Mark 4 from the end of the Gospel, we can see it already suggests the possibility of negative developments in the disciples' story. First, the hearing of the word is presented as a problem. The word doesn't always fall on good soil; it doesn't always bear fruit when it has once begun to grow. And Jesus speaks with urgency about the importance of hearing and about the revelation of the hidden. Second, in 4:13 Jesus appears to be critical of the disciples' lack of understanding. However, the explanation which follows allows the reader to assume that the problem has been cleared up, an assumption reinforced by closing the scene with a general reference to private instruction (4:34). Third, Jesus' teaching in Mark 4 is followed by the story of the stilling of the storm, in which the disciples are criticized for their cowardice and lack of faith (4:40) and appear to be ignorant of Jesus' status (4:41). Still, the reader reading Mark for the first time would not yet guess that the disciples are involved in any major and continuing difficulty. The view of the disciples is basically positive through 6:30, although there have been some suggestions of difficulty. However, the foundation has been laid for a very negative judgement of the disciples if their behaviour should conflict with Jesus' stated intentions for them.

The call of the four disciples (1:16–20), the choice of the twelve (3:13–19), and the mission of the twelve (6:7–13, 30) appear to be linked scenes which reinforce and develop a particular view of the twelve. This compositional technique of linking scenes by repeating (thereby emphasizing) and developing a set of motifs reappears in the three boat scenes in the first half of Mark. These three boat scenes, the stilling of the storm (4:35–41), the encounter with Jesus on the water (6:45–52), and the discussion in the boat (8:14–21), isolate Jesus and the disciples from the crowds by the setting of the scenes and highlight the attitude of the disciples. The first two boat scenes are connected by the motifs of the disciples' difficulty with the sea, Jesus' miraculous power, and the disciples' fear and lack of understanding. The third is not a miracle story, but it is linked to the second by references in both to Jesus' feeding of a multitude, and it presents in a most emphatic way the disciples' failure to understand.

The second and third boat scenes follow closely the two feedings of the multitudes and refer back to them. Both feedings are preceded by a conversation between Jesus and the disciples. In 6:37 Jesus charges the disciples with the responsibility of feeding the crowd, but their reply shows that they see no way in fulfilling this responsibility. However, through Jesus the crowd is fed, and the disciples are given a subordinate role in the feeding. The feeding is followed by a boat scene in which the behaviour of the disciples is clearly criticized. The fear and astonishment which the disciples show at their encounter with Jesus on the water is attributed in 6:52 to their failure to understand the feeding and to their hardened hearts (in evaluative commentary by the narrator). Then the cycle of events is repeated, emphasizing the theme of disciple blindness and bringing it to an effective climax. In 8:2–3 Jesus points out the need of the crowd to the disciples. It is not surprising that the disciples do not know what to do in the first feeding, but when the very same situation arises again (note that the author presents the feedings as two consecutive events, not two versions of the same event), the reaction of the disciples suggests a perverse blindness that must disturb the reader. The third boat scene (8:14–21) puts great emphasis in this perverse blindness of the disciples. After Jesus has twice fed a multitude, the disciples are pictured as anxious about their low supply of bread. Jesus castigates them for this, reminding them of the abundant supply of food left over from the feedings and, in the process, accusing them of the same blindness, deafness, and lack of understanding attributed to the outsiders in 4:11–12. The discussion begins with Jesus' warning against the leaven of the Pharisees and of Herod, a warning which the disciples are too preoccupied to heed. This scene functions as a climactic summary of preceding scenes. It is the climax of the boat scenes, bringing the theme of disciple blindness to emphatic expression. It refers to the feeding scenes, using these experiences as a basis for accusing the disciples. It recalls 4:11–12 (see 8:18) but shows that, contrary to Jesus' intention, the disciples share the blindness of the outsiders. They are heedless of the danger of sharing the blind opposition to God's messengers shown by the Pharisees and Herod (8:15), for, in fact, they already share their hardness of heart (see 6:52 and 8:17 with 3:5–6). A clear shift in the disciples' role has taken place. From a position with Jesus as his followers, the disciples have moved to a position which associates them with Jesus' enemies and the outsiders of 4:11–12.

As the author begins to present the disciples in strongly negative terms, some of the miracle stories become contrasting scenes. It is no accident that the final sequence of feeding and discussion in the boat, with Jesus' reproachful question concerning the disciples' inability to see and hear (8:18), is framed by stories of healing a deaf man and a blind man (7:31–7; 8:22–6). These two healing stories have a number of common features and phrases, so that the second one reminds us of the first. The healing of blind Bartimaeus in 10:46–52 is probably a third story in this series, for Bartimaeus follows Jesus on the way to the cross (10:52), a discipleship theme. The contrast between 8:22–6 and 8:18 is clearer than the connection between the former and Peter's confession. These miracles highlight the deafness and blindness of the disciples by contrast and, at the same time, indirectly promise the reader that Jesus is able to create true discipleship in spite of the story of blindness and denial in which the reader is implicated.

The scene in 8:14–21 leaves the relation between Jesus and the disciples in a very unsatisfactory state, but, as long as the story goes on, there is hope for some resolution of the problem. The reader awaits such a resolution. However, the reader may not be entirely clear as to the nature of the disciples' problem, for the story has given various kinds of clues. On the one hand, the boat scenes have emphasized the disciples' fear, lack of trust, and anxious self-concern (4:40; 6:49–50; 8:14–16), associating these with a lack of understanding. On the other hand, the question of who Jesus is has been raised (4:41; see 6:14–16 and the identification of Jesus by demons). Perhaps the problem arises from the disciples' failure to identify Jesus correctly. Insofar as this is the problem, there is ironic distance between the reader and the disciples, for the reader knows what the disciples do not know. However, in 8:27ff. the reader discovers that the problem is not resolved when Peter makes a correct confession of faith (8:29). Jesus insists that something more must be said about himself and, as a direct corollary, about discipleship (8:31ff.). Even this additional teaching does not solve the disciples' problem. For the role of suffering which Jesus chooses and the meaning of Jesus' role for his disciples (following in suffering, becoming servants) challenges and provokes the fear and anxious self-concern portrayed in the boat scenes.

In 8:31–10:45 there is clear evidence of careful composition, with close attention to the role of the disciples. Three passion announcements (8:31; 9:31; 10:33–4) become the basis of a major three-fold pattern building up to a climax. Each of these passion announcements is followed by resistance (8:32–3) or behaviour contrary to that of Jesus (9:33–4; 10:35–41) on the part of the disciples, followed in turn by Jesus' corrective teaching. This teaching points to Jesus' suffering as a model for Jesus' followers (especially at 8:34–5 and 10:45) and relates the approaching death of Jesus to two problems which probably reflect problems of the early Church as perceived by the author: the possibility of persecution and martyrdom (8:34–8), and the desire for status and domination (9:33–7; 10:35–45). The passion announcements are accompanied by indications that the disciples are both afraid and without understanding (9:32; 10:32), recalling features of the boat scenes, but the disciples' anxious self-concern now takes specific shape as fear of suffering and desire for status. Both of these problems are clearly important to the implied author. The latter is carried over from the second to the third instance of the pattern, where it is developed as a forceful climax (10:35–45). Placing this concern in final position in the pattern seems to give it the greatest emphasis.[33] However, the former concern is also supported by the larger composition of Mark. Not only is the teaching in 8:34–8 stressed by the voice from the cloud at the transfiguration ("Listen to him", 9:7), but this teaching picks up the previous theme of following (8:34) and provides a basis for evaluation of the disciples' behaviour in chapter 14. The strong emphasis in chapter 14 on the disciples' failure to follow Jesus to suffering and death, as they had promised, shows that the concern expressed in 8:34–8 is also of major importance.

Jesus' teaching about discipleship is the last element in each of the three instances of the pattern discussed above. This aspect of the composition has the following effects: (1) The teaching is emphasized through end position in the pattern and through contrast with the preceding actions of the disciples. (2) Since no response of the disciples is narrated immediately after 10:45, there is still a possibility that the disciples will change their ways. The possibility of various responses not only holds open the outcome of the disciples' story but allows the reader to consider various responses for himself. Of course, later actions of the disciples should be evaluated in the light of the authoritative commentary on discipleship in 8:31–10:45. (3) Not only the authority of the teacher but also the emphasis and openness noted above allow this material to function as direct teaching to the reader, not just teaching to the first disciples. This is also promoted by the generality of much of the teaching.

While the principal repetitive pattern in 8:31–10:45 gives special importance to the issues of suffering and desire for status, these are not the only causes of tension between Jesus and the disciples in this section. In various ways the disciples are put in a bad light, in connection with a number of specific problems. In 9:14–29 the disciples fail in the role of exorcists, to which the twelve were commissioned and which they had successfully performed (6:7, 13). In 9:37 Jesus instructs the disciples about the importance of receiving a child. In 10:13–16 they disobey this instruction and are rebuked by Jesus. (This is related to the theme of desire for status – see 9:35–7). In 9:38–40 we learn of the disciples' attempts to end the work of an exorcist who "was not following us". Again their attitude proves to be contrary to that of Jesus. The story of the rich man is followed by a conversation between Jesus and the disciples about riches (10:23–31), which ends with a promise and a warning (10:29–31). While the promise evidently applies to the disciples, it has a critical edge to it. It pokes fun at the feeling that a great reward is due by speaking in extravagant terms of a present reward "with persecutions".[34] Thus, in a variety of ways and in connection with a variety of specific issues the conflict between the desires, expectations, and actions of the disciples and the authoritative instruction of Jesus is shown to the reader. The reader must choose between the attitudes of Jesus and those of the disciples. It is clear how the choice should go according to the values of the author. But the difficulty of Jesus' demands reminds the reader that in many ways he is like the disciples.

Chapter 13 is also important for the author's shaping of the disciples' story. This discourse of Jesus has a setting prior to Jesus' death and resurrection but deals with events which will transpire after the death and resurrection. Placing the discourse at this point in the narrative is a compositional choice by the author. Even if, for some reason, the author did not want to present this as a discourse of the risen Christ, he could easily have placed this material after the resurrection, either through presenting it in the narrator's voice (Now, before his death Jesus had said . . .) or in the voice of a story character (Peter said, "Remember what Jesus told us . . .").[35] However, this discourse is placed before the passion story, at least in part as preparation for the events in chapter 14.[36] It prepares for chapter 14 in two respects. On the one hand, Jesus' warnings refer to situations similar to those the disciples face in chapter 14. Jesus tells the disciples that they will face persecution and death and must endure to the end (13:9–13). He warns them (and the reader – see 13:37) that they must watch and not be caught asleep (13:33–7). However, as the story continues we learn that the disciples desert and deny Jesus rather than face death and that they fail to watch in Gethsemane. The disciples' failure is heightened by the preceding instruction. On the other hand, Jesus' discourse anticipates a continuing role for the disciples beyond the disaster of chapter 14. So the preparation is not entirely negative.

The importance attached to Judas' betrayal, the flight of the other disciples, and Peter's denial appears in the fact that Jesus predicts all three of these events. In the narrative these predictions serve both to emphasize and evaluate these events. They emphasize because the event is, in effect, told more than once, the reader's attention being called to it before it actually happens in the sequence of events. This is coupled with strong negative evaluation. This is obvious in the remark about Judas in 14:21, and use of symbols of close relationship (table fellowship, 14:18–20; kiss, 14:44–5) heightens the sense of betrayal. The prediction of the scattering of the disciples and the denial by Peter

187

also heightens the negative evaluation of these acts, for the disciples respond by rejecting Jesus' predictions and promising just the opposite (14:31). Thus the desertion and denial which follow are not only contrary to Jesus' stern call to follow him in suffering in 8:34–7, making the disciples liable to the judgement announced in 8:38. These acts are also contrary to an explicit promise by the disciples. When the reader reads these predictions, he knows how the disciples' story will come out, for Jesus' predictions carry authority. But that does not lessen his emotional involvement. The emotions of tragedy are aroused as the reader witnesses the fatal promises being made and recognizes the approach of disaster. The composition of the rest of chapter 14 fits what we now expect. In the Gethsemane scene the author emphasizes, through narrating the return of Jesus three times, the failure of the disciples to watch.[37] The desertion of Jesus by the fleeing disciples is reported in 14:50. The following flight of the naked young man probably dramatizes the shamefulness of the disciples' flight and satirizes the pretensions of Christians who claim to be ready for martyrdom.[38] The story continues by noting that Peter, who is now the last hope for faithful discipleship among Jesus' close associates, followed Jesus "from a distance" (14:54). The story of Jesus before the Jewish council is framed by the introductory reference to Peter's presence (14:54) and the following scene of denial, thus encouraging the reader to note the contrast between Jesus' fearless disclosure (14:62), by which he is condemned, and Peter's denial. The construction of the denial narrative itself encourages both sympathetic awareness of Peter's plight, as he struggles to escape the persistent accusations, and full recognition of the horrible thing that he is doing. The narrative goes into unnecessary detail, recording three separate denials and building to a climax with the third, which is accompanied by a curse (14:71). The composition of the story promotes both the reader's sympathetic involvement and an emphatically negative evaluation of Peter's act. Jesus' closest friends have completely failed to take up the cross and follow him.

In one sense the story of the disciples is over, for nothing further is recorded of the actions of the twelve, who have been the central figures in this story. The disciples' story has come to a disastrous conclusion, and the author has spared nothing in emphasizing the disaster. This ending sends reverberations back through the whole preceding story. The reader who was at first content to view the disciples as reflections of his own faith and who may have continued to hope for a happy ending to their story must now try to disentangle himself from them, which will mean choosing a path contrary to their path. The possibility of this other path is recognized within the story, for there is a sense in which the disciples' story is *not* over. There are features of the story which hold the future open. At 14:28 and 16:7 first Jesus and then the "young man" at the tomb announce a journey to Galilee and a meeting there between the risen Jesus and his faithless disciples. The relation between 14:27 and 28 indicates that this anticipated meeting can be a remedy (note *alla* ["but"]) for the scattering of the sheep and the loss of their shepherd, that is, this meeting can restore the relationship between Jesus and his disciples, in spite of desertion and denial. So the Gospel holds open the possibility that those who deserted Jesus will again become his followers, reinstating the relationship established by Jesus' call.[39] I say "possibility" because we are not told that the disciples have changed their ways and become true followers. In fact, the women's failure to follow the instructions of the resurrection messenger (16:7–8) gives an ambiguous quality to the ending of the Gospel. It is not clear how the story will develop from this point. The cowardly disobedience which characterized the disciples reappears in the behaviour of the women. It has not been eliminated from the Church by the resurrection. The failure of the women to convey the message may also suggest that the disciples are insufficiently aware of the need and possibility of a new beginning after disaster. So, on the one hand, a figure of authority clearly states that a meeting will take place (16:7), a meeting which carries with it the possibility of renewed discipleship. On the other hand, there are indications that this renewal is not a simple and automatic affair. A positive development is indicated but negative possibilities are also suggested. The Gospel is open-ended, for the outcome of the story depends on decisions which the Church, including the reader, must still make.

The continuing story is developed most extensively in chapter 13, where Jesus, in a discourse addressed to Peter, James, John and Andrew (three of these four have prominent roles in scenes emphasizing conflict between Jesus and the disciples), warns them, and the Church, about the trials which they must face between the resurrection and parousia. The discourse assumes a restored relationship but also recognizes the continuing possibility of failure. Jesus speaks of the need to watch (13:33–7), although the disciples failed to watch in Gethsemane, and states that the disciples will be handed over to councils (13:9) just as Jesus was, although the disciples ran from this possibility in the passion story. The story is not over. It continues into the time of the reader, and the author anticipates that each reader will decide how it comes out for himself.

Finally, as the author emphasizes the disciples' failure he also points to a different possibility through very brief references to contrasting figures. These figures include Bartimaeus, who follows Jesus on the way to the cross (10:52), the anointing woman, whose act appropriately recognizes the approaching passion (14:7–8), Simon of Cyrene, who must "take up"[40] Jesus' cross (15:21), the centurion at the cross, who makes the confession of faith which Peter refused to make (15:39), and Joseph of Arimathea, who cares for Jesus' burial as we would expect his closest friends and relatives to do.[41] These are figures who replace the disciples in the roles which they fail to fill. They appear in such brief flashes that they do not allow the reader to shift his attention from Jesus and the disciples and become deeply involved with these other characters. But they do point to the way which contrasts with the disciples' failure.

I do not wish to imply that the disciples' story is the sole interest of the author of Mark. However, what we have discovered does indicate that it has major importance within the larger story which is being told.

We have noticed various features of the narrative composition of Mark which seem to indicate selective emphasis and imply an evaluation. We have seen how such composition shapes the narrative role of the disciples throughout the Gospel. We have noted the importance of relationships among characters, and shifts in those relationships, in the understanding of narrative roles. The changing relationship between the disciples and Jesus, moving from concord to expanding and intensifying conflict, has been a key element in this study. The role of the disciples is shaped by the composition of the author and reflects his concerns. The purpose of the author and the response which he anticipates from the reader begin to come clear when we consider the author's shaping of the disciples' role as indirect communication with the reader. The author assumes that there are essential similarities between the disciples and his anticipated readers, so that what he reveals about the disciples may become a revelation about the readers and so enable them to change.

NOTES

1 Norman Perrin, "The Evangelists as Author: Reflections on Method in the Study and Interpretation of the Synoptic Gospels and Acts", *Biblical Research* 17 (1972) 9–10.

2 Ibid., 15–17.

3 Quentin Quesnell (1969) 51f. seems to be making a similar point when he distinguished material which is "redactional by nature" from what is redaction "in fact".

4 Robert Scholes and Robert Kellogg give considerable attention to narrative prior to the novel in their book *The Nature of Narrative* (New York: Oxford University Press, 1966). There is currently a strong interest in clarifying, through the construction of abstract "grammars" of narrative, the structures and relationships basic to all narrative. In this discussion, examples simpler than the novel are often chosen. In this area of discussion I have found the following especially valuable: Vladimir Propp, *Morphology of the Folktale*, 2nd ed. (Austin: University of Texas Press, 1968); the work of Claude Bremond, including *Logique du récit* (Paris: Editions du Seuil, 1973); "Le Message narratif", *Communications* 4 (1964) 4–32; "Morphology of the French Folktale", *Semiotica* 2 (1970) 247–76; "Le Rôle d'influenceur", *Communications* 16 (1970) 60–9; and the work of Tzvetan Todorov, including "Poétique" in François Wahl, et al., *Qu'est-ce que le structuralisme?* (Paris: Editions du Seuil, 1968) 97–166; *Grammaire du Decameron* (The Hague: Mouton, 1969); "Language and Literature", in *The Languages of Criticism and the Sciences of Man*, ed. Richard Macksey and Eugenio Donato (Baltimore: John Hopkins Press, 1970) 125–33; *Poetik der Prosa* (Frankfurt: Athenaeum, 1972 [trs. of *Poétique de la prose*]).

5 Theodore J. Weeden (1971) 15f. refers to Livy's indirect methods of interpreting historical characters, influencing the reader's attitudes. Weeden believes that Livy's approach is similar both to Greek drama and to Mark.

6 The most comprehensive and systematic study of narrative roles known to me is in Bremond's *Logique du récit*. It would have been possible to utilize Bremond's categories in the following discussion. However, these categories, which are quite abstract, would have made it more difficult for me to make my points clearly and concisely.

7 The roles of Jesus, as he interacts with others in the gospel story, are, of course, especially important. It may be possible to gain new insight into the Christology of Mark by concentrating not on the titles applied to Jesus but on the narrative functions which Jesus performs within the Marcan story. This will require a comprehensive view of narrative role interaction in Mark. Many

characters in the Gospels appear only in a single scene. Still, study of the relationships and situations of these characters, together with possible developments within the scene, may be rewarding. Furthermore, different persons, whether members of a designated group or not, may have similar roles in similar narratives, e.g. the miracle stories. Study of the similarities and variations in these roles may be worth while.

8 Robert P. Meye, in *Jesus and the Twelve* (Grand Rapids, Mich.: Eerdmanns, 1968), argues that "the evangelist Mark equates discipleship and Twelveship throughout his narrative" (228). However, there is evidence to the contrary. It is made clear in 4:10 that the following discourse, with its private explanation of the parable of the sower, is addressed not only to the twelve but to a larger group. In 4:33–4 the author generalizes the pattern of the preceding narrative (public teaching in parables followed by private explanation) and notes that the private explanation is given to Jesus' "disciples".

9 Wolfgang Iser speaks of the "potential multiplicity of connections" in a literary text. The reader must work out connections for himself. Because the text requires the reader to be creatively active in this way, he becomes involved in events, and they seem real to him even when they are "far from his own reality". "The literary text activates our own faculties, enabling us to recreate the world it presents. The product of this creative activity is what we might call the virtual dimension of the text, which endows it with its reality. This virtual dimension is not the text itself, nor is it the imagination of the reader: it is the coming together of text and imagination"; see *The Implied Reader* (Baltimore: John Hopkins University Press, 1974) 278–9.

10 Wayne C. Booth, in his book *The Rhetoric of Fiction* (Chicago: University of Chicago Press, 1961), argues that "the rhetorical dimension in literature is inescapable" (105). Among other things this involves "the ordering of intensities" in a literary work (60) and the use of "reliable commentary" (169), in which a narrator or other person in the story suggests a set of norms and values in light of which action and character in the story should be judged. I believe that these features of "the rhetoric of fiction" can be found also in Mark's narrative.

11 The implied author may differ in significant ways from the author in everyday life, for one may write in order to be, for a time, a different person. The phrase "implied author" also calls attention to the fact that the position of the author must be inferred from the choices made in writing the story. Booth speaks of "the core of norms and choices [within a work] which I am calling the implied author" (ibid., 74).

12 Dan O. Via, Jr. (1975) 147 adopts the term "discourse level", as distinct from story level, to speak of this communication.

13 The study of narrative "deep structure" should not draw our attention away from this narrative hypotaxis found in the so-called surface structure of the text. It is only through taking the latter into account that we can clarify the special way in which an author has used narrative structures to communicate with his readers.

192

14 On the relation between repetition and emphasis, see Robert C. Tannehill, *The Sword of His Mouth* (Philadelphia: Fortress Press, 1975) 40–1; see further 39–51 of the same book, where I discuss other significant aspects of repetition, with special reference to synoptic sayings. Some of these observations also apply to repetition in narrative.

15 This is the case in the three examples just mentioned. See 14:71 in relation to the preceding denials of Peter, 10:33–4 in relation to 8:31 and 9:31; 8:14–21 in relation to 6:45–52.

16 See also Via (1975) 154–5; he suggests that Mark develops and finally resolves the enigma of who Jesus is. However, this enigma, I believe, operates on two levels. When we compare what the story tells the reader with what the characters of the story know, we see that the reader is partially "on the inside". However, there are also enigma and surprise for the reader.

17 See Gérard Genette's discussion of "duration" in narrative in *Figures III* (Paris: Editions du Seuil, 1972) 122–44. Genette also expands on a number of points mentioned above; see especially his discussion of order (including prospect and retrospect), frequency, the mimetic mode, and narrative levels.

18 Booth, 18.

19 Crites argues that "consciousness grasps its objects in an inherently temporal way" and memory retains a temporal order. Furthermore, "the inner form of any possible experience is determined by the union of . . . three distinct modalities": "the present of things past", "the present of things present", and "the present of things future', and "the tensed unity of these modalities requires narrative forms . . . for its expression" ("The Narrative Quality of Experience", *Journal of the American Academy of Religion* 39 [1971] 291–311; see esp. 298, 301).

20 Ibid., 304.

21 Karl-Georg Reploh (1969) is based on the correct insight that the disciples in Mark are representatives of the early Church. However, Reploh, like other New Testament scholars, does not deal adequately with the narrative form of Mark. Furthermore, his selection of Marcan material is too restricted. Especially striking is the omission of everything after 10:52. One cannot judge the meaning of a story without attention to its outcome. See also David J. Hawkin, "The Incomprehension of the Disciples in the Markan Redaction", *JBL* 91 (1972) 491–500. Hawkin rightly poses the question of "how the writer wishes the reader to relate to characters and groups within the story", especially to the disciples (493).

22 See Weeden (1971).

23 Ibid., 61.

24 Ibid., 141–2.

25 Ibid., 71.

26 Iser, *The Implied Reader*, xii; see also 34, 37, 46, 118–19.

27 Ibid., 37.

28 See E. K. Brown, *Rhythm in the Novel* (Toronto: University of Toronto Press, 1950) 33–59. According to Brown, "the expanding symbol is repetition balanced by variation, and that variation is in progressively deepening disclosure" (57). "By the use of an expanding symbol, the novelist persuades and impels his readers towards two beliefs. First, that beyond the verge of what he can express, there is an area which can be glimpsed, never surveyed. Second, that this area has an order of its own which we should greatly care to know" (59).

29 On the significance of the form of Mark 8:35 and 10:43, see Tannehill, *Sword*, 98–107.

30 A point correctly emphasized by Günther Schmahl (1974). However, Schmahl does not deal adequately with the negative aspect of the disciples' behaviour.

31 On the significance of the rhetorical structure of this scene, see Tannehill, *Sword*, 165–71.

32 Recognition of this positive self-image would be promoted by the fact that the contrast between the Church's privilege of revelation and the blindness of the world was common in the early Church, as we see from its presence in various parts of the New Testament; see Quesnell (1969) 183–7.

33 Anitra Bingham Kolenkow discusses Mark's emphasis on serving rather than seeking status: see "Beyond Miracles, Suffering and Eschatology", *Society of Biblical Literature 1973 Seminar Papers* 2 (1973) 155–202. It is worth noting that 10:35–40 combines the concerns of suffering and status. James and John are willing to suffer for status in the final glory.

34 On the significance of Mark 10:29–30 in its setting, see Tannehill, *Sword*, 147–52.

35 On the significance of comparing order of narration to the chronological order of events in the study of narrative composition, see Genette, 77–121 (n. 17 above).

36 The desire to end with 16:1–8 was probably another factor in the author's choice.

37 The historical question of whether Jesus actually did return three times to find the disciples sleeping is irrelevant to my point. Even if he did, it is easy enough for a narrator to report similar but separate events in summary form (Jesus kept coming and finding . . . [Greek imperfect]). Drawing out this feature of the narrative by repeated narration results in emphasis. The same applies to the three-fold narration of Peter's denial. See Genette, 145–82.

38 This interpretation may be supported by the reference to the fine linen (*sindōn*) worn by the young man. Elsewhere in the New Testament the word is used only of the cloth in which Jesus was buried (see 15:46 and par.). If this detail is significant, it suggests that this man is so sure of his loyalty that he comes all dressed for death, but suddenly changes his mind when his death is a real prospect. His nakedness emphasizes the shamefulness of his flight.

39 It seems to me unlikely that 14:28 and 16:7 refer to a meeting at the parousia. The pre-parousia suffering of the Church and its proclamation of the Gospel

(see 13:9–13) presuppose a restoration of the relationship between Jesus and his followers. The anticipated meeting can be postponed until the parousia only if we ignore its function of reconciling the scattered sheep with their shepherd and mitigate, as the author of Mark does not, the seriousness of the break between Jesus and the disciples which takes place in chapter 14. For other arguments against the parousia interpretation of these verses, see R. H. Stein, "A Short Note on Mark xiv. 28 and xvi. 7", *NTS* 20 (1973–4) 445–52.

40 Eduard Schweizer (1970) 343 notes that the verb is the same as in Jesus' call to take up the cross and follow in 8:34.

41 The author takes time to note that John the Baptist was buried by his disciples (6:29). Is he suggesting a contrast with Jesus?

8

*Mark's Significance for the Theology of Early Christianity**

SIEGFRIED SCHULZ

Mark occupies the key position within the history of early Christian theology. His real significance, however, rests not on his famous "messianic secret", his theory of parables, or his writing a "passion narrative with an extended introduction". His central significance lies in the fact that he was the first and the only one to write a Gospel.

It is true that we have in the New Testament four Gospels. But the label "Gospel" only really suits Mark. The inner intention of the so-called Gospel of Matthew is to be a *biblos* ("book": Matt: 1:1) of halachic and apocalyptic compilations of sayings, which Matthew can occasionally call a gospel (e.g. 24:14; 26:13). The so-called Gospel of John does not contain the concept *euangelion* ("gospel") at all: it is, in fact, a *biblion* ("book": 20:30), a collection of revelatory discourses. Luke also is consistent in not using this concept in his first "Word" (Acts 1:1), since his aim is to write a *historia*, i.e. a *life* of Jesus.

Despite this, it remains true that none of Mark's successors, right down to the apocryphal literature (see the Nag Hammadi material), could avoid this structural pressure. Mark's Gospel had its followers.

It is well known that Paul was the first to introduce the word *euangelion* into the New Testament. The concept and its parameters of meaning stem from hellenistic and oriental religions

* First published in *Studia Evangelica II*, 1 (Berlin, 1964) 135–45.

of redemption. The same history of religious background is normative for Mark's use of the concept *euangelion*. But this comparison with other New Testament writers and the wider religious background is no further help in understanding the origin of Mark's Gospel because Mark has joined a completely new subject-matter to this concept which in its origins and still in Paul was non-literary. Roughly speaking "gospel" in Mark no longer means the oral (and epistolary) message of glad tidings, but a history.

This line of enquiry takes us no further, however, on the history of the concept. For although Paul and Mark have used the same word the former has not written a Gospel but proclaimed it, and done so without using Palestinian and hellenistic Jesus traditions. His gospel was in no way the *historia* of Jesus, but contains the word of the cross, complete with the traditional scheme of gentile-Christian missionary preaching: call to repentance, threat of judgement and proclamation of Jesus' resurrection (1 Thess. 1; Heb. 6; Acts 14 and 17).

What at once strikes us about Mark is precisely the pluralism of individual traditions from different and differing communities, brought together for the first time into a connected and coherent story of the historical Jesus. Geographical links, chronological sequences, and biographical information are the constitutive elements of this *historia* between Galilee and Jerusalem seen as gospel. These redactional transitions are decisively increased by eight Marcan summaries: 1:14f., 32ff., 39; 3:7–12; 6:12f., 30–4, 52–6; 8:14–21. The perennial concern of Mark to present an itinerary and to create through detailed depictions of circumstances fictive spaces of time, is especially noticeable here. In a word, Mark applies in his Gospel the still classical law of every literary and historical narrative: the law of temporal sequence.

The well-known quest of the historical Jesus has in its own way proved that this story cannot be evaluated historically. It is, of course, kerygmatically based. But that then raises the decisive problem: what necessity is there in the kerygma for such a conception? For this historical Jesus set in a connected story is not a "righteous" (or "innocent"), "man" (*anthrōpos dikaios*: Luke 23:47); that would be an illegitimate jump to Luke, the father of the West and promoter of emergent early catholicism. This Jesus is the Son of God, presented by God in his baptism, proclaimed by God on the mount of transfiguration, and finally acclaimed on the cross by the Roman centurion.

Jesus' conflict sayings, miracles and his passion are eschatological epiphanies, but they have remained equally hidden to Pharisees, relatives and his disciples up to the resurrection. For the hellenist Mark, the story of the historical Jesus is at one and the same time the secret eschatological epiphany of the Son of God. This history on an epiphany christology background is gospel and kerygma.

But what is the history of religions and especially the theological rationale for this confessional equation of gospel and story of the historical Jesus, which Mark was the first to combine with hellenistic Jewish-Christian and gentile-Christian traditions as well as with the mass of Palestinian Jesus material available in the early Church?

1. Apocalytic Judaism is familiar with the literary form of an apocalypse with its all-surpassing redeemer figure of the Son of Man. But apocalyptic never wrote a history of the heavenly Son of Man, because when the Son of Man is manifest on earth that will be the end of history and cosmos. To write a connected story of the Son of Man as having already appeared and then to proclaim this as the gospel meant the abolition of a totally future-oriented apocalyptic.

The same is true for Pharisaic and Qumran Essene Judaism. A life or history of the Pharisaic Messiah or the two Qumran Messiahs did not and could not exist because for these groups the Messiah had not yet appeared. For them it was simply a matter of bridging the time that remained. But even if the Messiah had appeared, no Pharisaic or Qumran Essene Jew would have written this history, which could then be proclaimed as the salvation event for the whole world. When the Messiah arrived the end is instituted, whether it is seen as judgement upon the world power Rome or upon the children of darkness. In other words, the theological necessity for Mark's conception cannot be found in apocalyptic, Pharisaic or Qumran Essene Judaism.

2. A second test case is the Q source of the Aramaic-speaking early church in and outside Jerusalem, which can be reconstructed with some degree of certainty from Matthew and Luke. This sayings source consists of a sequence of groups of sayings arranged by subject-matter. In contrast to this, larger narrative

units such as the centurion of Capernaum and the temptation narrative only came in at the later stage of hellenistic redaction. Originally sayings were simply put together and assembled in uncomplicated groups. We can also see the typical late Jewish catchword procedure, which theologically is nothing more than the additive process of assembling material. Arranging it thematically – i.e. in the baptist sayings, the programmatic sayings, the mission sayings, polemical, discipleship and kingdom of God sayings – this compiling it into ordered unities of sayings is largely the work of the Q redactor.

These thematically arranged collections generally lack any introduction, or if they have one it is redactional. Only Jesus' defence against the reproach of being in league with the devil contains already in Q an introduction (Luke 11:14), though a typical one. One can on the basis of Luke 11:14 get some idea of what the introductions to such sayings looked like. They were quite brief, without any biographical, geographical or chronicle type of detail.

The combination of these thematically arranged collections is not arbitrary. It follows a catechetical outline which begins with the Baptist's preaching, continues through numerous sayings of Jesus, and ends with the kingdom of God sayings, i.e. with the expectation of an imminent Zion parousia of Jesus the Son of Man.

So Q lacks the typically Marcan biographical, geographical and chronological tendencies. It has a thematic but not a temporal sequence. The time and space plan is still quite flatly mapped out and moves almost exclusively by literary means. The total absence of historical interest in the early Church's sayings source is connected with the Pharisaic-nomist and apocalyptic structure of its thought. But Q is not simply an apocalypse either. It is rather, above all, Jesus' messianic Torah and *halacha*, in the style of the *Pirke Aboth*. The earthly Jesus is the teacher of the messianic Torah and wisdom, and messianic preacher of repentance, whereas the future coming Jesus is the apocalyptic judge of the world. Even this differentiating between the earthly Jesus as teacher of messianic Torah and the coming Jesus as apocalyptic Son of Man is something new in this early Jewish and Jewish-Christian linguistic area, born of the early Aramaic-speaking church's resurrection kerygma. But what is really new is the fact that here for the first time in the Pharisaic-Jewish-Christian tradition the arrival of the Messiah is understood in the perfect tense and mastered in a literary form for catechetical purposes. In characteristic distinction from Mark, however, the salvation event is not the story of Jesus but his messianic Torah, his prophetic-apocalyptic word, and his priestly instruction.

It is clear that this nomist and apocalyptic response to the equally unapocalyptic and anti-Torah proclamation of the historical Jesus cannot have led to the conception of Mark's Gospel.

3.   That is confirmed also and especially by the *biblos* ("book") (1:1) of Matthew. For this Matthean "Bible" resurrects the nomist-apocalyptic sayings catechism of the Aramaic-speaking early church, and is thus the final attack upon the dominant confession and characteristic literary form of hellenistic Christianity by halachic-apocalyptic Jewish Christianity. It is true that Matthew has based his Gospel on Mark's, and has been unable to destroy its kerygmatic foundations – Jesus' début in Galilee and his passion in Jerusalem. But he has decisively modified Mark's Gospel, by then the dominant literary form of hellenistic Christianity, by including above all the sayings source Q and also, of course, the special material of his communities. Nevertheless Mark corresponded so exactly to the creed of hellenistic Gentile and Jewish Christianity, that, in undertaking to summarize in a normative way his communities' confession, Matthew did not base his work on the Q outline and subsume Mark's Gospel under the halachic-apocalyptic outline, but vice versa. And that was decisive. When the Q *halacha* was subsumed under the Gospel, and not Mark's Gospel under the Q *halacha* – in this copernican revolution the victory in principle of hellenistic Christianity over the apocalyptic-nomistic linguistic area of Jewish Christianity becomes evident.

Matthew has, of course, decisively modified Mark's conception by pushing biographical, historical, geographical elements firmly into the background and with the help of the formula quotations pressing the historiographical elements that remain into his salvation history scheme of prophecy and fulfilment. Matthew has shattered the real structural frame of Mark – a sequential story or history of Jesus as the Son of God made manifest – by arranging the entire sayings material (of Mark, Q and Special Matthew) thematically in church style and compiling it into six large collections of sayings: the Sermon on the Mount (chapters 5–7), the mission discourse (chapter 10), the parable collection (chapter 13), church discourse (chapter 18), woes on the Pharisees (chapter 23), and apocalyptic discourse (chapters 24–25). These six discourses, especially the first, the Sermon on the Mount, which is programmatic and occupies a representative position in the construction of Matthew's "Bible", control the structure of the book both formally and materially.

At the same time Mark's novelistic narrative traditions with their *theios anēr* ("divine man") idea have been radically reinterpreted by Matthew. The miracles are no longer epiphanies of a hellenistic *theios anēr* but paradigms for particular themes in the proclamation of the Church. The redactor Matthew has harmonized as far as was possible hellenistic Christianity's confessional type of gospel with the Jewish Christian, early church Q *halacha* and apocalyptic construction. The decisive thing for Matthew is no longer the kerygmatic qualification of time and space as linguistic explication of the revelation event, but above all the Torah and apocalyptic declaration of the Messiah Jesus as the second Moses. That makes it unambiguously clear that the Marcan-type of Gospel cannot have arisen from the late Jewish and Jewish-Christian presuppositions of Palestinian-Pharisaic observance.

4. We come to a similarly negative result, only from quite different history of religions and theological presuppositions, when we investigate Pauline theology. A good two decades before Mark, Paul did not write and could not have written a Gospel. For in its soteriological concentration on the past Jesus event his theology reflects only the destiny of the historical Jesus, not his proclamation, his behaviour or the chronological succession and geographical connections of his ministry. It is striking that while Paul's letters contain much kerygmatic, liturgical and paraenetic material they entirely lack the mass of early Church and hellenistic Jesus tradition. And this is the main, if not the only, reason why Paul could not have written a Gospel. These Jesus traditions were unknown to him. It is at this point that the sermon theory of Martin Dibelius requires a crucial correction. This whole complex of Palestinian and hellenistic Jesus tradition evidently did *not* belong to the missionary kerygmatic stock and was not handed down to the missionary Paul, not even by the

church in Antioch. For this, Paul relies far more on the Old Testament, as is apparent especially from Romans, though not only here.

5.   The Johannine *biblion* ("book"; 20:30) is also significant for our topic. Johannine-Nazirite Christianity probably got the idea for this fourth *biblion* from Mark. But the modifications it made are more than typical. The biographical, chronological and scenic – in short the historiographic – element has been reduced to theological insignificance in this Johannine-Nazirite *biblion*, as it was in the Matthew "Bible", though from diametrically opposite history of religions presuppositions. Typical now are the characteristic "I am" and farewell discourses and the "signs" which evoke them. Mark's messianic secret (it would be more appropriate, *qua* both history of religions and theology, to speak of a Son of God secret) is balanced by the historiographic element. In this Johannine-Nazirite *biblion* it has become independent: the epiphany on earth of the pre-existent redeemer, being made manifest in revelatory discourses and signs, makes any history of secondary importance. This *biblion* is really a collection of revelatory discourses and signs which are only of necessity clothed in scenic garments. Mark cannot have come to his theological necessity of combining gospel and Jesus story from this direction of pre-Johannine-Nazirite Christianity.

6.   The apocryphal gospels of the Nag Hammadi papyri are also significant, especially the so-called *Gospel of Thomas*. As with the other gospels from Nag Hammadi, we do not have here a Gospel in the Marcan sense. The *Gospel of Thomas* is nothing but a collection of sayings, in this respect structurally related to Q, except that its sayings material has been edited in a gnostic-hellenistic, not a halachic-apocalyptic (i.e. Pharisaic Jewish-Christian) direction. But the structural parallels between these two diametrically opposed collections of sayings extend still further. Both the miracle stories (with their *theios anēr* Christology) and the conflict sayings and above all the passion narrative are ignored by Q, and by the *Gospel of Thomas*. In the composition of both collections, didactic-catechetical concerns are uppermost. As in Q there are in the *Gospel of Thomas* cases of the catchword principle (e.g. the parables of the Kingdom). But above all the typically Marcan biographical, geographical and chronological features are absent. The Gospel is not a continuous

narrative. For example, the introductions to the sayings are generally quite short, such as "Jesus said". More often the disciples ask a question. Female disciples crop up, too. It is by contrast quite rare that an event is mentioned which Jesus observes (Logion 22: Jesus saw some infants at the breast), or which he occasions (Logion 13: "And he [= Jesus] took him [= Thomas], went aside and said . . ."). Outsiders such as Pharisees are never involved in the conversations.

This applies even more strongly in the case of the so-called *Gospel of Philip*. This writing is a florilegium of gnostic sayings and ideas. It consists of clear shorter or longer units of meaning, mostly speculative or meditative, with less narrative content, unconnected or joined only by catchwords, standing alongside one another.

Once again we reach a negative result. Mark cannot have come to his conception of a Gospel from Pharisaic-apocalyptic Judaism nor from Nazirite-gnostic gentile Christianity.

7.   There remains only one Gospel: Luke's *vita* (life) or *historia* of Jesus. Unlike Mark, Luke has taken up both the apocalyptic-nomist Q catechism and his own special material. But whereas Matthew relates polemically and regressively to Mark's hellenistic confessional type of literary gospel form, and John merely tolerates it, Luke accepts it in every way and develops it. This insight allows us to remove a common misunderstanding. The first *historia* or life of Jesus was written not by Luke but by Mark. The first proof of this is the thoroughly anti-apocalyptic fact that Mark wrote a Gospel which at the same time mediates the presence of the exalted one. He did not write an apocalyptic-nomist catechism which was to provide the necessary personal preparation for the imminent coming of the Son of Man to Zion. Secondly, the historiographical elements of a summarizing account of the historical Jesus are found in the redactional layer of Mark's Gospel.

Luke has built further upon this epochal, profoundly and a priori, anti-apocalyptic foundation. He has done so with the whole technical arsenal and methodical skill of a hellenistic Roman historian. So Luke is, in fact, the first creator of a *vita* of Jesus in the full sense of hellenistic Roman historiography.

There is no other theologian or author in the New Testament except Luke who has even remotely taken up and perfected the impulses which led to Mark's Gospel. Of course, we miss in Mark the conscious use of the technical tools of hellenistic Roman historiography: consistent attention to causality and teleology, psychological empathy, the historian's work in collecting data, and the tendency towards edification. But in the *basic* tendency towards biography, geography, chronology – i.e. towards identifying the gospel with the *historia* of Jesus, in this epochal undertaking only Mark and Luke in the New Testament join hands.

But Mark's taking up of Palestinian and hellenistic narrative traditions and above all his conception of a sequential connected *historia* of Jesus do not stem like Luke's from hellenistic Roman historiography. They come from the popular tradition of *theios anēr* lives, such as Apollonius of Tyana, Alexander of Abonuteichos and Peregrinus Proteus. Luke also knows this *theios anēr* tradition. He applied it not only to Jesus in the Gospel but also to the apostles in Acts. But the real impulse to compose his *vita* came to the cultured gentile Christian Luke from Roman-hellenistic historiography.

At the same time and combined with this history, the hellenistic epiphany Christology scheme of humiliation and exaltation is constitutive for Mark: the Son of God secret, the theory of parables, and the cross as eschatological epiphany of the Son of God. Mark was the first radically to reinterpret the Jesus traditions he had picked up, through the hellenistic epiphany Christology. Certainly Mark has worked apocalyptic material into his Gospel, above all in Mark 13. But vv. 1–23 are completely de-apocalypticized by Mark and related to history. The present time (13:10) is the period of gentile mission, the age of the Church (1:8) and of the word being sowed (chapter 4). For the *basileia tou theou* ("kingdom of God") is present in the perfect tense, and the time is fulfilled (1:15). The transcendent breaking into history and church history does not come until 13:24ff., and nobody knows when that will happen (13:32). Even this so-called synoptic apocalypse has nothing about judgement, but "only" the gathering of the elect. For judgement has already been passed on unbelievers in the death on the cross, with the *skotos* ("darkness", 15:33ff.), the death cry, the rending of the Temple veil, and the acclamation of the Roman centurion. It takes place continuously throughout history upon those who reject the Logos, i.e. make no space for the Word event (4:1ff.).

Mark knows nothing either of a pilgrimage of the nations with an eschatological meal in a parousia at Zion when the Son of Man will establish the salvation-history kingdom of the twelve tribes, such as the Aramaic-speaking early church expected. He also knows nothing of a Pauline mystery (Rom. 11:25f.) in which the totality of the Gentiles currently living in the Roman Empire must be missionized (hence Paul's Spanish plans), so that all Israel can be received back and the parousia can come.

At the same time Mark 13 belongs, as the last unitary complex of statements, to the framework of the Q catechism which Mark has observed. Mark 1 begins with the Baptist and Mark 13 closes with the parousia of the Son of Man, but this Q catechism framework has been mutilated beyond recognition by Mark. He not only includes between these two two points the mass of controversy material and hellenistic miracle stories which Q has wilfully negated, but has added to chapter 13, the dogmatic conclusion of the Aramaic-speaking early church, the passion narrative – i.e. the passion kerygma of hellenistic Christianity. For in this passion narrative the whole Gospel reaches its climax. Not the parousia but the passion, which was not even mentioned in the early church Q catechism, is central here. Eschatology is shifted by Mark to the end of the gentile mission and church history, to a time which nobody can now check or verify. For the hellenist Mark it is in reality already nothing more than teleology.

Taking all this into account there is no other book in the whole New Testament that has been more influential than Mark. So it was not only at once copied in three different ways within the New Testament itself. It also had to serve as a model for numerous apocryphal writings.

Mark's Gospel is a deeply anti-apocalyptic and anti-Torah conception, stimulated by the hellenistic tradition of thought with its history and epiphanies. Unlike the Aramaic-speaking early church Mark did not respond to the unapocalyptic and anti-Torah message of the historical Jesus in an apocalyptic and in part nomistic way. Rather he has done full justice, in the changed situation faced by the Christian message in his own time, to what found expression in Jesus.

9

The Rhetoric of Direction and Indirection in the Gospel of Mark*[1]

ROBERT M. FOWLER

My task in this essay is to use reader-response criticism to talk about the experience of reading the Gospel of Mark. I presume a basic familiarity with the standard moves of reader-response criticism, which are described in a growing number of anthologies and general introductions to this brand of criticism.[2] Even though reader-response criticism has obtained the status of a standard approach to literary criticism, and has been applied with success to biblical literature,[3] there is still the need to sharpen and clarify the use of this critical approach to the reading experience. In this essay I want to point out and discuss two broad rhetorical strategies employed in the discourse of Mark's Gospel, strategies that I have called *direction* and *indirection*. I shall discuss these and several other critical terms that can help us to articulate better what we experience as we read Mark's Gospel.

A good place to begin is with the common narratological distinction between the *story* and the *discourse* of a narrative. Seymour Chatman (1978: 15–42) explains this terminology clearly and succinctly. The *story* is the *what* of a narrative – the characters and the events that make up the content of the narrative. The *discourse* is the *how* of a narrative – the way in which the narrative is narrated or the way in which the available

* First published in *Semeia* 48 (1989) 115–34.

means of narrative rhetoric are employed by the narrator[4] that we may suppose to be telling the story. So far, so good, but we must hasten to observe that the great bulk of modern criticism of biblical narrative, whether primarily historical or literary in aim, has focused primarily upon the story level of biblical narrative and the events or ideas to which it is thought to refer, whereas reader-response criticism invites us to shift our attention primarily to the experience of encountering the discourse level of biblical narrative in the act of reading. I have argued elsewhere that biblical narrative generally, and the Gospel of Mark particularly, is designed primarily to accentuate the effects of the discourse rather than the contents of the story, but that argument cannot be presented here (see Fowler, 1991). Suffice it to say here that reader-response criticism is a salutary way to learn how to focus critical scrutiny upon the discourse level, as opposed to the story level, of biblical narrative. With these few words of introduction, we may now look briefly at several instances of direction and indirection at the discourse level of Mark's Gospel.

When I speak of the rhetoric of direction in Mark, I think first and foremost of what Wayne Booth calls "reliable commentary" (1983: 169–209). The reliable commentary provided by the narrator directs the thinking and understanding of the narratee in relatively clear and determinate ways. By means of this sort of direction the narrator places into the possession of the narratee those unquestionable "facts" that she or he simply must embrace and make use of if she or he wishes to continue reading the narrative with any degree of understanding. In Mark's Gospel the commentary that is issued by the reliable, omniscient, third-person narrator of the Gospel comes to us frequently in the form of explanatory, parenthetical remarks upon elements of the story. Chatman calls this kind of narrative commentary "interpretation": "the open explanation of the gist, relevance, or significance of a story element" (228). The parenthetical comments made in the discourse about elements of the story are legion in Mark and invite exhaustive study (Fowler, 1981: 157–79; 1991). Nevertheless, I propose here to examine only two very clear instances of parenthesis, both of them introduced by the linguistic signal γάρ ("for"), one in Mark 10:22 and the other in 12:12. Then I shall examine Mark 2:10 and 2:28, two other instances of parenthesis that are less clear, since they are usually thought by critical readers *not* to be parentheses at the level of discourse, but rather explanatory comments made within the story by Jesus.

Mark 10:22[5] is the last verse of the episode that is often labelled "The Rich Man" (Mark 10:17–22). In this story a man comes to Jesus and asks him what one must do to inherit eternal life. Jesus responds by reciting the commandments of the Decalogue, and the man replies by saying that he has always observed these commandments. The story reaches its denouement when Jesus instructs the man to go and sell all that he has, and to give the proceeds to the poor. Upon hearing these words, the man departs, "sorrowful". Why? "For (γάρ) he had great possessions" (10:22).[6]

That this episode has been given the handy title of "The Rich Man" speaks volumes about the neglect of the experience of reading this story among non-professional and professional readers alike. Why do I say this? Let us take care to note that we do not know that the rich man is a rich man until after the story is over. The story itself contains no mention at all of the wealth of the man. It is only at the level of discourse, and then only after the story itself has ceased, that the narrator informs *only* the narratee that the man has great wealth. Then, in retrospect, the narratee can think back through the episode and see the whole episode in a new light. The reader of the Gospel (who is encouraged by the Gospel always to imagine himself in the role of the narratee) can actually re-read the story. The reader is enticed to re-read, re-view and re-interpret everything in the story from the vantage point of having read this episode through once already to its revelatory conclusion. We will re-read the episode, in short, knowing this time from the very beginning that the man is a rich man. In re-reading we will re-consider and re-evaluate his motivations in coming to Jesus. Whatever we thought of him upon a first reading, probably upon a second reading we will evaluate him less favourably, considering him this time less of a seeker of truth and more of a self-aggrandizer. We will also re-consider and re-evaluate Jesus' response to the man, perhaps finding new evidence of Jesus' unusual perspicacity. And so on and so forth. Thus does reliable commentary provided by the narrator "direct" – i.e. it both instigates and constrains – the development of a progressive series of re-interpretations in the course of reading and re-reading.

Mark 10:17–22 is an excellent example of an episode in biblical narrative that has been "read" and "re-read", clarified and concretized, so many times that hardly anyone really "reads" it anymore; we just go through the motions of reading it. We may even label the story "The Rich Man" in our Bibles, thus encouraging future readers to skip right past a first reading of the story, to leap ahead, as it were, into an enlightened re-reading. Why not make the work of reading easier for others than it was for ourselves? As a result, first-time readers now anticipate the outcome of the story even before they begin to read it. The standard title given to the episode tells us the punch line of the story before it can be delivered by the narrator in his discourse. Of course, this robs the punch line of its punch. Consequently, we have lost sight of the surprise that the revelation of the man's wealth must have brought to the earliest readers of this episode. And that has meant in turn that the possibility of being all but coerced by the narrative commentary into a re-visionary re-reading of the episode has also been obliterated. The episode is perhaps neither "read" nor "re-read" in any significant sense today.

But not only have we lost the ability to read this episode and to be surprised and powerfully directed by the discourse, we have at the same time lost sight of what is and is not happening in the story. On the one level, at least the narratee does grasp that the man is rich, in the very last phrase of the narrator's discourse in 10:22. On the other level, absolutely no one at the story level ever demonstrates clear and unmistakable knowledge of the man's wealth. A term introduced by J. L. Austin, the father of "speech act theory", is useful here.[7] As Austin might say, there is no indication at the level of story that there is any "uptake" for the statement that the man was rich (117–18). But how could there be any uptake in the story, since the statement is made only at the level of discourse? To be sure, in retrospect it may appear that Jesus, as is so typical of him in Mark, reads the heart of the man and discerns the man's fatal weakness. But Jesus does not *say* that he knows that the man is rich; readers *infer in retrospect* that Jesus knows that the man is rich. Then, typically, readers read their discourse-level inference back into the story and "find" it there on subsequent re-readings. In other words, we have often mixed up what is or is not understood in the story with what is or is not understood at the level of discourse. Since biblical critics have tended not to draw the distinction between story and discourse, we have seldom been able to keep the two straight, in spite of the fact that most modern critics of the Bible have tacitly professed a critical focus upon the story level.

Another clear instance of an explanatory parenthesis, one that also comes at the end of its episode and is also introduced by the narrator with γάρ, is found in 12:12. Mark 12:12 is the final verse of an episode often labelled "The Parable of the Vineyard and the Tenants" (Mark 12:1–12). In this episode we have not only direction but much indirection as well, for the bulk of this episode is inherently indirect, being a parable or a riddle (παραβολή) supposedly uttered by Jesus at story level. Let us not fail to observe, however, that indirect, parabolic discourse uttered within the story is simultaneously indirect, parabolic discourse at the discourse level of the narrative. When Jesus speaks indirectly, our narrator speaks indirectly. In this particular instance, Jesus issues a patently indirect narrative puzzle within the story, but it is only the narrator at the discourse level who provides the crucial key for solving the puzzle.

In the story told by Jesus, a man plants a vineyard and rents it to tenants, while he goes into another country. The man sends a succession of servants to collect the rent, all of whom are treated shamefully by the tenants. At last the man sends his "beloved son", whom the tenants kill and cast out of the vineyard. The end of the story finds the owner returning to the vineyard, "destroying" the tenants, and renting out the vineyard to others.

Since the story is introduced as a "parable" in the narrator's discourse in 12:1, the reader is alerted from the beginning that the story should not be taken literally. It is thoroughly metaphorical or figurative, which is to say that it needs to be "figured out". Jesus himself begins the process of figuring out the parable at the level of story (12:10–11), but his explanation ("the very stone which the builders rejected has become the head of the corner") is itself figurative and therefore it too needs to be figured out. The substitution of one figurative riddle for another does not solve anything for us.

The crucial comment that allows the reader to solve the riddle of the vineyard and the tenants comes from the narrator in 12:12, at the level of the narrator's discourse, after the words spoken within the story have ceased: "And they tried to arrest him, but feared the multitude, *for* [γάρ] *they perceived that he had told the parable against them*; so they left and went away." The first matter of business for the reader encountering this concentrated

211

moment of narrative exposition intertwined with narrative commentary is to clarify who the "they" is. Who is the "they" who tried to arrest Jesus, who feared the multitude, who perceived that the parable was aimed at them, and who then went away? *Ambiguity* is a favourite strategy of indirection employed frequently in the Markan discourse, but the ambiguous "they" in 12:12 is not among the more challenging of the Markan ambiguities. The reader will recall that in the episode immediately preceding the vineyard parable Jesus was disputing in the temple with "the chief priests and the scribes and the elders" (11:27). That same setting and those same interlocutors seem to be presupposed as we move into 12:1, which is the narrator's introduction to the vineyard parable: "And he began to speak *to them* in parables". Because of our experience of reading 11:27 and 12:1, as we read Jesus' vineyard parable in 12:2ff. it will not be difficult to infer that the parable is a figurative attack upon the interlocutors introduced back in 11:27 and mentioned again in 12:1, namely, the chief priests, scribes and elders. We infer that it is they who are the "tenants" in Jesus' story. This identification must remain only a supposition, however, until the narrator confirms our supposition by means of the parenthetical γάρ clause in 12:12. Once the identification *tenants = chief priests + scribes + elders* is confirmed by the narrator in 12:12, all the rest of the pieces of the puzzle fall more or less neatly into place, in retrospect. To be sure, most of the riddle is not exceedingly difficult for the reader to figure out even upon a first reading. Besides having a strong suspicion from the beginning of the parable about who the "tenants" are, who the "beloved son" must be (12:6) is also not too difficult to figure out, if we remember reading Mark 1:11 and 9:7. However, it is the incontrovertible identification of the "tenants", reliably provided by the narrator, that guarantees that the puzzle will be solved correctly by the reader, albeit in retrospect.

It should be noted also that the γάρ clause in 12:12 is a particular kind of narrative commentary, an "inside view" (Booth: 163–4 *et passim*) into the hearts and minds of story characters. In fact, in 12:12 we are granted altogether no less than three different inside views. We are told the *intention* of Jesus' opponents ("they tried to arrest him"), we are told of their *emotion* ("they feared the multitude"), and we are informed of their *knowledge* ("they perceived that he had told the parable against them"). Because we are usually too busy making use of this remarkable gift of insight into the hearts and minds of story characters, we have usually neglected to observe where the gift comes from. It comes to us directly and openly from the narrator, in the narrator's discourse. Moreover, we have tended to overlook that this gift of insight in 12:12 just so happens to place into our hands the one sure key that is indispensable for figuring out what the vineyard parable is all about. This is wonderfully indirect direction. We are all but coerced into understanding *Jesus'* parable, by being directed momentarily into the hearts and minds of his *opponents*, all of which encourages us to overlook that our grasp of everything in story and discourse alike is being carefully orchestrated by our *narrator*. Paradoxically, the more omniscient, the more intrusive, the most insistently direct our narrator becomes, the easier it becomes to overlook him.

Having now examined two fairly clear and non-controversial instances of direction by means of parenthetical comments emanating openly from the narrator of Mark's Gospel, I now want to look at two more instances of narrative commentary that are less obviously parentheses by the narrator. The two Son of Man sayings in Mark 2:10 and 2:28 are usually taken as explanatory comments uttered by Jesus at the level of story, but I want to argue instead that they are actually parenthetical comments uttered by the narrator at the level of the narrator's discourse. I also want to argue that it makes absolutely no difference at all whether Jesus speaks these lines in the story or whether the narrator speaks these lines as parenthetical interruptions of the story, as long as it is recognized that the only one who definitely takes up these comments is the narratee of the story. In tackling two parentheses whose function in story and discourse may at first appear less than clear, I am tackling turns of narrative discourse that lie somewhere between the clearest turns of direction and the shadowiest turns of indirection.

The Son of Man sayings in Mark 2:10 and 2:28 are noteworthy, among other reasons, for being the only two Son of Man sayings in the first half of the Gospel. Together 2:10 and 2:28 assert that the "Son of Man" possesses "authority to forgive sins" and is in some sense "lord of the sabbath". This leaves much about the Son of Man open to future development in the narrative, but that the Son of Man possesses authority and lordship in Mark's Gospel is hereafter hardly to be disputed. Although it is often noted that

Jesus is the only character in the Gospel to use the expression "Son of Man", and oddly enough only in the third-person, it is too seldom observed that Jesus never identifies himself explicitly as the Son of Man anywhere in the Gospel. Mark 10:32 ("he began to tell them *what was to happen to him*") comes the closest to being an explicit identification, but it is an oblique and not an explicit identification, and it is a statement by the narrator in the narrator's discourse and is not uttered at the level of story. Who the Son of Man is, is one of many puzzles given to the reader of this Gospel, and like many of Mark's puzzles, this one is easily figured out. Who else could the Son of Man be, other than Jesus? But the most important point to be made here is that who and what the Son of Man is, is a puzzle that is handed to the reader to be solved.

Regardless of who gets credit for speaking the Son of Man comments in 2:10 and 2:28, it should be fairly clear that they are both parenthetical comments. They are both "interpretations", in Chatman's terminology, of an element of the story. They both interrupt the story in order to offer a comment on the story. Literal translation and judicious use of typography may help us to see this better:

> "Which is easier, to say to the paralytic, 'Your sins are forgiven', or to say, 'Arise, take your bed, and walk'?" – *but* [δέ] *so that* [ἵνα] *you may know that the Son of Man has authority to forgive sins on earth* – he says [λέγει] to the paralytic: "I say to you, arise, take your bed, and go to your home" (2:9–11; my translation).

> And he said to them, "The sabbath was made for man, not man for the sabbath" – *so* [ὥστε] *the Son of Man is lord even of the sabbath* (2:27–8; my punctuation of the RSV's translation).

Both parenthetical comments abruptly interrupt the flow of the narration in order to shed some light on an element of the story, namely, to say something illuminating about the Son of Man. Both parenthetical comments are introduced by linguistic signals that are commonly used elsewhere by the narrator to signal his parenthetical comments. For example, the introduction of the parenthesis in 2:10 is signalled both with ἵνα and the adversative δέ. The conclusion of the parenthesis is signalled as the narrator shifts his focus back to the level of story and *re*-introduces Jesus as the speaker within the story: "he says [λέγει] to the paralytic . . .".

214

One possible problem with my suggestion that the parenthesis in 2:10 is spoken only at discourse level and not in the story is that the parenthesis is addressed to a second-person plural "you", and therefore one might argue that in 2:10 Jesus continues to address the interlocutors he first addressed in the story back in 2:8–9. It is possible to construe that in 2:10 Jesus is still talking to the scribes, but this could just as well be one of a number of places in the Gospel where an assembled audience *for the Gospel itself* is presupposed. I think particularly of Mark 13, where second-person plural pronoun and verbal forms occur with such exaggerated emphasis and frequency that discourse completely overwhelms story. I would argue that the "apocalyptic discourse" in Mark 13 is aimed less at Peter, Andrew, James and John in the story (13:3), and more at the narrator's audience of assembled narratees outside of the story. Mark 13:37 makes rather clear that the apocalyptic discourse supposedly uttered by Jesus within the story is actually aimed primarily at Mark's narratees: "And what I say to you [Peter, Andrew, James, John] I say to all [Mark's narratees]: Watch".[8] If a reader is still disposed to take 2:10 as a parenthetical comment made by Jesus within the story, then she or he must assume the burden of explaining where the "he says to the paralytic" phrase comes from and what its function is. This is obviously not Jesus speaking; it can only be the narrator who speaks these words. But if the narrator feels the need to use these words to introduce Jesus all over again in 2:11, it may well be because the narrator had broken off from the words of Jesus in the story in 2:8–9, in order to give us his own commentary on the story in 2:10. At least that is how I read 2:10.

The Son of Man comment in Mark 2:28 is also signalled linguistically as a parenthetical comment. The chief linguistic signal is ὥστε ("for this reason, therefore, so"), which serves here to introduce an independent clause. The independent clause in 2:28 is a comment from the narrator that stands apart from the comment by Jesus that immediately precedes it. A parenthetical comment by the narrator that breaks off from a statement by Jesus that immediately precedes it was exactly what we had also in 2:10, but 2:28 is the less obvious parenthesis of the two, for in 2:28 the parenthesis comes at the very end of the episode, and therefore it does not dramatically interrupt the flow of the narration half-way through an episode, the way 2:10 does. That our narrator should choose in 2:28 to delay an explanatory comment until the very end of an episode is a practice with which we are already familiar, from having examined the parentheses at the end of episodes in 10:22 and 12:12.

Consequently, regardless of who gets credit for speaking them, it should be fairly obvious that the Son of Man statements in 2:10 and 2:28 are both parenthetical comments on the story. In addition, I would argue that they are properly understood as parenthetical comments *made by the narrator* on the story. They are, after all, signalled in the same fashion that other parenthetical comments by the narrator are signalled in Mark's Gospel. But be that as it may, the most important point to be made here is that even if it is Jesus who speaks the Son of Man comments in 2:10 and 2:28, there is no indication whatsoever that anyone in the story hears and understands these comments. There is no demonstration of uptake for the Son of Man statements in 2:10 and 2:28 at the level of story. Indeed, *no Son of Man statement in Mark's Gospel ever receives clear and unmistakable uptake at the level of story.*[9] But if the characters in the story do not hear or understand the Son of Man statements, who does? The narratee, obviously. There has never been a recipient of Mark's narrative discourse who has not heard every single Son of Man statement in the Gospel and understood them all, at least to some extent. Even though the identity of the one who is the Son of Man is never made explicitly clear in either story or discourse, there has never been a reader who has not been able to figure that the Son of Man can only be Jesus. What readers have *not* been sufficiently cognizant of is that no one in the story hears and understands what we hear and understand. Once again, we have grasped neither what characters in the story understand nor what we as readers are led to understand by the narrator's discourse. The workings of story and discourse in Mark's Gospel remain largely a mystery to us. The orchestration of story and discourse in this narrative is so masterful that we are utterly enchanted by the spell it weaves over us as we read. In narrative commentary such as that in 2:10 and 2:28, the narrator has directed our thinking in ways we have not yet fathomed.

I want to turn now from direction to indirection in Mark's rhetoric. That is not to say that direction and indirection can always be easily distinguished and disentangled in the discourse of the Gospel. Sometimes one has the sense that various strategies of direction and indirection shade gradually over into each other and therefore are difficult to try to distinguish. At other times turns of direction and indirection are distinguishable but are tangled up in each other, indirection playing off against direction and vice versa. The experience in criticism gained above, learning how to identify and describe the more overt turns of direction by the narrator, stands us in good stead now as we turn to more covert and indirect guidance from the narrator. With indirection the narrator ceases to speak openly and directly and steps momentarily behind the curtain, as it were, in order to orchestrate the workings of story and discourse covertly from offstage, in the wings. Whereas in direction he speaks to us directly in his own voice, in indirection he "speaks" to us tacitly, through what the characters in his story say or do, or through the way that the events and situations in the story are structured and plotted. "Speaking" to us indirectly through both characters and the orchestration of circumstances and events in the narrative, the narrator employs verbal and dramatic turns of irony, metaphor, paradox and ambiguity. Like direction, indirection often leads us to insights and understandings. At other times, indirection does not lead us to a particular destination. In such cases it is offered to us as an experience to be experienced for its own sake. Indirection permeates Mark's Gospel, from beginning to end, but there are some places in the Gospel where the rhetoric of indirection is particularly concentrated, and I would like to look at one such passage here.

The passage I would like to consider is the difficult and much-discussed scene that occurs between the riddle of the sower in Mark 4:3–9 and its story-level explanation by Jesus in 4:14–20. I want to concentrate especially on 4:11–13:

> And he said to them, "To you has been given the secret of the Kingdom of God, but for those outside everything [τά πάντα] is in riddles [παραβολαῖς]." (So that [ἵνα] in seeing, they may see and not perceive, and in hearing they may hear and not understand, lest they should turn and be forgiven.) And he says [λέγει] to them, "Do you not know this riddle? How then will you understand all (πάσας] of the riddles?" (4:11–13; my translation).

Few verses in Mark have perplexed scholars more than 4:11. The problem here can be stated simply: Jesus says to his disciples that they have been given "the secret of the Kingdom of God", but the narratee does not know what this secret is or when it

217

might have been given to the disciples in the story. When critical readers encounter this verse, they often flip back through the preceding pages of the Gospel, hoping to discover when and where this secret might have been given to Jesus' disciples, but to no avail. We have found it most difficult to accept that in 4:11 the discourse alludes to something that apparently occurred in the story, but the narrator chose not to narrate it to us. I call this narrative strategy *opacity*. Whatever the secret might be, and whenever we may suppose it was given in the story, it lies behind an opaque veil as far as we are concerned. We might say that the giving of the secret apparently occurred at the level of story, but was omitted from the narrator's discourse, thus excluding the narratee from this moment in the story.

If we have had a hard time recognizing and coming to terms with the opacity in 4:11, it may be because we have assumed that narrative is invariably supposed to enlighten the narratee, not to put him or her in the dark. But 4:11 does put the narratee in the dark, or, more accurately, it reveals to the narratee that he or she has for some unknown period of time been in the dark concerning the existence of a "secret". To be sure, more typically Mark will portray the characters in the story as victims of opaque veils that blind their eyes, deafen their ears, and keep them from understanding the events in the story that are taking place in front of their noses. Opacity is another way of talking about the absence of uptake in the narrative. In Mark there is much opacity – absence of uptake – at the level of story, veils that seem to keep the characters in the story in the dark (e.g. all Son of Man sayings are smothered by an aural veil of opacity in the story). But what is most interesting to the student of narrative rhetoric, however, is that the narrator of this story is not afraid to put the narratee occasionally in the dark as well. Of course, by the very nature of opacity, we cannot know that we are being excluded by an opaque veil as long as the veil is in place. But the narrator will occasionally reveal to us, in a moment of retrospective illumination, that we had been excluded from an earlier moment in the story that the characters apparently had experienced. That is, occasionally the narrator will tear away a veil that had previously blinded us.

In narratological terms, opacity occurs when either the story or the discourse halts and the other level proceeds by itself. Opacity occurs whenever the narrator introduces a gap into either the story or the discourse, thus excluding either characters or the narratee from understanding a portion of the story. As powerful as the various covert twists and turns of Markan indirection can be, opacity is the ultimate strategy of indirection, since it is the outright denial, to either a character or a narratee, of the opportunity to experience and understand fully the story that is being told.

Lest we fall into despair over the narrator's denial to us of the secret of the Kingdom of God, we need to continue reading. Surprises may lie ahead. But before we proceed with our reading of 4:11–13, we need to observe the opposites that are introduced to us in 4:11. On the one hand, we have those who have been graced with the secret of the Kingdom of God. On the other hand, we have the outsiders, for whom *everything* (τὰ πάντα) is in riddles. Putting this language together and filling in the missing terms, apparently there are insiders, who possess the secret of the Kingdom of God and who understand Jesus' riddles, and there are outsiders, who do not possess the secret and who do not understand the riddles. Using this language we would have to say that in 4:11 it would seem that Jesus' disciples are insiders, who possess the secret of the Kingdom, while the narratee is an outsider, not possessing the secret. At this point in the passage the reader seems to stand on the outside of the privileged circle of insight and understanding, and laments that she or he has been so excluded. But matters do not rest there. We must read on.

In Mark 4:12 we come across yet another of our beloved parenthetical comments. Like the parentheses in 2:10 and 2:28, the parenthesis in 4:12 is usually regarded as a comment by Jesus uttered at the level of story. And like the parentheses in 2:10 and 2:28, I would argue that 4:12 should be understood instead as a parenthetical comment by the narrator. And, furthermore, like the parentheses in 2:10 and 2:28, it really does not matter whether we understand that Jesus or our narrator is the principal speaker of the parenthesis in 4:12, as long as we recognize that there is no indication of uptake for the comment in the story. This is yet another of those parenthetical comments that we only know for sure that the narratee hears and responds to. Even if Jesus does speak the parenthesis at story level, there is no indication at story level that anyone there hears it and takes it to heart.

219

That 4:12 is a parenthetical comment should be fairly obvious. It interrupts the speech by Jesus about understanding parables that both precedes and follows it, in vv. 11 and 13. Furthermore, the parenthesis is introduced by the linguistic signal ἵνα, just like the parenthesis in 2:10. Also like 2:10, the narrator's parenthesis in 4:12 concludes with the *re*-introduction of Jesus as the principal speaker in the story: "and he says [λέγει] to them . . ."

In form, therefore, this parenthetical comment resembles the other parenthetical comments in the Gospel. In function, however, this parenthesis differs from the others we have seen so far in several respects. For one thing, it is an allusion to, if not a direct quotation from, the Old Testament. It is an allusion to Isaiah 6:9–10, to be precise, but precise our narrator is not. The quotation, if that is what it is, is not an accurate quotation, nor is it even introduced as a quotation by either Jesus or the narrator, nor are we told what we should make of it. What relevance does it have to the topic under discussion in the story? Unlike the other parentheses we have examined, this one is more of a question than an answer, more of a puzzle than a solution, more of a challenge of indirection than a piece of clear, reliable direction.

It should be noted that the narrator on a number of occasions offers to the narratee gratuitous allusions to Old Testament passages. The Gospel in fact begins with a parenthetical comment in Mark 1:2–3 that loosely "quotes" a pastiche of passages from Exodus, Malachi and Isaiah. What we are to make of that scriptural allusion is also difficult to determine. Suffice it to say that as a result of these and other allusions to Jewish scripture, the reader of Mark's Gospel must read the Gospel intertextually. The textual fabric of Mark's Gospel is intertwined with the fabric of these precursor texts, which makes this narrative one that is perpetually open to the influence of its precursors. Allusions to the Old Testament may cast some light upon Mark's story, but the lighting is often at best indirect and inconclusive.

Besides observing that the parenthetical comment in 4:12 is an unheralded, unexplained, ambiguous allusion to a precursor text, we should also note that this allusion is thoroughly figurative, indeed, *metaphorical*. "Seeing" and "hearing" are introduced here as grand metaphors that will appear again and again in the narrative that follows. Hereafter, whenever we encounter "seeing" or "hearing" (or their opposites, "blindness" or "deafness") in either story or discourse, we must suspect that these are figures not to be taken up too literally. In spite of the openness and ambiguity of the Old Testament allusion in 4:12, the reader can surely figure out minimally that this comment is suggesting that some who think they "see" really do not perceive anything at all, and some who think they "hear" really understand nothing. What we are to do then with this insight remains far from clear, but one thing it may do is to encourage us to begin to re-consider the understanding we developed back in 4:11 that the disciples are insiders and we are outsiders. Maybe, just maybe, those in 4:11 who seemed to "see" and "hear" certain things did not "see" or "hear" as much as we thought.

As if it were not enough that 4:12 is an ambiguous inter-textual allusion, and a metaphorical one at that, it is also *ironic*. The irony comes at the beginning of the parenthesis, in the infamous "so that" (ἵνα) clause, and especially at the end of the parenthesis, in the shocking conclusion, "lest they should turn and be forgiven". The ἵνα is infamous, because it seems to suggest that the parables are told with the express purpose of excluding people from understanding them. Whether they will admit it or not, most modern readers are deeply offended by Mark's ἵνα, and consequently they prefer Matthew's substitution of ὅτι ("because"; Matt 13:13) for Mark's ἵνα, because this suggests that the purpose of telling parables is to enlighten people, not to exclude them from enlightenment. None of us likes to feel excluded, so we like Matthew's ὅτι much better than Mark's ἵνα. However, were we able to face up to the opacity that does indeed exclude us in 4:11, we might be less astonished and offended by the apparent implication in 4:12 that a storyteller would ever intentionally shut someone out of the inner circle of understanding.

The ἵνα is definitely perplexing, but the key to identifying the parenthetical comment as an ironic statement is the final clause, "less they should turn and be forgiven". This tips us off that the whole verse has been recited with tongue in cheek. We can figure this out because it is clear from our reading experience that both our narrator and his protagonist wish to persuade their respective audiences to hear and believe their respective discourses, and to repent or turn their lives around accordingly. The narrator already begins to reveal his goal of swaying his audience in the

221

very first verse of the Gospel: "The beginning of the gospel of Jesus Christ, the Son of God". This tells us already before the Gospel gets under way certain things the narrator hopes we will be willing to say about Jesus as a result of reading this narrative. Within the story, Jesus makes clear his rhetorical aims as well: "The time is fulfilled, and the kingdom of God is at hand; repent, and believe in the gospel" (1:15). Jesus offers this epitome of his preaching at the beginning of his ministry, as he takes up the mantle of John the Baptist, who had also preached repentance, specifically "for the forgiveness of sins" (1:4). All of this the reader reads in the first fifteen verses of the Gospel. Then when we arrive at 4:12, are we actually supposed to believe that either the narrator or Jesus would actually tell a story *so that* people would *not* turn their lives around, *so that* they would *not* be forgiven? The literal sense of Mark 4:12 is patent nonsense, quite incongruous with the clear and unmistakable rhetorical goal of both the narrator, at discourse level, and Jesus, within the story. Consequently, Mark 4:12 simply cannot be taken literally. It should not be taken in a straightforward, direct manner, because it is not uttered directly; it is uttered indirectly. It is spoken (by the narrator, I believe, but neither I nor the narrator would mind if Jesus got credit for it) with tongue in cheek. One might even dare to say that it is a little bit humorous. The narrator (or Jesus) may be pulling someone's leg, either the leg of the narratee at the level of discourse, or the leg of certain characters within the story, or maybe both simultaneously. So, just as the metaphors of "seeing" and "hearing" within the parenthesis are not to be taken literally, the whole parenthetical comment is not to be taken literally either. Two major turns of indirection work together here, metaphor and verbal irony. It is only fitting, after all, that a metaphorical statement that suggests that "seeing" and "hearing" are not always what they seem to be, should itself be uttered in a manner that is not what it seems to be.

Let us read on to v. 13. Jesus is re-introduced by the narrator and he poses two questions to the disciples: "Do you not know this riddle? How then will you understand all of the riddles?" These are "rhetorical" questions, in the sense that they serve the narrator as an effective rhetorical strategy for guiding the thinking of the narratee indirectly. Since they receive no explicit answer either in the story or in the narrator's discourse, the narratee is encouraged to try to answer the questions, or at least to explore

222

their implications, on his or her own. The first of the two unanswered questions seems to imply that Jesus thinks that the disciples do not understand the riddle of the sower (4:3–9). The narratee may already have suspected this in 4:10, when the disciples[10] of Jesus "asked him concerning the parables", but why they were asking about the parables was left artfully ambiguous by the narrator. Now in 4:13, however, we know for sure that they did not understand the sower riddle, but we learn this from the narrator indirectly, through an unanswered question uttered by a character at the level of the story. The second of the two questions suggests rather emphatically that if the disciples do not understand this one riddle, then *all* (πάσας) of the riddles will be a mystery to them. Apparently they stand in imminent danger of failing to understand everything that Jesus teaches, and perhaps everything that he stands for.

This is quite a turnabout. Back in 4:11 we were surprised and maybe a little offended to learn that the disciples had been given the secret of the Kingdom of God without our knowing anything about it. But now it appears that these touted insiders are really outsiders, after all. And the narratee, the one excluded by the veil of opacity in 4:11, now suddenly understands that the disciples do not understand, which turns the narratee into an insider, at least to a modest degree. We may not know much, but we know at least that the disciples do not know. In revealing to us that the "insiders" of 4:11 are in fact "outsiders", we the "outsiders" of 4:11 are turned into "insiders". The tables are turned; positions are reversed; the veil of opacity has not excluded new victims while ushering the old victims into a modest enlightenment.

Reading Mark 4:13 is an experience of *dramatic irony* for the reader. Dramatic irony is a sub-category of situational irony, which is built upon a provocative incongruity of situations or events. One might say that dramatic irony is situational irony used as rhetorical strategy in narrative discourse. Dramatic irony occurs when there is a sharp incongruity between various situations or events within the story, or more dramatically still when there is a sharp incongruity between what is known or understood at the level of story and what is known or understood at the level of discourse. In the theatre, for example, dramatic irony occurs when Oedipus does not know his origins, and therefore stumbles "blindly" into his fate, while everyone in the audience knows full well from the beginning of the play both what his origins are and what his fate must be. Mark's dramatic irony in 4:13 is even more powerful than this classic example, because Mark first sets up an incongruous opacity that favours the characters and excludes the audience in 4:11, and then he reverses the positions, by suddenly favouring the audience and excluding the characters behind the opaque veil in 4:13. Each of the two turns of opacity is dramatically ironic by itself, but there is the further dramatic irony that the narrator replaces one dramatically ironic opacity with another that is diametrically opposed to it. The two ironic moments of opacity are ironically, maybe even paradoxically, opposites of each other.

Like so many moments in the reading of Mark's narrative, the dramatic irony of 4:13 is a matter of re-visioning the reading experience in retrospect. The reader cannot detect the dramatic incongruity between 4:11 and 4:13 until 4:13 is read and its indirect challenge taken up. When it is read, Mark 4:13 functions as an indirect invitation from the narrator to re-read and re-vision the preceding verses. Not only may we detect for the first time a dramatic irony reverberating between 4:11 and 4:13, we may also begin to suspect that the verbal irony that we encountered in 4:12 had already begun back in 4:11. Perhaps 4:11 participates not only in dramatic irony, but also verbal irony as well. Maybe Jesus (or the narrator) was already pulling the leg of the disciples (or of the narratee) back in 4:11. Maybe Jesus never seriously intended to suggest that the disciples had actually received the "secret of the Kingdom of God". If the reader could suspect already in 4:10 that the disciples really did not understand the parables, and that is why they asked Jesus about them, could not Jesus also have been this shrewd, and have begun to chide the disciples ironically for their lack of perception already in 4:11? Whether or not Jesus is chiding the disciples ironically in 4:11, by the time we reach 4:13 it is without doubt that he chides the disciples and sharply so. By that point his tone has become unmistakably severe, for the stakes are high. If the disciples cannot figure out this one riddle, then *everything* (πάσας) will be a mystery for them. *Their position in 4:13 is that of the outsiders who were mentioned in 4:11, those for whom everything* (τὰ πάντα) *is in riddles.* The reader can only hope that she or he will not also end up as an outsider, but our experience of reading 4:11–13 leaves us less than sanguine about the possibilities of this happening, for we know by our own experience that it is possible for us, even us, to be "blind" and "deaf" to what is happening in Mark's narrative.

The experience of reading Mark 4:11–13 can be summarized briefly. The temptation here is to say that the text tells us that those who "see" often are in fact "blind", and those who "hear" often are in fact "deaf". The text, especially the parenthetical comment in 4:12, does say something like that, but far more important than what the text *says* is what it *does*. We are not merely *told* about those who "see and yet do not see", *we are given the opportunity to experience this for ourselves.* The reader lives through the experience of being shut out of insight and understanding by an opaque veil, followed by the gift of a modest amount of sight and understanding, in a surprising reversal of position with those who had started out on the favoured side of the veil.

The experience of reading Mark 4:11–13 is illustrative of the experience of reading Mark's Gospel as a whole in several respects. For one thing, reading Mark is less a matter of being informed of certain facts and ideas and more a matter of being given the opportunity to live through certain kinds of experiences. And those experiences typically proceed on paths that are both direct and indirect, but with a special inclination toward indirection. The experience of reading this narrative is characterized by frequent twists and turns, by surprises and reversals. This narrative does not just *say* that insiders are outsiders, and outsiders are insiders; it *performs* this reversal upon us time and time again. But as often as it might cast us out into the dark, it more often casts us into the inner circle of privileged insight and understanding. The overall tendency of this narrative is gradually to make of the narratee, by direct and indirect means alike, an inveterate insider.

Mark 4:1–13 is also illustrative of the whole Gospel insofar as we encounter here, in a remarkably brief span of narrative, examples of many of the favourite Markan turns of indirection. We encounter different moments of *opacity* that exclude at one point the narratee and at another point the characters; we are given an *intertextual allusion* that signals the openness of this narrative and that seems to reflect the narrator's willingness to live with *ambiguity*; several major *metaphors* are offered to us; we encounter both *verbal* and *dramatic irony*;[11] and we take up the challenge of *unanswered, "rhetorical" questions*. When this critical vocabulary is used along with the other terms I have introduced and employed in this essay (*story* and *discourse, direction* and *indirection, reliable commentary, uptake, inside views,* etc.), we are well on our way toward the development of the critical tools necessary to describe and discuss the experience of reading Mark's Gospel.

The latter describes well my goal in this paper and in the larger project of reader-response criticism in which I have been engaged for the last decade. My goal is to learn to attend as closely as possible to the experience of reading. I want to understand better what is or is not happening in Mark's story as I read it, and especially what is or is not happening in me at the same time, thanks to the narrator's discourse. I want to observe and understand the workings of the gamut of rhetorical moves made by the narrator, as I encounter them in the act of reading, ranging from the most overt and direct turns, to the most covert and indirect turns. For me, this is the proper goal of a reader-response criticism of the experience of reading Mark's Gospel.

NOTES

1 This essay is dedicated to Bob and Mary Lou Thomson, who made possible my participation in the SNTS seminar on "The Role of the Reader in the Interpretation of the New Testament". I am greatly indebted to them for their encouragement and support.

2 See J. Tompkins (ed.), *Reader-Response Criticism: From Formalism to Post-Structuralism* (Baltimore: John Hopkins University Press, 1980); S. R. Suleimann and I. Crosman (eds.), *The Reader in the Text: Essays on Audience and Interpretation* (Princeton: Princeton University Press, 1980); E. Freund, *The Return of the Reader: Reader-Response Criticism* (London and New York: Methuen, 1987).

3 See R. Detweiler (ed.), *Reader Response Approaches to Biblical and Secular Texts* (Leipzig, 31; Decatur, GA: Scholars Press, 1985); Fowler (1981) and (1991); S. D. Moore, "Narrative Homiletics: Lucan Rhetoric and the Making of the Reader" (Ph.D. Thesis, Trinity College, University of Dublin, 1986); J. L. Resseguie, "Reader-Response Criticism and the Synoptic Gospels", *JAAR*, 52 (1984) 307–24.

4 I am presuming familiarity with the common narratological distinctions between, on the one hand, the real author, the implied author, and the narrator, and on the other hand, the real reader, the implied reader, and the narratee (see Chatman: 147–51; Fowler, 1985: 10–15). For all practical purposes, in Mark the implied author is virtually indistinguishable from the narrator, and the implied reader is virtually indistinguishable from the narratee.

5 For this example I am indebted to the article by Resseguie (312–13).

6 Unless indicated otherwise, the English translation I am using is the Revised Standard Version.

7 J. L. Austin, *How to Do Things with Words*. Ed. J. O. Urmson and M. Sbizà. 2nd ed. Cambridge: Harvard University Press, 1975.

8 I pursue this argument at greater length elsewhere (Fowler, 1991). Suffice it to say here that there are a number of places in Mark where second-person plural forms seems to imply an assembled audience for the Gospel. To give only one example, see the brief parenthetical comment in 9:41, which should also, I believe, be credited solely to the account of the narrator: "because you are of Christ" (ὅτι Χριστοῦ ἐστε).

9 The closest thing to a Son of Man statement that receives uptake in the story is perhaps the Son of Man statement in Mark 14:62, in the scene where Jesus is questioned before the high priest. But I would argue that this, too, is a parenthetical comment that is spoken by the narrator and heard only by the narratee. There is no clear demonstration by the high priest that he hears and responds to the Son of Man statement that the narratee of the Gospel undoubtedly hears and responds to. Mark 14:62 interrupts the story in order to offer a comment on the story, and it functions only at the level of discourse.

Nevertheless, let us be clear that Jesus does indeed utter many Son of Man statements in the story. See, for example, the three passion predictions in 8:31, 9:31 and 10:33. However, not one of these receives clear and unmistakable uptake within the story. The narrator confirms this lack of uptake explicitly in 9:32, after the second passion prediction, when he says that the disciples "did not understand the saying".

10 To identify "those who were about him with the twelve" in 4:10 is difficult. I suspect we have a scribal gloss here that was introduced into an early manuscript of Mark's Gospel to save the twelve from the embarrassment of having to ask for Jesus' help in understanding the parables. Ultimately, it does not matter much to whom Jesus is speaking in 4:11 and 4:13. It is enough to know that he is speaking to disciples intimately associated with him, a group of supposed "insiders".

11 Elsewhere I have discussed both verbal and dramatic turns not only of irony, but also of metaphor, paradox, and, to a limited extent, ambiguity (Fowler, 1991).

10

The Promise and the Failure: Mark 16:7, 8

ANDREW T. LINCOLN

I *Introduction*

The questions that surround the ending of Mark's Gospel have long held a fascination for its readers. What was the original ending? If it was 16:8, did Mark intend to end here? If he did, is the response of the women to be evaluated positively or negatively? More recent emphasis on the Gospel as narrative has, if anything, increased this fascination. How is the ending of Mark to be evaluated in terms of closure? What is the relation between the end of the Gospel's plot and the end of its narrative world? Questions about the Gospel's narrative world inevitably generate further questions about the implied reader who is invited by the text to construct that narrative world and its ending, and then about actual readers and their response to the ending, both the intended first-century readers, as far as their setting can be determined, and aspiring ideal readers of the late twentieth century.[1]

In this article I wish to attempt to further the discussion by arguing that the ending of Mark can be appreciated for the closure it provides and the response it was meant to evoke only if both 16:7 and 16:8 are stressed equally and the juxtaposition between them is allowed its full force, if the pattern that emerges from the two verses is linked to similar patterns earlier in the narrative, and

* First published in *JBL* 108 (1989) 283–300.

if their content is related to some of the major themes found earlier in the narrative, including that of the so-called messianic secret. Having set out a reading that accomplishes this,[2] I shall also reflect briefly on its capacity for embracing not only a literary–critical but also a more traditional redactional approach, with its attempts to reconstruct the author's intention and purpose in relation to his readers and their setting, and on its implications for efforts to appropriate theologically the vision of Mark's narrative.

It will already have become clear that I see no virtue in being a purist and refusing to recognize any overlap between literary and historical concerns. Indeed, unless the literary critic is willing to provide several different readings of Mark to accord with the different endings in the textual tradition, he or she must first make a historical judgement about which text is to be interpreted. This reading of the ending will work with the text that ends at 16:8 and will proceed on the assumption that it is no longer necessary to argue in any great detail either that 16:8 is the original ending[3] or that an author could have intended to end a work with the clause ἐφοβοῦντο γάρ. The ending can be said to fit Mark's style. He frequently uses the postpositive γάρ in short clauses and five times has employed φοβέομαι absolutely (cf. 5:15, 33, 36; 6:50; 10:32). There is a striking parallel to Mark's conclusion at the end of a sentence in the LXX. In LXX Gen. 18:15 Sarah denied that she had laughed – ἐφοβήθη γάρ, "for she was afraid". Examples can also be cited not just of sentences that end with γάρ but also of whole discourses that end in this way; see Plato *Protagoras* 328c, νέοι γάρ; Musonius Rufus *12th Tractate*, γνώριμον γάρ.[4] It could be argued that whatever the original author's intentions, the best text that we now have with 16:8 as the ending has to be interpreted in its present form with that ending. But the more convincing such an interpretation is found to be, the more likely it becomes that an actual author could have intended it.[5]

II *Two Exegetical and Interpretative Assumptions*

Two other assumptions underlying the reading that follows – one about the promise in v. 7 and the other about the failure in v. 8 – need to be highlighted and justified. The first is that v. 7 contains a reference to a resurrection appearance of Jesus, not to the parousia.[6] There is much to be said for the latter interpretation. Mark has used ὄψεσθε twice already in connection with the parousia (cf. 13:26; 14:62), and the verb "to see" has also been used with reference to the imminent coming of the kingdom at the parousia (ἴδωσιν, 9:1; cf. 8:38). Certainly an actual reference to the parousia here would be appropriate to the significance of that event in the Gospel's narrative world. But ὄψομαι is also the natural verb to use for experiencing a resurrection appearance (see 1 Cor. 9:1; Matt. 28:17; John 20:18, 25, 29). Matthew clearly understood Mark's reference to be to a resurrection appearance in Galilee (cf. the way 28:7, 10 lead into 28:16–20). Peter's being singled out for special mention is less likely with a reference to the parousia, whereas the naming of Peter as well as the disciples makes sense in terms of resurrection appearances (see also 1 Cor. 15:5). In addition, a reference to an almost immediate parousia in Galilee does not take account of the fact that the plot of Mark's narrative presupposes other events to be fulfilled before the parousia, for example, international conflicts, earthquakes and famines (13:7, 8), disciples being put on trial (13:9, 11), the gospel being preached to all the nations (13:10), and the appearance of false Christs and false prophets (13:21, 22). According to 9:9 the point from which the disciples' proclamation can begin and which must be determinative for their regrouping is the resurrection of the Son of Man and not his parousia. Finally, Mark 14:28, to which 16:7 refers back, explicitly connects Jesus' going to Galilee with his resurrection rather than his parousia.[7]

The second important assumption is that the narrator's evaluation of the women's response in his "inside view" in v. 8b is a negative one. Some have attempted to argue that the women's "fear" can and should be assessed positively and that v. 8a with its mention of τρόμος καὶ ἔκστασις should be allowed to determine the connotation given to ἐφοβοῦντο in v. 8b.[8] On this view the women's saying nothing to anyone is not disobedience and does not have a negative cause. It is simply that they are temporarily struck dumb with awe before the numinous. When connected with their amazement (v. 5) and their trembling and astonishment (v. 8), their fear takes on more of the sense of the proper human response to an action of God which has displayed his overwhelming power.

On the reading advocated in this article, however, the notion of "fear" in the second half of the verse adds a different perspective to that reflected in the trembling and astonishment of the first half of v. 8. The women fail to obey the command and the fear that lies behind this is to be evaluated negatively as evidence of a wrong attitude. There is no dispute that terms such as amazement, awe, trembling, and fear are frequently used to describe the response to an epiphany or to divine revelation of some sort. The question is whether "fear" in Mark depicts a positive or a negative response. It turns out that in fact in Mark it usually does not depict a proper response of faith.[9] In the first instance of the use of φοβέομαι in the narrative, the element of awe before divine power, when the disciples are greatly afraid at Jesus' stilling of the storm, is given negative overtones by its juxtaposition with a rebuke about their lack of faith (4:40, 41). In 5:15 those who see what Jesus has done to the demoniac are afraid, but again this does not indicate a positive response, since they immediately beg Jesus to leave their neighbourhood (cf. 5:17). In the case of the woman with a haemorrhage, the combined phrase "fear and trembling" occurs for the only time, and this does accompany a response of faith (cf. 5:33, 34). But a few verses later in conversation with Jairus, Jesus again contrasts fear and faith: "Do not fear, only believe" (5:36). Herod's fear of John the Baptist (6:20) is neither wholly positive nor wholly negative. The disciples' terror and fear at seeing Jesus walk on the water are a response to an epiphany that is again given negative connotations in the light of a narrator's comment about their lack of understanding and their hard hearts (6:50, 52). Similarly, Peter's response to the transfiguration in 9:5, which shows his misunderstanding, is linked with the notion of fear in 9:6: "for he did not know what to say, for they were exceedingly afraid" (ἔκφοβοι γὰρ ἐγένοντο). Again in 9:32 the disciples' fear and misunderstanding are clearly connected, and when, according to 10:32, those who follow Jesus to Jerusalem are afraid, there is no indication that this is to be taken positively. Instead their attitude should probably be interpreted in relation to the predictions in the immediately following verses about what will befall Jesus as a consequence of this journey to Jerusalem (10:33, 34). The fear of the chief priests and scribes toward Jesus goes hand in hand with their search for a way to destroy him (11:18), and these same characters are also said to be afraid of the people (11:32; 12:12). So, of the other twelve references to fear in the narrative, only one can be judged to be part of a positive response (5:33) and then it belongs to the set phrase "fear and trembling"; one is ambiguous (6:20); and ten, including all the references to the disciples, have negative connotations.

Our reading of v. 8, then, is in line with the dominant force of the terms for "fear" earlier in the narrative. The women's fear is not just stunned silence before the transcendent. Nor on the negative understanding of "fear" is there any reason in terms of the plot for the women to have been afraid to pass on the message to the disciples. Instead, the underlining of their fear functions simply as an explanation of something more primary, and that something is disobedience to a command.[10] Not only is the women's fear associated with the disobedience of their silence, but it is also in the context of the failure of their flight. The mention of their flight (ἔφυγον, 16:8) inevitably recalls that of the disciples and the young man in 14:50, 52 (ἔφυγον, ἔφυγεν). This exegetical discussion about "fear" establishes a literary point. The use of the term conveys the narrator's point of view about his characters, and he has made clear enough that it expresses a predominantly negative evaluation of the attitudes and actions of Jesus' followers.[11]

III *The Immediate Impact of the Ending*

An appreciation of the impact of the ending will be enhanced by rehearsing a little of the preceding story line as it affects the characters who are the centre of interest in the last two verses – Jesus' would-be followers.[12] The disciples, at least the males, have disappeared from the narrative since the end of chapter 14: "They all forsook him and fled" (14:50). Although they have been taught repeatedly that discipleship means going the way of the cross, when the plot reaches its climactic point and the crucifixion is depicted, there is not a disciple to be seen. The situation is vividly illustrated in the "Gospel streaker" episode of 14:51, 52.[13] A young man has followed Jesus wrapped only in a shroud (the only reference to a σίνδων in the New Testament is to the fine linen shroud in which Joseph of Arimathea wraps the body of Jesus; cf. 15:46, par.). At least he has recognized that following this man will lead to death and has come suitably dressed for the occasion. But as soon as there is the possibility of any such outcome and he is arrested, he is out of the shroud in a shot and makes his naked escape.[14] Only Peter makes a heroic attempt to follow Jesus any farther than Gethsemane. He follows at a distance and gains entrance to the high priest's courtyard (14:54). But it does not take torture or even arrest to discourage him. While Jesus is boldly making a true confession inside (14:55–65), conversation with one of the female servants outside is enough to send Peter's discipleship toward its ignominous end with its three denials, the final one accompanied by a curse (14:66–72).

Peter's humiliation at the hands of the young woman signals the replacement in the narrative of Jesus's male followers by his female followers. A woman has led to Peter's downfall, and now these women followers will be the link to his restoration. The women do look on at the crucifixion, even though, like Peter's following after the arrest, it is from afar (ἀπὸ μακρόθεν, 15:40, 41; cf. 14:54); they observe the burial (15:47); and they arrive at the tomb at the first possible moment after the sabbath in order to anoint Jesus' body (16:1, 2). In fact, pericopes about women and anointing frame the passion narrative. Earlier an anonymous woman through her action of anointing Jesus' head had already shown more insight into his identity and destiny than the disciples who accompanied him (14:3–9). The women are portrayed then in a positive light. At the climactic events of Mark's plot, they have replaced men as the representatives of the followers of Jesus. In contrast to the other disciples, they have displayed the loyalty expected of followers, and it becomes their honour to be the first to discover the empty tomb and to receive the announcement of Jesus's resurrection. Yet it is at this very point that the reader begins to discover that ultimately women are no different from men – at least in terms of discipleship. The angelic young man commands them to go and remind the failed disciples of Jesus' earlier promise in 14:28: "But after I am raised up, I will go before you to Galilee". Now in 16:7 this previous promise is underlined: καθὼς εἶπεν ὑμῖν. In its repetition in the command to the women, those who forsook Jesus and fled and the one who denied and cursed him (Peter is singled out) are promised that Jesus will go before them to Galilee where they will see him. This meeting with the risen Jesus signals the restoration of the disciples under their leader. Προάγει recalls the earlier language used of the relation of Jesus and his followers with Jesus going on before the disciples (προάγων, 10:32) and the disciples coming after him (ὀπίσω, 1:17, 20; 8:34). As Galilee has been presented earlier in the narrative as the primary setting for Jesus' ministry and as the place from which that ministry went out to the Gentiles, the implication of its mention in the repeated promise is likely to be that the regrouping of the disciples will be for mission.[15] So the command to the women contains in it the promise that the failure of the disciples is not the end. They are to go and tell the disciples that there is hope on the basis of the momentous announcement they have received: "He has risen, he is not there . . . He is going ahead to Galilee".

"So they departed quickly from the tomb with fear and great joy, and ran to tell his disciples." That is the ending the reader expects, and that is the ending one of the story's first-century readers, Matthew, has in fact supplied (Matt 28:8). So much were Matthew and his readers governed by that expectation of the response to the command that he changed the ending that was in his source. Mark himself had ended with a "kalte Dusche" effect: "And they went out and fled from the tomb; for trembling and astonishment had come upon them; and they said nothing to any one, for they were afraid". The significance of the women's silence must not be overlooked in the light of the other Gospels. Nor should it be interpreted simply as a device whereby the disciples themselves, the twelve, will after all be allowed to be the first to divulge the secret.[16] It would be hard to make the women's disobedience and failure any clearer.[17] The divine messenger has commanded them to tell but οὐδενὶ οὐδὲν εἶπαν, "they said nothing to anyone". The double irony is that they are to tell of a promise that failure is not the end, but then *they* fail to tell and that *is* the end – of the narrative!

IV   *The Undermining of Earlier Expectations (v. 8)*

We should not be too hard on Matthew for once more thinking that Mark's way of telling the story was too difficult for his readers and for conforming to their expectations by supplying a happy ending. After all, in this case Mark has deliberately set him up, as he has set up all his readers, by reinforcing those expectations. It does not escape the attentive reader that the wording of v. 8b bears a very close resemblance to that of a passage near the beginning of the narrative which is not a response to a command but the command itself. The passage is 1:44, the first occasion on which a human being is commanded to keep secret the activity of Jesus: Ὅρα μηδενὶ μηδὲν εἴπῃς, "See that you say nothing to anyone". There is a series of similar commands which constitute the core of the Gospel's so-called messianic-secret motif (cf. 5:43; 7:36; 8:30; 9:9; cf. also 1:34; 2:12; 8:26).[18] So throughout the narrative there is supposed to be this element of secrecy about Jesus' messianic activity and identity, and various people, including the disciples, are not to tell anyone anything. But in the last in the series of references (9:9), at the same time as reiterating the command, Jesus tells the inner group of three followers that the time will come when the secret can be let out and when there will be no restriction on telling. The reader even learns in advance exactly when that time will be: "he charged them to tell no one what they had seen until the Son of Man should have risen from the dead". When, therefore, he or she reaches the account of the resurrection, the reader is expecting the ban on telling to be lifted and the message about Jesus to be blazed abroad. Such an expectation is reinforced when the one announcement in the resurrection story contains the explicit command to the women to go and tell. Now that the resurrection has taken place, the silence can be broken and the women are given the commission to begin the process of telling. Yet, as has now become clear, the narrator's telling of the story has carefully created such an expectation only to shatter it immediately.[19] In this review of the building and destruction of an expectation, yet another element of the ending's irony has become apparent.[20] Earlier the strict injunctions to silence had sometimes proved to be quite unrealistic and had been disobeyed (cf. 1:45; 7:36). The ending contains the post-resurrection command to do the easier thing and to tell, but now even this is disobeyed. The reader cannot resist the thought that in the women's response of telling nobody anything it is as if, perversely and at precisely the wrong time, Jesus' women followers have become the ones who do carry out the pre-resurrection injunction to silence. In this new context, however, theirs is a failure to divulge the secret.

V *The Promise and Its Fulfilment (v. 7)*

Having felt the powerful ironic reverberations of v. 8, we need to connect it again with v. 7 and its promise and to discuss the significance both of the power of the promise and of the person who conveys that promise.

Although the failure comes after the promise in the narrative sequence, it is by no means the end in the Gospel's narrative world. The preceding promise points to a time beyond the women's disobedient response when the disciples will regroup with Jesus in Galilee. In fact, the promise itself is precisely a promise of restoration after failure! And the reader obviously knows that the promise of 16:7 was fulfilled despite the disobedience and failure of 16:8. The implied reader knows this because of the post-resurrection role ascribed to the disciples by Jesus himself in chapter 13, and the actual reader knows it because his or her acquaintance with the Christian message depends on such an event having taken place.[21] But what the reader knows is *that* the promise of 16:7 was fulfilled, not necessarily *how* it was fulfilled. He or she is not necessarily required to think or know that it was the women who told after all.[22] What is important is that the silence of the women was overcome by Jesus' word of promise. The word was fulfilled. Jesus did meet with his disciples and Peter, and they did regroup for mission to Gentiles. The angelic young man had pointed to Jesus' words: "as he told you" (v. 7c). This is not a new emphasis. In fact, the first part of the young man's message can be seen as an announcement of the fulfilment of Jesus' earlier predictions of his resurrection (8:31; 9:31; 10:34). Earlier and in a variety of ways, the narrative has highlighted the authority of Jesus' words (e.g. 1:22, 27) and their ultimate significance (e.g. 9:7, where the voice from heaven says, "Listen to him").[23] The reader has already been told of the effectiveness and lasting powers of Jesus' words of promise, for in 13:23 Jesus says, "I have told you all things beforehand", and in 13:31 such words of Jesus are said to be words that will not pass away even though heaven and earth will pass away. In fact, this last verse functions most immediately as a comment on the only other outstanding promise within the narrative world that is yet to be fulfilled.[24] Whatever else they may be uncertain of and even if they fail on their way to the end (cf. 13:13, 20), would-be disciples can know that the end will still come with the parousia of the Son of Man. In this light the juxtaposition of 16:7 and 16:8 provides a paradigm for Christian existence according to Mark – the word of promise and the failure of the disciples, and yet the word of promise prevailing despite human failure.[25]

It may well be that the conveyer of the promise is himself a sign that for disciples the promise holds despite their failure. The commentators always ask whether the figure in white in 16:5 is simply a young man, as the text describes him, or whether he is to be thought of as an angel. I believe a good argument can be made for deliberate ambiguity on the part of the writer. The reader is meant to think of both. The figure in 14:51 and that in 16:5 are both described in the same threefold way – a young man (νεανίσκος), wearing (περιβεβλημένος), and the description of the garment worn. But a transformation has taken place in regard to this last item. As we saw, in 14:51 the young man was dressed for death – in a shroud. In 16:5 he is dressed as befits the new occasion of resurrection – in a white robe (cf. Rev. 7:9, 13, 14). The figure who failed abysmally in the face of death is now restored as the messenger of resurrection and restoration. But angels also can traditionally be described as young men (see, e.g. 2 Macc. 3:26, 33, 34) dressed in white (cf., e.g. Lucian *Philops*. 25). Ambiguity would not be surprising, since Mark's Jesus tells us that "when they rise from the dead, they . . . are like angels in heaven" (12:25). So perhaps the very presence of the angelic young man is also a veiled promise that failure will not be the end. Just as his presence in the garden underlined the failure of the disciples,[26] so now his presence at the tomb highlights the imminent restoration of the disciples.[27]

VI *The Juxtaposition of Verses 7 and 8 in Relation to the Preceding Narrative*

So what we have argued is that vv. 7 and 8 need to be taken together and that, when this is done, they provide a paradigm for the interplay between divine promise and human failure in Christian existence according to Mark. The unexpectedness of v. 8 makes the reader review the preceding narrative. When this is done, it can be seen that vv. 7 and 8 are the final and climactic example of a promise–failure juxtaposition pattern which runs through the second half of the Gospel's narrative, once the theme of discipleship as the way of the cross has been introduced in 8:27ff.[28] In fact, the first half of the narrative contains the more general juxtaposition of revelation through the ministry of Jesus with human failure to understand this. In 1:14–3:6 the revelation has its focus in the authority of Jesus, and human failure is represented by the hardness and opposition of the Pharisees, who are out to destroy Jesus. In 3:7–6:6a the revelation in Jesus centres in his ministry through parables and miracles, and blindness and misunderstanding are now on the part of the common people, including Jesus' family and his fellow citizens. In 6:6b–8:26 the revelation in Jesus centres in his miracles, especially the two feeding miracles, but also in his teaching about the law, and this time it becomes clear that the blindness and misunderstanding are shared even by his disciples (see especially 6:51, 52; 7:18; 8:17, 18, 21). It is only in 8:27–10:52 that the revelation takes on the form of prediction about the future and can be termed a word of promise. As is well known, there is a threefold juxtaposition of promise and failure in this section: an announcement of the passion and resurrection of the Son of Man (8:31; 9:31; 10:33, 34) is followed by a negative response or misunderstanding on the part of the disciples (8:32, 33; 9:32–4, including a reference to their fear; 10:35–41). The predictions are, of course, fulfilled in detail within Mark's story in the passion and resurrection narrative,[29] and each time the disciples' failure is not the end and is followed by a renewed call from Jesus to discipleship (8:34; 9:35; 10:42). When, as in 16:7, the promise itself has in view renewed discipleship and yet is followed by failure in 16:8, a recalling of the earlier threefold cycle and knowledge of the fulfilment of its predictions will reinforce for the reader that the end of the narrative need not be the end of the discipleship and that on the basis of the earlier story there will always be the possibility of discipleship's renewal.

The juxtaposition takes even more striking form in the narrative of the transfiguration (9:2–13), which is followed by that of the failure of the disciples to perform an exorcism (9:14–29). The transfiguration functions in the narrative as a confirmation or guarantee of Jesus' word of promise. The divine endorsement – "This is my beloved Son, listen to him" – refers specifically to what Jesus has just had to say in 8:31–9:1, namely, that he has to suffer and die but will be raised, that those who follow him must also go the way of the cross, but that the Son of Man will come in glory and the kingdom of God come in power. The Son of Man's future glory is anticipated through Jesus' transfiguration in the presence of his disciples, but it is only an anticipation. The incident is meant to reassure the disciples that both for Jesus and for them glory *will* follow suffering but it will not bypass the way of the cross. This message remains valid despite the misunderstanding and failure of the disciples in the midst of which it stands. In the incident itself Peter misunderstands and wants to build for permanent glory ahead of time, while the other disciples outside the inner group of three are depicted in the meantime back down in the valley having failed to perform an exorcism. As 9:9 makes clear, the promise that the transfiguration represents is to come into its own only after the resurrection. Then in particular, in the time between the resurrection and the parousia, it will be important to remember the guaranteed promise of glory despite failure in discipleship.

Three further instances of the promise–failure juxtaposition that are found in chapters 13 and 14 should be mentioned. The apocalyptic discourse of chapter 13 contains the promises of the imminent coming of the Son of Man in great power and glory together with the vindication of his elect (13:26, 27, 30). That it also contains three warnings to watch at the end (cf. 13:33, 35, 37) suggests that these should be correlated with the threefold failure of the disciples to watch with Jesus in 14:32–42. Again through the sequence of the plot the readers are being told that Jesus' words of promise will not pass away (cf. 13:31) despite the failure of discipleship. 14:27, 28 contain Jesus' prediction that his disciples will all fall away but that he will be raised up and go before them to Galilee (the promise to which 16:7 refers back). The first part of the prediction is, of course, soon fulfilled when all the disciples fail by forsaking Jesus and fleeing (14:50–2). The rest of the promise remains to be fulfilled beyond the failure of the disciples. Finally, the Marcan sandwich of 14:53–72 emphasizes Jesus' prophetic role. There are two prophetic statements in Jesus' trial before the Sanhedrin. Despite its introduction as false witness, the statement of 14:58 about building another temple made without hands in three days is a prophetic formulation which in all probability should be understood as a reference to the new temple of the church to be established as the result of Jesus' resurrection.[30] The other promise in 14:62 is about the vindication and coming of the Son of Man. At the very moment that Jesus is being condemned and mocked for these prophecies, however, outside in the courtyard an earlier prediction of Jesus (14:30) is being fulfilled to the letter, as Peter fails by his threefold denial. The reader is expected to draw the appropriate inferences about the promises of 14:58, 62: despite appearances and despite the failure of his followers, these words of Jesus will also be fulfilled. It is significant that the promise of 16:7 will single out Peter. There will remain hope for him despite his failure. Jesus' word of promise holds out hope of restoration in a new community and of final vindication. So the argument has been that vv. 7, 8 provide a closure in which the reader discovers that one set of expectations produced by the preceding plot has been reversed but that, on the review that this provokes, there is a coherence with another consistent pattern of plot which gives an explanation for the initital shock.[31] Verse 8 alone – the failure of the women – is not the closure after all. It is vv. 7 and 8 – the failure of the women juxtaposed with the promise that is able to overcome it.

VII *The Actual Author's Redaction of the Tradition*

Not only does the reading of 16:7, 8 as a promise–failure juxtaposition cohere with the rest of the narrative; these very elements in the ending of the Gospel are most likely to be the evangelist's own stress, his redaction of the tradition he received. There is no clear consensus about the exact extent of a pre-Marcan resurrection narrative,[32] but whether the tradition about the empty tomb with which Mark is working in the pericope began with v. 1 or v. 2, whatever its precise relation to the tradition of the burial, and whatever minor details have been added to the tradition in vv. 2–6, it is usually held that vv. 7, 8b are Marcan redaction.[33] Verse 7 takes up 14:28, which is itself a redactional insertion (14:29 follows on far more naturally from 14:27), and the use of προάγω for Jesus' relationship to his followers recalls not only 14:28 but also the Marcan seam of 10:32. Verse 8a follows straight on from v. 6.[34] The original tradition therefore concluded with the announcement of the resurrection, the vindication of the suffering righteous one, which is followed, just as in Old Testament accounts of encounters with God or his angel, by an awestruck response. The women's amazement has already been mentioned in vv. 5b, 6a. Now trembling and terror seize them, and they flee from the place where they have been confronted by God's messenger. But v. 8b is redactional, containing characteristic Marcan style, vocabulary, and content. The use of the postpositive γάρ in a short clause, the employment of φοβέομαι (which has already been discussed in section II), and the similarity of the notion of saying nothing to anyone to Mark's secrecy motif (again discussed already under section IV) all point in this direction.[35] The tradition then ended on the notes of revelation and response to revelation. Mark's redaction makes an addition to each element to give it his own emphasis. It is precisely the aspect of promise that Mark adds to the notion of revelation through 16:7 and the aspect of failure that he adds to the notion of response through 16:8b.

VIII   *The Force for the Actual Readers*

For the actual readers the ending does not function as a challenge to overcome their fear of witnessing.[36] Instead, the impact of its juxtaposition is encouragement to persevere despite failure and disobedience. This sort of ending is pastoral,[37] and it is characterized by a realism that is ultimately positive, not negative. The whole story has faced its readers with the way of the cross and the necessity for suffering discipleship. It has offered no false encouragement through stressing the powerful presence of a resurrected Christ who transforms human limitations and delivers from persecution and death. But its austere message does still provide encouragement. If, as disciples, the readers fail to stand up to the rigours of the way of the cross set out in the story, all is not necessarily lost. Christ's powerful word of promise will still prevail. Since the promise of 16:7 was fulfilled despite failure, the readers can be confident that the other major unfulfilled prediction by the end of the narrative – the imminent parousia and vindication of the Son of Man in glory, and with it the vindication of his followers (cf. 9:1; 13:26, 27, 30; 14:62) – will also be fulfilled. Mark's story allows for human failure even after the resurrection yet holds out the triumph of God's purposes despite this.

The story and its ending were meant to give reassurance to its readers, who in all probability were facing persecution but at the same time were being presented with a view of Christ that was preoccupied with his resurrection power and glory.[38] From their knowledge of the gospel tradition (cf. e.g. 1 Cor. 15:3–8; Acts 10:38–42) part of the readers' expectation about the ending would have been that it would include accounts of resurrection appearances. Significantly, these are not provided. In fact, in some ways Mark's resurrection narrative is anticlimactic. It is clear that the crucifixion and burial have been reversed and that the resurrection has taken place, but the real climaxes of the narrative are at a point in the past – the cross – and a point in the future – the parousia (cf. chapter 13). The structure of the plot de-emphasizes the resurrection. Even after God's revelation has taken place in Jesus' resurrection, mystery, fear and failure remain.[39] For Mark's narrative world also the time between resurrection and parousia is not one dominated by visible resurrection power. As far as everyday life is concerned, the resurrection has not changed the course of history in any obvious visible way. To be sure, the promise is that the risen Jesus will regroup his disciples for mission, but the two features of the period between the resurrection and the parousia previewed in chapter 13 are the mission itself (13:9, 10) and suffering discipleship in the midst of persecution (13:9, 11–13, 19–20). Only the parousia will once and for all remove suffering, ambiguity and failure and provide ultimate vindication.

There are no elements of the reading being proposed that are obviously anachronistic. In fact, such a reading could only have its full force in a first-century setting with a strong hope in an imminent parousia. The story was not over. It continued into the time of the readers. The effectiveness of its final juxtaposition of promise and failure within the context of the Gospel's narrative world depended on the belief that the one outstanding promise about the parousia of the Son of Man would soon be fulfilled. The reading is also not anachronistic in the sense of demanding too great a literary sophistication on the part of its first readers.[40] To expect the reader to be able to relate the fulfilment of a promise and the failure of the women disciples when similar relationships have been a consistent feature of the story is scarcely to be too demanding.

IX *Some Concluding Reflections of a Modern Reader*

The proposed reading has a number of advantages. It satisfies the needs of consistency and coherence with its demonstration of the narrative's repetitive pattern of promise and failure. It can be supported both by a more literary and by a more redaction–critical approach. What is more, the values and norms that emerge from this reading of the ending are appropriate to the pastoral purpose of the Gospel, and its perspective on Christian existence is suggestive for the modern reader.

Whereas for ancient readers it was the notion of the women's failure that was initially alienating, for modern readers it may well be the aspect of failure in the story that is most appealing. This can be highlighted by comparing Mark's vision of life with that of Paul in their ability to embrace ambiguity. Paul's theology of the cross has its correlate in Christian existence in the paradox of grace being experienced in weakness, power only in the midst of suffering. Mark's focus on the passion has a similar correlate in Christian existence in discipleship as the way of the cross, a way that holds out promise despite failure. For Paul weakness and suffering do not include sinning. Especially if, as the majority scholarly view holds, Rom. 7:7–25 is not about present Christian existence, then in Paul's thought sin in the believer's life is totally incongruous. He allows no room for sin in the normal Christian life.[41] Mark's perspective then seems more realistic than Paul's, for it makes allowance not just for human weakness but for human failure. Its view of discipleship can embrace failure in the form of disobedience and therefore sinfulness.

As we have seen, though the end of the narrative underlines human failure, that is not the last word in the narrative world. The last word involves Christ's sovereign promise about the end. But there lies the major problem not only for a modern reader but also for any reader from the end of the first century CE on for whom the delay of the parousia had become a concern.[42] Our attraction to Mark's realism about Christian living is certainly balanced by our alienation from his portrayal of a Christ whose prediction about the end is given such importance and yet was so clearly mistaken. Are we left with a reading which takes away with one hand what it has offered with the other? Does any reassurance about failure of discipleship in fact become hollow and illegitimate once the eschatology of the promise that underlies it becomes problematic?[43] What happens to the effectiveness of Mark's ending when that on which it depends – the correspondence between the sense of a real ending in the narrative world and the expectation of a real end in the reader's world – is undermined or removed? What happens when the issue becomes not how to understand human failure after Christ's resurrection but how to understand divine failure to complete the vindication of Christ and his followers? Modern readers can envisage an end, but nuclear annihilation or the total pollution of the environment is scarcely the same as the coming of the Son of Man. Among Christian readers some, having asked such questions, find that they must still talk about the delay of a real parousia and in the context of the Christian message as a whole find this hope more attractive and no more difficult to sustain than alternative Marxist or humanist visions of the end. Others are unable to go as far but recognize the need for the sense of an ending.[44] They recognize that for the present to have meaning there is the need for a story about ourselves and the history of the world, a story with a beginning and an end. Since such narrative fictions are not abandoned because they are fictions but only if they lose their "operational effectiveness",[45] these readers have decided that perhaps the best that can be done is to live "as if" there were some version of the Christian ending.[46] Both sorts of readers we have described can reflect that, though their views on the promise of an end are foreign to that of Mark's story, at least the ambiguities involved in the former and the ironies essential to the latter might not be totally lost on its writer. Readers who have experienced the initially unexpected ending of Mark's story should not be surprised to find themselves thinking not just about the failure of discipleship but also about the failure of the promise. There is at least some plausibility about a story without a straightforwardly happy ending leading to a reading without a straightforwardly positive conclusion.

NOTES

1 See R. M. Fowler, "Who is 'the Reader' of Mark's Gospel?" in *Society of Biblical Literature 1983 Seminar Papers* (ed. K. H. Richards; Chico, CA: Scholars Press, 1983) 31–53; idem, "Who Is 'The Reader' in Reader Response Criticism?" *Semeia* 31 (1985) 5–23, for discussion of this terminology; see also N. R. Petersen, "The Reader in the Gospel", *Neot* 18 (1984) 38–51.

2 In comparison with the three most recent detailed studies, this reading differs from that of T. E. Boomershine ("Mark 16:8 and the Apostolic Commission", *JBL* 100 [1981] 225–39), who puts most stress on his particular interpretation of v. 8 as a challenge to gospel proclamation to the detriment of the significance of v. 7, whose function he misinterprets in terms of the apostolic commission to announce Jesus' messiahship. It differs also from that of J. L. Magness (*Sense and Absence* [Atlanta: Scholars Press, 1986]), who allows v. 7 to override v. 8, which he interprets positively in terms of a temporary awestruck silence which gave birth to speech; he thereby allows a suspended or expected ending to override the distinctiveness of the actual ending. It has closer affinities with the interpretation of N. R. Petersen ("When is the End not the End? Literary Reflections on the Ending of Mark's Narrative", *Int* 34 [1980] 15–66), but in the end he places more weight on the prediction and fulfilment connected with v. 7, interprets v. 8 and its irony differently, and as a consequence does not relate these verses to the rest of the plot in the same way.

245

3 See also B. M. Metzger, *A Textual Commentary on the Greek New Testament* (London: United Bible Societies, 1971) 122–6; K. Aland, "Der Schluss der Markusevangeliums", in *L'Évangile selon marc* (ed. M. Sabbe; Leuven: Leuven University Press, 1974) 345–70, *pace* W. R. Farmer's attempt to argue for the originality of 16:9–20 in *The Last Twelve Verses of Mark* (Cambridge: University Press, 1974). See especially the review of Farmer by J. N. Birdsall, *JTS* 26 (1975) 151–60.

4 For fuller discussion of Greek sentences ending with γάρ, see R. H. Lightfoot, *The Gospel Message of Mark* (Oxford: Clarendon, 1950) 80–97, 106–16; F. W. Danker, "Menander and the New Testament", *NTS* 10 (1963–4) 365–8; P. W. Van der Horst, "Can a Book End with γάρ? A Note on Mark 16:8", *JTS* 23 (1972) 121–4 (who in particular calls attention to the concluding sentence of Plotinus's thirty-second treatise [*Ennead* 5.5], though, as he also says, it should be "obvious that, if a sentence can end with γάρ, a book can end with such a sentence"); T. E. Boomershine and G. L. Bartholomew, "The Narrative Technique of Mark 16:8", *JBL* 100 (1981) 213–23 (though it is not necessary to argue with them that ἐφοβοῦντο γάρ is a final complete sentence rather than merely the concluding clause of 16:8 as a whole).

5 Or to put it another way with A. Farrer (*A Study in St Mark* [London: Dacre Press, 1951] 175): "And if the mice in the bishop's house at Rome ate the appendix, what highly discriminating mice they must have been!" Farrer would have done well to remember this when in a later work (*St Matthew and St Mark* [London: Dacre Press, 1954] 144–59) he revised his view under the influence of Matthew's use of Mark's ending and argued for an additional summarizing phrase in Mark's original.

6 *Pace* W. Marxsen, *Mark the Evangelist* (Nashville: Abingdon, 1969) 75–95; T. J. Weeden, *Mark – Traditions in Conflict* (Philadelphia: Fortress, 1971) 111–17; N. Perrin, *The Resurrection According to Matthew, Mark and Luke* (Philadelphia: Fortress, 1977) 27.

7 See also R. Bultmann, *History of the Synoptic Tradition* (Oxford: Blackwell, 1963) 285; R. H. Fuller, *The Formation of the Resurrection Narratives* (London: Collier-Macmillan, 1971) 62–4; E. Schweizer, *The Good News According To Mark* (London: SPCK, 1970) 365–6; R. H. Stein, "A Short Note on Mark 14:28 and 16:7", *NTS* 20 (1973–4) 445–52; H. Anderson, *The Gospel of Mark* (London: Oliphants, 1976) 357; D. Catchpole, "The Fearful Silence of the Women at the Tomb", *Journal of Theology for Southern Africa* 18 (1977) 4, 5; N. R. Petersen, *Literary Criticism for New Testament Critics* (Philadelphia: Fortress, 1982) 77; E. Best, *Mark: The Gospel As Story* (Edinburgh: T. & T. Clark, 1983) 77.

8 E.g Lightfoot, *Gospel Message of Mark*, 87–97; W. L. Lane, *Commentary on the Gospel of Mark* (Grand Rapids: Eerdmans, 1974) 590–2; R. Pesch, *Das Markusevangelium* (Freiburg: Herder, 1977) 2. 535–6, 541; J. R. Donahue, "Jesus as the Parable of God in the Gospel of Mark", *Int* 32 (1978) 380–1; Magness, *Sense and Absence*, 101.

9 See also J. M. Robinson, *The Problem of History in Mark* (London: SCM, 1957) 68–74 (on the relation between cowardly fear and numinous awe in Mark); Weeden, *Mark – Traditions in Conflict*, 49–50; H. Fleddermann, "The Flight of a Naked Young Man (Mark 14:51–2)", *CBQ* 41 (1979) 416 n. 25 (who goes as far as to say, "Mark equates fear and unbelief"); P. Perkins, *Resurrection* (London: Geoffrey Chapman, 1984) 121–2.

10 The function of narrative comments introduced by γάρ is, after all, to explain a previous statement; see also Boomershine and Bartholomew, "The Narrative Technique of Mark 16:8", 215.

11 On point of view in Mark, see N. R. Petersen, "'Point of View' in Mark's Narrative", *Semeia* 12 (1978) 97–121; J. Dewey, "Point of View and the Disciples in Mark", *Society of Biblical Literature 1982 Seminar Papers* (ed. K. H. Richards; Chico, CA: Scholars Press, 1982) 97–106; D. Rhoads and D. Michie, *Mark as Story* (Philadelphia: Fortress, 1982) 39–44.

12 On the women's role in the narrative as an extension of that of the disciples, see E. Best, "The Role of the Disciples in Mark", *NTS* 23 (1976–7) 386; Perrin, *Resurrection*, 29–31; W. Munro, "Women Disciples in Mark?" *CBQ* 44 (1982) 225–41; E. S. Malbon, "Fallible Followers: Women and Men in the Gospel of Mark", *Semeia* 28 (1983) 29–48; Perkins, *Resurrection*, 122; W. H. Kelber, "Apostolic Tradition and the Form of the Gospel", in *Discipleship in the New Testament* (ed. F. F. Segovia; Philadelphia: Fortress, 1985) 36.

13 Since F. Kermode's *The Genesis of Secrecy* (London: Harvard University Press, 1979) 49–73, with its comparison with Joyce's *Ulysses*, one is tempted to call this figure "Mark's Man in the Macintosh".

14 See especially R. Tannehill, "The Disciples in Mark: The Function of a Narrative Role", *JR* 57 (1977) 403 n. 38; Fleddermann, "The Flight of a Naked Young Man", 412–18. For a history of interpretation, see F. Neirynck, "La fuite du jeune homme en Mc 14,51–52", *ETL* 55 (1979) 43–66.

15 See Fuller, *Formation of the Resurrection Narratives*, 59–62; G. Stemberger, "Galilee – Lord of Salvation?" in W. D. Davies, *The Gospel and the Land* (Berkeley: University of California Press, 1974) 409–38.

16 *Pace* U. Wilckens, *Resurrection* (Atlanta: John Knox, 1978) 35; Fuller, *Formation of the Resurrection Narratives*, 64; Pesch, *Markusevangelium*, 2. 536.

17 See Schweizer, *Good News According To Mark*, 373; Perrin, *Resurrection*, 30–2 (who speaks of "the totality of discipleship failure" in this connection); Boomershine, "Mark 16:8", 229 ("the women's silence is unequivocally and unambiguously wrong"); *pace* Catchpole, "The Fearful Silence", 6 (who argues that because in 1:44 the command "but go, show yourself to the priest" follows the injunction "See that you say nothing to anyone", and therefore the injunction to keep silence relates to the broad mass of persons and does not prevent disclosure to a specified individual, 16:8 should be understood to be a response of obedience which brings the message to certain specified individuals, namely, the disciples, and excludes the public at large. But this by

no means follows. It is precisely the specific qualification of the general statement that allows 1:44 to be understood in this way, and such a qualification is absent from the description of the women's response in 16:8. Magness (*Sense and Absence*, 100) is also prepared to alter v. 8 to mean that they said nothing to anyone only until "passing soldiers [*sic*] changing the guard and merchants opening their stalls and shoppers heading for the market, they reached the disciples".

18 On the messianic secret, see W. Wrede, *The Messianic Secret* (London: James Clarke, 1971); C. Tuckett, ed., *The Messianic Secret* (London: SPCK, 1983).

19 Boomershine see this clearly ("Mark 16:8", 229). The women's action is described as "a shocking reversal of expectations". He even sees it as a reversal of expectations about the messianic secret (p. 238) but misinterprets the significance of such a reversal, as do Marxsen (*Mark the Evangelist*, 91–2), Wilckens (*Resurrection*, 34–5), and Fuller (*Formation of the Resurrection Narratives*, 64).

20 Magness fails to allow for any relation between the ending and reader's expectations other than reinforcement (*Sense and Absence*, 87–125). The strong elements of irony earlier in the narrative should have prepared the reader for an undermining or reversal of expectations in its ending. On ironic elements elsewhere in Mark, see W. Booth, *A Rhetoric of Irony* (London: University of Chicago Press, 1974) 28–9; J. R. Donahue, "Temple, Trial and Royal Christology (Mark 14:53–65)", in *The Passion in Mark* (ed. W. H. Kelber; Philadelphia: Fortress, 1976) 79 ("Irony is the rhetorical medium through which Mark conveys his message of faith"); D. Juel, *Messiah and Temple* (Missoula, MT: Scholars Press, 1977) 47–8, 55–6, 205–7 (who calls irony "the most prominent literary feature of the passion story" [p. 47]); R. C. Tannehill, "The Gospel of Mark as Narrative Christology", *Semeia* 16 (1979) 78–80; R. M. Fowler, *Loaves and Fishes* (Chico, CA: Scholars Press, 1981) 96–9, 154–7; Rhoads and Michie, *Mark as Story*, 59–62; D. O. Via, *The Ethics of Mark's Gospel – In the Middle of Time* (Philadelphia: Fortress, 1985) 49, 54, 57, 62, 77, 102, 181, 191. On endings that are confrontational rather than reinforcing and that deliberately thwart reader expectations, see M. Torgovnick, *Closure in the Novel* (Princeton: University Press, 1981) 18, 117.

21 *Pace* Kelber ("Apostolic Tradition and the Form of the Gospel", 40), who claims that the assumption of a postresurrectional reunion between Jesus and the disciples depends on a historicizing harmonization of different gospel stories and a preference for fulfilment over disappointment; Tannehill ("The Gospel of Mark", 84), who prefers to stress that, since the narrative does not relate the promised appearance, the reader is meant to understand it simply as possibility. The reader's knowledge is also not sufficiently taken into account by A. Lindemann ("Die Osterbotschaft des Markus: Zur theologischen Interpretation von Mk 16,1–8", *NTS* 26 [1979–80] 315–17) in his analysis of v. 8 as placing the reader in the same position as the women in immediate confrontation with the Easter proclamation of the young man.

22 *Pace* Petersen ("When is the End not the End?" 159, 162), who suggests that the ending is ironic but by this means not an undermining of expectations but that "our narrator does not mean what he says in Mark 16:8". On our reading, the narrator does mean that the *women* were disobedient to the message and did not tell; see also Via, *Ethics of Mark's Gospel*, 53.

23 This is also seen clearly by R. P. Meye, "Mark 16:8 – The Ending of Mark's Gospel", *BR* 14 (1969) 39–43.

24 On this relationship between prediction and fulfilment in the story, see Petersen, *Literary Criticism*, 767; idem, "When is the End not the End?" 155–6; see also J. D. Kingsbury, *The Christology of Mark's Gospel* (Philadelphia: Fortress, 1983) 135–6.

25 See also Tannehill, "The Gospel of Mark", 84: "the author wants us to believe that the words of Jesus in 14:28, repeated and clarified in 16:7, will also prove true in spite of fear and failure."

26 See also Kermode, *Genesis of Secrecy*, 62–3; Fleddermann, "The Flight of a Naked Young Man", 415–16 (who points out that the young man's failure to accept the passion contrasts with Jesus' willingness so to do).

27 A. K. Jenkins makes the connection with 14:51 but treats the young man in white as representative of the outcome of discipleship – martyrdom ("Young Man or Angel?" *ExpTim* 94 [1983] 237–40).

28 Petersen sees something of this when he asserts, "In the plotting of the entire narrative what Jesus says comes to pass despite the understanding and deeds of the disciples" (*Literary Criticism*, 78).

29 See also Petersen, *Literary Criticism*, 73: Boomershine, "Mark 16:8", 234–5.

30 See, e.g. Juel, *Messiah and Temple*, 117–57.

31 The process of forming expectations and then having them undermined is, of course, frequently analysed in reader-response criticism and shown to be a common way in which an author attempts to educate a reader. See, e.g. W. Iser, *The Implied Reader* (Baltimore: Johns Hopkins University Press, 1974) 37–9, 288; S. Fish, *Is There a Text in This Class?* (Cambridge, MA: Harvard Univeristy Press, 1980) 158–9, 345. For the role that endings play in such a process and the "retrospective patterning" of parallelism they provoke, see Torgovnick, *Closure in the Novel*, 5, 8, 13. The ending of Mark is similar to what Torgovnick calls a "close-up" ending in which "first-time readers may not even understand why the ending *is* the ending, or may be at a loss for what the ending implies about meaning. . . . Readers can usually, however, discover both the appropriateness of the ending and its implications for meaning through retrospective analysis and through perception of the pattern that controls the ending . . ." (p. 15).

32 Indeed, J. D. Crossan exploits this in the course of his argument that Mark 16:1–8 is a complete creation of Mark himself ("Empty Tomb and Absent Lord [Mark 16:1–8]", in *The Passion in Mark* [ed. W. H. Kelber; Philadelphia: Fortress, 1976] 135–52). At the other end of the spectrum of views is Pesch, who claims that "der Evangelist Markus hat seine Vorlage nicht redaktionell

bearbeitet" (*Markusevangelium*, 2. 520). For a history of recent discussion, see
F. Neirynck, "Marc 16,1–8 tradition et rédaction", *ETL* 56 (1980) 56–88.

33 See E. J. Pryke, *Redactional Style in the Marcan Gospel* (Cambridge: University Press, 1978) 23, for a list of those who hold this view; see also L. Schenke, *Auferstehungesverkündigung und leeres Grab* (Stuttgart: Katholisches Bibelwerk, 1969) 30–55; Weeden, *Mark – Traditions in Conflict*, 47–50, 103–6; J. Gnilka, *Das Evangelium nach Markus* (Zürich: Benziger, 1979) 2. 338–9.

34 See also Marxsen, *Mark the Evangelist*, 84–5; Fuller, *Formation of the Resurrection Narratives*, 53; J. E. Alsup, *The Post-Resurrection Appearance Stories of the Gospel Tradition* (Stuttgart: Calwer, 1975) 91–4; Catchpole, "The Fearful Silence", 3, 4.

35 See C. H. Bird, "Some γάρ Clauses in St. Mark's Gospel", *JTS* 4 (1953) 171–87; Pryke, *Redactional Style*, 44–5.

36 *Pace* Boomershine ("Mark 16:8", 237), who holds that "the story appeals for the proclamation of the resurrection regardless of fear"; he is followed by Rhoads and Michie, *Mark as Story*, 61–2, 140; Perkins, *Resurrection*, 123. This is mistaken on two counts. Strictly speaking, the women are not told to proclaim the resurrection but to pass on a message about a post-resurrection reunion. It also misjudges the function of v. 7. As can be perceived from chapter 13, the implied reader knows that this meeting must have taken place (see also Petersen, "The Reader in the Gospel", 49). The importance of the command is the promise it contains and its fulfilment, not its obligation upon the reader to do the actual task the women failed to do.

37 See Best, *Mark: The Gospel as Story*, esp. 51–4, 93–9.

38 This is not to endorse the details of the reconstruction of a hypothetical heretical Christology by scholars such as Weeden (*Mark – Traditions in Conflict*), but it is to agree that the shaping and emphases of Mark's narrative suggest a response not only to false notions of discipleship but also to the Christology that would have accompanied them.

39 See also Via, *Ethics of Mark's Gospel*, 56: "There will be failures to understand after the resurrection. . . . The resurrection does not introduce a radically new departure, and the redeeming kerygmatic word and the demanding ethical word will never be made unambiguously clear".

40 This objection to 16:8 as the original ending was stated forcefully by W. L. Knox, "The Ending of St Mark's Gospel", *HTR* 35 (1942) 22–3. But Magness, who examines a number of endings in ancient literature, argues that ancient writers and readers were well able to produce and understand "open endings" (*Sense and Absence*, 25–63).

41 See, e.g. J. C. Beker, *Paul the Apostle* (Edinburgh: T. & T. Clark, 1980) 215–21.

42 See also Rhoads and Michie, *Mark as Story*, 142: "In one sense, the time-limits of the story world do not account for a reader beyond the generation of Jesus, because the story assumes that the rule of God will be fully established shortly

after the temple is destroyed"; Petersen, "The Reader in the Gospel", 44: "When we perceive the generation gap, we should be concerned with questions about the *delay* of the parousia, while Mark's implied and authorial readers must be concerned with the *imminent occurrence* of the parousia".

43 We cannot agree with Best (*Mark: The Gospel as Story*, 146–7), who claims that Mark's presentation of discipleship "is capable of indefinite extension; it is in no way linked to the return of Jesus, for it is set in terms of the cross and the resurrection". See also the discussion in n. 46.

44 See F. Kermode, *The Sense of an Ending* (New York: Oxford University Press, 1967) 3–64, 155–80.

45 Ibid., 40.

46 The most sustained recent reflection on the implications for the modern reader of the temporal elements of Mark's plot and narrative world is that of Via, *Ethics of Mark's Gospel*, esp. 27–66, 164–7, 209–25. Despite the illuminating nature of much of his discussion, in the end Via only highlights the reader's dilemma, appearing to equivocate on the issues of most interest to our reading. On the one hand, he acknowledges that belief in a literal, imminent end may well be Mark's actual position (p. 165), but, on the other, he suggests with some rather unconvincing arguments that "it is by no means unequivocally clear that he has an imminent eschatology" (p. 166). He goes on to assert that Mark's "ethic is not constituted by an integral relationship to the literal near end of the world and therefore is not undermined by the failure of that event to occur, even if the Gospel predicted it" (p. 167). This may be true of the material in Mark 10 on which Via focuses, but it scarcely holds for our reading of the ending and its view of Christian existence as undergirded by the sovereign word that overcomes human failure. This view must be affected if the word is not fulfilled. As far as the contemporary reader's appropriation of the temporality of Mark's narrative is concerned, Via holds both that the beginning, middle, and end of Mark's narrative world correspond in some way to the temporality of the real world as we experience it (p. 219) and that its future aspect must be demythologized so that it is seen to represent the more revealing future which draws out the significance of the present (pp. 7, 163–6).

11

*Galilee and Jerusalem: History and Literature in Marcan Interpretation**

ELIZABETH STRUTHERS MALBON

A number of New Testament scholars have investigated the significance of the Marcan spatial designations Galilee and Jerusalem. Here the influence of E. Lohmeyer may be traced through R. H. Lightfoot and W. Marxsen to W. Kelber. In general, *historical* concerns about the composition of "Mark's" Gospel seem to motivate the approaches of Lohmeyer, Lightfoot, Marxsen and Kelber to the narrative opposition of Galilee and Jerusalem in the Gospel of Mark. The present approach to the significance of Galilee and Jerusalem is marked by concern for the Gospel of Mark as a *literary and theological* whole and for its narrative space as a system of relationships. The focus is more on the function of the narrative than on the intention of the narrator, more on how the story is read than on why it was written. The task is to consider Marcan geopolitical locations (especially Galilee and Jerusalem) in their system of relations and to consider the significance of this manifest, narrative system in terms of an underlying, non-manifest, "mythological" system.[1]

But, first, let us survey the trajectory of historical concerns for the Marcan opposition of Galilee and Jerusalem – a trajectory

* First published in *CBQ* 44 (1982) 242–55.

from Lohmeyer to Lightfoot to Marxsen to Kelber. Lohmeyer maintained, in *Galiläa und Jerusalem*,[2] that, historically, early Christianity in Palestine had two main centres: Galilee, where a Son of Man eschatology predominated, and Jerusalem, where a nationalistic messianic hope prevailed. Thus each historical, geographical centre may also be characterized theologically, or, more particularly, christologically: in Galilee the basic pre-supposition was *Kyrios Iēsous*, Jesus is Lord; in Jerusalem the basic presupposition was *Christos Iēsous*, Jesus is Christ (Messiah).[3] The Gospel of Mark, Lohmeyer then argued, building especially upon the significance of 14:28 and 16:7, reflects the convictions of the older Galilean tradition as it portrays Galilee as the place of the divine revelation and of the future return of the apocalyptic Son of Man as a prelude to the parousia. Galilee is the centre of Jesus' ministry and the future centre of the fulfilled kingdom of God, the "holy land" of the Marcan Gospel. Jerusalem, on the other hand, is the centre of opposition to the Marcan Jesus.[4]

R. H. Lightfoot, in *Locality and Doctrine in the Gospels*,[5] applied Lohmeyer's thesis particularly to the problem of under-standing the conclusion of Mark's Gospel. That the Gospel of Mark ends and was meant to end at 16:8, Lightfoot argued on the basis of both "form" (literary and philological grounds) and "content" (theological grounds). However, according to Light-foot, the significance of this ending is made most clear by the (theological) opposition of Galilee and Jerusalem throughout the Gospel. The best summary of Lightfoot's interpretation is his own.

> Galilee and Jerusalem, therefore, stand in opposition to each other, as the story of the gospel runs in St. Mark. The despised and more-or-less outlawed Galilee is shown to have been chosen by God as the seat of the gospel and of the revelation of the Son of man, while the sacred city of Jerusalem, the home of jewish piety and patriotism, has become the centre of relentless hostility and sin. Galilee is the sphere of revelation, Jerusalem the scene only of rejection. Galilee is the scene of the beginning and middle of the Lord's ministry; Jerusalem only of its end.[6]

And Galilee is also "the hallowed land of his eschatological coming".[7] Thus, Lightfoot concluded, the "importance which is assigned to Galilee rests not only on historical grounds, but on doctrinal or, more precisely, eschatological considerations; it rests above all on the conception of Jesus as the Son of man".[8]

Marxsen, in his study of "The Geographical Outline" of *Mark the Evangelist*,[9] shared the historical and eschatological emphases of Lohmeyer and Lightfoot but protested that both had over-looked the importance of distinguishing tradition and redaction in Mark.[10] According to Marxsen, (1) the appropriate focus is the redaction; (2) the redaction is found basically in the framework; (3) Mark's framework is "topical", i.e. theological in intent, although geographical in expression; (4) the centre of the theological/geographical framework of Mark is Galilee – and "almost all references to place (except for Galilee) are already anchored in the tradition"[11] and therefore not particularly important from Marxsen's viewpoint; and (5) Galilee is the centre for the Marcan Jesus because it was the centre for the Marcan community, the gathering place for awaiting the imminent parousia.[12] Thus, "Mark writes a 'Galilean Gospel'".[13] "Galilee is Jesus' 'place'".[14] "The decisive preaching always occurs in Galilee".[15] But primarily Galilee is "the locale of the imminent Parousia".[16] "Galilee is thus Jesus' 'home' in a far deeper sense than the merely historical. It is the place where he worked, where – hidden in the proclamation – he is now working, and will work at his Parousia".[17] In working out these ideas exegetically Marxsen attended almost exclusively to Galilee (note point 4 above) as a *terra christiana* where the parousia is awaited,[18] and he forfeited, to a large extent, the relational sense of Galilee *versus Jerusalem* so stressed by Lohmeyer and Lightfoot.

Kelber redresses this balance in *The Kingdom in Mark*,[19] further strengthening the prevailing conception of Galilee by an exegesis of "kingdom" passages throughout the Gospel and further darkening the prevailing view of Jerusalem with argu-ments that the family and the (failed) disciples of the Marcan Jesus join the Jerusalem authorities in opposing him.[20] As his prede-cessor Lohmeyer, Kelber hypothesizes, historically, that "Mark is representative of a northern Christianity which is in opposition to a southern Jerusalem-type Christianity".[21] But Kelber does move, exegetically, in several new directions – noting, for example, that while "the Galilee-Jerusalem polarity" is the "most conspicuous dynamic" operating within the spatial framework of the Marcan narrative, it does not represent the full extent of that spatial framework.[22] Like Lohmeyer and Marxsen before him, Kelber appears to be concerned most basically with the historical boundaries of the composition of the Gospel of Mark,[23] yet more thoroughly than either of them (or Lightfoot) Kelber seeks to establish both the boundary of the past (temple destruction) and the boundary of the future (parousia) for the Marcan community. Like Lohmeyer and Marxsen before him, Kelber seems to compress theology into eschatology,[24] yet more strongly than either of them (or Lightfoot) Kelber stresses the connotation of Galilee, of "all of Galilee", as the place of Jewish Christians and Gentile Christians together.[25] *The Kingdom in Mark* presents a more detailed exegesis of a larger portion of the Gospel of Mark than either "The Geographical Outline" or *Locality and Doctrine in the Gospels*, and yet it fails to treat chapters 14–16 in their narrative integrity. To a certain extent one might say that Kelber combats Lohmeyer, Lightfoot and Marxsen's overemphasis of 14:28 and 16:7 by combining it with an overemphasis of 1:14–15[26] and chapter 13.[27] As chapter 13 is perceived by Kelber as pivotal in understanding "Mark's" detachment from Jerusalem, so 1:14–15, "the gospel program", is regarded as the key to sensing "Mark's" attachment to Galilee. "Under the apocalyptic dynamic of revealing and concealing the gospel shrinks into a prologue of the parousia".[28] In other words, the initial (fulfilled, but concealed) appearance of the kingdom in Galilee (1:14–15) points to the final (revealed) appearance of the kingdom in Galilee (14:28; 16:7). In the final analysis, the most difficult evaluation to make of Kelber's, as of the work of so many Marcan scholars, is this: Is the exegete's relation of the internal evidence (the text itself) to external evidence (historical occurrences and documents, sociological reconstructions, etc.) warranted, legitimate and helpful in understanding the text?

In general, historical concerns about the composition of "Mark's" Gospel seem to motivate the approaches of Lohmeyer, Lightfoot, Marxsen and Kelber to the narrative opposition of Galilee and Jerusalem in the Gospel of Mark. Eschatology is taken as the key to understanding this Marcan opposition, and eschatology is portrayed as (to oversimplify but a little) the locus of the *history* of the community in and for which "Mark's" Gospel was composed. From historical presuppositions, historical conclusions emerge.[29] Marxsen's redaction-critical study appears to fit this generalization most closely, Lightfoot's broader literary and theological approach most loosely. Kelber's *Kingdom in Mark* serves as a clear example of the historical interpretation of the significance of Galilee and Jerusalem in the Gospel of Mark.

Now another step is called for. The present study of the Marcan opposition of Galilee and Jerusalem is, like Kelber's, concerned with theology and geography; but for Kelber geography itself is theological (Galilee is *the place* of the parousia) and theology itself is geographical (to await the parousia one must *go* to Galilee), while for me the *distinctions and interrelations* of the geographical (and, in a larger sense, spatial) system of the Marcan narrative may signal theological *distinctions and interrelations* of the Marcan Gospel; relationships are compared with relationships, not places with dogmas. While Kelber considers Marcan geography an indicator of the historical world of the text, I am considering Marcan geography in the context of the text as a literary world. As important as historical investigation may be, the investigation of the relation of the text to its historical world may not proceed in ignorance or disdain of the text itself or of the relation of the text to its literary world. In this, I must agree with Dan O. Via, writing in *Kerygma and Comedy in the New Testament*:

> To suppose that the historical phenomena somehow caused the text of Mark is to assume that language is an icon, that the text is primarily a reflection of the historical reality outside of itself. This view fails to recognize that both texts and history as meaningful are generated by "grammars" or systems of meaning, linguistic competences which are substructures of a fundamental matrix of possibilities of meaning. It has never been proved that the grammar of history is ontologically or epistemologically prior to the grammar (genre [i.e. literary world]) of texts.[30]

And, in fact, in relation to a text such as the Gospel of Mark, the "grammar of history" may be all but impossible to recover, whereas the "grammar of the text" invites investigation.

In investigating the "grammar of the text" of the Gospel of Mark, we must examine the narrative both diachronically (from 1:1 to 16:8) and synchronically (abstractly, theoretically). These two dimensions, diachronic and synchronic, or, graphically, horizontal and vertical, are analogous to the two simultaneous dimensions of an orchestra score. The image is that of structural anthropologist Claude Lévi-Strauss, who suggests that "an orchestra score, in order to become meaningful, has to be read diachronically along one axis – that is, page after page, and from left to right – and also synchronically along the other axis, all the

257

notes which are written vertically making up" one harmonic unit.[31] Thus, the diachronic dimension of a narrative is the chronological order in which events occur, the "apparent content" of the narrative, while the synchronic dimension is the underlying, formal, theoretical organization of the narrative, its "latent content".[32] The "apparent content" tells the story; the "latent content" suggests the fundamental opposition the story seeks to mediate.

A diachronic investigation of Galilee and Jerusalem in the Gospel of Mark focuses attention on the journeys of the Marcan Jesus and on various ways in which these journeys are anticipated. A close chronological reading brings out narrative patterns of foreshadowing or echoing – to suggest both a visual and an auditory metaphor.

Jesus' initial journey from Nazareth of Galilee to Judea, near Jerusalem (1:9), foreshadows Jesus' final journey to Judea, to Jerusalem. In the beginning Jesus journeys to Judea to be baptized by John into a ministry that leads, in the end, to a journey to Jerusalem to be crucified. But Jesus' initial return to Galilee from the wilderness in Judea (1:14) also foreshadows Jesus' final return to Galilee "as he told you" from the tomb in Judea (16:7). The ministry of the Marcan Jesus opens with Jesus' return to Galilee from Judea; the Marcan closing anticipates a like return.

On other occasions in the Marcan narrative, a journey of Jesus is anticipated not by an earlier journey of Jesus but by a journey of other Marcan characters in one of two ways: (1) Jesus' fame, or word of his deeds, is spread by a person or persons, either unsolicited or commanded, in an area Jesus will later traverse, or (2) persons come to Jesus from regions Jesus will later enter. Jesus' fame (1:28) precedes him (1:39) throughout Galilee, for it spreads "everywhere throughout all the surrounding region of Galilee" (1:28) before the Marcan Jesus has travelled beyond Capernaum for the first time. What Jesus has done is preached in the Decapolis by the healed Gerasene demoniac (5:20) before Jesus himself preaches there (7:31). At 1:28 Jesus' fame spreads unsent; at 5:20 Jesus sends the Gerasene home to tell and he goes out proclaiming. Before Jesus is reported to have travelled beyond Galilee teaching and healing, a multitude comes to him from Judea, Idumea, beyond the Jordan, and Tyre and Sidon (3:7–8).[33] Later Jesus himself goes to each of these places (with the exception of Idumea) that have first come to him in a metaphorical way through their inhabitants: Judea (10:1), beyond the Jordan (10:1), and Tyre and Sidon (7:24, 31). Thus Jesus retraces, in reverse, the steps of those who come to him from Judea and from foreign regions. Jesus' reception by the people of Galilee, Judea and the surrounding foreign regions is anticipated by his reception of persons from each area. The significance of Jesus' journeys, of his openness to persons everywhere, is underlined by these foreshadowings.

Jesus' final (completed) journey, the journey to Jerusalem, is anticipated in an analogous, and ominous, way. Scribes come down (3:22, *katabantes*) from Jerusalem to confront Jesus (3:22; 7:1), and Jesus and his followers go up (10:32, *anabainontes*; 10:33, *anabainomen*; 15:41, *synanabasai*) to Jerusalem and to confrontation with the religious establishment. The scribes, with their concerns for order in the religious group in the face of a disruptive exorcist (3:22) and for ritual purity (7:1), represent the religious establishment of Jerusalem. Thus the accusations delivered to Jesus by the scribes who come down from Jerusalem anticipate the accusations against Jesus when he is delivered to the chief priests and the scribes upon going up to Jerusalem. This decisive "going up" to Jerusalem of Jesus contrasts with the "coming down" from Jerusalem of the scribes. Jesus and the scribes move in opposite directions, not only spatially but also theologically. Jesus seeks to break down and break open the exclusive categories of the sacred and the profane that the scribes, and the entire religious establishment, seek to maintain. Jesus' rejection in Jerusalem is anticipated by his rejection by the scribes from Jerusalem. Jesus' rejection, like his reception, is foreshadowed by the journeys of others to him. Jesus is at the centre of all Marcan movement.

From the centre, movements radiate outwards, and to the centre they return. As broadly as Jesus travels, his name and fame travel farther, borne on the lips of those who come to him from as far away as Syrophoenicia (7:26) in the north and Idumea (3:8) in the south and who go away from him not only throughout Galilee (1:28) to the west but also throughout the Decapolis (5:20) to the east. During his Galilean ministry, Jesus moves not only throughout Galilee but to Judea and to foreign regions as well, and persons from each of these three major areas come to him. During his Judean passion, persons from each of these areas again come to Jesus: from North Africa, Simon the Cyrenian to carry his cross (15:21); from Galilee, Mary Magdalene and the other women to observe his crucifixion (15:40–1) and to make preparations for his burial (15:47; 16:1); from Judea, Joseph of Arimathea to lay him in a tomb (15:46). Again Jesus is the focal point. Galilee, Judea and foreign regions look to him.

In one sense, the narrative action of Mark seems to end in Judea. However, the close of the Marcan Gospel turns our attention away from Judea and back to Galilee. From the Mount of Olives, Jesus informs his disciples that after he is raised up he will go before them to Galilee (14:28). At the cross, the reader is given a flashback to Galilee in the description of the women "who, when he was in Galilee, followed him, and ministered to him" (15:41). At the empty tomb, the women and the reader are given a flash-forward to Galilee where Jesus is going and where "you will see him, as he told you" (16:7). The final reference to Galilee, a promise suggested in spatial terms, serves to move the story beyond its literal ending in Jerusalem while at the same time recalling not only the narrative's beginning but its dominant geopolitical mode. In some sense the Marcan experience of Jesus' Galilean ministry seems to be proleptic of the post-resurrection experience of the followers of Jesus. The beginning of Mark gives away the end, and the end gives way to the beginning, not just spatially but theologically. At the initial return to Galilee, Jesus "comes preaching the gospel of God" (1:14). At the final return to Galilee, it would appear, Mark comes preaching "the gospel of Jesus Christ, the Son of God" (1:1).

Thus, although Galilee is the dominant spatial setting of chapters 1–9 of Mark and Judea of chapters 10–16, the narrative, in fact, opens in Judea and closes with past and future looks to Galilee. Action in Judea, and especially Jerusalem, as the climax to action in Galilee might represent the cultural expectation of many first-century hearers of Mark's story. Jerusalem was, after all, the culmination of many a pilgrimage. However, the Marcan diachronic pattern reverses this expectation: Judean actions culminate in Galilee (1:14); Judean actions culminate in Galilee (14:28; 16:7). Thus, not only does the Judea-to-Galilee pattern frame the narrative at the geopolitical level, but it is intensified by repetition within the narrative.

A synchronic investigation of Galilee and Jerusalem in the Gospel of Mark focuses attention on the broader system of relationships within which "Galilee" and "Jerusalem" are meaningful terms and on the deeper significance of their opposition. A thoughtful theoretical reading brings out "logical" or "mythological" patterns of opposition and mediation – to borrow the terminology of Lévi-Strauss.

The most dramatic spatial contrast of the Gospel of Mark is the opposition of land (*gē*) and sea (*thalassa*). As an opposition that is both natural and basic, land versus sea implicitly underlies the narrative as a whole. The Sea of Galilee is central to the spatial movements of the Marcan Jesus. Jesus calls his first disciples while "passing along by the Sea of Galilee" (1:16). Jesus often teaches the crowds on the land "beside the sea" (2:23; 3:7; 4:1; 5:21). Physically, the sea is a barrier between the land of Galilee and the foreign lands on its eastern shore, but Jesus easily crosses this barrier (4:35; 5:1; 5:21; 6:51–3; 8:10; 8:13). At certain points in Mark the opposition "land versus sea" comes to explicit expression (4:1, Jesus is on the sea, the crowd is on the land; 6:47, the disciples are on the sea, Jesus is on the land).

The land, the normal and secure environment of human beings, is quite naturally opposed to the sea, a temporary place of movement for human beings and also a place that threatens (4:37–8; 6:48) and is capable of destruction (5:13; 9:42; 11:23). According to the Hebrew/Jewish tradition underlying the Gospel of Mark, the land was created by God as the habitation for men and women over which they are "lord" (Genesis 1). But God remains Lord over the sea; Old Testament imagery, particularly in the Psalms but also in Genesis 1 and Book of Job, frequently portrays the sea as chaos, which only the Lord can order or reorder (see especially Psalm 107 and Job 38).[34] Mark accepts this connotation of the sea as chaos in opposition to the land as order, but the Marcan Gospel suggests that in the acts of Jesus the mediation of this fundamental opposition has begun. By his word Jesus calms the sea (4:39), orders the chaos. By his deed Jesus treats the sea as if it were the land; he walks on the sea (6:48); for him chaos is made order.

The fundamental opposition "chaos versus order" is manifest in the Marcan narrative by the opposition "sea versus land", which is "replaced" by the opposition "foreign land versus Jewish homeland". The opposed pair, foreign land versus Jewish homeland, may be understood as less antithetical than sea versus land since both poles do represent land.[35] Jewish homeland is narrativized in Mark as Galilee and Judea. The narrative manifestations of foreign land include Idumea, beyond the Jordan, Tyre and Sidon, the country of the Gerasenes, the Decapolis, Bethsaida, Syrophoenicia, Caesarea Philippi and Cyrene.

Mark's geographical assumptions concerning the lands surrounding Galilee sometimes prove confusing if plotted on a map reflecting physical reality.[36] The "foreignness", as it were, of these cities and areas is more crucial in Mark than their precise location or Jesus' exact itinerary in reaching them. Narrative signs such as the swine in the country of the Gerasenes (5:11–13) or the conversation with the Syro-Phoenician woman about the children's crumbs for the dogs (7:26–9) signal the strange, foreign, Gentile nature of these places as opposed to the familiarity of the Jewish homeland of Galilee, with its synagogues (1:21ff.; 1:39; 3:1; 6:2), and Judea, with its temple. Jewish homeland, the place of residence of the central characters of the story, is related to foreign land, a temporary place of travel for the central characters, as land, the familiar environment of human beings, is related to sea, a temporary place of travel for human beings. Familiar is to strange as order is to chaos. But here again movement toward mediation is sensed in the actions of Jesus. He miraculously feeds both Jews (6:35–44) and Gentiles (8:1–9); he heals persons from foreign regions as well as from Galilee and Judea (3:7–8); he journeys both in his home country and away from it.

The opposition "foreign land versus Jewish homeland", which "replaces" the opposition "sea versus land" in the "logical" or "mythological" order underlying Mark's narrative, is in turn "replaced" by the opposition "Judea versus Galilee". Structural analysis confirms the proposition of redaction criticism that the distinction between Galilee and Judea is pivotal for the Marcan Gospel. However, redaction critics, for example, Kelber, draw theological and *historical* conclusions from this observation, while structural critics draw *literary* and theological conclusions.

The Marcan narrative, which manifests the traditional Jewish associations of sea and foreign land with chaos and of land and Jewish homeland with order, reverses the expected associations of Galilee and Judea. Would not Judea, the region of Jerusalem – religious centre of the Jewish people, home of the temple that ordered their worship and of the Tables of the Law that ordered their very lives – be expected to be the centre of order? And would not Galilee, in contradistinction to the home of the religious establishment, Galilee "ringed" by foreign lands and their influence,[37] be anticipated as a manifestation of chaos? But, in the Marcan Gospel, Galilee, Jesus' homeland within the Jewish homeland, is the centre of order. Wherever he journeys – to the Jordan to be baptized, to Tyre and Sidon to heal, to Jerusalem to be crucified – the Marcan Jesus always returns to Galilee. Galilee forms a framework for the narrative action, ordering movements in space. In controversy with the leaders and representatives of the supposed religious order centralized in Jerusalem, Jesus calls the established religious order into question. A new and authentic order is both demanded and proclaimed by Jesus of Nazareth in Galilee;[38] to Jesus the old order is as chaos. Chaos breaks loose when Jesus arrives in Jerusalem in Judea. The chaos of the trial, in which the Marcan chief priests and elders appear to ignore their own required order, leads to the chaos of the crucifixion, complete with darkness when there should be light and the rending of the temple curtain that makes chaos of the rigid demarcation of the sacred and profane within the religious structure. Thus Judea is linked with the chaos pole of the fundamental opposition, and Galilee with order.

At the level of the opposition "Galilee versus Judea" movement toward the mediation of chaos and order is implied in the Marcan exchange of connotations between the two regions. When Galilee, supposedly chaotic, connotes a new order, and Judea, supposedly orderly, represents chaos, the fundamental opposition is severely weakened. Yet tension remains between Jerusalem and Galilee. At the close of the Gospel of Mark, Jesus' spatial location is neither Jerusalem nor Galilee, but somewhere in between; Jesus is in movement; he is "going before" (16:7); he is on the way. By understanding the system of relationships at the narrative level of the Gospel of Mark, including the relationship of Jerusalem and Galilee, we may be better able to understand the significance of Mark's Gospel at the theological level, including the relationship of chaos and order.

On the other hand, Kelber understands "Jerusalem" – and the temple, and the family of Jesus, and Jesus' disciples – as representatives of the historical reality of the Jerusalem church that was the enemy of the Marcan community[39] and "Galilee" as a symbol for the historical "Galilean Christians" who awaited the imminent parousia in Galilee after A.D. 70 and for whom "Mark" was the "spokesman".[40] It seems, indeed, ironic that Kelber's

"Mark" devotes all his energy to rescuing the parousia hope from its literal and dogmatic attachment to Jerusalem only to attach it just as literally and dogmatically to Galilee.[41] The gospel of such a "Mark" would not be "good news" for long, and this is, in fact, Kelber's evaluation.

> While it remains true that Mark creates the process of time [the "New Place" and "New Time" of Kelber's subtitle], his vision of time is subject to rapid erosion by time itself. He can build the bridge which spans past and future, because Jesus' past and the Christians' future are still conceivable as the beginning and end of one generation. But as the gulf between Jesus and the eschaton widens, this bridge will be too short and the Markan basis for Christian existence too narrow.[42]

It may well be that, at this point, it is Kelber's conception, not Mark's, that is too narrow. While it is not my contention that the task of examining the relation of the text to its historical world is an illegitimate one, or even an impossible one, it is surely a more difficult one, a more tentative one, than Kelber or others would lead us to believe. By failing to do justice to the integrity and complexity of the text in relation to its literary world, Kelber increases both the difficulty of his task and the tentativeness of his conclusions.

More importantly, it may be that a narrow focus on historical concerns in Marcan interpretation is at odds with the Gospel of Mark itself! As Robert Tannehill has observed:

> There are texts whose primary purpose is to convey information, but this is not characteristic of Gospel texts. . . . When the scholar uses these texts as sources of information about historical events, persons, or views which lie behind them, he is forcing concerns which are subordinate in the text into a dominant position. This may be legitimate, for there are many purposes which a text may serve. However, it means that the scholar and the text are moving at cross-purposes, and the information must be extracted in spite of the stubborn efforts of the text to speak in its own way. . . . One can properly claim to interpret a text [rather than use it as a source of information] only if he takes account of the intention embodied in the text.[43]

The Marcan text intends to be "the beginning of the good news of Jesus Christ, the Son of God". In *interpreting* such a text, an historical approach is inadequate, a literary approach promising.

NOTES

1 Prospects for investigating mythic structure in the Gospels are especially intriguing, for the Gospels are perhaps best understood as N. Perrin has depicted them: myth interpreting history and history functioning as myth (*The New Testament: An Introduction* [New York: Harcourt, Brace, Jovanovich, 1974] 26–34.

2 (Göttingen: Vandenhoeck & Ruprecht, 1936).

3 Other theological issues, of course, also characterized the two centres in Lohmeyer's view. For example, in Jerusalem the Holy Spirit, the world mission of the Church, and the sacrificial cult received emphasis lacking in Galilee; in Galilee the requirement of poverty was given distinction not found in Jerusalem. However, according to Lohmeyer, the divergent christologies were of primary importance. Furthermore, F. C. Grant, in presenting and discussing Lohmeyer's thesis states: "and it is clear that the earliest Christology was really, as the term suggests, *an eschatology*, in which the central figure was the same – the risen, glorified Christ who had lived and talked and done mighty works in Galilee but had died on a cross outside Jerusalem, who was now at the right hand of God, and was soon to come in glory to inaugurate the New Age" (*The Earliest Gospel* [New York/Nashville: Abingdon-Cokesbury, 1943] 147).

4 For a sympathetic presentation and discussion of Lohmeyer's thesis, see Grant, *Earliest*, 125–47. For an independently initiated reconstruction of early Galilean Christianity, with some conclusions not dissimilar to those of Lohmeyer, see L. E. Elliott-Binns, *Galilean Christianity* (Chicago: Allenson, 1956). While Elliott-Binns suggests that "Eschatology was perhaps especially characteristic of Galilee" (38), he characterizes the christology of primitive Christianity (following Dibelius) in Galilee as "undeveloped" (48). Elliott-Binns' work on *Galilean Christianity* was stimulated by his research on the Letter of James (7), which he believes "is very early and comes from Galilee" (52). His focus in this monograph is entirely "historical" rather than exegetical.

5 (New York/London: Harper & Bros., 1948).

6 Ibid., 124–5.

7 Ibid., 74. However, Lightfoot is much less dogmatic about the literal location of "the parousia" in Galilee than Lohmeyer, Marxsen or Kelber. See R. H. Lightfoot, *Locality*, 77, 112 (note the "perhaps").

8 Ibid., 142.

9 (New York/Nashville: Abingdon, 1969).

10 Ibid., 56.

11 Ibid., 62.

12 Although the numbers are mine, this train of thought is particularly clear in Marxsen, *Mark*, 55–6.

13 Ibid., 92; cf. 66.

14 Ibid., 59.

15 Ibid., 62.

16 Ibid., 92.

17 Ibid., 94.

18 Ibid., 108.

19 (Philadelphia: Fortress, 1974).

20 The influence of T. J. Weeden is, of course, obvious at this point. "Theodore J. Weeden who brought the discipleship phenomenon in Mark into focus" follows Lohmeyer, Lightfoot and Marxsen in Kelber's list of "scholars, past and present, who guided my thinking in fundamental ways" (Kelber, *Kingdom*, xi). See "The Heresy that Necessitated Mark's Gospel", above 89–104; and *Mark – Traditions in Conflict* (Philadelphia: Fortress, 1971). However, while Weeden sees the Marcan disciples as representatives of a false *theios anēr* christology, Kelber links them with a false eschatology.

21 *Kingdom*, 64–5. Kelber notes at this point that, although "the thesis of a northern Christian community was advocated by Marxsen", "he failed to perceive the gospel's anti-Jerusalem bias" (p. 64).

22 Ibid., 129. Kelber recognizes, for example, the importance of the Marcan voyages on the sea (chapter III) and journeys "on the way" (chapter IV). However, Kelber's spatial comments are limited by his prior "historical" focus on parousia expectation in Galilee and discipleship failure in Jerusalem.

23 Note the concerns raised in Lohmeyer's conclusion (pp. 80–104), Marxsen's conclusion (pp. 207–16), and Kelber's conclusion (pp. 129–47; even the title, "Conclusion: The Genesis of the Gospel of the Kingdom", makes this clear).

24 Kelber posits that "Eschatology is of ultimate concern to Mark" (p. 11) and writes of "Markan theology-eschatology" (pp. 9, 12). But see also p. 139 on the close interweaving of eschatology and christology.

25 See, e.g. *Kingdom*, 46–7, 51, and esp. p. 63. Kelber's view is less extreme than those of G. H. Boobyer ("Galilee and Galileans in St Mark's Gospel", *BJRL* 35 [1952] 334–48) and C. F. Evans ("'I Will Go before You Into Galilee'" *JTS* 5 [1954] 3–18), who regard "Galilee" in Mark's Gospel as a symbol for the Gentile world. Elliott-Binns urgently rejects any association of "Galilee" with "Gentiles" on the basis of his historical interpretation of the firm, yet independent, Jewishness of Galileans, both Jewish and Christian (see esp. 8, 13, 18–19, 24–6). "Galilean Christianity," he concludes, "was a form of Jewish Christianity in its origin, and so it remained" (p. 75).

26 "Mark 1:14–15 provides the hermeneutical key not primarily to the ministry of Jesus, but first and foremost to Markan theology" (Kelber, *Kingdom*, 4). See esp. pp. 3–15.

27 "While throughout the Gospel the past of Jesus speaks to the present of Mark, in this one instance [chapter 13 or more particularly, 13:5b–22] the Markan reality bursts through the medium of the Jesus story. . . . The facts speak for themselves. What comes to expression in the apocalyptic speech must be of ultimate concern to Mark" (p. 110). See esp. Kelber, *Kingdom*, chapter VI.

28 Ibid., 143.

29 Cf. E. V. McKnight, *Meaning in Texts: The Historical Shaping of a Narrative Hermeneutics* (Philadelphia: Fortress, 1978) 241: "It may be argued that, in practice, the acceptance of the presuppositions of the historical approach precluded the accomplishment of the task of discovering anything but historical meaning, or the original meaning".

30 *Kerygma and Comedy in the New Testament: A Structuralist Approach to Hermeneutic* (Philadelphia: Fortress, 1975) 93–4. Compare the comments on the epistemological priority of structural criticism by B. W. Kovacs, "Philosophical Foundations for Structuralism", *Semeia* 10 (1978) 85–105.

31 "The Structural Study of Myth", *Journal of American Folklore* 68 (1955) 432; reprinted, *Myth: A Symposium* (ed. T. A Sebeok; Philadelphia: American Folklore Society, 1955) 50–66; reprinted with slight modifications, C. Lévi-Strauss, *Structural Anthropology* (New York: Basic Books, 1963) 206–31.

32 "The Story of Asdiwal", tr. N. Mann, *The Structural Study of Myth and Totemism* (ed. E. Leach; London: Tavistock, 1967) 17, 21; reprinted, C. Lévi-Strauss, *Structural Anthropology* 2 (New York: Basic Books, 1976) 146–97.

33 At this point the Marcan Jesus has already been "throughout all Galilee" (1:39), and here the multitude from Galilee is said to have "followed" (*ēkolouthēsen*) him while the multitude from other regions "came" (*ēlthon*) to him. This passage represents a "Markan insertion" as isolated by J. R. Donahue (*Are You the Christ? The Trial Narrative in the Gospel of Mark* [SBLDS 10; Missoula, MT: Scholars, 1973] 241). According to D. E. Nineham (*The Gospel of St. Mark* [Baltimore: Penguin Books, 1963] 112–13), the people of the multitude of 3:7–8 are not so much Jews and Gentiles as "crowds from every part of the Holy Land inhabited by Jews. [Cf. R. H. Lightfoot, *Locality*, 119.] The idea is clear – and for St Mark it is theologically very significant. All Israel gathers to Jesus and there he creates the new community which was expected in the last time, and appoints its leaders". Marxsen, in support of his view that Mark's Gospel is a (historical) call to await the (temporal) parousia in (geographical) Galilee, reads 3:7–8 as a suggestion "that in Mark's day Christians were living in all these places or in all these regions" and that (of "primary importance") "these Christians have a meeting place – the Sea of Galilee" (*Mark*, 64).

34 For further references to the Hebrew Scriptures, see B. W. Anderson, "Water",
IDB, 4: 808–10, and D. E. Nineham, *Gospel*, 146–7, 180.

35 C. Lévi-Strauss, "Structural Study", 440: "Mythical thought always works from the awareness of oppositions towards their progressive mediation . . ."

36 The most obvious example is 7:31, on which E. Schweizer comments: "The impossibility of this route of travel must be illustrated by an example closer to home, e.g. going from New York to Washington by way of Boston down the Mohawk Valley" (*The Good News According to Mark* [Atlanta: John Knox, 1970] 154).

37 The name "Galilee', which means "ring, circle" was, according to K. W. Clark, probably given to the district "in recognition of the circle of Gentile nations which had infiltrated the region" ("Galilee, Sea of ", *IDB*, 2: 348).

38 Commentators who seek in Mark's Gospel the "history of Jesus" suggest that Jesus "manifested a freshness and independence of mind as to the meaning and application of the Law, consonant with the religious spirit of the *galil*," that is, consonant with "the modified orthodoxy of Jews in the *galil* of the Gentiles" (K. W. Clark, "Galilee", *IDB*, 2: 347). Whatever the history, the Marcan meaning remains. The traditional order (associated with Judea) is challenged by a new order (associated with Jesus of Nazareth in Galilee).

39 See n. 20 above.

40 *Kingdom*, 130: "So much in sympathy with Galilee is the author, and so tangibly does he argue from the perspective of its Jewish-Christian community that it seems plausible to see in him the spokesman of Galilean Christians. Galilee in its broadest sense, including the Decapolis and the area of Tyre and Sidon as outlined by Mark, furnishes the setting in life for Mark the evangelist".

41 Is such literalism consistent with the Marcan narrator who, as Kelber himself observes, employs voyages on the sea, "the way", bread, blindness and sight, etc. in ways beyond their literal significance?

42 *Kingdom*, 141. Paralleling Kelber on this point is his teacher, N. Perrin (*The Resurrection According to Matthew, Mark, and Luke* [Philadelphia: Fortress, 1977] 37–8), who states that Mark transformed Jesus' tensive symbol of the "kingdom of God" into a steno-symbol of the "parousia". (The terms "tensive symbol" and "steno-symbol" are borrowed from Philip Wheelwright's *Metaphor and Reality*.) In disagreement with Perrin's view on this point is another of his former students, J. R. Donahue ("Jesus as the Parable of God in the Gospel of Mark", *Int* 32 [1978] 378). See also (1) the argument of D. O. Via (*Kerygma*, 78–90) against interpreting Mark as an apocalypse or the Marcan vision of time as apocalyptic and (2) the view of J. M. Robinson (*The Problem of History in Mark* [SBT 21; Naperville, IL: Allenson, 1957]) that Mark distinguishes the church's existence "on the one hand from the non-eschatological history preceding Jesus, and on the other hand from the non-historicity of the new aeon" (p. 56, see also p. 55).

43 *The Sword of His Mouth* (Philadelphia: Fortress, 1975; Missoula, MT: Scholars, 1975) 6–7.

12

*Literary Reflections on Mark 13:5–37: A Narrated Speech of Jesus**

WILLEM S. VORSTER

I   *Literary Interpretation of Mark 13:5–37*

From the point of view of interpretation, there seems to be hardly any other chapter in the New Testament which offers as many challenges to the interpreter as does Mark 13. On the semantic level there are a few intriguing problems which have puzzled scholars through the ages. Although the meaning of the *bdélugma tes eremóseos* of v. 14, for instance, is clear, there still remains uncertainty about the reference of the term. Whether the chapter was written from an apocalyptic perspective is a bone of contention between scholars, and about the origin and the literary history of the chapter there will always be difference of opinion. On the Christological level the problem of the imminent parousia has given rise to many and divergent "solutions" for the difficulties of v. 30 and so there are many other detail problems which scholars attempt to solve in view of their understanding of the chapter and its relation to the rest of the Gospel of Mark.

The purpose of this essay is not to give answers to the many "unsolved" problems of Mark 13 (cf. Beasley-Murray, 1983; Brandenburger, 1984; Wenham, 1975). What I have in mind is to approach this chapter from a different perspective than is usually

* First published in *Neotestamentica* 21 (1987) 203–24.

done by New Testament scholars in order to throw light on aspects of Mark 13 which are normally neglected. It has been the custom to study this chapter from the perspective of its origin and growth. With the exception of a few articles (cf. Hallbäck, 1981; Petersen, 1980, 1984), even in the latest extensive studies on Mark 13 the focus is on the literary history and the origin of this chapter (cf. Brandenburger, 1984) and not on the text as a text or a communication. Important and interesting as this might be, there is no reason why the interpretation of this chapter should be restricted to this very limited perspective (cf. Lambrecht, 1967; Pesch, 1968). I will approach the chapter from a literary point of view with the focus on Mark 13:5–37 as a narrated speech and not on the literary history or the extratextual context to which it could possibly refer. It is impossible to give an exhaustive interpretation of the speech in a single essay. Therefore I shall concentrate on a few aspects only. In the first part of the essay attention will be paid to the fact that Mark 13 is presented to the reader as a narrated speech and what this implies for the interpretation of this chapter. The second section deals with the place of Mark 13 in the Gospel of Mark. The problem of time is of special interest here. In the third place narrative point of view and the function of apocalyptic and paraenesis in Mark 13 will be discussed. The essay will be concluded by a few summary remarks.

II   *A Narrated Speech*

After more than a century of critical scholarship following the hypothesis of T. Colani that Mark supposedly used and expanded an existing apocalypse in compiling Mark 13, it is almost impossible to escape the haunting questions concerning the origin and growth of this chapter. This is what scholars have been studying and not the text in its final redaction as part of the Gospel of Mark. In spite of the paradigm switch which is taking place in New Testament studies – where the emphasis is on the texts of the New Testament as communications and not on their origin and growth – it still very often is the literary history of texts and not what they are and how they communicate, which intrigue the minds of New Testament scholars. This should not prevent scholars from testing hypotheses and applying new methods of interpretation. On the contrary, it should rather invite us to test and revise basic presuppositions and to develop new answers to old questions.

To say that Mark 13:5–37 is a narrated speech may not seem very important. The term, however, is not as innocent as it may seem. The basic presupposition behind the term is that the Gospel of Mark is a narrative and that the speech in Mark 13 is part of that particular narrative and should be read in the light of these presuppositions. This too may not seem to be of particular interest to those who are used to referring to the gospels or parts of them as narratives. But, as we shall see below, the approach followed in this essay implies a different perspective of Mark 13 than the usual "historical" one. The application of a set of different questions to the text is also implied, since the approach is that of structural semiotics (cf. Genette, 1980).

There are not many ways in which material can be organized in a discourse.[1] Narration is one. The way in which material is organized is important both with regard to the production and the reception of texts. It is important regarding the production of texts because of the conventions which are followed. When a person, for example, produces a narrative, he almost involuntarily uses the codes of the narrative genre. And the same happens to the receiver in the decoding process. He also has to read the text in accordance with its codes in order to produce an adequate reading. Asserting that a particular text is a narrative would, therefore, mean that the text reveals certain characteristics.

In order to tell a story one needs a storyteller, a story and an audience.[2] A narrative consists of a series of events forming a story which is told by a narrator to a narratee. The events are arranged in terms of space and time, performed by a limited set of "actors" and told from a specific perspective. In this way a narrative world is created. This in short is what a narrative is and how it works. To avoid any misunderstanding a few extra remarks will have to be made.

It is important to note that when an author of flesh and blood writes or tells a narrative he creates (cf. Chatman, 1978: 19) a narrative message (the contents or "what" of the narrative) by using certain narrative techniques (the "how" of the narrative). He selects and arranges the events and existents (e.g. space, time and actors) and uses a narrator and a narrative point of view inside the text as the means by which he tells the narrative. The important thing to notice here is that by telling or writing a story the author creates an image of events and personages in order to communicate something to his audience. This image is his image. The following diagram visually explains some of the aspects involved in the communication of a narrative:

NARRATIVE (e.g. Gospel)

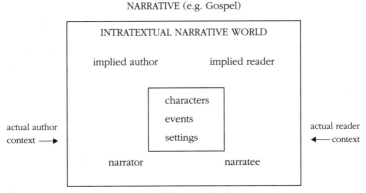

context of communication

   With this in mind let us now turn to the Gospel of Mark. That Mark's Gospel is a narrative, cannot be doubted. The discourse is organized in narrative style and the story is communicated by means of a narrator. In writing a story Mark created an image of events and personages in the life of Jesus in order to communicate something to his readers. The story he created is Mark's image and the narrative world is his narrative world. He selected and arranged his material in terms of order and space and it is he who decided on what each character will do or say and when. Even if Mark closely followed tradition and "historical events", it was still he who created the image of a not too loquacious Jesus or disciples who lack understanding. When we read Mark's Gospel we are guided by his text through pro- and retrospection, gaps and indeterminacy, selection and organization, and the modification of expectations (cf. Iser, 1974, 1978) to assign meaning to the image he created. This is how we create our own image of Mark's image. What is done or said in a gospel should therefore be interpreted in view of the fact that it is narrated. This is of particular interest with regard to Mark 13.
   In view of the fact that the sayings in the gospels have been studied in terms of historical reliability, authenticity and the

reconstruction of the teaching of Jesus, it is not surprising that Mark 13:5–37 causes so many problems in this connection. Amongst other things, it was the idea of the imminent parousia in Mark 13 and the resulting problem of the possibility that Jesus might have been mistaken (cf. Hooker, 1982: 79), which have given rise to the conclusion that Mark 13:5–37 is in its present form a secondary speech based on a Jewish or Christian fly leaf. As Brandenburger (1984: 21) remarks: "Als inzwischen fast einhellig vertretenes Ergebnis der kritischen Forschung kann festgehalten werden, dass in Markus 13 keine historische Rede Jesu vorliegt".

From a literary point of view the words ". . . that in Mark 13 we do not find an historical speech of Jesus", are of particular interest. On what grounds can we expect a narrated speech like Mark 13:5–37 to be "an historical speech of Jesus"? Even if we take into account the fact that in an oral culture people were able to recall the exact words of a speaker far better than those who are exposed to writing and reading, there seems no reason why ancient speeches in narrative form should be historical or even verbatim reports, as some seemingly expect them to be. This does not apply only to the speeches in the New Testament as is clear from the following remarks by the ancient Greek historian Thucydides (*Thuc Hist* I.22, Loeb translation):

"As to the speeches that were made by different men, either when they were about to begin the war or when they were already engaged therein, it has been difficult to recall with strict accuracy the words actually spoken, both for me as regards that which I myself heard, and for those who from various other sources have brought me reports. Therefore the speeches are given in the language in which, as it seemed to me, the several speakers would express, on subjects under consideration, the sentiments most benefitting the occasion, though at the same time I have adhered as closely as possible to the general sense of what was actually said".

These words clearly indicate the problems involved in narrating direct speech in ancient times. But it also points to the role and purpose of speeches in narrative texts like the history of the Peloponnesian war. This is, however, not the main point I wish to make. Narrated speeches have to do with the presentation of material in a discourse – a problem which has puzzled man for many centuries. The perspective from which something is narrated and the way in which it is presented clearly influence the information given.

In his *Republic* (392–5) Plato contrasts two ways of presentation by distinguishing between simple narration (*diegesis*) and imitation (*mimesis*). In connection with the Iliad he writes:

> "... the poet himself is the speaker and does not even attempt to suggest to us that anyone but himself is speaking. But what follows he delivers as if he were himself Chryses and tries as far as may be to make us feel that not Homer is the speaker, but the priest, an old man ... 'But when he delivers a speech as if he were someone else, shall we not say that he then assimilates thereby his own diction as far as possible to that of the person whom he announces as about to speak?'... 'And is it not likening one's self to another in speech or bodily bearing an imitation of him to whom one likens one's self?' 'Surely'. 'In such case then, it appears he and the other poets effect their narration through imitation' " (*Pl Resp* 393, Loeb translation).

In order to explain the difference between what he calls *diegesis* and *mimesis*, Plato rewrites the end of the scene between Chryses and the Achaeans as *diegesis*. He indicates the difference in directness between the two modes of presentation. Imitation is much more direct and gives the impression of less distance between the reader and what is told. It is in this connection that Genette (1980: 162) correctly observes that, "... the narrative can furnish the reader with more or fewer details, and in a more or less direct way, and can thus seem ... to keep at a greater or lesser distance from what it tells".

The use of the word "seem" is very important since in the end any narrative is a presentation of reality and creates the illusion of *mimesis*. For our purpose two things are very important. Firstly, it is clear that speeches have narrative functions. They create the illusion of directness. Secondly, they are invented as an aid to other narrative means of conveying a narrative message. Both these aspects have to do with the nature of narrative and how they work. Narratives are not descriptions of reality. In a certain sense they are the remaking of reality. And this holds good even for narratives which pretend to make use of historical persons and events.

Mark 13:5–37 is a speech which should not in the first place be analysed outside its narrative context. As a narrated speech it has a narrative function within the story of Jesus according to Mark.

One can compare it to the parables of Jesus which receive their messages in the gospels from their narrated contexts of communication. Mark 13 has meaning within the narrative context of this gospel. In fact, it can be argued that the reader of the Gospel of Mark is educated through the reading of the preceding twelve chapters on how to read the speech,[3] as we shall see below. It has to do with the image Mark created of Jesus. This makes it in principle impossible to start any discussion about what Jesus had said, could have said and would have said in connection with either the future of Jerusalem or the return of the Son of Man on the grounds of Mark 13:5–37 as it stands. The narrative character of the speech makes it necessary to reconstruct Jesus' words, if one is interested in what the earthly Jesus had to say. That is, however, something different from reading or interpreting the meaning or message of the narrated speech as a narrated speech of a narrated figure. To enjoy and understand a narrative the reader has to suspend his own feelings and beliefs and accept those of the text, argues Booth (1983: 137). This is a very important guideline for us, New Testament critics, who were educated to read the gospels not as narratives but as layers of tradition.

If we accept the fact that the author of the gospel presented Mark 13:5–37 as a narrated speech in order to convey a part of his message about Jesus, it will be necessary to consider some of the implications with regard to its place in the Gospel of Mark.

III *Narrative Time and Context*

Both the length of the speech and the place in the gospel narrative have been noticed as remarkable by scholars in the past. It is well known that the Jesus of Mark's gospel is not very talkative. Barring the speech on the parables in chapter 4, Mark 13 is the only long speech in Mark. What, if anything, is the significance of this in terms of the narrative? And secondly, is there any significance in the fact that Mark 13 is placed before chapters 14–16 (cf. Grayston, 1973–4)?

The importance of temporal aspects of the Gospel of Mark has in the past been related mostly to the question of the dating of the gospel and the temporal stance of the readers with regard to the narrated material. Interesting as this may be, there are other aspects of time in the gospel which, from a literary point of view, need our attention first.

Time, like space, plays an important role in the communication of a narrative message. In fact, it is part of the narrative message. When studying time in a narrative it is necessary to distinguish between various elements. It is particularly helpful to make a distinction between the *story* (*fabula*), that is the basic story material or signifiers; the *narrative text* or *narrative discourse*, that is the *fabula* transformed into an artistic structure of chronology and logic (*sjuzet*, the signified); and the *act of narration* or *narration*. These are also referred to as *histoire*, *recit* and *narration* (cf. Genette, 1980). There is an interdependence between these narrative elements, and authors make use of different devices to manipulate material in terms of these elements, as we shall see below. These distinctions make it possible to differentiate between story time and narrative time and to study the significance of the time aspect of a narrative by comparing story time and narrative time and the effect of arrangement (order), duration and frequency (cf. Genette, 1980: 33–160; Petersen, 1978a: 49–80). Let us consider the order of Mark's narrative first with reference to Mark 13.

The order in which Mark emplotted his material becomes remarkable when the chronological sequence of the story is compared to that of the narrative. The events in the narrative leading to chapter 13 have to do with things which occurred in and around Jerusalem (A). Then in chapter 13, when they leave the temple the remark (B) by one of the disciples about the wonderful buildings gives rise to the Olivet speech (C). In narrative time most of the preceding events have to do with the past, the Olivet discourse, however, concerns the future. There is a switch both in narrative content (fall of Jerusalem and parousia (D) which is predicted) and in narrative tense. Until chapter 13 the narrative was, with the exception of predictions and narrative commentary, told in the past tense (imperfect, aorist and historic present) and in the narrative mode (*erzählte Welt*). In chapter 13:5–37, on the other hand, there is a change in narrative tense (mostly future tenses) and mode (*besprochene Welt*). The narrator returns to past events in chapter 14–16 when he relates the events (E) preceding the trial of Jesus, his trial (F), crucifixion (G), death (H), burial (I) and resurrection (J). The chronological order of these events in the story time is: 1, 2, 10, 3, 4, 5, 6, 7, 8, 9. In other words, the chronological order of the basic material (story) out of which Mark made his narrative text is different from that of the order in the narrative. In Mark 13 the author introduces another narrator, Jesus who looks forward and narrates events which are still to come. That is what changes the chronological order in the narrative. Whereas the narrator of Mark's story usually looks backward in time and narrates past events, in the Olivet discourse Jesus looks forward.

If we compare narrative time with story time, the order of Mark's emplotted narrative is most remarkable and thus also the place of Mark 13 in his narrative. The result of our comparison can be expressed as follows: A(1) B(2) C(3) D(10) E(5) F(6) G(7) H(8) I(9). Is there anything significant in Mark's ordering of the material in this manner? Is this perhaps a means of foregrounding and accentuating the contents of the speech for the sake of the readers?

The rearrangement of story time in narratives is not unusual. It is in fact quite customary to find all sorts of rearrangements of time, like pro- and retrospection, in narratives. This is the way in which the reader is directed through the narrative. This is how the reader is invited to take part in the narrative, to form expectations and to modify his expectations. And it is also true of Mark's gospel. It has, for example, been noticed by Petersen (1978a, b, 1980, 1984) that one of the important plot devices of this gospel is prediction and fulfilment, which is a form of rearrangement of story material. The reader is directed through the narrative by this device because predictions as well as their fulfilments are emplotted within the narrative (8:31; 9:31; 10:33ff. and the passion narrative). In the case of Mark 13 it is different. These predictions are not fulfilled (emplotted) inside the narrative. Contrary to the reader's expectation which is grounded on the way in which he is educated by the text, Mark does not tell what happened with the predictions Jesus makes in Mark 13. Literally, Petersen (1980, 1984) finds this aspect of Mark 13 very significant and offers an interesting interpretation of the chapter on the basis of the "unfulfilled" predictions. I shall return to this below. Fact is that the fulfilment of the predictions of Mark 13 are not emplotted in Mark's narrative, which underscores the question whether the placing of Mark 13 in the order of the narrative has any significance.

Another aspect of narrative time which might help us answer the question is that of *duration*. Duration has to do with the amount of time it takes to narrate an event (or events) in the story.

It often happens that a narrator mentions a period (e.g. youth) in the life of a person but spends pages on one single event in the person's life. The amount of time devoted to the passion narrative in Mark, for example, is relatively extensive in comparison with other events. The only way of measuring the time spent in a narrative on an event or events, is to measure the amount of space taken to tell the event. The relative importance of an event is often determined by the space given to its narrative time. The comparison between story time and text time is therefore based on the basis of space. If an author devotes twenty pages to one day in the life of the protagonist and one line to his birth, he clearly regards the former as more important for his purpose. The events which receive more attention are those which take most narrative space. The effect of longer or shorter narrative space is that of acceleration and deceleration, accentuation or generalization. Let us now turn to Mark 13.

I have already observed that Mark 13:5–37 takes relatively much space in comparison with what Jesus has to say in the rest of the Gospel of Mark. If we compare the length of Mark 13:5–37 to that of the summaries given, for instance, of the miracles which Jesus performed (cf. 1:32–4), or the resurrection narrative (16:1–8), it becomes clear that the speech in Mark 13 is undoubtedly accentuated and focused upon. There is a deceleration in narrative speed. In the material preceding the Olivet discourse the tension builds up through the amount of events that are told. But all of a sudden the narrative speed is decelerated by the introduction of a long speech. There is a pause in the narrative. In view of the fact that it is Jesus that speaks, the narrative becomes more dramatic (cf. 1 above) and a scenic impression is made on the reader. Taken together, there seems to be little reason to doubt the importance of and the accent on the contents of the speech given by the narrative devices of order and duration. This explains the significance of the order in which Mark narrated Jesus' speech. Before the trial, death and resurrection the reader is called to a halt. The material is foregrounded for the sake of the reader to reflect upon in order to "understand" what "followed" (in the narrative of Mark!), and to instruct the reader about his own conduct.

The question now arises as to what the author wanted to achieve with the speech since he obviously placed a lot of weight on the contents thereof.

IV   *Narrative Point of View,*
Apocalyptic and Paraenesis

In Mark's gospel, like in any other narrative, the story of Jesus is presented by the narrator from a certain perspective or viewpoint. Narrative point of view signifies the perceptual, conceptual and ideological way in which the story gets told.[4] It is the means by which the reader is directed to identify with the message of the narrative and to accept the norms of judgement presented in the text. Petersen (1978b) has correctly observed that until chapter 13 the reader is educated to accept the view presented by Jesus and the unclean spirits and to view Jesus in terms of the things of God (cf. 8:33) and not in terms of man, as the other characters in the narrative, including the disciples, do. The other characters wrongly view Jesus as the worldly messiah and do not understand his mission. The disciples' lack of understanding is woven like a golden thread through the fabric of the text. The reader knows, because he is given the information by the narrator, that Jesus is the Son of God and what his fate as Son of Man is (cf. 4–10); that death, resurrection and parousia await Him. The disciples, however, are presented as characters who are unable to comprehend.

"... they do not comprehend what the reader is given to comprehend, namely that messiah and kingdom are to be understood in terms of death, resurrection, and parousia of Jesus, the Son of man who is the Son of God" (Petersen, 1984: 47).

In literary terms, it means that Jesus is a reliable character because his perspective is presented by the narrator as trustworthy, while the disciples are unreliable (cf. Petersen, 1980: 161). With regard to Mark 13 this is rather important. Is Jesus presented as reliable? And what about the disciples? We will return to this.

It is not only through the eyes of the narrator that the events in the text are perceived. It is also possible to present the story from the perspective of a character in the story, in which case such a character is referred to as a "focalizer" (cf. Genette, 1980: 189ff.). It is the narrator of the Gospel of Mark that presents Jesus in Mark 13 as a narrator. Embedded into Mark's narrative, which is told from a particular perspective, is the speech (the story about the future) of Jesus being told from the perspective of Jesus who is the focalizer in Mark 13:5–37. In the chapters preceding Mark 13 the narrator presented the viewpoint of Jesus as being trustworthy and established the norms of judgement through that point of view. What is the message and the perspective of Mark 13? Let us start with a few remarks about the closure of Mark's story with regard to Mark 13 in order to explain the difficulties of interpretation that are involved.

In two thought-provoking articles Petersen (1980, 1984) argued that Mark 13 should be seen as the key to the plot of Mark's story. In view of the fact that Petersen gives a literary interpretation of Mark's gospel, and also because of the importance of his findings, I will rehearse in some detail parts of his argument. He maintains:

> "Unlike the understanding of all other characters in the story, the twelve disciples' understanding is contrary to the intent and expectations of the reliable character, Jesus. For the plot to be resolved and this theme to be closed, something closural must either happen or be firmly implied" (Petersen, 1980: 161).

He then goes on to show that Mark 13 is Jesus' story about a conflict of eschatological interpretations. On the one hand there is the eschatology of the false messiahs and prophets who proclaim that the messiah has come. They pretend that with his coming the end, that is the kingdom of God, has also set in and as a token they perform signs and wonders. On the other hand, there is the viewpoint of the disciples, who in chapter 13 ". . . have reversed the position they held before Jesus' death and resurrection" (Petersen, 1984: 47). When did this reversal take place? Petersen (1984: 49) maintains that although the reversal is not described in the text of Mark, and although the predictions of Mark 13 are not fulfilled in the text of Mark, the reversal is addressed in the meeting of Jesus with his disciples in Galilee, which is predicted (but not described) in the section after Mark 13 (cf. 14:28; 16:7).

> "Because he insists that the disciples, or at least four of them, remained in their false messianist position until the meeting in Galilee, Mark is saying of the later false messianists that their credentials are false because they have not been processed through Galilee" (Petersen, 1984: 49).

According to Petersen the closure of the story is thus, firmly implied, namely in the meeting of the disciples with Jesus in Galilee. The closure of Jesus' story in Mark 13 is implied in the return of the Son of man. Both events take place in the continuum of Mark's narrative world. The intended reader, however, is aware of the change the disciples had undergone through their meeting with Jesus in Galilee because in the continuum of Mark's story the Galilee encounter did happen. The return of the Son of man still has to happen. The Galilee meeting supplies the basis for the reader to believe that the Son of man will return. Jesus thus remains a reliable character throughout the whole narrative and the reader can be convinced that the things of God dominate.

> "The message of Mark's narrative is therefore not that the disciples were indeed a dull lot, or that they were such until Galilee, but that those proclaiming that Messiah and Kingdom have come are not to be believed because Jesus already disclosed the error of their views to four of his disciples and because these disciples themselves experienced a dramatic realization of that error which had once been their own" (Petersen, 1984: 166).

For Petersen, Mark 13 tells the story of Jesus about the reversal the disciples will undergo with the respect to their views about Jesus. He has indeed made a number of very important observations about the Gospel of Mark and his views are especially challenging with respect to the interpretation of Mark 13. There are, however, a few things in his interpretation, which, from a literary point of view, are problematic. I fully agree that the closure of Mark's gospel is strongly implied in the Galilee episode and that the reader is invited to read Mark 13 in view of the reliability of the narrator, Jesus. However, it seems to me that Petersen wrongly interprets the story of Mark 13:5–37 as a story which relates the reversal of the viewpoint of the disciples because the reader knows that it had taken place in the Galilee episode. Let us therefore return to the text of Mark 13:5–37.

Unlike most of the information in Mark's narrative, Mark 13:5–37 is a speech about the future. It is a "narrative" about future conflict written from an apocalyptic point of view in paraenetic style. The cast of characters includes, on the one side, the false messiahs and prophets (cf. 13:5, 22), the unidentified "they" of 13:9 and 11, and persecutors and helpers of the false messiahs and prophets. Opposed to these characters are the disciples to whom the story is told. Included in this narrative role are the "elect" (13:20, 22, 27) referred to as the "many" (13:5) and those who are persecuted (13:9–13). The helpers in this role are the Holy Spirit (13:11), the Lord (13:20), the angels (13:27) and the fig tree (13:28–9). It is a story about conflict and torment in which persecution and deception will play an enormous role. In addition to persecution the false messiahs and prophets will pretend that they are Jesus, the Messiah (13:5). They will even perform signs and miracles (13:22) to lead astray the elect. The time co-ordinates of the narrative are indicated by phrases introduced by *hotan* and *tote* and references to events which will come about (beginning), and (end) by the return of the Son of man (13:26). The latter (end) is imminent, it will occur in the time of the contemporaries of Jesus: "I tell you this: the present generation will live to see it all" (13:30 NEB). The former (beginning) lies in the near future although not even the Son knows the exact time of "that day" (13:32). There is a necessity for the conflict to take place – it must happen (13:7). The gentile mission also first has to take place (13:10). The narrative space includes earthly and heavenly scenes. In terms of the plot of the "narrative" the task set for the false messiahs and prophets is to lead astray the elect (disciples), which will only be accomplished if the opponents of the false messiahs (the elect) are unable to read the signs, and do not endure and keep in mind the paraenesis they receive.

In addition to the fact that the speech of Jesus is told in the future tense while most of Mark's text is told in the past tense, there is a shift in what may be called the "conceptual perspective". I am here referring to the way of representing things, the symbolic universe of Mark 13:5–37. Jesus is still presented as the One who sees things in God's terms. There is a change in the conceptual perspective by the introduction of a new way of presenting material. What I mean is the theological perspective from which the material is presented – the way in which Jesus sees the world and its future in the narrative of Mark. This is not the place to enter into the scholarly debate about whether Mark 13 is apocalyptic or not (cf. Brandenburger, 1984), but a few remarks seem to be necessary.

The main difficulty concerning the theological perspective of Mark 13:5–37 is that of definition. Apocalyptic is used in many confusing ways and that explains the difference of opinion with regard to the supposedly apocalyptic nature of Mark 13. Following the research of Hanson (1976) and others,[5] apocalyptic to my mind (cf. Vorster, 1986)[6] refers to a crisis phenomenon and apocalyptic eschatology to a meaning system, a theological perspective. Apocalyptic usually arises when the values and structures of a society lose all meaning for some minority group within a particular society and are replaced by a new symbolic meaning system. It is therefore at once a crisis phenomenon and an all-embracing approach to life in which the future determines the present. It is not concerned with the future only. Adherents of apocalyptic are not merely interested in the future. The contents of their visions and revelations also affect their views on the present and the past. Because life is seen in relation to the future there is great emphasis on correct conduct and ethics. Eschatology is of paramount importance. The past, present and future are interpreted in terms of the expectation of a new future or age and a new world in which supernatural space (heaven) and figures play an important role. Against this background one may ask how apocalyptic is Mark 13?

It is difficult not to read Mark 13 in its intertextual relationships and to overlook the traces of apocalyptic imagery in the chapter (cf. Brandenburger, 1984). The eschatological conflict and the promise of the return of the Son of man are obviously two of the master symbols of a new symbolic universe which the text offers, making it different from the previous sections. Mark 13:5–37 presupposes a new context of communication. The material given in Mark 13:5–37 refers to a narrative world which is different from that in the previous chapters and the reader is expected to have a different frame of reference from the previous sections in Mark's story in order to understand the codes of the text. Chapters 1–12 undoubtedly generate certain expectations about the future by previews and hints through which the reader is educated on how to read Mark 13. He is aware of the return of the Son of man (cf. 8:38), of future suffering for the sake of Jesus (8:27–9:1) and of the imminent coming of the kingdom (9:1). Most of this information is, however, related to the death and resurrection of Jesus which the reader is expected to see as something which has to happen to the Son of God. In Mark 13 conduct is determined by the coming of the end which will be sudden, and not by the death and resurrection of Jesus. End-time events are given in images which are familiar to those who are acquainted with apocalyptic imagination and theology. That determines the new context of communication. On the ground of the reliability of Jesus as character the reader is entrusted through

283

the eyes of Jesus with a view of what will happen in the immediate future. The future and future events are presented to the four and thus to the reader as new knowledge. Things that will happen, of which they did not have the faintest clue, are now made known to the four. They are in addition told how to react to the new situation which will arise.

One of the recurring problems in the interpretation of Mark 13:5–37 is that of reference. This does not only apply to v. 14 which remains a *crux interpretum* with regard to the speech as can be seen in the history of interpretation (cf. Brandenburger, 1984: 49ff.). It also applies to the speech as a whole and to texts written from an apocalyptic perspective in particular. It is obvious that these texts, like any other text, refer in some way or another and that extratextual realities play a role in this regard. It should, however, not be forgotten that the primary function of texts written from an apocalyptic perspective is not to refer to extratextual realities. In the case of Mark 13:5–37 it is clear that the speech has a function with regard to the complete narrative and that it creates a narrative world of its own within the narrative world of Mark's gospel. It is the image of a future of conflict, persecution, tribulation, cosmic changes and the unexpected coming of the Son of man which is used to persuade the four to be on the alert, and not the events in the extratextual world to which each narrated event could possibly refer. That is why one should determine the semantic function of the text rather than its possible reference to extratextual realities. In the history of the interpretation of Mark 13 it appears to have been the other way round. Far more importance was attached to the possible historical inferences that could be made, than to the semantic function of these intertextual realities. I am not saying that texts written from an apocalyptic perspective do not reflect the real world out of which they arose, only that their primary function should not be looked for in terms of extratextual reference. I will return to this problem below. First, there is a need to reflect on the semantic function of Mark 13:5–37.

Our text is an interesting mixture of apocalyptic imagery and paraenesis. It is remarkable that almost everything which is said to, and thus about the four to whom the speech is directed, is done by way of imperatives (cf. *blépete* in 13:5, 9, 23, 33; *me throeîsthe* in 13:7; *me promerimnate* in 13:11; *proseúchesthe* in 13:18; *me pisteúete* in 13:21; *máthete* in 13:28; *ginoskete* in 13:28,

29; *blépete agrupneîte* in 13:33; *gregoreîte* in 13:35, 37 and the singular subjunctives in 14–16). It is expected from the four disciples to act in a certain way during the end time. This is of particular interest with regard to the interpretation of the text, since language is used to some end. To use language is to do things; it is to make language perform one or more functions.[7] The question may rightly be asked what the function of language is in Mark 13:5–37. Is it to inform the reader about all events which are referred to in the chapter, or is it to persuade the reader? To me there seems to be little doubt about the answer. The use of imperatives is self-explanatory. Mark 13:5–37 was not in the first instance written to inform the four about the future, but rather how to expect the future – that is, to be prepared for the future by being alert and aware of what to expect. It is the paraenetic mode of expression which dominates the text, not in the sense of "ethical" admonitions, but of the stringing together of imperatives of conduct. The imperatives in Mark 13:5–37 have the same characteristics as paraenetic admonitions which are devised as ethical precepts.[8] On the basis of the authority and trustworthiness of Jesus these imperatives are given to ". . . define the ideal behaviour for those entering into a new social position or group" (Perdue, 1981: 249). Perhaps the most important remark made by Perdue (1981: 249) for our purpose is that these admonitions call the recipient to serious reflection about his initial entrance into his present position, which is a matter of resocialization. Does the language of Mark 13:5–37 lead the reader to such reflection before he reads the closure of Mark's story? The language used in Mark 13 is used to do something and that is to convince the reader about the perspective of Jesus, that is the life and works of the Son of God seen in terms of the things of God – the suffering and return of the Son of man. To accept the story the reader has to take a different stance than the one taken by the disciples.

One has to keep in mind the development of the plot of Mark's narrative in an attempt to understand Mark 13. The reader has of God, namely the idea of a kingdom and messiahship which is not of man. Until Mark 13 he is prepared to accept the predictions of the suffering, death and resurrection on the ground of the reliability of Jesus. In terms of redundancy the reader is in fact well prepared for the death and resurrection of Jesus. Mark 13 is however of vital importance for the time after the resurrection and for the implications of his being Son of God, who will return as Son of man. It substantially undergirds the total resocialization of the reader who has to accept the view that the Son of God had to suffer and that the end is not yet, neither with the death and resurrection of Jesus nor with rumours about end time signs like wars (cf. 13:7). It implies a closure of the plot in the future.

It seems to me that Petersen's interpretation about the disciples and their reversal in Mark 13 cannot be accepted. He infers too much from Mark 13 and in the end ignores the text and its directives for the reader. He regards the disciples as the protagonists of the story – not a set of orders of conduct to disciples who lack understanding (cf. Petersen, 1980: 165). This is best seen in the following remark:

> "Some, who were declared false by Jesus, proclaim that the messiah has come, and with him the end, that is, the Kingdom of God, while prophets attest to the eschatological presence by performing signs and wonders (13:6, 21–3). Opposed to the messiahs and prophets are the four disciples who, in this story, say that the end is not yet but that it will come next when, with cosmic signs, the Son of man will come in clouds with great power and glory" (13:25–7, 29) (Petersen, 1980: 165–6).

This is the hub of Petersen's interpretation. It stands and falls with the question whether "in this story" the four disciples say that the end is not yet – as he maintains – or whether they are expected to say so – as I have argued above. I do not doubt that the disciples, according to the text, are expected to say that the end is not yet and so on, and that their role is that of opposing the protagonist, that is the false messiahs and the false prophets. They are not the protagonists in the story of Jesus in Mark 13:5–37. They are once again given the instruction to comprehend the implications of the story of Mark. They are undoubtedly not presented in their after-Galilee meeting (in the real world or continuum of Mark's narrative world), but in their state of incomprehension. They are again, as in chapters 1–12, put in the privileged position of receiving inside information on the after-resurrection period and are expected in the continuum of Mark's story to make the viewpoint of the things of God their own.

Much of what Petersen has to say in connection with Mark 13 is useful. He seems, however, in his literary interpretation of the text to have been led by historical inferences about the first flesh and blood readers and the problem of the "historical" as well as the literary closure of Mark's gospel. In the long run Mark's disciples are not personages in a narrative world but real persons. The task of the interpreter becomes one of establishing what the real readers knew and what their positions were. Once this is established the text is interpreted in the light thereof. The reason for this is found, amongst others, in Petersen's use of the term "implied reader". For him the implied reader is not a textual construct (cf. Booth, 1983: 137; Iser, 1978: 34), a reader encoded in the text, but a real flesh and blood reader implied by the text. This is misleading and nothing less than the construction of a possible reader. His results are not literary but rather historical, based on inferences made from the text. There is a very sophisticated mixture of literary and historical information in these studies as is seen in the following remark:

> "From a literary perspective, therefore, Jesus' predictions are the implied author's fictions, based on his knowledge of events that are either past or present" (Petersen, 1984: 45).

Is fiction now becoming factual and is that the reason for the historical inferences? One should remember that all we have is the text, a contextless text and that in the first place the Gospel of Mark is a narrative, rather than a history of Jesus and his disciples.

There are enough literary grounds to argue the importance of the fact that Mark 13:5–37 is a narrated speech and that its position in the order of the narrative is significant. The narrative message of the text ties in with the theme of the incomprehension of the disciples. From an apocalyptic perspective they are admonished to reconsider their position as followers of Jesus and encouraged to resist the persecution, tribulation and false messages of the false messiahs and prophets who will try to lead them astray. Similar to the closure of the Gospel of Mark in 16:8, Mark 13 is an open-ended story. The reader is left with the gap of the fulfilment of the Galilee episode, but also with the gap of the fulfilment of the predictions of Mark 13. This is one of the significant ways in which the reader is guided to read the text constructively. It leaves the reader with the strong expectation of an imminent parousia. It is very difficult for a modern reader, who is accustomed to the delay of the parousia, not to realize that Mark wrote a story for people who lived a long time ago.

V   *Conclusion*

A literary interpretation of Mark 13 can never pretend to solve all the problems in the text. It can only offer a particular reading of the text based on certain presuppositions as we have seen above. What is more, there is more than one literary reading possible in accordance with literary vantage points. I have not tried to give an exhaustive treatment of the narrated speech. I have simply dealt with a few, to my mind important, problems. In the first place it seems clear that much more attention should be spent on the narrative character of Mark 13, also on the fact that the speech in Mark 13 is told from the perspective of a reliable character who is trusted to talk about the future, even though he himself confesses that he does not know everything (13:32). The point of view from which he offers his information will also have to be studied in greater detail, but from a literary and not a literary comparative viewpoint. In the third place much more attention should be paid to semantic function in New Testament studies.

NOTES

1 Cf. C. Brooks and R. P. Warren, *Modern Rhetoric* (New York: Harcourt, 1970), 3rd ed., 56f.

2 Cf. R. Scholes and R. Kellogg, *The Nature of Narrative* (New York: Oxford University Press, 1966) 240.

3 Cf. F. Burnett, "Prolegomena to Reading Matthew's Eschatological Discourse: Redundancy and the Education of the Reader in Matthew", Semeia, 31 (1985) 91–109.

4 Cf. M. H. Abrams, *A Glossary of Literary Terms* (New York: Holt, 1971), 3rd ed., 133; Chatman, 1978: 151ff.

5 P. D. Hanson, "Apocalypticism" ad loc., *Interpreter's Dictionary of the Bible*, Supplementary Volume, ed. K. Crim (Nashville: Abingdon, 1976).

6 W. S. Vorster, "Texts with an Apocalyptic Perspective" in F. E. Deist, W. S. Vorster (eds.), *Words from Afar: The Old Testament Literature* (Capetown: Tafelberg, 1986), Vol. I, 166–85.

7 Cf. Chatman, 1978: 162ff.; M. A. K. Halliday, *Language as Social Semiotic: The Social Interpretation of Language and Meaning* (London: Arnold, 1978) 19f.

8 Cf. L. G. Perdue, "Paraenesis and the Epistle of James", ZNW 72 (1981) 241–56 (here 242–6).

13

*The Prologue as the Interpretative Key to Mark's Gospel**

FRANK J. MATERA

Few things are more essential to appreciating a story than under-standing the manner in which the narrator begins. Readers who misunderstand the beginning almost inevitably misunderstand the conclusion. At the beginning of a narrative, the narrator establishes the setting, introduces the characters, and lays the foundation for the plot.

Markan scholars have learned that the Gospel's prologue[1] provides the reader with essential information for interpreting the rest of the Gospel. B. Standaert says that from a dramatic perspec-tive the prologue functions as an "avant-jeu" which is formally separate from what follows[2] and provides the reader with information unknown to the characters of the story. M. D. Hooker writes, "here Mark is letting us into secrets which remain hidden, throughout most of the drama, from the great majority of the characters in the story".[3] And W. L. Lane notes that the prologue "suggests the general plan of the work by anticipating the crucial points in the history he relates".[4]

Restricted by the genre of their works, however, most com-mentators deal with the several textual problems the prologue presents, its extent, and the significance of the opening

* First published in *JSNT* 34 (1988) 3–20.

verse. Only a few scholars have endeavoured to relate the prologue to the rest of the Gospel.[5]

With the application of literary criticism to Biblical studies,[6] however, it appears that the time is ripe for examining anew the question: how does the Markan prologue prepare the reader for the story which follows? Divided into three parts, this study begins by discussing the extent of the prologue. Next, it reviews the major themes of the prologue. Finally, it demonstrates the essential connection between these themes and the rest of the Gospel. It suggests that the dramatic irony of the narrative derives from the fact that the readers possess inside or privileged information, given in the prologue, which the characters of the story (Jesus excepted) do not know. As in all good narratives, the narrator does not reveal everything to the readers at the beginning. The information given in the prologue tells who Jesus is (the Son of God), but does not disclose the full significance of his person through this title. This information must be supplemented by what is told in the rest of the narrative. Thus, by the end of the narrative the readers discover that they must integrate their knowledge of Jesus learned in the prologue with their knowledge of him learned in the light of the cross and resurrection.

I *The Extent of the Prologue*

At the beginning of this century, most commentators assumed that the prologue consisted of 1:1–8. Their reasoning was clear: the preaching of John the Baptist was the beginning of Jesus' public ministry. Thus these verses were understood as referring to John's work; the beginning of the Gospel of Jesus Christ was the preaching of the Baptist. Toward the middle of this century, however, R. H. Lightfoot argued that despite the manner in which Westcott and Hort paragraphed their text of the New Testament (a major break after Mark 1:8), the prologue should be extended to v. 13.[7] Lightfoot's reasoning was insightful: "only in verses 9 to 13 do we learn that He is Jesus from Nazareth of Galilee, and that He, Jesus of Nazareth, is the unique or only Son of God".[8] For several years, Lightfoot's position was accepted by most commentators.[9] In 1966, however, L. E. Keck wrote an article which argued that the prologue should be extended to 1:15.[10] He contended that the use of εὐαγγέλιον ("gospel") in 1:14–15, as well as in 1:1, suggests that the verses belong to the prologue. [11] Furthermore, he maintained that the handing over of John (παραδοθῆναι) related in 1:14 is primarily of theological interest, and only secondarily, if at all, of biographical interest. [12] The imprisonment of John is not a break in the text, rather "vv. 14f. are a climactic statement that fulfils the word of John about Jesus, while at the same time it rounds out the over-arching interest in το εὐαγγέιον". [13]

Keck's position seems to have won the day among many commentators. [14] Most now extend the prologue to 1:15, interpreting 1:1 as a superscription which covers the content of the whole work. [15]

It seems to me, however, that R. H. Lightfoot's position remains essentially sound. As he and others correctly noted, 1:1–13 is delimited in terms of locality and by its references to the Spirit. In 1:1–13, the locality is the wilderness: John preaches in the wilderness, and Jesus is baptized and tested in the wilderness. In 1:14 the locality changes. "Jesus leaves the desert and goes back to Galilee to begin his ministry there". [16] In addition to locality, the Spirit plays an important role in these verses. John says that Jesus will baptize with the Spirit (1:8); the Spirit descends upon Jesus (1:10); and the Spirit thrusts Jesus into the wilderness (1:12). The fact that the Spirit plays a relatively minor role in the rest of the Gospel also suggests that these verses form a unit. [17] Finally, J. M. Robinson notes that there is a difference between John's preaching (something will happen) and Jesus' proclamation (something has happened: the Kingdom has drawn near). [18]

In addition to these traditional arguments, I would add yet another from the point of view of literary criticism. In 1:1–13 the narrator[19] communicates privileged information about John and Jesus to the reader. Thus the narrator informs the reader that John the Baptist is to be understood in light of the quotation attributed to Isaiah (1:2–3), that the Spirit has come upon Jesus (1:10), that the Father identifies Jesus as his beloved Son (1:11), and that Jesus has confronted Satan in the wilderness (1:12–13). All of this information, vital for understanding the person of Jesus, is communicated *only* to the reader; none of the human characters within the narrative (Jesus excepted) is privy to it. The crowds that come for John's baptism have not heard the narrator identify John in terms of the scriptural quotation attributed to Isaiah. And no one, not even John, realizes that the

Spirit has descended upon Jesus, that the Father calls Jesus the beloved Son, and that Jesus struggles in the wilderness with Satan. From the point of view of the narrator, the events of these verses are different from those communicated in the rest of the narrative (1:14ff.) inasmuch as they are told solely for the reader's benefit;[20] the characters of the story (Jesus excepted) are not aware of them. In contrast to these verses, the events beginning with 1:14 are public in nature.[21] The narrator's summary of Jesus' preaching (1:14–15) and the report of John's imprisonment, for example, are not meant for the reader alone; John's imprisonment is public knowledge and Jesus' proclamation is the kind of preaching which the characters of the story hear, and will hear again. In a word there is a change in the way the narrator speaks to the reader after the testing of Jesus in the wilderness. To this point, the narrator has communicated inside information to the reader. After this point, the events which are narrated are public in nature in the sense that they are accessible to the characters of the story.

But what of Keck's argument that the appearance of εὐαγγέλιον in 1:1 and 1:14–15 binds these verses together? Keck and others correctly argue that 1:1 is a superscription which includes the content of the entire Gospel. But if 1:1 is a superscription to the entire work, then it is not surprising that the word "gospel" is found again at the beginning of Jesus' public ministry (1:14–15). Furthermore, even if 1:1 and 1:14–15 form a bracket, this does not mean that 1:14–15 is part of the prologue. Rather one could argue that since 1:1 is a superscription to the entire work, it is not part of the prologue proper (1:2–13), which is delimited by references to the wilderness and the Spirit, as well as by the unique nature of the information it communicates.[22] The most telling clue to the extent of the prologue is not the bracket formed by 1:1 and 1:14–15 but the shift of narrative point of view. Prior to 1:14 the narrator tells the reader of events which the characters of the story (Jesus excepted) do not know. After 1:14 the narrator tells the reader of events which the characters of the story will participate in or observe. As for Mark 1:1, it is indeed a superscription covering the entire work. It might be paraphrased as follows: the origin of the proclamation about Jesus Christ the Son of God which is proclaimed in the church today is the account of Jesus which will be narrated as follows.[23] The prologue proper consists of 1:2–13.

II *The Prologue and the Reader*

The Markan prologue (1:2–13) presents the reader with information essential for understanding who Jesus is. This section will try to state that information as clearly as possible.

The relationship between John and Jesus (1:2–8)

The prologue begins with a scriptural quotation attributed to Isaiah (1:2–3) which introduces the work of John and explains his relationship to Jesus. The quotation does not derive wholly from the prophet. It is a mixed quotation. Verse 2 is based upon Exod. 23:20 and Mal. 3:1; v. 3 comes from Isa. 40:3. In its original context, Exod. 23:20 referred to the angel God sent ahead of Israel to protect it on its way to the promised land. The quotation from Mal. 3:1 refers to the messenger God sent to prepare for the day of his appearance. In Mal. 3:23, LXX 4:5, that messenger is identified as Elijah; and in rabbinic exegesis the texts from Exodus and Malachi were later combined, identifying the messenger of both texts as Elijah.[24] The quotation from Isaiah is the beginning of Deutero–Isaiah's prophecy announcing that God is about to redeem Israel from exile by a new exodus. For our purpose it is not necessary to determine if the evangelist, or his tradition, realized the mixed nature of this citation. As it stands, the entire text is attributed to Isaiah. Its function is to identify who John is. It answers that he is the messenger of the covenant, the eschatological prophet foretold by "Isaiah". His task is to prepare the way of the Lord[25] for God's final act of salvation, a new exodus. From the opening of the narrative, therefore, the reader knows the correct relationship between John and Jesus. John is not the Messiah; he is the precursor, the promised Elijah as even his garb suggests (cf. 1:6 with 2 Kgs. 1:8). When John makes his appearance (1:4–8), the reader, unlike the crowds, knows exactly what his function is.

To further distinguish John from Jesus, the narrator has John contrast himself with the Coming One. The one who will come after John is more powerful (1:7a). John is not worthy to loosen his sandal straps (1:7b). John baptizes with water, but Jesus will baptize with the Holy Spirit.[26] John's baptism is described as a baptism for the forgiveness of sins (1:4), but Jesus' preaching is described as the gospel of God (1:14). At John's preaching, all the inhabitants of Judea and Jerusalem go out to be baptized (1:5).

293

Jesus stands apart from those to be baptized inasmuch as he alone is from Galilee. In sum, the first part of the prologue identifies John and explains his relationship to Jesus. It authenticates his mission by interpreting it in light of a quotation attributed to Isaiah. Those who are privy to this information will have a proper understanding of the relationship between Jesus and John. Those who are not will misinterpret their relationship, their identities, and their missions (2:18–19; 6:14–16; 8:27–28; 9:11–13; 11:27–33; 15:35).

The Identity of Jesus (1:9–11)

Having identified John and his relationship to Jesus, the narrator now focuses upon Jesus. The description of Jesus as coming from Nazareth of Galilee (1:9) immediately distinguishes him from the crowds of Judeans and Jerusalemites. It establishes a contrast between all the people of Judea and Jerusalem on the one hand, and a single representative from Galilee on the other.[27] The crowds from Judea and Jerusalem do not recognize the lone Galilean, but the reader does.

Immediately following Jesus' baptism, a number of important events occur. Jesus rises from the water (ἀναβαίνων ἐκ τοῦ ὕδατος), he sees the heavens open (εἶδεν σχιζομένους τοὺς οὐρανούς), the Spirit descends upon him (καταβαῖνον εἰς αὐτόν), and a voice from heaven declares: "Thou art my beloved Son; with thee I am well pleased." These verses confront the interpreter with several difficulties, e.g. the imagery of the dove,[28] the meaning of ἀγαπητός,[29] the descent of the Spirit,[30] the source of the scriptural allusion.[31] But despite these difficulties the basic thrust of the text is clear: Jesus is identified as the Spirit-empowered Son of God. Precisely why God is pleased with him, the text does not say, nor does it explain the nature of Jesus' sonship. Such information is withheld from the reader. What is clear is that no human character (Jesus excepted) within the story, including John, has seen the Spirit descend upon Jesus or heard the voice.[32] For John and the crowds this is just another baptism.

Once more the reader is privy to inside information essential for understanding Jesus' identity. While the crowds and John see Jesus as another penitent, not even aware that he comes from Galilee, the reader knows that he is the Spirit-empowered Son of God.

Jesus and Satan (1:12–13)

In the final section of the prologue, Jesus confronts Satan. Once more the reader is given privileged information. The same Spirit which descended upon Jesus now sends him into the wilderness to confront Satan. No sooner is Jesus identified as the Son of God than he is driven (ἐκβάλλει) into the wilderness to meet the adversary. No human character within the narrative apart from Jesus is aware of the struggle, either now or later. As with Jesus' baptism, the scene has an otherworldly dimension: the testing of God's Son by Satan and the presence of angels who serve his needs.

Again the text presents problems of interpretation. Do the wild beasts symbolize a restoration of the situation which prevailed before Adam's fall, thereby suggesting that Jesus has conquered Satan? Or, do they symbolize the hostile environment in which Jesus finds himself during his time of testing?[33] Do the angels serve Jesus to sustain him against Satan, or because he has overcome Satan? The text does not explicitly say. Nonetheless, the basic movement of the narrative is clear. The Son of God does not fail during his period of testing, for he returns from the wilderness with the gospel of God (1:14).[34] The reader now knows the secret of Jesus' authority over unclean spirits; he has been tested by the prince of unclean spirits in the wilderness, and has not failed. Thus when Jesus tells the scribes that "no one can enter a strong man's house and plunder his goods, unless he first binds the strong man" (3.27), the reader understands what the scribes do not. Jesus is the one who plunders Satan's house because he has already confronted Satan.

A summary of our results discloses that the reader has been given the following information, unknown to the characters of the story besides Jesus. First, John the Baptist is the promised Elijah, Jesus' precursor. Second, Jesus is the Spirit-empowered Son of God, the one in whom the Father is pleased. Third, Jesus has confronted Satan in the wilderness and has not succumbed to his temptations.

III   *Mark's Narrative in Light of the Gospel Prologue*

Markan scholars have not been able to agree upon the outline and structure of the Second Gospel.[35] Nevertheless, most would concur that Peter's confession at Caesarea Philippi and the centurion's confession at the cross are major turning points in the narrative. At both moments human characters within the narrative come to a deeper understanding of Jesus' identity: he is the Messiah (8:29); he was God's Son (15:39). The reader, of course, knows this information from the prologue while the human characters within the narrative, except Jesus, continually struggle with the question of his identity. In this section, I will trace the quest by the human characters of the story to identify Jesus. An overview of Mark's narrative will show that the human characters of the story are puzzled by Jesus' identity because, unlike the readers, they have not been privy to the prologue. If they are to attain an understanding of who Jesus is, they must arrive at it by the way of the cross.

Jesus is the Messiah (1:14–8:30)
The first half of Mark's Gospel is marked by a series of questions and misunderstandings concerning Jesus' identity and ministry. These misunderstandings and questions involve all of the human characters within the narrative: the religious leaders, Jesus' family and compatriots, Herod, the crowds, and the disciples. Only the demons, beings who belong to another realm, know who Jesus is and what his mission entails. They correctly refer to him as ὁ ἅγιος τοῦ θεοῦ ("the Holy One of God", 1:24), ὁ υἱὸς τοῦ θεοῦ ("the Son of God", 3:11), and Ἰησοῦ υἱὲ τοῦ θεοῦ τοῦ ὑψίστου ("Jesus, Son of the Most High", 5:7). Furthermore, the demons seem to know the purpose of Jesus' mission: he has come to destroy them (1:24). Indeed, his very presence torments them (5:7). Because the demons have this knowledge, Jesus commands them to be silent (1:25, 34; 3:12). For reasons which are not disclosed at this point, a public proclamation of Jesus' identity as God's Son is premature.

The source of the demons' knowledge comes from the events which occur in the prologue. In the wilderness Satan tested the Son of God (1:12–13). Consequently, his subordinates are aware of Jesus' identity. They know who he is and why he has come. Their public proclamation of his identity is an attempt to undermine his mission by revealing who he is apart from the cross.

In contrast to the demons, none of the other human characters of the narrative knows Jesus' identity or mission. They must come to an understanding of it by witnessing and properly interpreting what Jesus says and does. A perverse interpretation comes from the religious leaders who form a monolithic block of opposition against Jesus. They question his authority to forgive sins, interpreting his words as blasphemy (2:6–7). They do not understand why Jesus' disciples do not fast (2:18); they accuse the same of violating the Sabbath (2:24) and the traditions of the elders (7:5); and they go so far as to say that Jesus is possessed by an unclean spirit (3:22, 30). They even ask Jesus for a sign from heaven (8:11) after he has fed 4,000 with bread in the wilderness. Finally, their intention to destroy Jesus (3:6) reveals their animosity.

The reaction of Jesus' family and compatriots is also characterized by misunderstanding and opposition. Jesus' family comes to take him home because of reports that he is mad (ἔλεγον γὰρ ὅτι ἐξέστη, 3:21). The manner in which this episode involving Jesus' relatives (3:21, 31–35) encloses the Beelzebul controversy (3:22–30) suggests that the narrator intends the readers to see a parallel between the reactions of the religious leaders and Jesus' family: both misunderstand Jesus. Finally, when Jesus returns to his own country (6:1), his compatriots are scandalized by him. Because they know Jesus' natural family, they think that they know who he is. Believing that they know who he is, they question his wisdom and power (6:2–3).

The reaction of the crowd and Herod is also one of misunderstanding. The crowd is amazed at Jesus' authoritative teaching which manifests itself in his power over demons (1:22, 27–8). The crowd speculates that Jesus is John the Baptist, Elijah, or one of the prophets (6:14–15; 8:28). Herod, however, is convinced that Jesus is John come back to life (6:16).

The reaction of the disciples to Jesus is the most complicated of all. On the one hand, the disciples enjoy a special relationship to Jesus. Not only does he call them to follow him and to be with him (1:16–20; 3:13–19), he also makes a distinction between them and the crowd, explaining to them the mysteries of the Kingdom of God (4:10–12, 33–34). At several points, however, even the disciples show that they do not understand Jesus' true identity or the full significance of his mission. When Jesus calms a storm on the lake, they ask, "Who is this, that even the wind and sea obey him?" (4:41). And despite the feeding of the 5,000 and the 4,000, they misunderstand the meaning of his mission (8:14–21).[36] Nevertheless, by the middle of the Gospel, the disciples arrive at a certain knowledge of who Jesus is. At Caesarea Philippi, after they rehearse what others think of Jesus (8:28; cf. 6:14–15), Peter correctly confesses that Jesus is the Messiah (8:29).[37] His confession seemingly derives from what he has seen Jesus say and do thus far. The first part of the Gospel concludes with the beginning of an awareness of Jesus' identity: knowledge which the reader already possesses from the prologue.

Except for Peter's confession, the first half of Mark's narrative is filled with questions and misunderstandings concerning Jesus' identity and mission. The answers to these questions and the information necessary to avoid these misunderstandings are found in the prologue. Thus the religious leaders do not comprehend how Jesus can expel demons because they do not know that he is the Spirit-empowered Son of God who has confronted Satan in the wilderness. Jesus' family and compatriots are scandalized because they do not realize that he is more than the son of Mary: he is the Son of God. Herod confuses Jesus with John because he does not understand the proper relationship between John and Jesus: John is Jesus' precursor; Jesus is not John *redivivus*. Even the disciples are puzzled about Jesus' identity and mission because they have not been privy to the Father's baptismal declaration. The one who calms the storm and feeds the multitude is the Son of God. In a word, all of these misunderstandings result from ignorance of information found in the prologue: the proper relationship between John and Jesus; the declaration of Jesus' sonship; the conflict between Jesus and Satan in the wilderness.

The Son of Man Will Suffer and Rise (8:31–10:52)
In the second part of the Gospel, Jesus does something which he did not do in the first part. He explains to his disciples that he will suffer and rise again (8:31; 9:12; 9:31; 10:33–4). Confronted by these predictions, the disciples rebel against this fate (8:32), do not understand it (9:10, 32), and act in a way incongruous with Jesus' words (9:33–4; 10:35–41). This misunderstanding is complicated by the fact that at the transfiguration there is a reprise of a major theme found in the prologue. The Father declares that Jesus is his beloved Son (9:7), and this time three disciples hear the declaration.[38] After the transfiguration, Jesus discloses that John was Elijah (9:11–13). Despite this privileged information, the disciples continue to misunderstand Jesus. Why?

298

The answer is suggested by the Father's declaration, "This is my beloved Son; listen to him" (9:7). Unlike the baptismal declaration which was addressed directly to Jesus, the Father now speaks to three of the human characters within the story. Moreover, the declaration concludes with a command, "listen to him". If the disciples are to understand that Jesus is the Son of God then they must listen to and accept what he says about the fate of the Son of Man: he must suffer, die, and on the third day he will rise from the dead. The disciples, however, do not understand or accept the fate of the Son of Man (8:32; 9:10, 32; 10:35–41). Therefore, they do not comprehend the full significance of the declaration made at the transfiguration. In a word, the privileged information granted on the mountain does not aid them because of their refusal to "listen to him". Only Bartimaeus, who acclaims Jesus as the Son of David (10:47–8), seems to understand something of Jesus' person inasmuch as he follows him "on the way" (10:52), an expression which refers to the destiny facing Jesus.

By way of summary, this section suggests that as important as the inside information of the prologue is, it is not sufficient for a full appreciation of Jesus' identity. Even those who know that Jesus is the Son of God and that John is Elijah can remain blind to Jesus' true identity if they do not "listen to him". The readers of the Gospel must beware, therefore, lest they take their privileged information, gained from the prologue, for granted. They must integrate the information learned from the prologue with the mystery of the dying and rising Son of Man.

From the Entry into the Temple to the Prediction of its Destruction (11:1–13:37)
Except for a brief incident (10:2–9), the religious leaders do not play an important role in 8:31–10:52. In chapters 11–12, however, they do. After Jesus cleanses the temple, they ask him by what authority he acts, and who gave him the authority for such action (11:28). Then in a series of controversies, they test Jesus further (12:13–34).[39] At the conclusion of these controversies, Jesus challenges the traditional scribal understanding of the notion that the Messiah is the son of David (12:35–7), and then condemns the scribes (12:38–40). In the midst of these controversies, however, there are important allusions to information found in the prologue. Thus, when the religious leaders challenge Jesus'

299

authority, he questions them about the significance of John's baptism (11:30), and then tells the parable of the vineyard (12:1–11) in which he echoes the Father's baptismal declaration (12:6). The religious leaders, however, refuse to answer the question about John's baptism (11:31–3) and take offence at the parable, realizing that it is directed at them (12:12).

These "echoes" of the prologue (the origin of John's baptism, the beloved son) explain why the religious leaders misunderstand Jesus. First, although all Judea and Jerusalem went out to be baptized by John (1:5), the religious leaders never understood or accepted the origin of his baptism. Second, because they did not comprehend the significance of John's ministry, they do not understand that Jesus is the Father's beloved son (1:11; 9:7), even when Jesus imparts this information by way of parable (12:6). As in the previous section (8:31–10:52), the narrator is making an important point. Knowledge found in the prologue is essential for understanding Jesus and his mission, but even this knowledge can be rendered useless by hardness of heart. There is still an opportunity for the religious leaders to acknowledge the origin of John's baptism, and Jesus even discloses that he is the beloved son, but they refuse to "listen to him". Once more the reader is being warned that knowledge gained from the prologue must not be taken for granted, Such knowledge can be rendered useless by hardness of heart.

The Recognition of Jesus as the Son of God (14:1–16:8)
Throughout the narrative thus far, no one has been able to pierce the secret of Jesus' identity or fully understand his mission. This misunderstanding continues throughout the passion narrative. Judas betrays Jesus (14:10–11), all of the disciples flee (14:50), and Peter denies him (14:66–72). Moreover, the religious leaders (14:65), the Roman soldiers (15:16–20), the passers-by (15:29–30), the chief priests and the scribes (15:31–2), and even the criminals (15:32) mock Jesus as a false messiah. After Jesus has died, however, a Roman centurion finally realizes that he was truly the Son of God (15:39). This confession is the climax of the Gospel and the final reprise of the Father's baptismal declaration.

The scene of Jesus' death (15:33–9) is related to the prologue in three ways: the reference to Elijah (15:36), the tearing of the temple curtain (15:38), and the centurion's confession (15:39). First, those standing around the cross misinterpret Jesus' great cry as a last desperate call for Elijah. Their misunderstanding manifests ignorance of information found in the prologue. The reader knows that Jesus is not calling Elijah because Elijah has *already* come in the person of John the Baptist. If the bystanders knew this, they would not confuse or mock Jesus' cry as a call for the prophet. But because the bystanders do not understand the proper relationship between John and Jesus, they do not understand that cry.

Second, at the moment of Jesus' death the curtain of the temple is torn (ἐσχίσθη) from top to bottom.[40] The word employed here is the same word used to describe the opening (σχιζομένους) of the heavens at the moment of Jesus' baptism (1:10). At that moment the Spirit descended upon Jesus, and the Father declared that Jesus is his beloved Son. Now the curtain of the temple is torn from top to bottom and the centurion confesses what the reader already knows from the baptism, that Jesus was truly the Son of God.[41]

Third, the centurion's confession is a moment of revelation similar to and related to the theophanies at Jesus' baptism and transfiguration. Then the Father declared that Jesus is his beloved Son, now the centurion confesses what no human character has been able to say: Jesus was truly God's Son. The precise motivation for this confession is not clear, but it has something to do with what the centurion has seen (see note 40). Most importantly, the confession occurs after Jesus has died, for only in the light of his death can the full significance of the title "Son of God" be understood. After Jesus had died, the secret of his identity can be disclosed because there will be no mistaking the nature of this sonship: Jesus is the Father's beloved Son inasmuch as he is the Son who obediently accepts the suffering and death (see 14:36). Once more the reader discovers that the privileged information gained from the prologue requires deeper insight. In the prologue the narrator tells who Jesus us (the Son of God) but not the full significance of this title (the Son of God is the Crucified Messiah who must suffer, die and rise from the dead).

Conclusion

This study has argued that the Markan prologue contains essential information for understanding Jesus and his mission. This information concerns the proper relationship between John and

Jesus, Jesus' divine sonship, and his confrontation with Satan in the wilderness. In the first part of the Gospel (1:14–8:30), the characters of the story misunderstand Jesus because they do not have this information. Nonetheless, on the basis of Jesus' words and deeds, the disciples come to an initial awareness of him as the Messiah. In the second (8:31–10:52) and third (11:1–13:37) parts, the prologue is recapitulated in terms of John (9:11–13; 11:29–33) and Jesus (9:7; 12:6), but the human characters of the story do not understand. The disciples remain blind because they do not "listen" to what Jesus says about the Son of Man. The religious leaders do not repent because they do not "listen" to what Jesus has to say about the beloved son in the parable of the vineyard. In a word, direct information does not help them. In the final section of the Gospel (14:1–16:8), the prologue is recapitulated once more.[42] This time, after Jesus dies, someone recognizes that he was truly the Son of God. This study suggests that the hermeneutical key to Mark's Gospel is the information found in the prologue, information which must be read by the light of the cross.

NOTES

1 Scholars do not agree about the extent of the prologue. Below, I argue that it consists of 1:2–13.

2 B. Standaert, *L'Évangile selon Marc: Commentaire* (Lire la Bible, 61; Paris: Les éditions du Cerf, 1983), p. 42.

3 M. D. Hooker, *The Message of Mark* (London: Epworth, 1983), p. 6.

4 W. L. Lane, *The Gospel According to Mark: The English Text with Introduction, Exposition and Notes* (NICNT; Grand Rapids: Eerdmans, 1974).

5 The most notable examples are L. E. Keck, "The Introduction to Mark's Gospel", *NTS* 12 (1965/6), pp. 352–70; J. M. Robinson, *The Problem of History in Mark* (London: SCM, 1957). My references are to the reprinted edition, J. M. Robinson, *The Problem of History in Mark and Other Marcan Studies* (Philadelphia: Fortress, 1982).

6 I am referring to the application of contemporary literary criticism to biblical studies. For an introduction to how this method is applied to the Gospel of Mark, see P. J. Achtemeier, *Mark* (2nd ed; Proclamation Commentaries; Philadelphia: Fortress, 1986), pp. 41–52; F. J. Matera, *What Are They Saying About Mark?* (New York: Paulist, 1987), pp. 75–92; D. Rhoads and D. Michie, *Mark as Story: An Introduction to the Narrative of a Gospel* (Philadelphia: Fortress, 1982). For the application of the method to the other

The Prologue as the Interpretative Key to Mark's Gospel

Gospels, see R. A. Culpepper, *Anatomy of the Fourth Gospel: A Study in Literary Design* (Foundations and Facets; Philadelphia: Fortress, 1983); J. D. Kingsbury, *Matthew as Story* (Philadelphia: Fortress, 1986); F. J. Matera, "The Plot of Matthew's Gospel", *CBQ* 49 (1987), pp. 233–53; R. C. Tannehill, *The Narrative Unity of Luke–Acts: A Literary Interpretation. Vol. 1 The Gospel According to Luke* (Foundation and Facets; Philadelphia: Fortress, 1986).

7 R. H. Lightfoot, *The Gospel Message of St. Mark* (Oxford: Clarendon 1950), pp. 15–20.

8 Ibid., p. 17.

9 Thus most of the standard commentaries accept this position: C. E. B. Cranfield, *The Gospel According to St. Mark: An Introduction and Commentary* (Cambridge Greek New Testament Commentary; Cambridge: Cambridge University Press, 1959); W. L. Lane, *The Gospel According to Mark*; J. Schmid, *The Gospel According to Mark* (RNT; New York: Alba House, 1968); E. Schweizer, *The Good News According to Mark* (Richmond: John Knox, 1970); V. Taylor, *The Gospel According to Mark: The Greek Text with Introduction, Notes, and Indexes* (2nd ed; New York: St Martins, 1966).

10 L. E. Keck, "The Introduction to Mark's Gospel". Other authors later argued for this position. See J. M. Gibbs, "Mark 1:1–15, Matthew 1:1–4:16, Luke 1:1–4:30, John 1:1–51: The Gospel Prologues and Their Function", *SE* VI, ed. E. A. Livingstone (TU 112; Berlin: Akademic Verlag, 1973), pp. 154–88; R. Pesch, "Anfang des Evangeliums Jesu Christi: Eine Studie zum Prolog des Markusevangeliums (Mk 1:1–15)", in *Die Zeit Jesu: Festschrift für Heinrich Schlier*, ed. G. Bornkamm and K. Rahner (Freiburg: Herder, 1970), pp. 108–44.

11 Keck, "The Introduction to Mark's Gospel", pp. 359–60.

12 Ibid., pp. 360–2.

13 Ibid., p. 361.

14 Thus the most recent commentaries view the prologue as consisting of 1:1–15: H. Anderson, *The Gospel of Mark* (NCB; Grand Rapids: Eerdmans, 1976), J. Ernst, *Das Evangelium nach Markus* (RNT; Regensburg: Pustet, 1981); J. Gnilka, *Das Evangelium nach Markus 1: Mk 1–8:26* (EKK 2/1; Zürich: Benziger Verlag, 1978); C. S. Mann, *Mark: A New Translation with Introduction and Commentary* (AB, 27; Garden City, New York: Doubleday, 1986); R. Pesch, *Das Markusevamgelium 1: Einleitung und Kommentar zu Kap. 1:1–8:26* (HTKNT 2/1; 4th ed; Freiburg: Herder, 1984).

15 It should be noted that even commentators who view 1:1–13 as the prologue tend to understand 1:1 as a superscription to the entire work.

16 U. Mauser, *Christ in the Wilderness: The Wilderness Theme in the Second Gospel and its Basis in the Biblical Tradition* (SBT; Naperville, Ill.: Alec R. Allenson, 1963), p. 79.

17 Lane, *The Gospel According to Mark*, p. 48.

18 *The Problem of History*, p. 72.

19 Throughout this study I employ the term "narrator" to designate the voice of the one who tells the story. Literary critics make a conceptual distinction between the real author and the voice the author employs to narrate the story. In modern literature this distinction is important because the real author does not always employ a reliable narrator, i.e. one who can be trusted to tell the story accurately. This technique does not occur in the Gospels, nevertheless it is important to maintain this conceptual distinction because it reminds us that our concern is the narrative world of the narrator, not the historical world of the real author. Thus I am not employing Mark's Gospel as a window through which to peer into the situation of his church or community, the so-called referential fallacy; I am concerned with the narrative world which the narrator creates for the reader. On the literary use of the narrator, see W. C. Booth, *The Rhetoric of Fiction* (2nd ed; Chicago: University of Chicago Press, 1983), pp. 149–65; S. Chatman, *Story and Discourse: Narrative Structures in Fiction and Film* (Ithaca: Cornell University Press, 1978), pp. 196–262; S. Rimmon-Kenan, *Narrative Fiction: Contemporary Poetics* (London: Methuen, 1983), pp. 86–116.

20 I am aware that there are many moments in the Gospel when the narrator communicates privately with the reader. The use of *gar* clauses (11:13) and other side comments (7:19) are examples. Furthermore, the whole narrative, inasmuch as it is a narrative, is primarily directed to the reader. My point is that the extraordinary events of this section, unlike the events in the rest of the Gospel, are not known to the characters of the narrative (Jesus excepted).

21 Even events such as the transfiguration are public in nature inasmuch as human characters within the narrative witness them. By contrast, no human character of the story hears the Isaiah quotation, the Father's baptismal declaration, or witnesses the struggle in the wilderness. Jesus, of course, is aware of these events.

22 J. Drury ("Mark", in *The Literary Guide to the Bible*, ed. R. Alter and F. Kermode [Cambridge: The Belknap Press of Harvard University, 1987], pp. 402–17) writes: "Verse 1 belongs in the present of Mark's Christian readers. 'The gospel of Jesus Christ, the Son of God', is their book about their master. From that near present they are suddenly taken far back in time. Verses 2 and 3, quoting Exodus, Isaiah and Malachi, fasten Jesus' story to the sacred past as strongly as v. 1 has fastened it to the sacred present" (p. 407).

23 Keck ("The Introduction to Mark's Gospel", pp. 366–67) makes a similar point.

24 Str.-B, I, p. 597.

25 Here, the narrator intends that the reader refer "Lord" to Jesus the Messiah, whereas in its original context "Lord" referred to God.

26 A few texts read "with the Holy Spirit and with fire" but the reading appears to be an assimilation of the texts of Matt 3:11 and Luke 3:16. So, B. M. Metzger, *A Textual Commentary on the Greek New Testament* (United Bible Societies, 1971).

27 Lane, *The Gospel According to Mark*, p. 55.

28 Taylor (*The Gospel According to Mark*, p. 161) offers rabbinic evidence that the imagery of the dove "is connected with the picture of the Spirit of God brooding or hovering creatively over the primaeval waters (Gen. i. 2)".

29 ἀγαπητός can be translated as "beloved" or "only". It can be taken with υἱός ("my beloved Son", "my only Son") or it can be taken as a separate designation ("my Son, the Beloved", "my Son, the Only One").

30 Most commentators interpret εἰς αὐτόν as the descent of the Spirit "upon" Jesus rather than "into" him.

31 The text can allude to Gen. 22:2, Ps. 2:7 or Isa. 42:1. The choice made here is crucial since it can result in understanding Jesus' sonship in terms of Isaac imagery (Gen. 22:2), royal imagery (Ps. 2:7), or servant imagery (Isa. 42:1). I do not think it inconceivable that the narrator intends the reader to see an allusion to all of these texts. Thus, Jesus is the royal Son of God who comes as the Lord's Servant to surrender his life.

32 The voice is spoken solely to Jesus whereas in the transfiguration it is spoken to the disciples (9:7). In Matt 3:17, by contrast, the Father's declaration is in third person.

33 Anderson (*The Gospel of Mark*, p. 82) writes, "The idea may also be present that Jesus has restored the situation that obtained before the fall when Adam was king of paradise and Lord of the wild animals". But Mauser (*Christ in the Wilderness*, p. 101) contends: "They [the wild beasts] represent the horror and the danger which faces man in the desert. Possibly in New Testament times the animals were associated with demons".

34 Keck ("The Introduction to Mark's Gospel", p. 362) writes, "Mark's Jesus is the victorious Son of God who returns from the testing-ground with the εὐαγγέλιον".

35 For a summary of different proposals see, H. C. Kee, *Community of the New Age: Studies in Mark's Gospel* (Philadelphia: Westminster, 1977), pp. 56–64. In my opinion, the placement of Peter's confession (8:27–30) is crucial for determining the Gospel's structure. Does it conclude the first part of the Gospel, or, as most commentators believe, does it begin the second part? If it concludes the first part of the Gospel, it is easier to view Peter's confession more positively as the climax of part one. But if it begins the second part of the story, there is a tendency to view the confession negatively since Peter's objection to Jesus' passion prediction immediately follows. I believe that the confession climaxes the first part of the story. I hope to deal with this pericope and the structure of the gospel in a later article.

36 The two feeding stories (6:31–44; 8:1–10) bracket Jesus' discourse on clean and unclean (7:1–23). The first occurs in Jewish territory and the second on the other side of the lake, in Gentile territory. These stories suggest that Jesus' mission extends to Gentiles as well as Jews, a point reinforced by Jesus' declaration that all foods are clean (7:18–23).

37 Not all commentators agree that Peter's confession is correct. For a discussion of those who view this confession negatively, and so in need of correction, see Matera, *What Are They Saying About Mark?*, pp. 18–27.

38 The narrator uses the third person here whereas the second person was employed at the baptism (1:11).

39 In 8:11; 10:2; 12:15 the narrator employs the verb πειράζειν to describe the activity of the religious leaders. The only other occurrence of the verb in Mark is 1:13, Satan's testing of Jesus. The narrator draws a parrallel between the activity of the religious leaders and that of the Satan *vis-à-vis* Jesus. Both test him in order to dissuade him from his mission.

40 Mark 15:38, the tearing of the temple curtain, presents two exegetical problems. First it seems to interrupt the narrative flow of vv. 37 and 39. Second, it raises the question, which curtain? The inner curtain before the Holy Place or the great outer curtain? H. L. Chronis ("The Torn Veil: Cultus and Christology in Mark 15:37–9", *JBL* [1982], pp. 97–114) and H. M. Jackson ("The Death of Jesus in Mark and the Miracle of the Cross", *NTS* 33 [1987], pp. 16–37) have shed light on these questions by the use of literary criticism. Although their answers differ, both convincingly show that the centurion's cry is related to the tearing of the Temple curtain, arguing that what the centurion sees is related to the tearing of the curtain. For Chronis 15:38 is a "cipher for theophany" (p. 110). When the narrator says that the temple curtain was torn, he means that the centurion is the recipient of a theophany. "Standing in the presence of the dying Jesus, he feels himself to be standing in the divine 'presence'. Looking into the face of the crucified Jesus at the instant of his death, he sees (as it were) the very 'face' of God" (p. 111). Jackson also argues for the narrative logic of 15:38 and 15:39. For him the event is more than a metaphor for a theophany. The breath/spirit of the dying Jesus (ἐξέπνευσεν) "rends the outer curtain of the Temple, and this is what the centurion saw" (p. 27). Thus the centurion's confession is based upon a divine prodigy: the tearing of the gigantic outer curtain by the expulsion of Jesus' breath/spirit.

41 S. Motyer ("The Rending of the Veil: A Markan Pentecost?", *NTS* 33 [1987], pp. 155–7) draws out the similarity between the rending of the heavens at Jesus' baptism and the rending of the temple curtain. He writes: "In both places something is rent, the verb being σχίζω; in both cases the rending involves a theophany, an opening of the Holy Place; in both something descends, whether the Spirit-dove or the tear in the curtain; in both Elijah-symbolism lies close at hand and informs the meaning" (p. 155).

42 The third element of the prologue, the testing of Jesus in the wilderness, is not recalled as explicitly in the second, third, and fourth sections of the Gospel as in the first. In part, this is due to the fact that all of the exorcisms, except 9:14–29, occur in the first section. Nevertheless, the testing of Jesus by the religious leaders (10:2; 12:15), as well as the mockery of Jesus (15:29–32), recall Satan's testing of God's Son. Most importantly, by his death, Jesus overcomes Satan's power.

Select Bibliography

A Commentaries

Achtemeier, P. J., *Mark* Proclamation Commentaries. Philadelphia: Fortress Press, 1975.

— *Invitation to Mark. A Commentary on the Gospel of Mark with Complete Text from the Jerusalem Bible.* Garden City: Image Books/Doubleday, 1978.

Allen, W. C., *The Gospel according to Saint Mark*, Oxford Church Biblical Commentary. London: Rivingtons, 1915.

Anderson, H., *The Gospel of Mark*, New Century Bible. London: Marshall, Morgan & Scott, 1976.

Bartlet, J. V., *St. Mark*, The Century Bible. Edinburgh: T. C. & E. C. Jack Ltd., 1922.

Blunt, A. W. F., *The Gospel according to Saint Mark*, Clarendon Bible. Oxford: Clarendon Press, 1929.

Bowman, J., *The Gospel of Mark. The New Christian Jewish Passover Haggadah*, Studia Post-Biblica, 8. Leiden: E. J. Brill, 1965.

Branscomb, B. H., *The Gospel of Mark*, Moffatt. London: Hodder & Stoughton, 1937.

Carrington, P., *According to Mark*. Cambridge: University Press, 1960.

Cranfield, C. E. B., *The Gospel according to Saint Mark*, Cambridge Greek Testament Commentary. Cambridge: University Press, 1959.

Ernst, J., *Das Evangelium nach Markus. Übersetzt und erklärt*, Regensburger Neues Testament. Regensburg: F. Pustet, 1981.

Gnilka, J., *Das Evangelium nach Markus*, Evangelisch-Katholischer Kommentar, II 1/2. 2 Vols. Zurich, Einsiedeln, Köln: Benziger/ Neukircher-Vluyn: Neukirchener Verlag, 1978/9.

Goguel, M., *L'Évangile de Marc*, Bibliotheque de l'École des Hautes Études, 22. Paris: Ernest Leroux, 1909.

Gould, E. P., *The Gospel according to St. Mark*, International Critical Commentary. Edinburgh: T. & T. Clark, 1896.

Grundmann, W., *Das Evangelium nach Markus*, Theologischer Handkommentar zum Neuen Testament, 2. 2nd ed. (1st ed. F. Hauck). Berlin: Evangelische Verlaganstalt, 1959.

Guelich, R. A., *Mark 1–8:26*, World Biblical Commentary, 34A. Dallas: Word, 1989.

Gundry, R. H., *Mark. A Commentary on His Apology for the Cross*. Grand Rapids: W. B. Eerdmans, 1992.

Haenchen, E., *Der Weg Jesu*. Berlin: Alfred Töpelmann, 1966.

Harrington, D. J., "The Gospel according to Mark", in *The New Jerome Biblical Commentary*, ed. R. E. Brown, J. A. Fitzmyer and R. E. Murphy, 596–629. London: G. Chapman, 1989.

Hauck, F., *Das Evangelium des Markus*, Theologischer Handkommentar zum Neuen Testament. Leipzig: A. Deichert, 1931.

Hurtado, L. W., *Mark*, A Good News Commentary. San Francisco: Harper & Row, 1983; *Mark*, New International Biblical Commentary 2. Peabody: Hendrickson, 1989.

Johnson, S. E., *The Gospel according to St. Mark*, Black. 2nd ed. London: Adam & Charles Black 1972.

Klostermann, E., *Das Markusevangelium*, Handbuch zum Neuen Testament, 3. 4th. ed. Tübingen: Mohr, 1950.

Lagrange, M.-J., *Évangile selon Saint Marc*, Études Bibliques. 5th ed. Paris: J. Gabalda et Fils, 1929.

Lane, W. L., *Commentary on the Gospel of Mark*, New London Commentary on the NT. Grand Rapids: Eerdmans, 1974.

Lohmeyer, E., *Das Evangelium des Markus*, Kritisch exegetischer Kommentar über das Neue Testament. Repr. 10th ed., 1937. Göttingen: Vandenhoeck & Ruprecht, 1957.

Loisy, A., *L'Évangile selon Marc*. Paris: Émile Nourry, 1912.

Lührmann, D., *Das Markusevangelium*, Handbuch zum Neuen Testament, 3. Tübingen: Mohr, 1987.

Mann, C. S., *Mark. A New Translation with Introduction and Commentary*, Anchor Bible 27. Garden City: Doubleday, 1986.

Nineham, D. E., *The Gospel of St Mark*, Pelican Gospel Commentaries. 2nd ed. London: Adam & Charles Black, 1968.

Pesch, R., *Das Markusevangelium* (Herders Theologischer Kommentar, II 1/2). 2 vols. 4th ed. Freiburg, Basel, Wien: Herder, 1984.

Plummer, A., *The Gospel according to St Mark*, Cambridge Bible for Schools and Colleges. Cambridge: University Press, 1915.

Pohl, A., *Das Evangelium des Markus*, Wuppertaler Studienbibel, Ergänzungsband. Wuppertal: R. Brockhaus, 1986.

Rawlinson, A. E. J., *St Mark*, Westminster. London: Methuen & Co. Ltd., 1925.

Schmid, J., *Das Evangelium nach Marcus*, Regensburger Neues Testament, 2. Regensburg: Friedrich Pustet, 1963.

Schmithals, W., *Das Evangelium nach Markus*, Ökumenischer Taschenbuchkommentar zum Neuen Testament. 2 Vols. Gütersloh: Mohr, 1979.

Select Bibliography

Schniewind, J., *Das Evangelium nach Markus*, Das Neue Testament Deutsch, 1. 7th ed. Göttingen: Vandenhoeck & Ruprecht, 1956.

Schweizer, E., *The Good News according to Mark*. ET. D. H. Madvig. London: SPCK, 1971; *Das Evangelium nach Markus. Übersetzt und Erklärt*, Das Neue Testament Deutsch 1. 14th ed. Göttingen: Vandenhoeck & Ruprecht, 1975.

Swete, H. B., *The Gospel according to St. Mark*. 2nd ed. London: Macmillan and Co. Ltd., 1902.

Taylor, V., *The Gospel according to St. Mark*. 2nd ed. London: Macmillan, 1966.

Weiss, J., *Das älteste Evangelium*. Göttingen: Vandenhoeck & Ruprecht, 1903.

Wellhausen, J., *Das Evangelium Marci*. 2nd ed. Berlin: Georg Reimer, 1903[1], 1909[2].

Wohlenberg, G., *Das Evangelium des Markus*, Kommentar zum Neuen Testament. Leipzig: A. Deichert, 1910.

B *Articles and Books*

Achtemeier, P. J., "Toward the Isolation of pre-Marcan Miracle Catenae", *JBL* 89 (1970) 265–91.

— "The Origin and Function of the pre-Marcan Miracle Catenae", *JBL* 91 (1972) 198–221.

— "'He taught Them Many Things': Reflections on Marcan Christology", *CBQ* 42 (1980) 465–81.

Ambrozic, A. M., *The Hidden Kingdom. A Redaction-Critical Study of the References to the Kingdom of God in Mark's Gospel*. Washington, D.C.: Catholic Biblical Association of America, 1972.

Aune, D. E., *The New Testament and its Literary Environment*. Philadelphia: Westminster, 1987.

Barbour, R. S., "Gethsemane in the Tradition of the Passion", *NTS* 16 (1969–70) 231–51.

Beasley-Murray, G. R., *Jesus and the Future. An Examination of the Criticism of The Eschatological Discourse, Mark 13, with Special Reference to the Little Apocalypse Theory*. London: Macmillan, 1954.

— "Second Thoughts on the Composition of Mark 13", *NTS* 29 (1983) 414–20.

Beavis, M. A., "The Trial before the Sanhedrin (Mark 14:53–65): Reader-Response and Graeco-Roman Readers", *CBQ* 49 (1987) 581–96.

— "Women as Models of Faith in Mark", *BTB* 18 (1988) 3–9.

— *Mark's Audience. The Literary and Social Setting of Mark 4.11–12*. Sheffield: JSOT, 1989.

Beck, N. A., "Reclaiming a Biblical Text: The Mark 8:14–21 Discussion about Bread in the Boat", in *CBQ* 43 (1981) 49–56.

309

Belo, F., *A Materialist Reading of the Gospel of Mark*. ET. M. J. O'Connell. Maryknoll: Orbis, 1981.

Best, E., *The Temptation and the Passion: the Markan Soteriology*. Cambridge: University Press, 1965.

— "Discipleship in Mark: Mark 8:22–10.52", *SJT* 23 (1970) 323–37.

— "Mark's Preservation of the Tradition", in M. Sabbe (ed.), *L'Évangile selon Marc. Tradition et Rédaction*, 21–34. Leuven: University Press, 1974, 1988.

— "Mark III. 20, 21, 31–35", *NTS* 22 (1975–6) 309–19.

— "The Role of the Disciples in Mark", *NTS* 23 (1976–7) 377–401.

— "Mark's Use of the Twelve", *ZNW* 69 (1978) 11–35.

— "Peter in the Gospel according to Mark", *CBQ* 40 (1978) 547–58.

— "Mark: Some Problems", in *Irish Biblical Studies 1* (1979) 77–98.

— *Following Jesus. Discipleship in the Gospel of Mark*. Sheffield, JSOT, 1981.

— *Mark: The Gospel as Story*. Edinburgh: T. & T. Clark, 1983.

— *Disciples and Discipleship. Studies in the Gospel according to Mark*. Edinburgh: T. & T. Clark, 1986.

— "Mark's Narrative Technique", in *JSNT* 37 (1989) 43–58.

— "Mark's Readers: a Profile", in F. Neirynck, Festschrift, *The Four Gospels 1992*, ed. F. Van Segbroeck, et al. (Leuven: University Press/Peeters, 1992; 3 vols), 2, 839–58.

Betz, H. D. (ed.), *Christology and a Modern Pilgrimage*. Claremont: Society of Biblical Literature, 1971.

— "Jesus as Divine Man", in E. C. Colwell, Festschrift, *Jesus and the Historian*, ed. F. T. Trotter, 114–33. Philadelphia: Westminster, 1968.

Bilezikian, G. G., *The Liberated Gospel: A Comparison of the Gospel of Mark and Greek Tragedy*. Grand Rapids: Baker, 1977.

Betz, O., "The Concept of the so-called 'Divine Man' in Mark's Christology", in A. P. Wikgren, Festschrift, *Studies in New Testament and Early Christian Literature*, ed. D. E. Aune, 229–40. Leiden: E. J. Brill, 1972.

Black C. C., "The Quest of Mark the Redactor: Why Has It Been Pursued, and What Has It Taught Us?", in *JSNT* 33 (1988) 19–39.

— *The Disciples according to Mark. Markan Redaction in Current Debate*. Sheffield: JSOT, 1989.

Blatherwick, D., "The Markan Silhouette?", *NTS* 17 (1970–1) 184–92.

Blevins, J. L., *The Messianic Secret in Markan Research 1901–76*. Washington, DC: University Press of America, 1981.

Boobyer, G. H., "The Eucharistic Interpretation of the Miracles of the Loaves in St. Mark's Gospel", *JTS* 3 (1952) 161–71.

— "Galilee and Galileans in St. Mark's Gospel", *BJRL* 35 (1952–3) 334–48.

Boobyer, G. H., "The Miracles of the Loaves and the Gentiles in St. Mark's Gospel", *SJT* 6 (1953) 77–87.

Boomershine, T. E., "Mark 16:8 and the Apostolic Commission", *JBL* 100 (1981) 225–39.

Boomershine, T. E., "Peter's Denial as Polemic or Confession: the Implications of Media Criticism for Biblical Hermeneutics", in *Semeia* 39 (1987) 47–68.

Boomershine, T. E., and Bartholomew, G. L., "The Narrative Technique of Mark 16:8", *JBL* 100 (1981) 213–23.

Booth, R. P., *Jesus and the Laws of Purity. Tradition History and Legal History in Mark 7*. Sheffield: JSOT, 1986.

Booth, W. C., *The Rhetoric of Fiction*. 2nd ed. Chicago: University of Chicago Press, 1983.

Boring, M. E., *Sayings of the Risen Jesus. Christian Prophecy in the Synoptic Tradition*. Cambridge: University Press, 1982.

— "The Christology of Mark: Hermeneutical Issues for Systematic Theology", *Semeia* 30 (1984) 125–53.

Boucher, M., *The Mysterious Parable*. Washington: Catholic Biblical Association, 1977.

Brandenburger, E., *Markus 13 und die Apokalyptick*. Göttingen: Vandenhoeck & Ruprecht, 1984.

Brandon, S. G. F., "The Date of the Markan Gospel", *NTS* 7 (1961–2) 26–41.

Breytenbach, C., *Nachfolge und Zukunftserwartung nach Markus. Eine methodenkritische Studie*. Zurich: Theologischer Verlag, 1984.

— "The Gospel of Mark as Episodical Narrative. Reflections on the 'Composition' of the Second Gospel", in *Scriptura* (special issue 4; 1989) 1–26.

— "Vormarkinische Logientradition. Parallelen in der urchristlichen Briefliteratur", in F. Neirynck, Festschrift, *The Four Gospels 1992*, ed. F. Van Segbroeck, et al. (Leuven: University Press, 1992; 3 vols), 2, 725–49.

Budesheim, T. L., "Jesus and the Disciples in Conflict with Judaism", *ZNW* 62 (1971) 190–209.

Bultmann, R., *The History of the Synoptic Tradition*. ET. J. Marsh from the 2nd Ger. ed. (1931). 2nd Eng. ed. with corrections and with additions from 1962 Suppl. Oxford: Blackwell, 1968.

— "Die Frage nach dem messianischen Bewusstsein Jesu und das Petrus-Bekenntnis", in E. Dinkler (ed.), *Exegetica*, 1–9. Tübingen: J. C. B. Mohr (Paul Siebeck), 1967. (Orig. pub. in *ZNW* 19 (1919–20) 165–74).

Burkill, T. A., *Mysterious Revelation. An Examination of the Philosophy of St. Mark's Gospel*. Ithaca: Cornell University Press, 1963.

— "Mark 3:7–12 and the alleged Dualism in the Evangelist's Miracle Material", *JBL* 87 (1968) 409–17.

Burkill, T. A., *New Light on the Earliest Gospel. Seven Markan Studies.* Ithaca/London: Cornell University Press, 1972.

Busemann, R., *Die Jungergemeinde nach Markus 10. Eine redaktionsgeschichtliche Untersuchung des 10. Kapitels in Markusevangelium.* Königstein/Ts-Bonn: Hanstein, 1983.

Butterworth, R., "The Composition of Mark 1–12", *HeyJ* 13 (1972) 5–26.

Camery-Hoggatt, J., *Irony in Mark's Gospel.* Cambridge: University Press, 1992.

Cancik, H. (ed.), *Markus-Philologie. Historische, literargeschichtliche und stilistische Untersuchungen zum zweiten Evangelium.* Tübingen: Mohr-Siebeck, 1984.

Catchpole, D., "The Fearful Silence of the Women at the Tomb", *Journal of Theology for Southern Africa,* 18 (1977) 3–10.

— "The 'triumphal' entry", in *Jesus and the Politics of his Day,* ed. E. Bammel and C. F. D. Moule (Cambridge, 1984) 319–34.

Chatman, S., *Story and Discourse: Narrative in Fiction and Film.* Ithaca: Cornell University Press, 1978.

Collins, A. Y., *Is Mark's Gospel a Life of Jesus? The Question of Genre.* Milwaukee: Marquette University Press, 1990.

— "The Eschatological Discourse of Mark 13", in F. Neirynck, Festschrift, *The Four Gospels 1992,* ed. F. Van Segbroeck, et al. (Leuven: University Press/Peeters, 1992; 3 vols), 2, 1125–40.

Conzelmann, H., "Geschichte und Eschaton nach Mc 13", *ZNW* 50 (1959) 210–21.

— "History and Theology in the Passion Narratives of the Synoptic Gospels", *Int* 24 (1970) 178–97.

Cook, M. J., *Mark's Treatment of the Jewish Leaders.* Leiden: E. J. Brill, 1978.

Corner, M. A., and Rowland, C. R., *Liberating Exegesis.* London: SCM, 1990.

Cousar, C. B., "Eschatology and Mark's Theologia Crucis. A Critical Analysis of Mark 13", *Int* 24 (1970) 321–35.

Crossan, J. D., "Mark and the Relatives of Jesus", *NovT* 15 (1973) 81–113.

— "A Form for Absence: The Markan Creation of Gospel", *Semeia* 12 (1978) 41–55.

— *In Fragments. The Aphorisms of Jesus.* San Francisco: Harper & Row, 1983.

Culpepper, R. A., "Mark 10:50. Why Mention the Garment?", in *JBL* 101 (1982) 131–2.

Dahm, C., *Israel im Markusevangelium.* Frankfurt/Bonn/New York/Paris: Lang, 1991.

Dautzenberg, G., "Zur Stellung des Markusevangelium in der Geschichte der urchristlichen Theologie", *Kairos* 18 (1976) 282–91.

Select Bibliography

Derrett, J. D. M., *The Making of Mark. The Scriptural Basis of the Earliest Gospels*. 2 Vols. Shipston-on-Stour: P. Drinkwater, 1985.

Dewey, J., "The Literary Structure of the Controversy Stories in Mark 2:1–3:6", *JBL* 92 (1973) 394–401.

— *Markan Public Debate. Literary Technique, Concentric Structure and Theology in Mark 2:1–3:6*. Chico: Scholars Press, 1980.

— "Oral Methods of Structuring Narrative in Mark", *Int* 43 (1989) 32–44.

Dibelius, M., *From Tradition to Gospel*. ET. B. L. Woolf. London: Ivor Nicholson and Watson, 1934.

Dinkler, E., "Peter's Confession and the 'Satan' Saying: The Problem of Jesus' Messiahship", in R. Bultmann, Festschrift, *The Future of our Religious Past*, ed. J. M. Robinson, 169–202. London: SCM, 1971.

Donahue, J. R., *Are You the Christ? The Trial Narrative in the Gospel of Mark*. Missoula: Society of Biblical Literature, 1973.

— "Jesus as the Parable of God in the Gospel of Mark", *Int* 32 (1978) 369–86.

— *The Theology and Setting of Discipleship in the Gospel of Mark*. Milwaukee: Marquette University Press, 1983.

— "The Community of Mark's Gospel", in F. Neirynck, Festschrift, *The Four Gospels 1992*, ed. F. Van Segbroeck, et al. (Leuven: University Press, 1992; 3 vols), 2, 817–38.

Dormeyer, D., *Die Passion Jesu als Verhaltensmodell*. Münster: Aschendorff, 1974.

— *Der Sinn des Leidens Jesu. Historisch-kritische und textpragmatische Analysen zur Markuspassion*. Stuttgart: Katholisches Bibelwerk, 1979.

— "Die Kompositionsmetapher 'Evangelium Jesu Christi, des sohnes Gottes' Mk. 1.1. Ihre Theologische und Literarische Aufgabe in der Jesus-Biographie des Markus", *NTS* 33 (1987) 452–68.

Dowd, S. E., *Prayer, Power and the Problem of Suffering: Mark 11:22–25 in the Context of Markan Theology*. Atlanta: Scholars Press, 1988.

Drury, J., "Mark 1:1–15: an Interpretation", in *Alternative Approaches to New Testament Study* (London: SPCK, 1985) 25–36.

— "Mark", in *The Literary Guide to the Bible*, ed. R. Alter, F. Kermode (Cambridge, Mass.: Harvard University Press, 1987) 402–17.

Dschulnigg, P., *Sprache, Redaktion und Intention des Markus-Evangeliums. Eigentümlichkeiten der Sprache des Markus-Evangeliums und ihre Bedeutung für die Redaktionskritik*. Stuttgart: Katholisches Bibelwerk, 1984.

Dunn, J. G. D., "Mark 2:1–3:6: A Bridge between Jesus and Paul on the Question of the Law", *NTS* 30 (1984) 395–415.

Edwards, J. R., "Markan Sandwiches. The Significance of Interpolations in Markan Narratives", *NovT* 31 (1989) 193–216.

Egger, W., *Nachfolge als Weg zum Leben. Chancen neuerer exegetischer Methoden dargelegt an Mk 10,17–31*. Klosterneuburg: Österreichisches Katholisches Bibelwerk, 1979.

Ellis, E. E., "The Date and Provenance of Mark's Gospel", in F. Neirynck, Festschrift, *The Four Gospels 1992*, ed. F. Van Segbroeck, et al. (Leuven: University Press, 1992; 3 vols), 2, 801–15.

Ernst, J., "Die Petrustradition im Markusevangelium – ein altes Problem neu angegangen", in H. Zimmermann, Festschrift, *Begegnung mit dem Wort*, eds. J. Zmijewski and E. Nellessen (Bonn: Hanstein, 1980a) 35–65.

— "Die Passionserzählung des Markus und die Aporien der Forschung", *Theologie und Glaube*, 70 (1980b) 160–80.

Evans, C. F., "I will go before you into Galilee", *JTS* 5 (1954) 3–18.

Farmer, W. R., *The Last Twelve Verses of Mark*. Cambridge: University Press, 1974.

Farrer, A., *A Study in St. Mark*. London: Dacre Press, 1951.

— *St. Matthew and St. Mark*. London: Dacre Press, 1954.

Fay, G., "Introduction to Incomprehension: the Literary Structure of Mark 4:1–34", *CBQ* 51 (1984) 65–81.

Feldmeier, R., *Die Krisis des Gottessohnes. Die Gethsemaneerzählung als Schlüssel der Markuspassion*. Tübingen: Mohr-Siebeck, 1987.

Fenton, J. C., "Paul and Mark", in R. H. Lightfoot, Festschrift, *Studies in the Gospels*, ed. D. E. Nineham, 89–112. Oxford: Blackwell, 1957.

Fleddermann, H., "The Discipleship Discourse (Mark 9:33–50)", *CBQ* 43 (1981) 57–75.

Focant, C., "Les Doublets dans la Section des Pains", in F. Neirynck, Festschrift, *The Four Gospels 1992*, ed. F. Van Segbroeck, et al. (Leuven: University Press/Peeters, 1992; 3 vols), 2, 1039–63.

Fowler, R. M., *Loaves and Fishes. The Function of the Feeding Stories in the Gospel of Mark*. Chico: Scholars Press, 1981.

— "Who is 'the Reader' in Mark's Gospel?", in *Society of Biblical Literature 1983 Seminar Papers: SBL 22*, ed. K. H. Richards (Chico: Scholars Press, 1983) 31–53.

— "The Rhetoric of Direction and Indirection in the Gospel of Mark", *Semeia* 48 (1989) 115–34.

— *Let the Reader Understand. Reader-Response Criticism and the Gospel of Mark*. Minneapolis: Fortress Press, 1991.

Geddert, T. J., *Watchwords. Mark 13 in Markan Eschatology*. Sheffield: JSOT, 1989.

Genette, G., *Narrative Discourse*. Oxford: Blackwell, 1980.

Gerhardsson, B., *The Origins of the Gospel Traditions*. Philadelphia: Fortress Press, 1979.

— *The Gospel Tradition*. Lund: Gleerup, 1986.

Select Bibliography

Goulder, M. D., "A Pauline in a Jacobite Church", in F. Neirynck, Festschrift, *The Four Gospels 1992*, ed. F. Van Segbroeck, et al. (Leuven: University Press, 1992; 3 vols), 2, 859–75.

Grässer, E., "Jesus in Nazareth (Mark VI. 1–6a). Notes on the Redaction and Theology of St. Mark", *NTS* 16 (1969–70) 1-23.

Grassi, J. A., "The Secret Heroine of Mark's Drama", *BTB* 18 (1988) 10–15.

Grayston, K., "The Study of Mark XIII", *BJRL* 56 (1973–4) 371–87.

Green J. B., *The Death of Jesus. Tradition and Interpretation in the Passion Narrative*. Tübingen: Mohr-Siebeck, 1988.

Guelich, R. A., "'The Beginning of the Gospel'. Mark 1:1–15", *Biblical Research* 27 (1982) 5–15.

Haenchen, E., "Die Komposition von Mk viii 27 – ix 1 und Par.", *NovT* 6 (1963) 81–109.

Hahn, F. (ed.), *Der Erzähler des Evangeliums. Methodische Neuansätze in der Markusforschung*. Stuttgart: Katholisches Bibelwerk, 1985.

Hällback, G., "Der anonyme Plan: Analyse von Mk. 13:5–27 im Hinblick auf die Relevanz der apokalyptischen Rede für die problematik der Aussage", *Linguistica Biblica* 49 (1981) 38–53.

Hamilton, N. Q., "Resurrection Tradition and the Composition of Mark", *JBL* 84 (1965) 415–21.

Hartman, L., *Prophecy Interpreted. The Formation of Some Jewish Apocalyptic Texts and of the Eschatological Discourse Mark 13 Par.* Uppsala: CWK Gleerup Lund, 1966.

Hawkin, D. J., "The Incomprehension of the Disciples in the Marcan Redaction", *JBL* 91 (1972) 491–500.

Hedrick, C. W., "Narrator and Story in the Gospel of Mark: Hermeneia and Paradosis", *Perspectives in Religious Studies* 14 (1987) 239–58.

Heil, J. P., "Mark 14,1–52: Narrative Structure and Reader-Response", in *Biblica* 71 (1990) 305–32.

Hengel, M., *Studies in the Gospel of Mark*. ET. J. Bowden. Philadelphia: Fortress Press, 1985.

Hooker, M. D., *The Son of Man*. London: SPCK, 1967.

— "Trial and Tribulation in Mark xiii", *BJRL* 65 (1982) 78–99.

— *The Message of Mark*. London: Epworth Press, 1983.

Horstmann, M., *Studien zur markinischen Christologie (Mk 8,27 – 9,13)*. 2nd ed. Münster: Aschendorff, 1973.

Hultgren, A. J., *Jesus and his Adversaries. The Form and Function of the Conflict Stories in the Synoptic Tradition*. Minneapolis: Augsburg, 1979.

Humphrey, H. M., *A Bibliography for the Gospel of Mark 1954–1980*. New York/Toronto: Edwin Mellen Press, 1981.

Hurtado, L. W., "The Gospel of Mark: Evolutionary or Revolutionary Document?", *JSNT* 40 (1990) 15–32.

Iser, W., *The Implied Reader: Patterns of Communication in Prose Fiction from Bunyan to Beckett*. Baltimore: John Hopkins University Press, 1974.

— *The Act of Reading: A Theory of Aesthetic Response*. London: Routledge & Kegan, 1978.

Johnson, E. S., "Mark 10:46–52: Blind Bartimaeus", *CBQ* 40 (1978) 191–204.

Johnson, W. A., " 'The Jews' in Saint Mark's Gospel", *Religion and Intellectual Life* (New Rochelle), 6 (1989) 182–92.

Juel, D., *Messiah and Temple*. Missoula: Scholars Press, 1977.

Kazmierski, C. R., *Jesus, the Son of God. A Study of the Markan Tradition and its Redaction by the Evangelist*. Würzburg: Echter Verlag, 1979.

Kealy, S. P., *Mark's Gospel. A History of its Interpretation from the Beginning until 1979*. Ramsay: Paulist Press, 1982.

Keck, L. E., "The Introduction to Mark's Gospel", *NTS* 12 (1965–6) 352–70.

— "Mark 3:7–12 and Mark's Christology", *JBL* 84 (1965) 341–58.

Kee, H. C., "The Transfiguration in Mark: Epiphany or Apocalyptic Vision?", in M. S. Enslin, Festschrift, *Understanding the Sacred Text*, ed. J. Reumann (Valley Forge: Judson Press, 1972) 135–52.

— "Aretalogy and Gospel", *JBL* 92 (1973) 402–22.

— "The Function of Scriptural Quotations and Allusions in Mark 11–16" in W. G. Kümmel, Festschrift, *Jesus and Paulus*, eds. E. E. Ellis, E. Grässer (Göttingen: Vandenhoeck & Ruprecht, 1975) 165–88.

— *Community of the New Age. Studies in Mark's Gospel*. Philadelphia: Westminster, 1977.

— "Mark's Gospel in Recent Research", *Int* 32 (1978) 353–68.

Kelber, W. H., "Mark 14:32–42: Gethsemane. Passion Christology and Discipleship Failure", *ZNW* 63 (1972) 166–87.

— *The Kingdom in Mark. A New Place and a New Time*. Philadelphia: Fortress Press, 1974.

— (ed.), *The Passion in Mark. Studies on Mark 14–16*. Philadelphia: Fortress Press, 1976.

— *Mark's Story of Jesus*. Philadelphia: Fortress Press, 1979a.

— "Mark and Oral Tradition", *Semeia*, 16 (1979b), 7–55.

— *The Oral and the Written Gospel*. Philadelphia: Fortress Press, 1983.

— "Biblical Hermeneutics and the Ancient Art of Communication: a Response", *Semeia* 39 (1987a) 97–105.

— "Narrative as Interpretation and Interpretation of Narrative: Hermeneutical Reflections on the Gospels", *Semeia* 39 (1987b) 107–33.

— "Narrative and Disclosure: Mechanisms of Concealing, Revealing and Reveiling", *Semeia* 43 (1988) 1–20.

Kermode, F., *The Genesis of Secrecy. On the Interpretation of Narrative*. Cambridge/London: Harvard University Press, 1979.

Select Bibliography

Kertelge, K., "Die Epiphanie Jesu im Evangelium (Markus)" in *Gestalt und Anspruch des Neuen Testaments*, ed. J. Schreiner (Würzburg: Echter-Verlag, 1969) 153–72.

— *Die Wunder Jesu im Markusevangelium. Eine redaktionsgeschichtliche Untersuchung*. Munich: Kösel-Verlag, 1970.

Kiilunen, J., *Die Vollmacht in Widerstreit. Untersuchungen zum Werdegang von Mk 2:1–3:6*. Helsinki: Suomalainen Tiedeakatemia, 1985.

Kingsbury, J. D., *The Christology of Mark's Gospel*. Philadelphia: Fortress Press, 1983.

— *Conflict in Mark. Jesus, Authorities, Disciples*. Minneapolis: Fortress Press, 1989.

— "The Religious Authorities in the Gospel of Mark", *NTS* 36 (1990) 42–65.

Klauck, H.-J., "Die erzählerische Rolle der Jünger im Markusevangelium. Eine narrative Analyse", *NovT* 24 (1982) 1–26.

Klein, H., "Das Bekenntnis des Petrus und die Anfänge des Christusglaubens im Urchristentum", *EvT* 47 (1987) 176–92.

Knigge, H. D., "The Meaning of Mark. The Exegesis of the Second Gospel", *Int* 22 (1968) 53–70.

Koch, D. A., *Die Bedeutung der Wunderzählungen für die Christologie des Markusevangeliums*. Berlin/New York: Walter de Gruyter, 1975.

Kopas, J., "Jesus and Women in Mark's Gospel", *Review for Religious* 44 (1985) 912–20.

Kuhn, H.-W., *Ältere Sammlungen im Markusevangelium*. Göttingen: Vandenhoeck & Ruprecht, 1971.

Kümmel, W. G., *Introduction to the New Testament*. ET. H. C. Kee from the 17th Ger. ed. (1973). London: SCM, 1975.

Lambrecht, J., *Die Redaktion der Markus-Apokalypse. Literarische Analyse und Strukturuntersuchung*. Rome: Pontifical Biblical Institute, 1967.

— "The Christology of Mark", *BTB* 3 (1973) 256–73.

— "The Relatives of Jesus in Mark", *NovT* 16 (1974) 241–58.

— "Redaction and Theology in Mk., IV", in *L'Évangile selon Marc: Tradition et Rédaction*, ed. M. Sabbe (Leuven: University Press, 1974) 269–307. 2nd ed. 1988.

Lane, A. B., "The Significance of the Thirteen Women in the Gospel of Mark", *Unitarian Universalist Christian* (Boston) 38 (1983) 18–27.

Laufen, R., *Die Doppelüberlieferungen der Logienquelle und des Markusevangeliums*. Königstein/Ts-Bonn: Hanstein, 1980.

Lemcio, E. E., "The Intention of the Evangelist, Mark", *NTS* 32 (1986) 187–206.

Lightfoot, R. H., *History and Interpretation in the Gospels*. London: Hodder and Stoughton, 1934.

Lightfoot, R. H., *Locality and Doctrine in the Gospels*. London: Hodder & Stoughton, 1938.
— *The Gospel Message of St. Mark*. Oxford: Clarendon Press, 1950.
Limbeck, M. (ed.), *Redaktion und Theologie des Passionsberichtes nach den Synoptikern*. Darmstadt: Wissenschaftliche Buchgesellschaft, 1981.
Lincoln, A. T., "The Promise and the Failure: Mark 16:7–8", *JBL* 108 (1989) 283–300.
Linnemann, E., *Studien zur Passionsgeschichte*. Göttingen: Vandenhoeck & Ruprecht, 1970.
Lohmeyer, E., *Galiläa und Jerusalem*. Göttingen: Vandenhoeck & Ruprecht, 1936.
Lührmann, D., "Biographie des Gerechten als Evangelium. Vorstellungen zu einem Markus-Kommentar", *Wort und Dienst* 14 (1977) 25–50.
Luz, U., "Markusforschung in der Sackgasse?", *TZ* 105 (1980) 641–55.
— "The Secrecy Motif and the Marcan Christology" in C. M. Tuckett (ed.), *The Messianic Secret* (Philadelphia: Fortress Press/London: SPCK, 1983) 75–96.
Mack, B. L., *A Myth of Innocence. Mark and Christian Origins*. Philadelphia: Fortress Press, 1988.
Mack, B. L., and Robbins, V. K., *Patterns of Persuasion in the Gospels*. Sonoma: Polebridge, 1989.
Magness, J. L., *Sense and Absence. Structure and Suspension in the Ending of Mark's Gospel*. Atlanta: Scholars Press, 1986.
Malbon, E. S., "Mythic Structure and Meaning in Mark: Elements of a Lévi-Straussian Analysis", *Semeia* 16 (1979) 97–132.
— "Galilee and Jerusalem: History and Literature in Marcan Interpretation", *CBQ* 44 (1982) 242–55.
— "The Jesus of Mark and the Sea of Galilee", *JBL* 103 (1984) 363–77.
— *Narrative Space and Mythic Meaning in Mark*. San Francisco: Harper & Row, 1986a.
— "Disciples/Crowds/Whoever: Markan Characters and Readers", *NovT* 28 (1986b) 104–30.
— "Fallible Followers: Women and Men in the Gospel of Mark", *Semeia* 28 (1989) 29–48.
— "The Jewish Leaders in the Gospel of Mark: A Literary Study of Marcan Characterization", *JBL* 108 (1989) 259–81.
Maloney, E. C., *Semitic Interference in Marcan Syntax*. Chico: Scholars Press, 1981.
Marcus, J., *The Mystery of the Kingdom of God*. Atlanta: Scholars Press, 1986.
Marshall, C. D., *Faith as a Theme in Mark's Narrative*. Cambridge: University Press, 1989.

Select Bibliography

Martin, R. P., *Mark – Evangelist and Theologian*. Exeter: Paternoster Press, 1979.

Marxsen, W., "Redaktionsgeschichtliche Erklärung der sogenannten Parabeltheorie des Markus", *ZThK* 52 (1955) 255–71.

— *Mark the Evangelist. Studies on the Redaction History of the Gospel.* ET. J. Boyce, et al. Nashville/New York: Abingdon Press, 1969; London: SPCK, 1970.

März, C.-P., *"Siehe, dein König kommt zu Dir . . ." Eine traditionsgeschichtliche Untersuchung zur Einzugsperikope.* Leipzig: St Benno-Verlag, 1980.

Masuda, S., "The Good News of the Miracle of the Bread. The Tradition and its Markan Redaction", *NTS* (1982) 191–219.

Matera, F. J., *The Kingship of Jesus. Composition and Theology in Mark 15.* Chico: Scholars Press, 1982.

— *Passion Narratives and Gospel Theologies: Interpreting the Synoptics through their Passion Stories.* New York – Mahwah: Paulist Press, 1986.

— *What Are They Saying About Mark?* New York – Mahwah: Paulist Press, 1987.

— "The Prologue as the Interpretive Key to Mark's Gospel", *JSNT* 34 (1988) 3–20.

— "Mystery and Humanity. The Jesus of Mark", *Church* (New York) 5 (1989) 20–3.

McKnight, E. V. (ed.), *Reader Perspectives on the New Testament.* Atlanta: Scholars Press, 1989.

Meagher, J. C., *Clumsy Construction in Mark's Gospel. A Critique of Form and Redaktionsgeschichte.* New York/Toronto: Edwin Mellen Press, 1979.

Minear, P. S., "Audience Criticism and Markan Ecclesiology" in O. Cullmann, Festschrift, *Neues Testament und Geschichte*, ed. H. Baltensweiler, B. Reicke (Zürich/Tübingen: Mohr-Siebeck, 1972) 79–89.

Minette de Tillesse, C., "Structure théologique de Marc", in F. Neirynck, Festschrift, *The Four Gospels 1992*, ed. F. Van Segbroeck, et al. (Leuven: University Press/Peeters, 1992; 3 vols), 2, 905–33.

Mohr, T. A., *Markus- und Johannespassion. Redaktions- und traditionsgeschichtliche Untersuchung der Markinischen und Johannischen Passionstradition.* Zürich: Theologischer Verlag, 1982.

Moore, S. D., *Literary Criticism and the Gospels. The Theoretical Challenge.* New Haven/London: Yale University Press, 1989.

Mudiso Mbâ Mundla, J.-G., *Jesus und die Führer Israels. Studien zu den sog. Jerusalemer Streitgespräche.* Münster: Aschendorff, 1984.

Munro, W., "Women Disciples in Mark?", *CBQ* 44 (1982) 225–41.

Myers, C., *Binding the Strong Man. A Political Reading of Mark's Story of Jesus.* Maryknoll: Orbis, 1988.

Neirynck, F., *Duality in Mark. Contributions to the Study of the Markan Redaction.* Leuven: University Press, 1972. Revised ed. 1988.

— "Marc 13. Examen critique de l'interprétation de R. Pesch", in *L'Apocalypse johannique et l'Apocalyptique dans le Nouveau Testament*, ed. J. Lambrecht (Leuven: University Press/Gembloux, Belgium: Éditions J. Duculot, S.A., 1980) 369–401.

— "Marc 16,1–8. Tradition et rédaction", *ETL* 56 (1980) 56–88. Repr. *Evangelica*, ed. F. Van Segbroeck (Leuven: University Press/Peeters, 1982) 239–72.

— "The Redactional Text of Mark", *ETL* 57 (1981) 144–62. Repr. *Evangelica*, ed. F. Van Segbroeck (Leuven: Peeters/University Press, 1982) 618–36.

— "Words Characteristic of Mark. A New List", *ETL* 63 (1987) 367–74. Repr. *Evangelica 11*, ed. F. Van Segbroeck (Leuven: Peeters/University Press, 1991) 339–46.

Neirynck, F., et al. (eds.), *The Gospel of Mark. A Cumulative Bibliography 1950–1990.* Leuven: University Press/Peeters, 1992.

Orchard, B., "Mark and the Fusion of Traditions", in F. Neirynck, Festschrift, *The Four Gospels 1992*, ed. F. Van Segbroeck, et al. (Leuven: University Press/Peeters, 1992; 3 vols), 2, 779–800.

Oswald, J., "Die Beziehungen zwischen Psalm 22 und dem vormarkinischen Passionsbericht", *Zeitschrift für katholische Theologie* 101 (1979) 53–66.

Parkin, V., "Mark chapter 4:10–12. An exegesis", *Irish Biblical Studies* 8 (1986) 179–82.

Paulsen, H., "Mark xvi 1–8", *NovT* 22 (1980) 138–75.

Peabody, D. B., *Mark as Composer.* Mercer: Mercer University Press, 1987.

Perrin, N., "The Wredestrasse becomes the Hauptstrasse: Reflections on the Reprinting of the Dodd Festschrift", *JR* 46 (1966) 296–300.

— "The Creative Use of the Son of Man Traditions by Mark", *USQR* 23 (1967–8) 357–65.

— *What is Redaction Criticism?* Philadelphia: Fortress Press/London: SPCK, 1970.

— "The Christology of Mark: A Study in Methodology", *JR* 51 (1971) 173–87.

— "Towards an Interpretation of the Gospel of Mark", in *Christology and a Modern Pilgrimage*, ed. H. D. Betz (Claremont: Society of Biblical Literature, 1971) 1–78.

— "The Interpretation of the Gospel of Mark", *Int* 30 (1976) 115–24.

Pesch, R., *Naherwartungen. Tradition und Redaktion in Mk 13.* Düsseldorf: Patmos Verlag, 1968.

— *Das Evangelium der Urgemeinde. Wiederhergestellt und erläutert.* Freiburg-Basel-Wien: Herder, 1979a.

Select Bibliography

Pesch, R. (ed.), *Das Markus-Evangelium* (Wege der Forschung, 411). Darmstadt: Wissenschaftliche Buchgesellschaft, 1979b.

Pesch, R., and Kratz, R., *So liest man synoptisch. Anleitung und Kommentar zum Studium der synoptischen Evangelien. VI: Passionsgeschichte. Erster Teil.* Frankfurt/M: Knecht, 1979.

Petersen, N. R., *Literary Criticism for New Testament Critics.* Philadelphia: Fortress Press, 1978a.

— " 'Point of View' in Mark's Narrative", *Semeia* 12 (1978b) 97–121.

— (ed.), *Perspectives on Mark's Gospel* (*Semeia*, 16). Missoula: Scholars Press, 1979.

— "The Composition of Mark 4:1–8:26", *HTR* 73 (1980a) 185–217.

— "When is the End not the End? Literary Reflections on the Ending of Mark's Narrative", *Int* 34 (1980b) 151–66.

— "The Reader in the Gospel", *Neotestamentica* 18 (1984) 38–51.

— " 'Literarkritik', the New Literary Criticism and the Gospel according to Mark", in F. Neirynck, Festschrift, *The Four Gospels 1992*, ed. F. Van Segbroeck, et al. (Leuven: University Press/Peeters, 1992; 3 vols), 2, 935–48.

Pryke, E. J., *Redactional Style in the Markan Gospel.* Cambridge: University Press, 1978.

Quesnell, Q., *The Mind of Mark. Interpretation and Method through the Exegesis of Mark 6,52.* Rome: Pontifical Biblical Institute, 1969.

Räisänen, H., *The "Messianic Secret" in Mark.* ET. C. Tuckett. Edinburgh: T. & T. Clark, 1990.

Rau, G., "Das Markus-Evangelium. Komposition und Intention der ersten Darstellung christlicher Mission", in *Aufstieg und Niedergang*, ed. H. Temporini, W. Haase (Berlin/New York: Walter de Gruyter, 1985), II, 25, 3, 2036–257.

Reiser, M., *Syntax und Stil des Markusevangelium im Licht der hellenistischen Volksliteratur.* Tübingen: Mohr-Siebeck, 1984.

Reploh, K.-G., *Markus – Lehrer der Gemeinde. Eine Redaktionsgeschtliche Studie zu den Jüngerperikopen des Markus-Evangeliums.* Stuttgart: Katholisches Bibelwerk, 1969.

Rhoads, D., "Narrative Criticism and the Gospel of Mark", *JAAR* 50 (1982) 411–34.

Rhoads, D., and Michie, D., *Mark as Story: An Introduction to the Narrative of a Gospel.* Philadelphia: Fortress Press, 1982.

Riesner, R., "Der Ursprung der Jesus-Überlieferung", *TZ* 38 (1982) 495–513.

— *Jesus als Lehrer. Eine Untersuchung zum Ursprung der Evangelien-Überlieferung.* 2nd rev. ed. Tübingen: J. C. B. Mohr, 1984.

Robbins, V. K., "The Healing of Blind Bartimaeus (10:46–52) in the Marcan Theology", *JBL* 92 (1973) 224–43.

Robbins, V. K., "Mark 1:14–20: an Interpretation at the Intersection of Jewish and Graeco-Roman Traditions", *NTS* 28 (1982) 220–36.

— *Jesus the Teacher. A Socio-Rhetorical Interpretation of Mark*. Philadelphia: Fortress Press, 1984.

— "Psalm 22 in the Markan Crucifixion", in F. Neirynck, Festschrift, *The Four Gospels 1992*, ed. Van Segbroeck, et al. (Leuven: University Press/Peeters, 1992; 3 vols), 2, 1161–83.

Robinson, J. M., *The Problem of History in Mark*. London: SCM, 1957.

— "On the 'Gattung' of Mark (and John)" in *Jesus and Man's Hope*, ed. D. G. Buttrick (Pittsburgh: Pittsburgh Theological Seminary, 1970) 1, 99–129.

— "The Literary Composition of Mark", in M. Sabbe (ed.), *L'Évangile selon Marc. Tradition et Rédaction* (Leuven: University Press, 1974) 11–19.

— *The Problem of History in Mark and other Marcan Studies*. Philadelphia: Fortress Press, 1982.

Roloff, J., "Das Markusevangelium als Geschichtsdarstellung", *EvT* 19 (1969) 73–93.

Ruhland, M., *Die Markuspassion aus der Sicht der Verleugnung*. Eilsbrunn: Ko'amar, 1987.

Sabbe, M., (ed.), *L'Évangile selon Marc. Tradition et Rédaction*. 2nd ed. Leuven: University Press, 1974[1], 1988[2].

Sariola, H., *Markus und das Gesetz. Eine redaktionskritische Untersuchung*. Helsinki: Suomalainen Tiedeakatemia, 1990.

Schenke, L., *Auferstehungsverkündigung und leeres Grab. Eine traditionsgeschichtliche Untersuchung von Mk 16,1–8*. Stuttgart: Verlag Katholisches Bibelwerk, 1969.

— *Studien zur Passionsgeschichte des Markus. Tradition und Redaktion in Markus 14,1–42*. Würzburg: Echter Verlag, 1971.

— *Die wunderbare Brotvermehrung. Die neutestamentlichen Erzählungen und ihre Bedeutung*. Würzburg: Echter Verlag, 1983.

— "Der Aufbau des Markusevangeliums – ein hermeneutischer Schlüssel?", *Biblische Notizen* (Munich) 32 (1986) 54–82.

Schierling, M. J., "Women as Leaders in the Marcan Communities", *Listening* (River Forest) 15 (1980) 250–6.

Schmahl, G., *Die Zwölf im Markusevangelium*. Trier: Paulinus-Verlag, 1974.

Schmidt, K. L., *Der Rahmen der Geschichte Jesu. Literarkritische Untersuchungen zur ältesten Jesusüberlieferung*. Berlin: Trowitzsch & Sohn, 1919.

Schmitt, J. J., "Women in Mark's Gospel", *Bible Today* 19 (1981) 228–33.

Schreiber, J., "Die Christologie des Markusevangeliums", *ZTK* 58 (1961) 154–83.

Select Bibliography

Schreiber, J., *Theologie des Vertrauens. Eine redaktionsgeschichtliche Untersuchung des Markusevangeliums.* Hamburg: Furche-Verlag, 1967.

— *Der Kreuzigungsbericht des Markusevangeliums: Mark 15,20b–41. Eine traditionsgeschichtliche und methodenkritische Untersuchung nach William Wrede (1859–1906).* Berlin/New York: de Gruyter, 1986.

Schulz, S., "Markus und das Alte Testament", *ZTK* 58 (1961) 184–97.

— "Die Bedeutung des Markus für die Theologiegeschichte des Urchristentums", in *Studia Evangelica II* (TU, 87), ed. F. L. Cross (Berlin: Akademie Verlag, 1964) 135–45.

Schweizer, E., "Anmerkungen zur Theologie des Markus", in O. Cullmann, Festschrift, *Neotestamentica et Patristica* (Leiden: E. J. Brill, 1962) 35–46.

— "Mark's Contribution to the Quest for the Historical Jesus", *NTS* 10 (1963–4) 421–32.

— "Die theologische Leistung des Markus", *EvT* 24 (1964) 337–55.

— "The Question of the Messianic Secret in Mark", in C. M. Tuckett (ed.), *The Messianic Secret* (Philadelphia: Fortress Press/London: SPCK, 1983) 65–74.

— "Eschatology in Mark's Gospel" in M. Black, Festschrift, *Neotestamentica et Semitica,* ed. E. E. Ellis, M. Wilcox (Edinburgh: T. & T. Clark, 1969) 114–18.

Scott, M. P., "Chiastic Structure: a Key to the Interpretation of Mark's Gospel", *BTB* 15 (1985) 17–26.

Sellew, P., "Composition of Didactic Scenes in Mark's Gospel", *JBL* 108 (1989) 613–34.

— "Oral and Written Sources in Mark 4:1–34", *NTS* 36 (1990) 234–67.

Sellin, G., "Textlinguistische und semiotische Erwägungen zu Mk 4:1–34", *NTS* 29 (1983) 508–30.

Senior, D., "'Swords and Clubs' . . . The Setting of Mark's Community and His Critique of Abusive Power", *BTB* 17 (1987) 10–20.

Sergeant, J., *Lion Let Loose. The Structure and Meaning of St. Mark's Gospel.* Exeter: Paternoster, 1988.

Smith, M., "The Composition of Mark 11–16", *HeyJ* 22 (1981) 363–77.

Smith, M., "Prolegomena to a Discussion of Aretalogies, Divine Men, The Gospels and Jesus", *JBL* 90 (1971) 174–99.

Smith, S. H., "The Literary Structure of Mark 11:1–12:40", *NovT* 31 (1989) 104–24.

Soards, M. L., "The Question of a Pre-Markan Passion Narrative", in *Bible Bhashyam* 11 (1985) 144–69.

Standaert, B., *L'Évangile selon Marc. Composition et Genre Littéraire.* Nijmegen: Stichting Studentenpers, 1978.

323

Stein, R. H., "The 'Redaktionsgeschichtlich' Investigation of a Markan Seam (Mc 1 21f.)", *ZNW* 61 (1970) 70–94.

Stenger, W., "Die Grundlegung des Evangeliums von Jesus Christus. Zur kompositionellen Struktur des Markusevangeliums", *Linguistica Biblica* 61 (1988) 7–56.

Stock, A., *Call to Discipleship: A Literary Study of Mark's Gospel*. Dublin: Veritas/Wilmington: Michael Glazier, 1982.

— "Chiastic Awareness and Education in Antiquity", *BTB* 14 (1984) 23–7.

— "Hinge Traditions in Mark's Gospel", *BTB* 15 (1985a) 27–31.

— "The Structure of Mark", *BTB* 23 (1985b) 291–6.

— *The Method and Message of Mark*. Wilmington: Glazier, 1989.

Stock, K., *Boten aus dem Mit-Ihm-Sein*. Rome: Biblical Institute Press, 1975.

Stoldt, H.-H., *History and Criticism of the Markan Hypothesis*. ET D. L. Niewyk & J. Riches. Edinburgh: T. & T. Clark, 1980.

Strecker, G., "The Passion and Resurrection Predictions in Mark's Gospel", *Int* 22 (1968) 421–42.

— "Schriftlichkeit oder Mündlichkeit der synoptischen Tradition? Anmerkungen zur formgeschichtlichen Problematik", in F. Neirynck, Festschrift, *The Four Gospels 1992*, ed. F. Van Segbroeck, et al. (Leuven: University Press/Peeters, 1992; 3 vols) 1, 159–72.

Stuhlmacher, P. (ed.), *Das Evangelium und die Evangelien. Vorträge vom Tübinger Symposium 1982*. Tübingen: Mohr-Siebeck, 1983.

Suhl, A., *Die Funktion der alttestamentlichen Zitate und Anspielungen im Markusevangelium*. Gütersloh: Gerd Mohn, 1965.

Tannehill, R. C., "The Disciples in Mark: the Function of a Narrative Role", *JR* 57 (1977) 386–405.

— "The Gospel of Mark as Narrative Christology", *Semeia* 16 (1979) 57–95.

Tagawa, K., "Mark 13. La tâtonnement d'un homme réaliste éveillé face à la tradition apocalyptique", *Foi et Vie* 76 (1977) 11–44.

Talbert, C. H., *What is a Gospel? The Genre of the Canonical Gospels*. Philadelphia: Fortress Press, 1977/London: SPCK, 1978.

Telford, W. R., *The Barren Temple and the Withered Tree. A Redaction-Critical Analysis of the Cursing of the Fig-tree Pericope in Mark's Gospel and its Relation to the Cleansing of the Temple Tradition*. Sheffield: JSOT, 1980.

— "Mark, Gospel of", in *A Dictionary of Biblical Interpretation*, ed. R. J. Coggins, J. L. Houlden (London: SCM/Philadelphia: Trinity Press International, 1990) 424–8.

— "More Fruit from the Withered Tree. Temple and Fig-Tree in Mark from a Graeco-Roman Perspective", in *Templum Amicitiae. Essays on the Second Temple presented to Ernst Bammel*, ed. W. Horbury (Sheffield: JSOT, 1991) 264–304.

Select Bibliography

Telford, W. R., "The Pre-Markan Tradition in Recent Research (1980–90)", in F. Neirynck, Festschrift, *The Four Gospels 1992*, ed. F. Van Segbroeck, et al. (Leuven: University Press/Peeters, 1992; 3 vols), 2, 693–723.

Theissen, G., *Miracle Stories of the Early Christian Tradition*. ET. F. McDonagh. Edinburgh: T. & T. Clark, 1983.

Thissen, W., *Erzählung der Befreiung*. Würtzburg: Echter, 1976.

Thompson, M. J., *The Role of Disbelief in Mark. A New Approach to the Second Gospel*. New York – Mahwah: Paulist Press, 1989.

Tolbert, M. A., *Sowing the Gospel: Mark's World in Literary-Historical Perspective*. Minneapolis: Fortress Press, 1989.

Trocmé, E., "Is there a Markan Christology?", in C. F. D. Moule, Festschrift, *Christ and Spirit in the New Testament*, ed. B. Lindars, S. S. Smalley (Cambridge: University Press, 1973) 3–13.

— *The Formation of the Gospel according to Mark*. ET. P. Gaughan. London: SPCK, 1975.

— *The Passion as Liturgy. A Study in the Origin of the Passion Narratives in the Four Gospels*. London: SCM, 1983.

Tuckett, C. M. (ed.), *The Messianic Secret*. Philadelphia: Fortress Press/London: SPCK, 1983.

Turner, C. H., "Marcan Usage: Notes, Critical and Exegetical, on the Second Gospel", *JTS* 25 (1923–4) 378–86; 26 (1924–5) 12–20, 145–56, 225–40, 337–46; 27 (1925–6) 58–62; 28 (1926–7) 9–30, 349–62; 29 (1927–8) 275–89, 346–61.

Tyson, J. B., "The Blindness of the Disciples in Mark", *JBL* 80 (1961) 261–8. Reprinted in Tuckett (1983).

Van Iersel, B., "Locality, Structure and Meaning in Mark", *Linguistica Biblica* 53 (1983) 45–54.

— *Reading Mark*. Edinburgh: T. & T. Clark, 1988.

Van Oyen, G., "Intercalation and Irony in the Gospel of Mark", in F. Neirynck, Festschrift. *The Four Gospels 1992*, ed. F. Van Segbroeck, et al. (Leuven: University Press/Peeters, 1992; 3 vols), 2, 943–74.

Verheyden, J., "Persecution and Eschatology. Mk 13,9–13", in F. Neirynck, Festschrift, *The Four Gospels 1992*, ed. F. Van Segbroeck, et al. (Leuven: University Press/Peeters, 1992; 3 vols) 2, 1141–59.

Via, D. O., Jnr., *Kerygma and Comedy in the New Testament. A Structuralist Approach to Hermeneutic*. Philadelphia: Fortress Press, 1975.

— *The Ethics of Mark's Gospel – In the Middle of Time*. Philadelphia: Fortress Press, 1985.

Vielhauer, P., "Erwägungen zur Christologie des Markusevangeliums" in R. Bultmann, Festschrift, *Zeit und Geschichte*, ed. E. Dinkler (Tübingen: Mohr-Siebeck, 1964) 155–69.

Vorster, W. S., "Mark: Collector, Redactor, Author, Narrator?", *JournTheolSAfrica* 31 (1980) 46–61.

Vorster, W. S., "The Function of the Use of the Old Testament in Mark", *Neotestamentica* 14 (1981) 62–72.

— "Literary Reflections on Mark 13:5–37, a Narrated Speech of Jesus", in *Neotestamentica* 21 (1987) 203–24.

Waetjen, H., *A Re-ordering of Power. A Sociopolitical Reading of Mark's Gospel*. Minneapolis: Fortress Press, 1989.

Wanke, J., *"Bezugs- und Kommentarworte" in den synoptischen Evangelien. Beobachtungen zur Interpretationsgeschichte der Herrenworte in der vorevangelischen Überlieferung*. Leipzig: St Benno-Verlag, 1981.

Watson, F., "The Social Function of Mark's Secrecy Motif", *JSNT* 24 (1989) 49–69.

— "Ambiguity in the Marcan Narrative", *King Theol Rev* 10 (1987) 11–16.

Weeden, T. J., "The Heresy that necessitated Mark's Gospel", *ZNW* 59 (1968) 145–58.

— *Mark – Traditions in Conflict*. Philadelphia: Fortress Press, 1971.

Weihnacht, H., *Die Menschwerdung des Sohnes Gottes in Markus-evangelium*. Tübingen: Mohr-Siebeck, 1972.

Weiss, W., *"Eine neue Lehre in Vollmacht", Die Streit- und Schul-gespräche des Markusevangeliums*. Berlin/New York: de Gruyter, 1989.

Wenham, D., "Recent Study of Mark 13", Parts 1 & 2, *TSF Bulletin* 71 (1975) 6–15 and 72 (1975) 1–9.

— *The Rediscovery of Jesus' Eschatological Discourse*. Sheffield: JSOT Press, 1984.

Wrede, W., *The Messianic Secret*. ET. J. C. G. Greig. Cambridge, London: James Clarke, 1971.

Wrege, H.-T., *Die Gestalt des Evangeliums. Aufbau und Struktur der Synoptiker sowie der Apostelgeschichte*. Frankfurt/M-Bern-Las Vegas: Lang, 1978.

Zwick, R., *Montage im Markusevangelium. Studien zur narrativen Organisation der ältesten Jesuserzählung*. Stuttgart: Katholisches Bibelwerk, 1989.

Index of Names

327

Index of Marcan Passages

335

Select Index of Subjects

History, Mark in *see* Interpretation,
History of

Intercalation 47 n. 36, 126
Interpretation, History of 1ff., 40
Irony 10, 217ff., 236, 248 n. 20

Jewish Leaders 19, 26, 35, 70f., 106,
113, 181, 238, 259, 263, 296ff.
John *see* Fourth Gospel

Kingdom of God 9, 26, 32, 71, 205,
219, 297

Law 63, 73, 144f.
Literary Approaches 9ff., 25, 49 n. 44,
127, 169ff., 207ff., 253ff., 269ff.,
289ff.
Literary Techniques 47 n. 36, 148
Luke 37, 125, 154, 158, 163, 198, 204f.

Matthew 3, 37, 67, 125, 154, 157f.,
162f., 197, 201f., 221, 231, 235
Messianic Secret *see* Secrecy Motif
Miracles and Miracle Stories 5, 9, 16ff.,
27f., 30, 34, 57 n. 98, 69, 86, 108,
110f., 114, 126

Narrative and Narrative Criticism 10,
169ff., 191 n. 4, 207ff., 229, 269ff.

Old Testament, Use of 21f., 28, 56 n.
89, 65, 68, 74, 110, 134, 145, 221,
293
Outline 80, 170, 295

Papias 2, 4, 105
Parables 1, 5, 9, 20f., 27, 32, 67, 71f.,
111f., 114, 126, 211ff., 217ff.
Parentheses 8, 11, 126, 157, 208ff., 219
Passion Predictions 25, 29, 110, 130,
136f., 158, 185, 239, 277, 298f.
Passion Narrative 5, 8, 11, 17, 22f.,
26f., 57 n. 98, 65, 108, 113f., 126,
187ff., 206, 300f.

Paul 31, 59 n. 116, 63f., 70, 86, 95, 99,
106f., 110, 120, 197, 202f., 244
Peter 2, 4, 79, 90ff., 128, 130, 156, 164,
188, 231, 240, 298
Plot 10, 127, 229, 280, 289ff.
Priority of Mark 3f., 42f. n. 15
Provenance 2, 39, 41 n. 8, 106
Purpose of Mark's Gospel 39, 122 n. 3,
129, 243

Q 4, 20f., 52 n. 62, 53 n. 71, 83 n. 24,
109, 112, 125, 161, 163, 199ff.,
202ff., 206

Reader-Response Criticism 10f., 207ff.
Redaction Criticism 7ff., 10, 13, 24,
65ff., 113, 125ff., 153ff.
Resurrection 25, 38, 176, 231, 242f.,
285
Rhetorical Criticism 10f.
Rhetorical Devices 207ff., 222f.
Romance 16

Secrecy Motif 4f., 26ff., 44 n. 18, 56 n.
90, 115ff., 121, 126, 128ff., 205,
219, 229f., 236
Settings 147
Socio-Historical Setting 30f., 33, 37,
39, 97f.
Soteriology 9, 29ff.
Sources and Source Criticism 4, 13f.,
17ff., 52 n. 66
Structuralism 10f., 50 n. 47, 253ff., 267
n. 30
Structure 9, 48f. n. 42, 147, 295
Style 8, 10, 48 n. 40, 126, 241
Summary Passages 8ff., 47 n. 34, 131,
198
Synoptic Problem 3f., 42 n. 15

Temple 8, 77f., 158, 256, 263, 301, 306
n. 40
Tradition Criticism 7f.
Tragedy 16

Women 12, 189, 229, 231, 247 n. 12